# THE LAST MAGICIAN

### WRITTEN BY:
## SEAN MEIGHEN

### ILLUSTRATED BY:
## THIEN UNCAGE

### LETTERED BY:
## MICAH MYERS

MARKOSIA

FOR MARKOSIA ENTERPRISES LTD

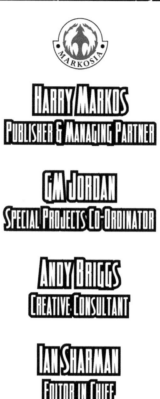

HARRY MARKOS
PUBLISHER & MANAGING PARTNER

GM JORDAN
SPECIAL PROJECTS CO-ORDINATOR

ANDY BRIGGS
CREATIVE CONSULTANT

IAN SHARMAN
EDITOR IN CHIEF

 Published by Markosia Enterprises, PO BOX 3477, Barnet, Hertfordshire, EN5 9HN. FIRST PRINTING, February 2023. Harry Markos, Director.

ISBN 978-1-915860-01-9

www.markosia.com

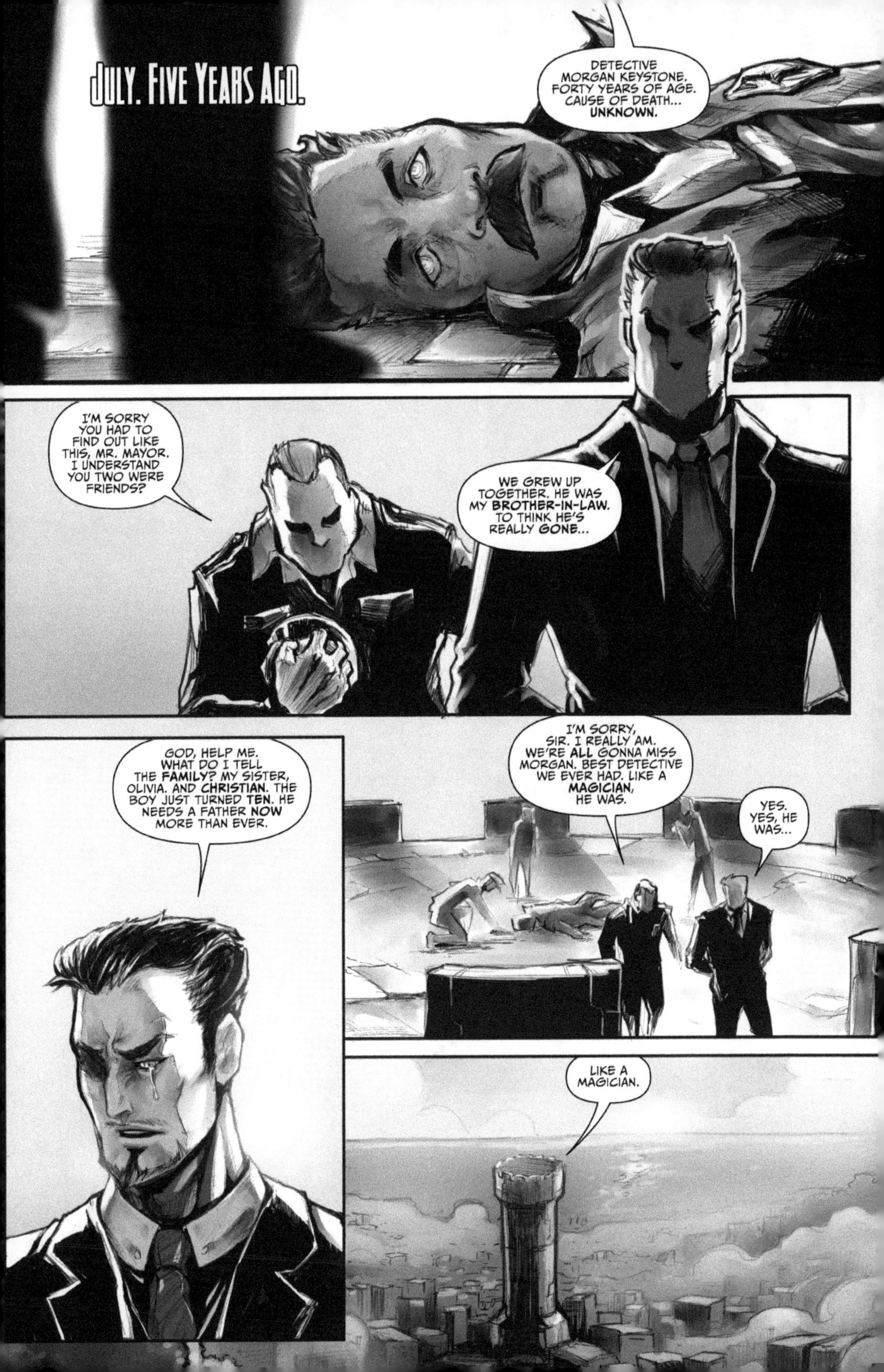
JULY. FIVE YEARS AGO.
DETECTIVE MORGAN KEYSTONE. FORTY YEARS OF AGE. CAUSE OF DEATH... UNKNOWN.
I'M SORRY YOU HAD TO FIND OUT LIKE THIS, MR. MAYOR. I UNDERSTAND YOU TWO WERE FRIENDS?
WE GREW UP TOGETHER. HE WAS MY BROTHER-IN-LAW. TO THINK HE'S REALLY GONE...
GOD, HELP ME. WHAT DO I TELL THE FAMILY? MY SISTER, OLIVIA. AND CHRISTIAN. THE BOY JUST TURNED TEN. HE NEEDS A FATHER NOW MORE THAN EVER.
I'M SORRY, SIR. I REALLY AM. WE'RE ALL GONNA MISS MORGAN. BEST DETECTIVE WE EVER HAD. LIKE A MAGICIAN, HE WAS.
YES. YES, HE WAS...
LIKE A MAGICIAN.

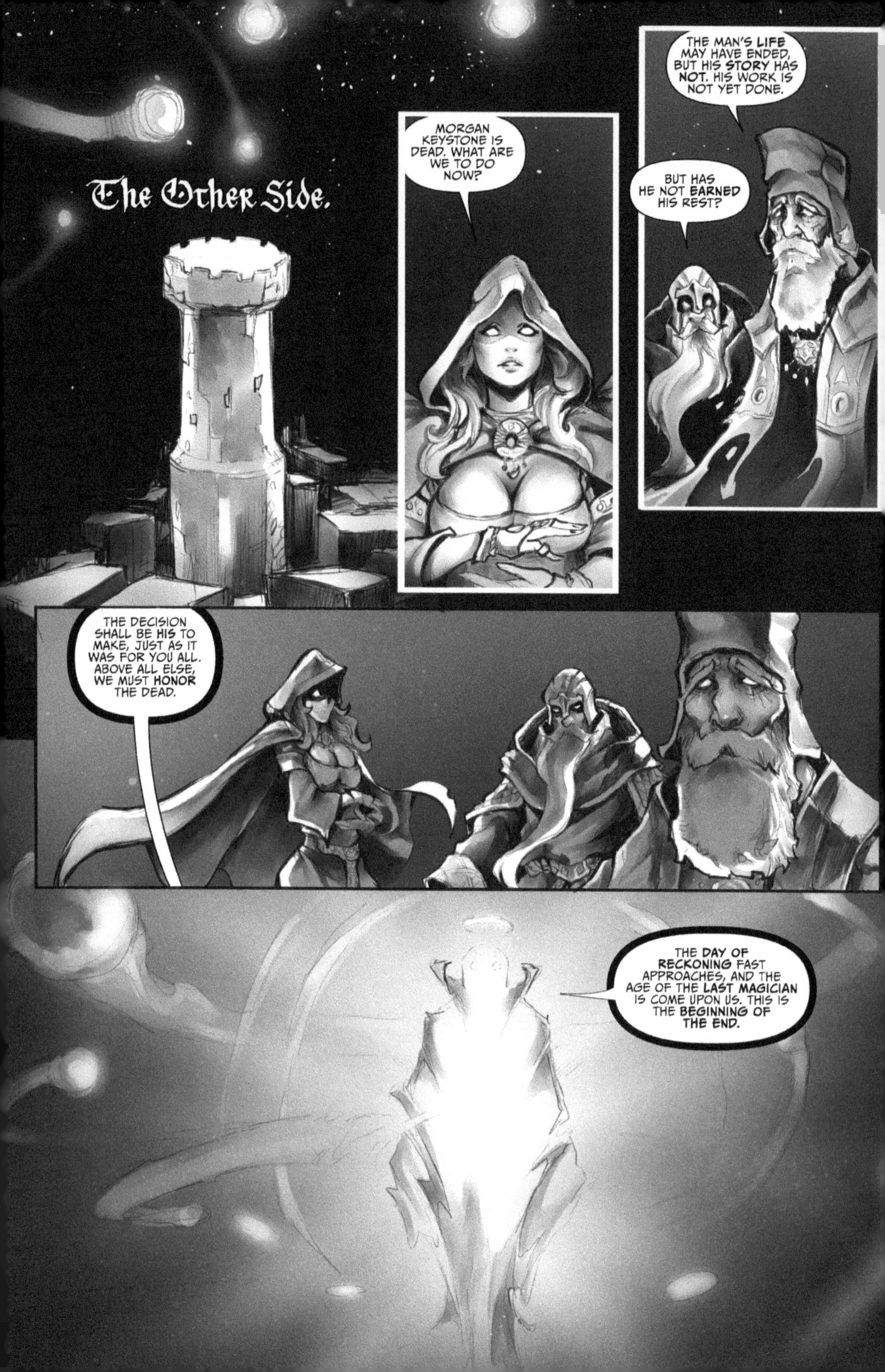
The Other Side.
MORGAN KEYSTONE IS DEAD. WHAT ARE WE TO DO NOW?
THE MAN'S LIFE MAY HAVE ENDED, BUT HIS STORY HAS NOT. HIS WORK IS NOT YET DONE.
BUT HAS HE NOT EARNED HIS REST?
THE DECISION SHALL BE HIS TO MAKE, JUST AS IT WAS FOR YOU ALL. ABOVE ALL ELSE, WE MUST HONOR THE DEAD.
THE DAY OF RECKONING FAST APPROACHES, AND THE AGE OF THE LAST MAGICIAN IS COME UPON US. THIS IS THE BEGINNING OF THE END.

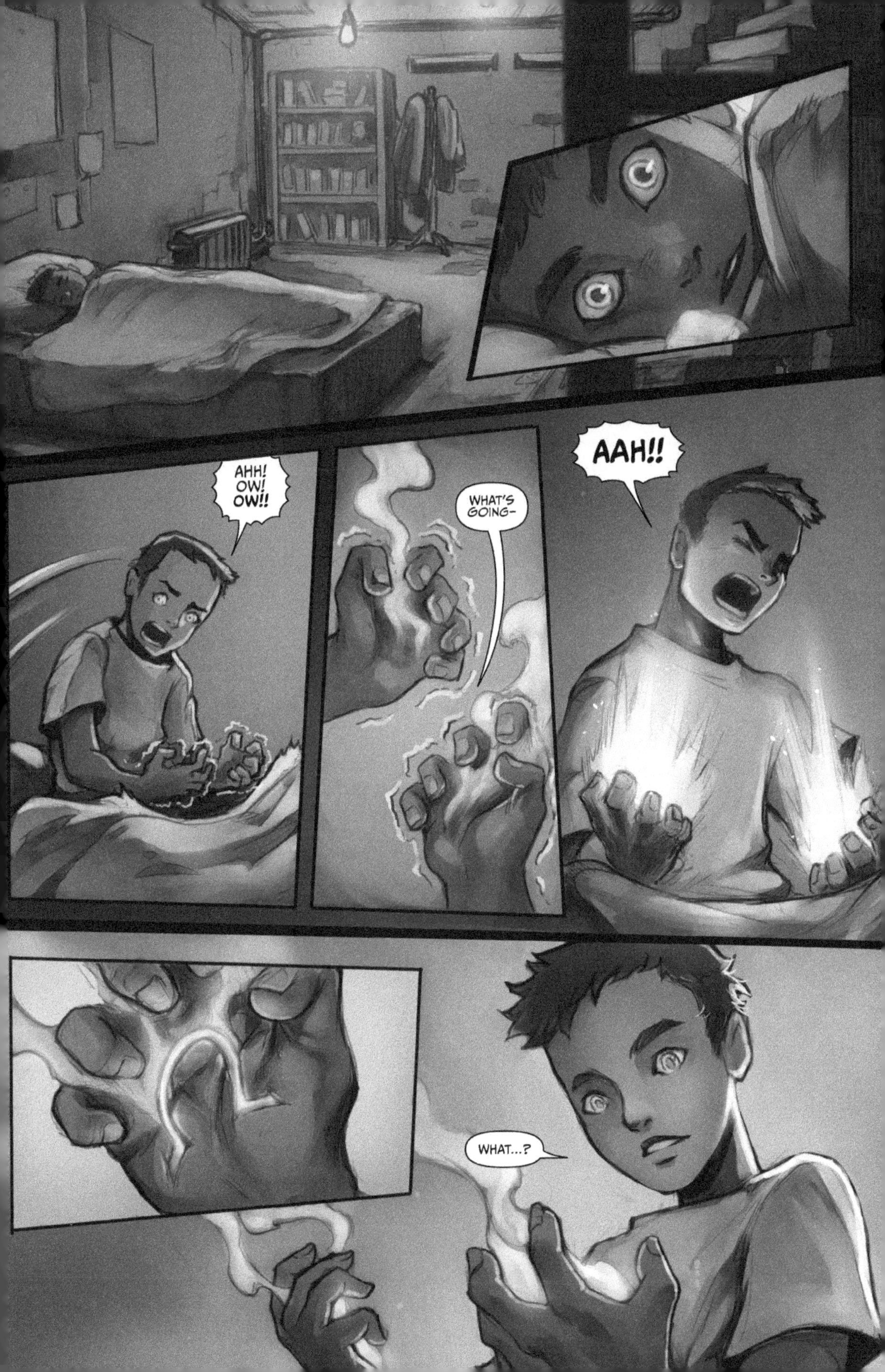
AHH! OW! OW!!
WHAT'S GOING-
AAH!!
WHAT...?

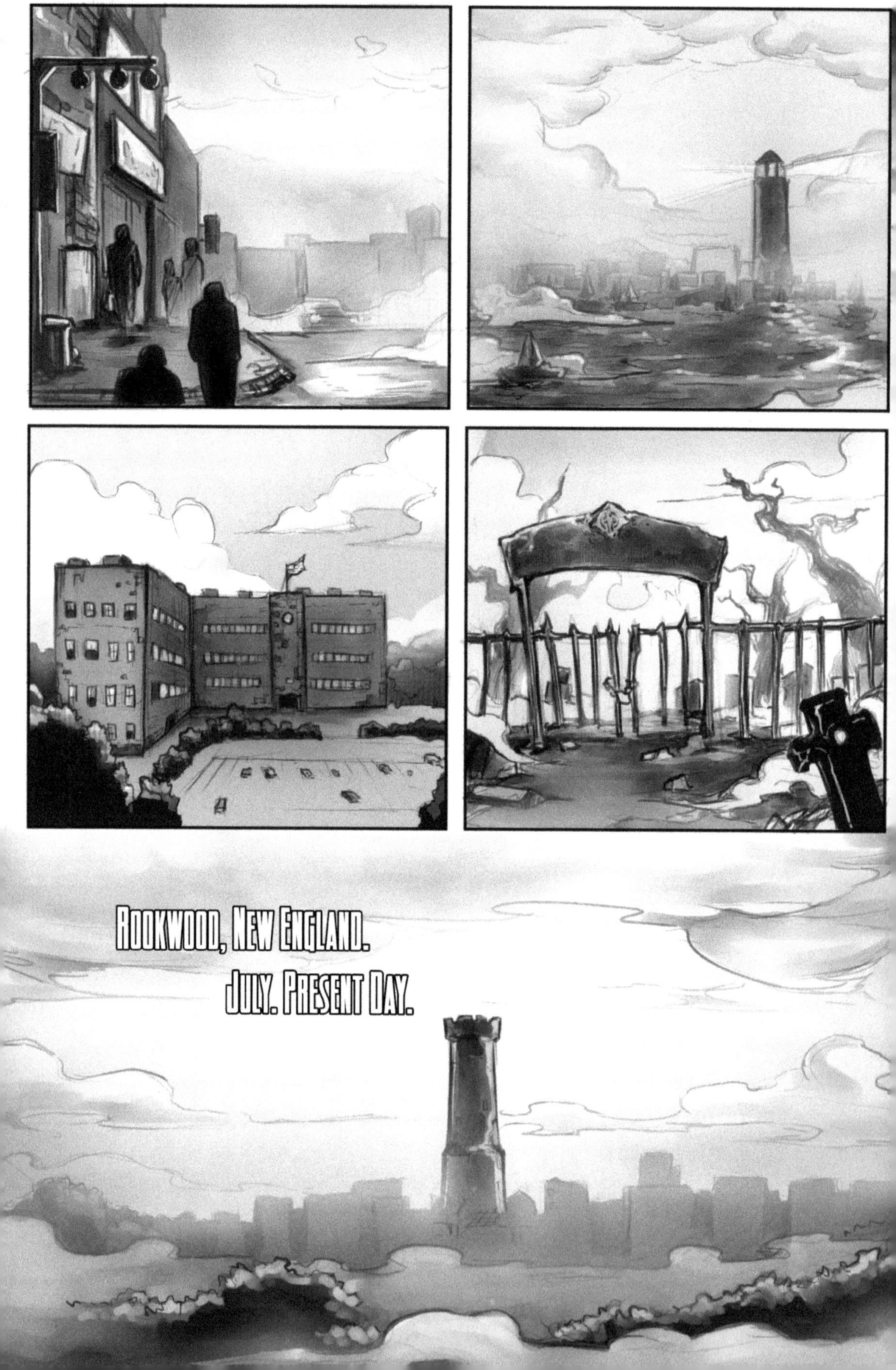
ROOKWOOD, NEW ENGLAND.
JULY. PRESENT DAY.

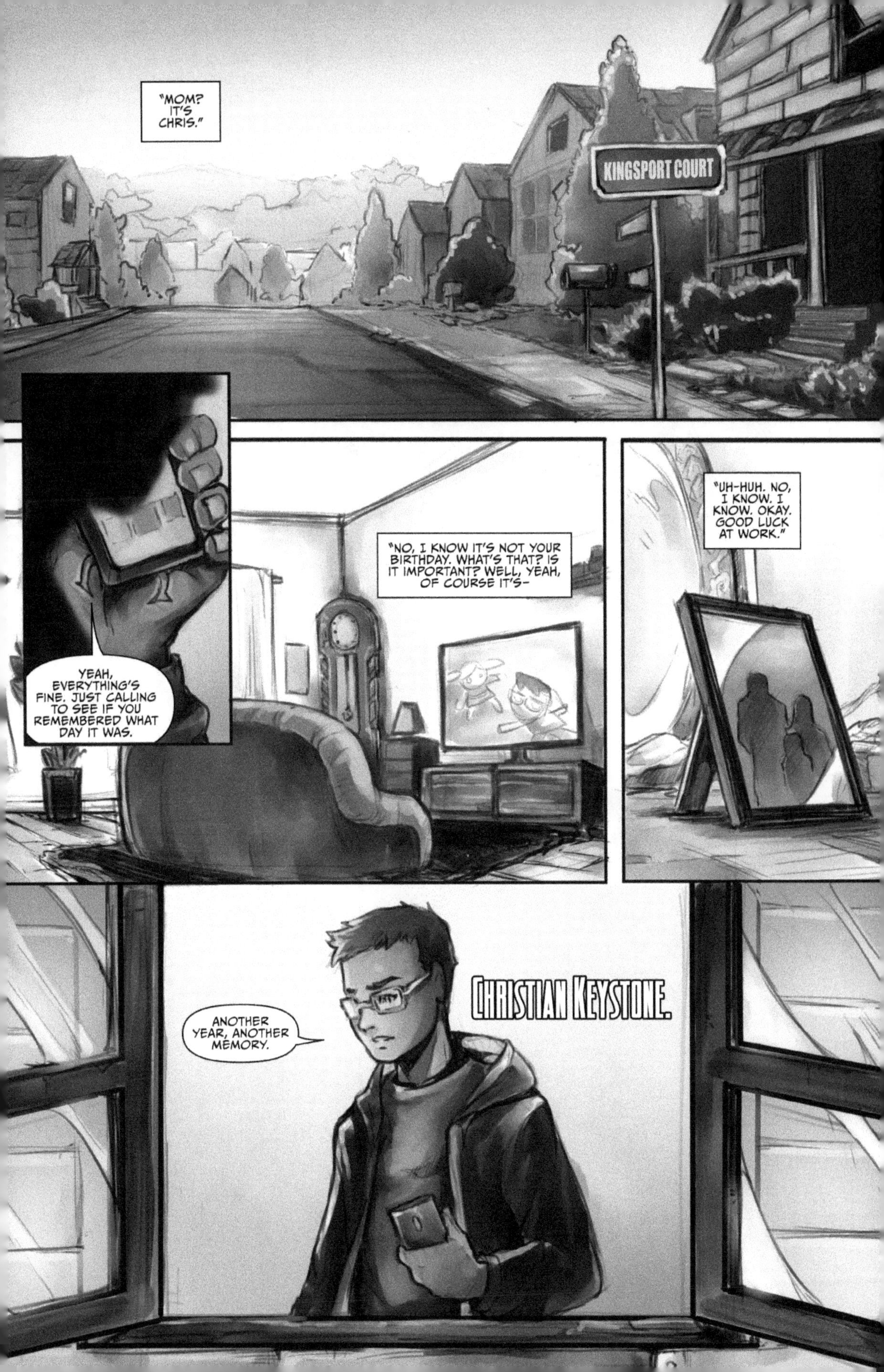
"MOM? IT'S CHRIS."
KINGSPORT COURT
YEAH, EVERYTHING'S FINE. JUST CALLING TO SEE IF YOU REMEMBERED WHAT DAY IT WAS.
"NO, I KNOW IT'S NOT YOUR BIRTHDAY. WHAT'S THAT? IS IT IMPORTANT? WELL, YEAH, OF COURSE IT'S-
"UH-HUH. NO, I KNOW. I KNOW. OKAY. GOOD LUCK AT WORK."
CHRISTIAN KEYSTONE.
ANOTHER YEAR, ANOTHER MEMORY.

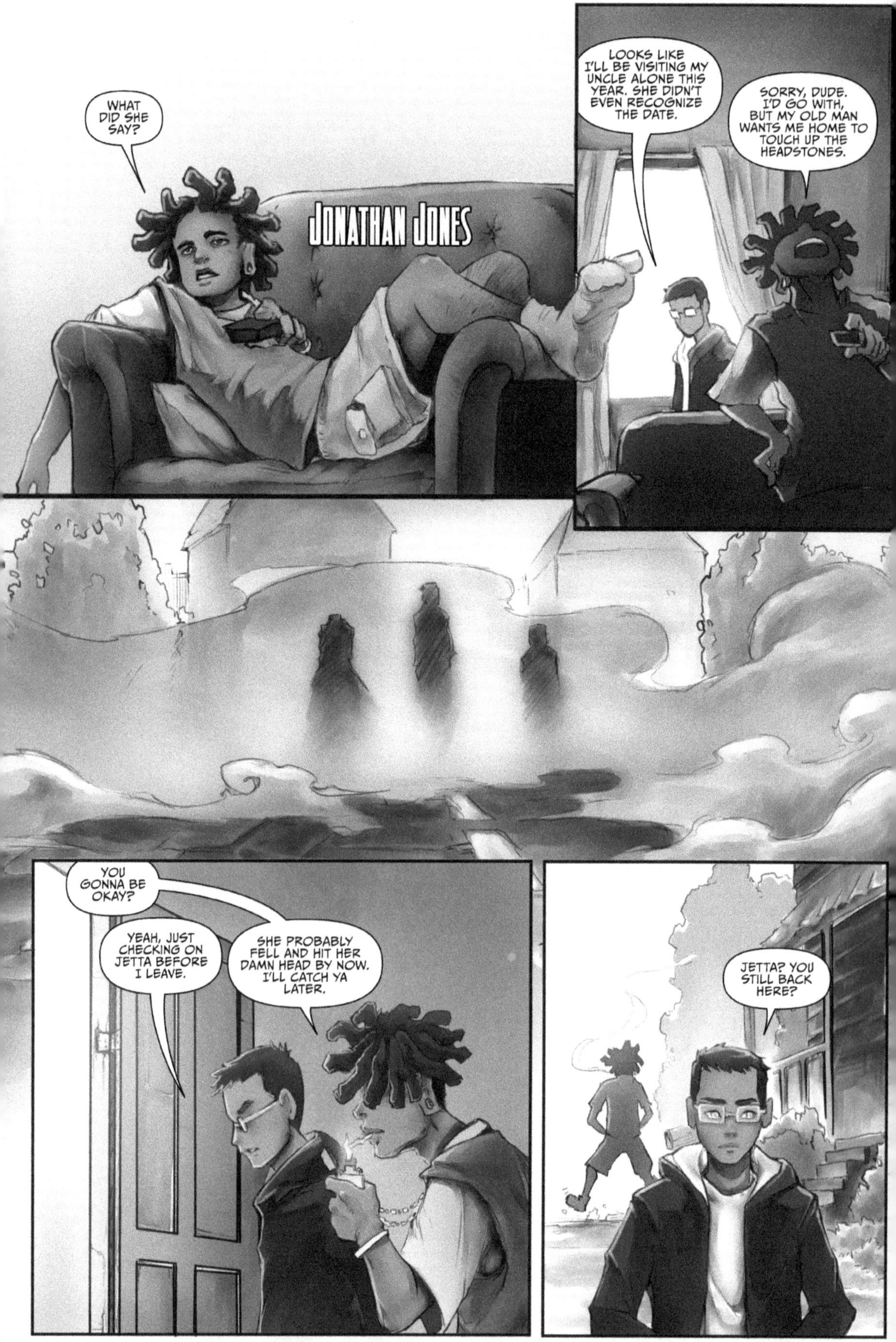
WHAT DID SHE SAY?
JONATHAN JONES
LOOKS LIKE I'LL BE VISITING MY UNCLE ALONE THIS YEAR. SHE DIDN'T EVEN RECOGNIZE THE DATE.
SORRY, DUDE. I'D GO WITH, BUT MY OLD MAN WANTS ME HOME TO TOUCH UP THE HEADSTONES.
YOU GONNA BE OKAY?
YEAH, JUST CHECKING ON JETTA BEFORE I LEAVE.
SHE PROBABLY FELL AND HIT HER DAMN HEAD BY NOW. I'LL CATCH YA LATER.
JETTA? YOU STILL BACK HERE?

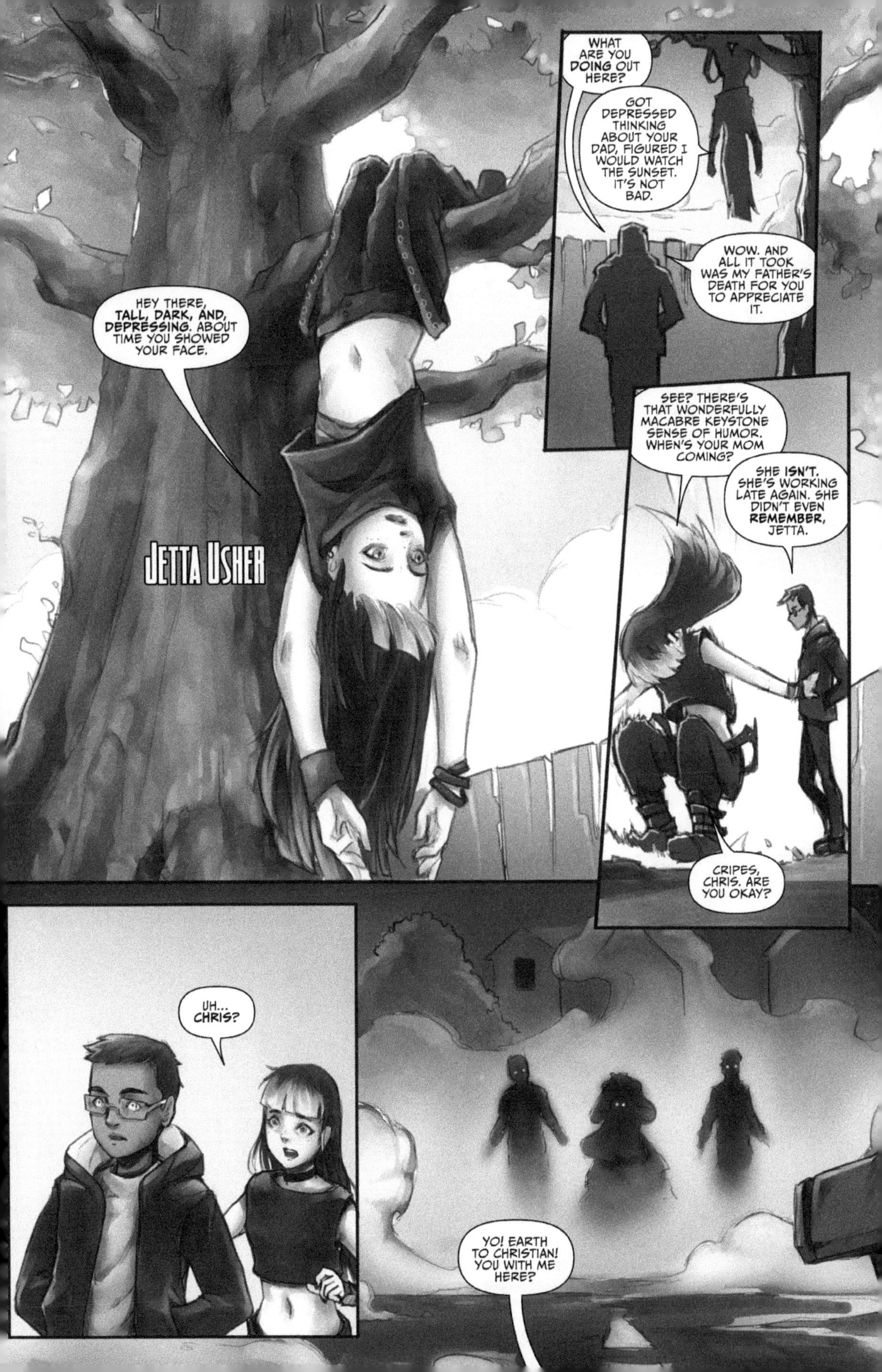
HEY THERE, TALL, DARK, AND, DEPRESSING. ABOUT TIME YOU SHOWED YOUR FACE.
JETTA USHER
WHAT ARE YOU DOING OUT HERE?
GOT DEPRESSED THINKING ABOUT YOUR DAD, FIGURED I WOULD WATCH THE SUNSET. IT'S NOT BAD.
WOW. AND ALL IT TOOK WAS MY FATHER'S DEATH FOR YOU TO APPRECIATE IT.
SEE? THERE'S THAT WONDERFULLY MACABRE KEYSTONE SENSE OF HUMOR. WHEN'S YOUR MOM COMING?
SHE ISN'T. SHE'S WORKING LATE AGAIN. SHE DIDN'T EVEN REMEMBER, JETTA.
CRIPES, CHRIS. ARE YOU OKAY?
UH... CHRIS?
YO! EARTH TO CHRISTIAN! YOU WITH ME HERE?

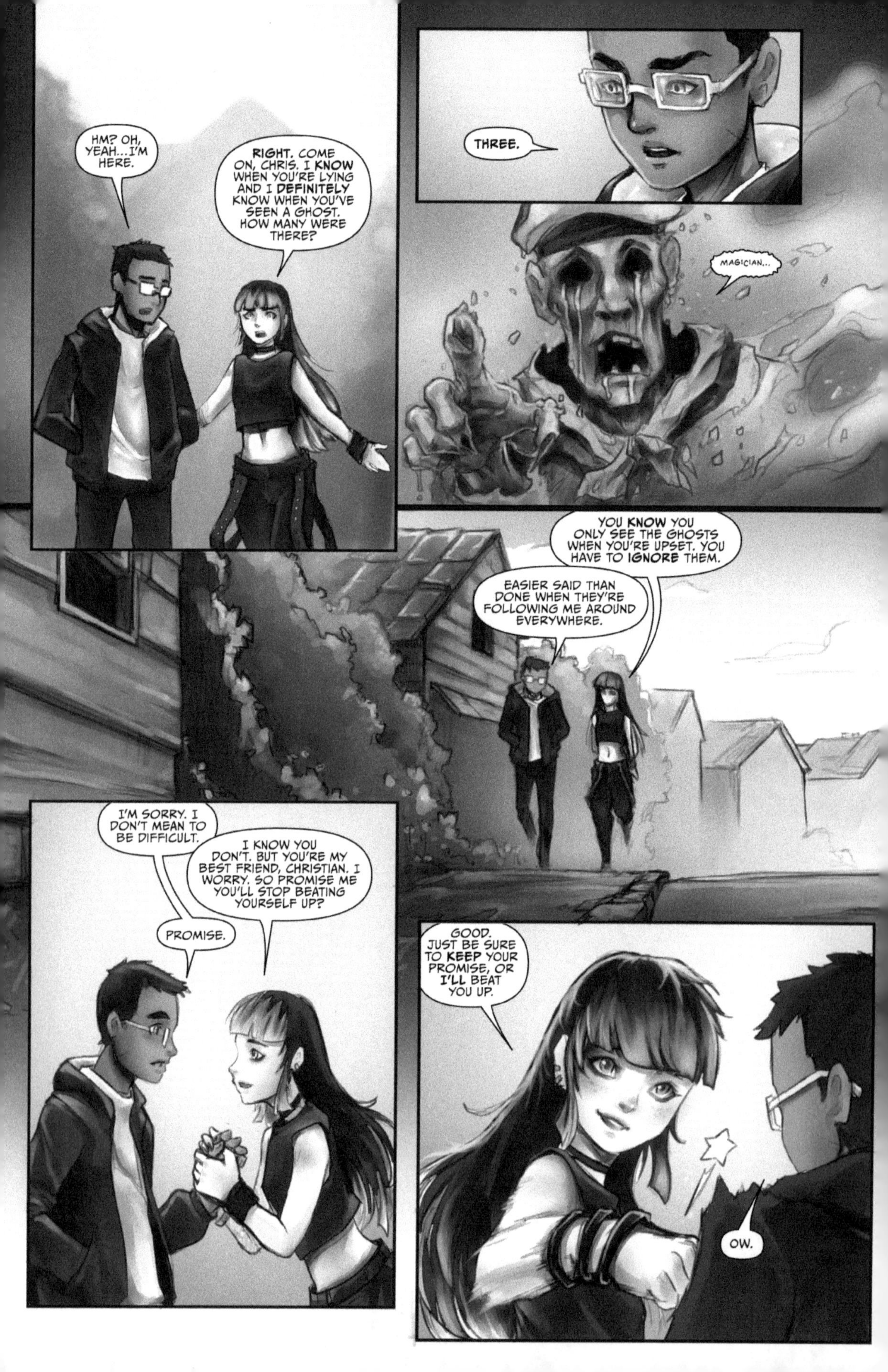
HM? OH, YEAH...I'M HERE.
RIGHT. COME ON, CHRIS. I KNOW WHEN YOU'RE LYING AND I DEFINITELY KNOW WHEN YOU'VE SEEN A GHOST. HOW MANY WERE THERE?
THREE.
MAGICIAN...
YOU KNOW YOU ONLY SEE THE GHOSTS WHEN YOU'RE UPSET. YOU HAVE TO IGNORE THEM.
EASIER SAID THAN DONE WHEN THEY'RE FOLLOWING ME AROUND EVERYWHERE.
I'M SORRY. I DON'T MEAN TO BE DIFFICULT.
I KNOW YOU DON'T. BUT YOU'RE MY BEST FRIEND, CHRISTIAN. I WORRY. SO PROMISE ME YOU'LL STOP BEATING YOURSELF UP?
PROMISE.
GOOD. JUST BE SURE TO KEEP YOUR PROMISE, OR I'LL BEAT YOU UP.
OW.

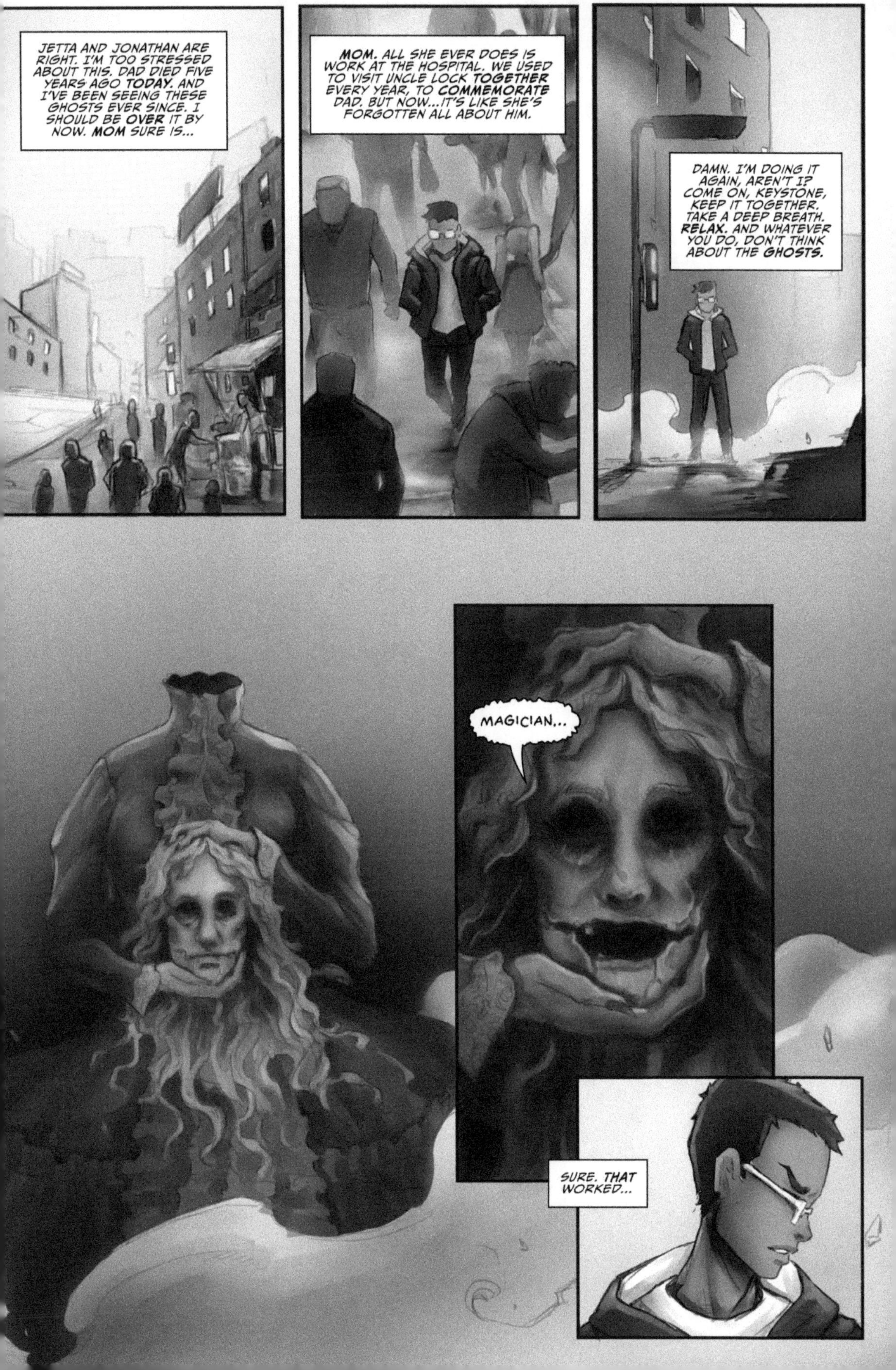
JETTA AND JONATHAN ARE RIGHT. I'M TOO STRESSED ABOUT THIS. DAD DIED FIVE YEARS AGO **TODAY.** AND I'VE BEEN SEEING THESE GHOSTS EVER SINCE. I SHOULD BE **OVER** IT BY NOW. **MOM** SURE IS...
**MOM.** ALL SHE EVER DOES IS WORK AT THE HOSPITAL. WE USED TO VISIT UNCLE LOCK **TOGETHER** EVERY YEAR, TO **COMMEMORATE** DAD. BUT NOW...IT'S LIKE SHE'S FORGOTTEN ALL ABOUT HIM.
DAMN. I'M DOING IT AGAIN, AREN'T I? COME ON, KEYSTONE, KEEP IT TOGETHER. TAKE A DEEP BREATH. **RELAX.** AND WHATEVER YOU DO, DON'T THINK ABOUT THE **GHOSTS.**
MAGICIAN...
SURE. **THAT** WORKED...

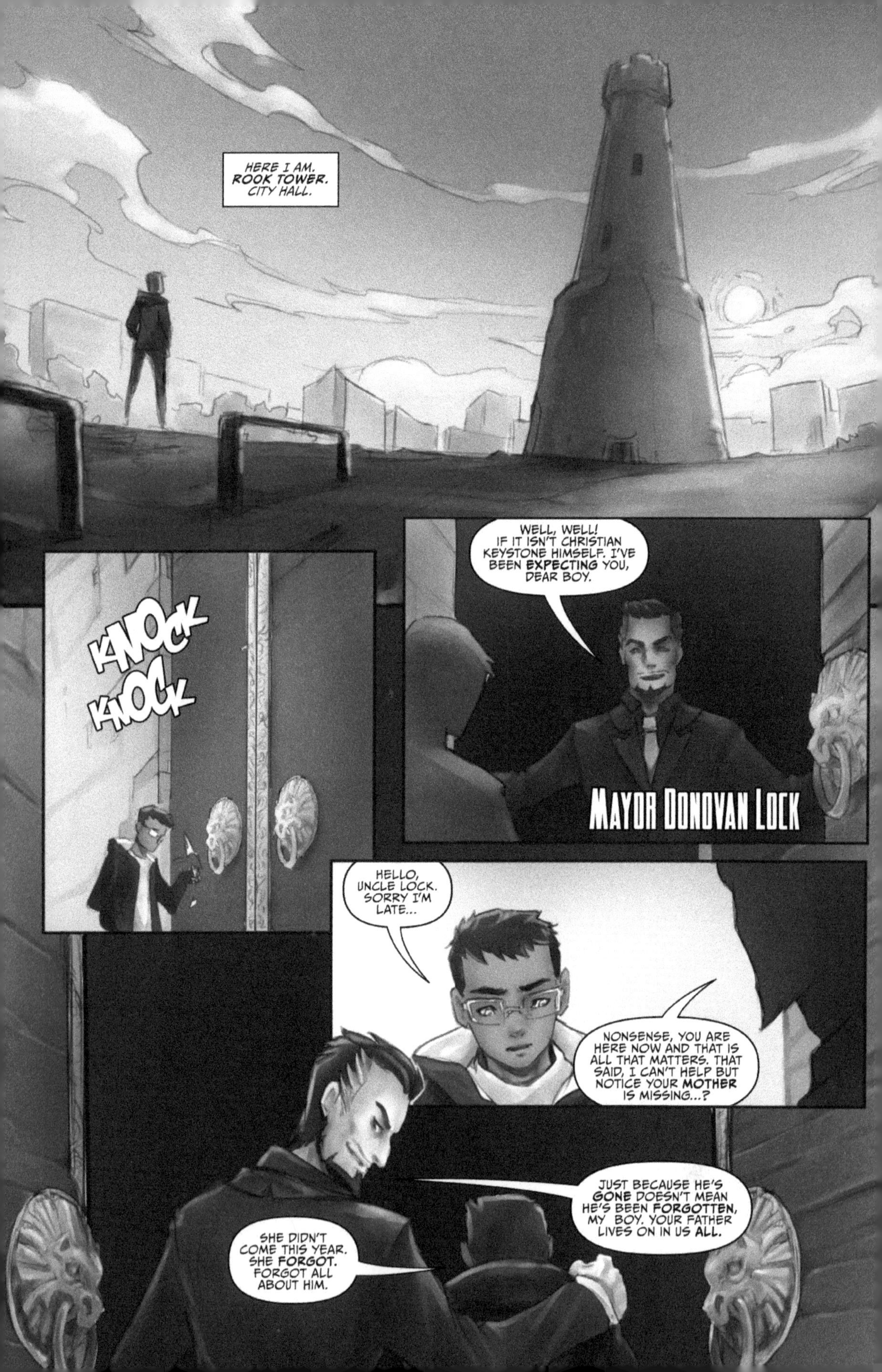
HERE I AM. ROOK TOWER. CITY HALL.
KNOCK KNOCK
WELL, WELL! IF IT ISN'T CHRISTIAN KEYSTONE HIMSELF. I'VE BEEN EXPECTING YOU, DEAR BOY.
MAYOR DONOVAN LOCK
HELLO, UNCLE LOCK. SORRY I'M LATE...
NONSENSE, YOU ARE HERE NOW AND THAT IS ALL THAT MATTERS. THAT SAID, I CAN'T HELP BUT NOTICE YOUR MOTHER IS MISSING...?
SHE DIDN'T COME THIS YEAR. SHE FORGOT. FORGOT ALL ABOUT HIM.
JUST BECAUSE HE'S GONE DOESN'T MEAN HE'S BEEN FORGOTTEN, MY BOY. YOUR FATHER LIVES ON IN US ALL.

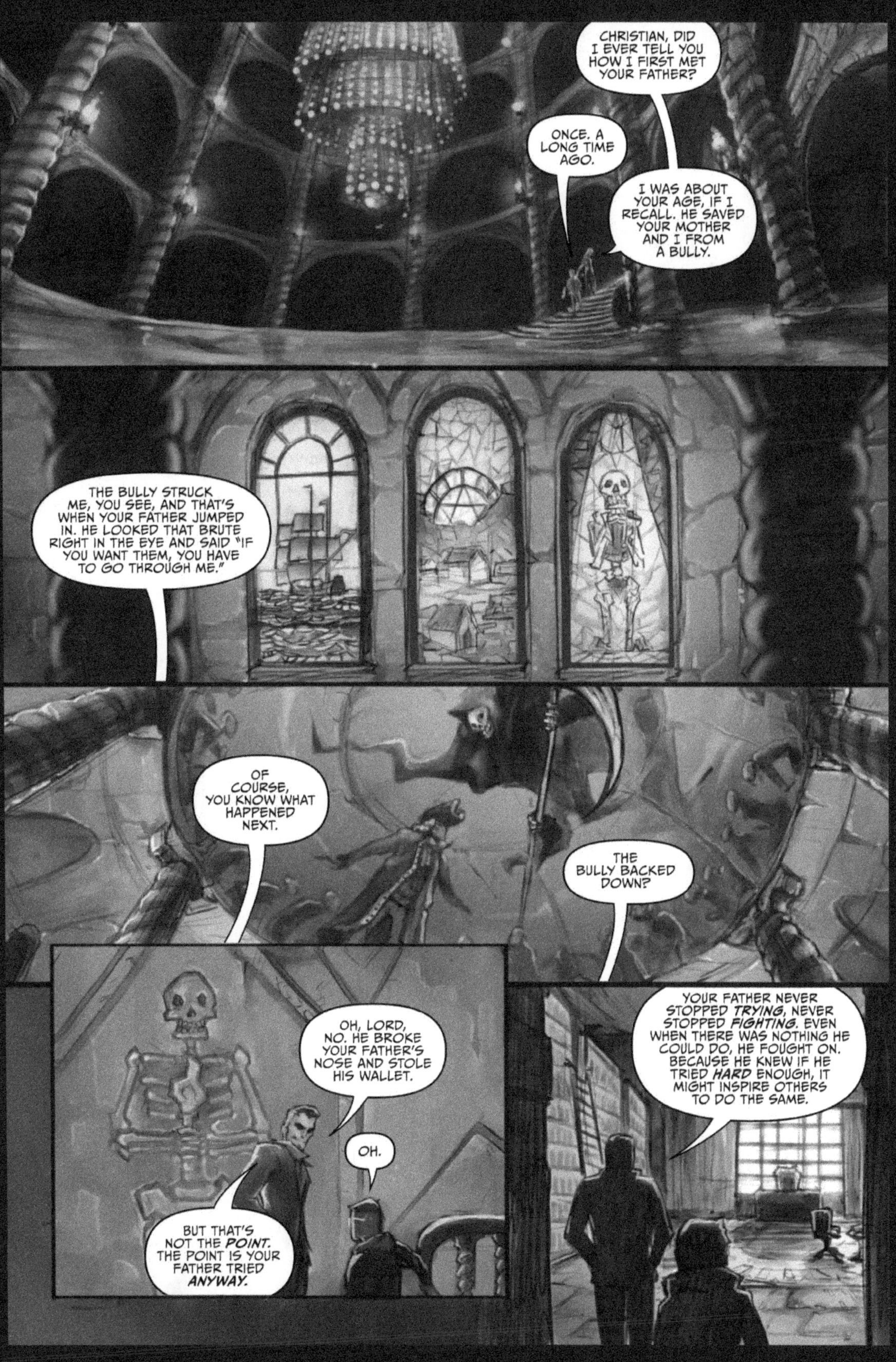
CHRISTIAN, DID I EVER TELL YOU HOW I FIRST MET YOUR FATHER?
ONCE. A LONG TIME AGO.
I WAS ABOUT YOUR AGE, IF I RECALL. HE SAVED YOUR MOTHER AND I FROM A BULLY.
THE BULLY STRUCK ME, YOU SEE, AND THAT'S WHEN YOUR FATHER JUMPED IN. HE LOOKED THAT BRUTE RIGHT IN THE EYE AND SAID "IF YOU WANT THEM, YOU HAVE TO GO THROUGH ME."
OF COURSE, YOU KNOW WHAT HAPPENED NEXT.
THE BULLY BACKED DOWN?
OH, LORD, NO. HE BROKE YOUR FATHER'S NOSE AND STOLE HIS WALLET.
OH.
BUT THAT'S NOT THE *POINT*. THE POINT IS YOUR FATHER TRIED ***ANYWAY.***
YOUR FATHER NEVER STOPPED *TRYING*, NEVER STOPPED *FIGHTING*. EVEN WHEN THERE WAS NOTHING HE COULD DO, HE FOUGHT ON. BECAUSE HE KNEW IF HE TRIED ***HARD*** ENOUGH, IT MIGHT INSPIRE OTHERS TO DO THE SAME.

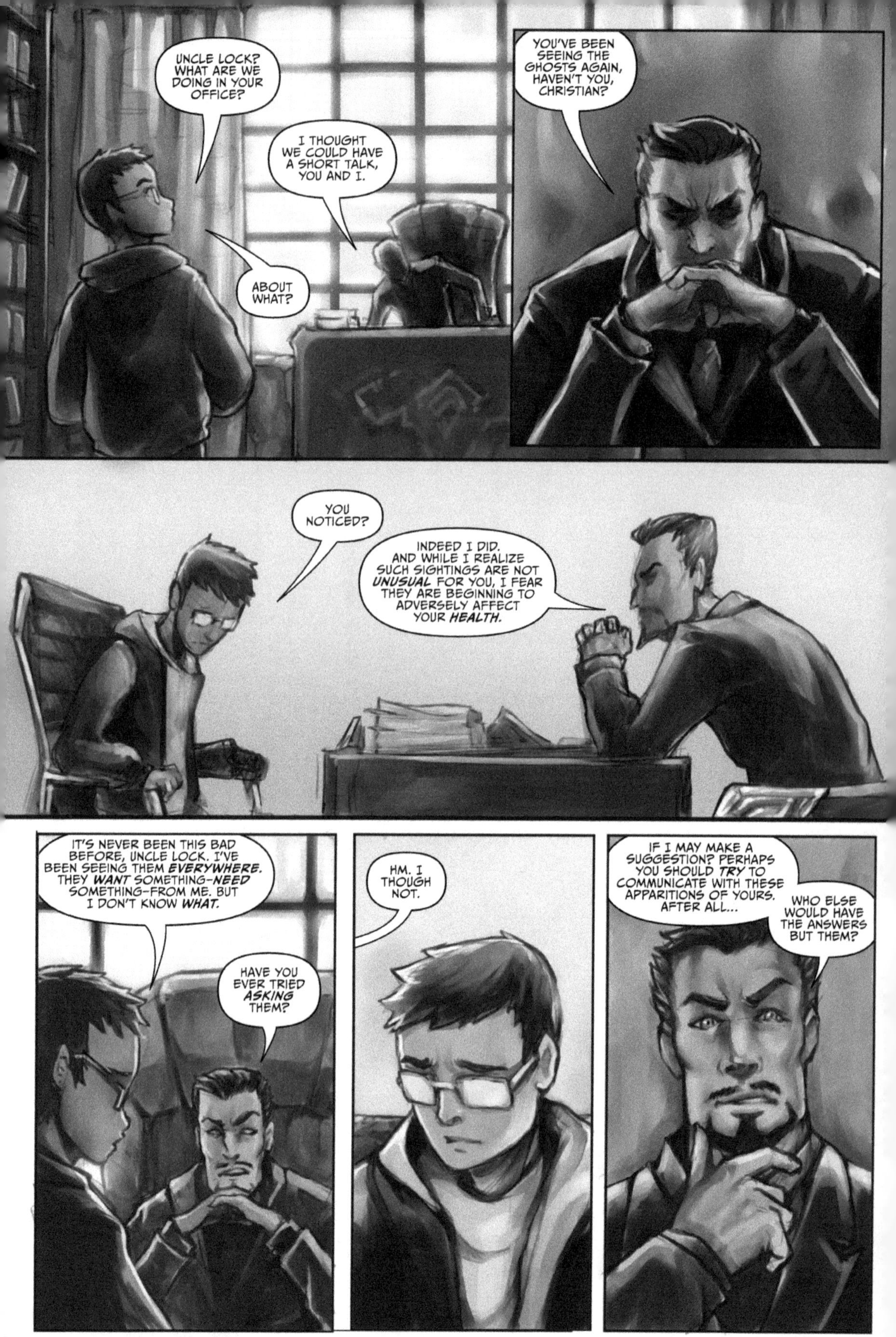
UNCLE LOCK? WHAT ARE WE DOING IN YOUR OFFICE?
I THOUGHT WE COULD HAVE A SHORT TALK, YOU AND I.
ABOUT WHAT?
YOU'VE BEEN SEEING THE GHOSTS AGAIN, HAVEN'T YOU, CHRISTIAN?
YOU NOTICED?
INDEED I DID. AND WHILE I REALIZE SUCH SIGHTINGS ARE NOT UNUSUAL FOR YOU, I FEAR THEY ARE BEGINNING TO ADVERSELY AFFECT YOUR HEALTH.
IT'S NEVER BEEN THIS BAD BEFORE, UNCLE LOCK. I'VE BEEN SEEING THEM EVERYWHERE. THEY WANT SOMETHING–NEED SOMETHING–FROM ME. BUT I DON'T KNOW WHAT.
HAVE YOU EVER TRIED ASKING THEM?
HM. I THOUGH NOT.
IF I MAY MAKE A SUGGESTION? PERHAPS YOU SHOULD TRY TO COMMUNICATE WITH THESE APPARITIONS OF YOURS. AFTER ALL...
WHO ELSE WOULD HAVE THE ANSWERS BUT THEM?

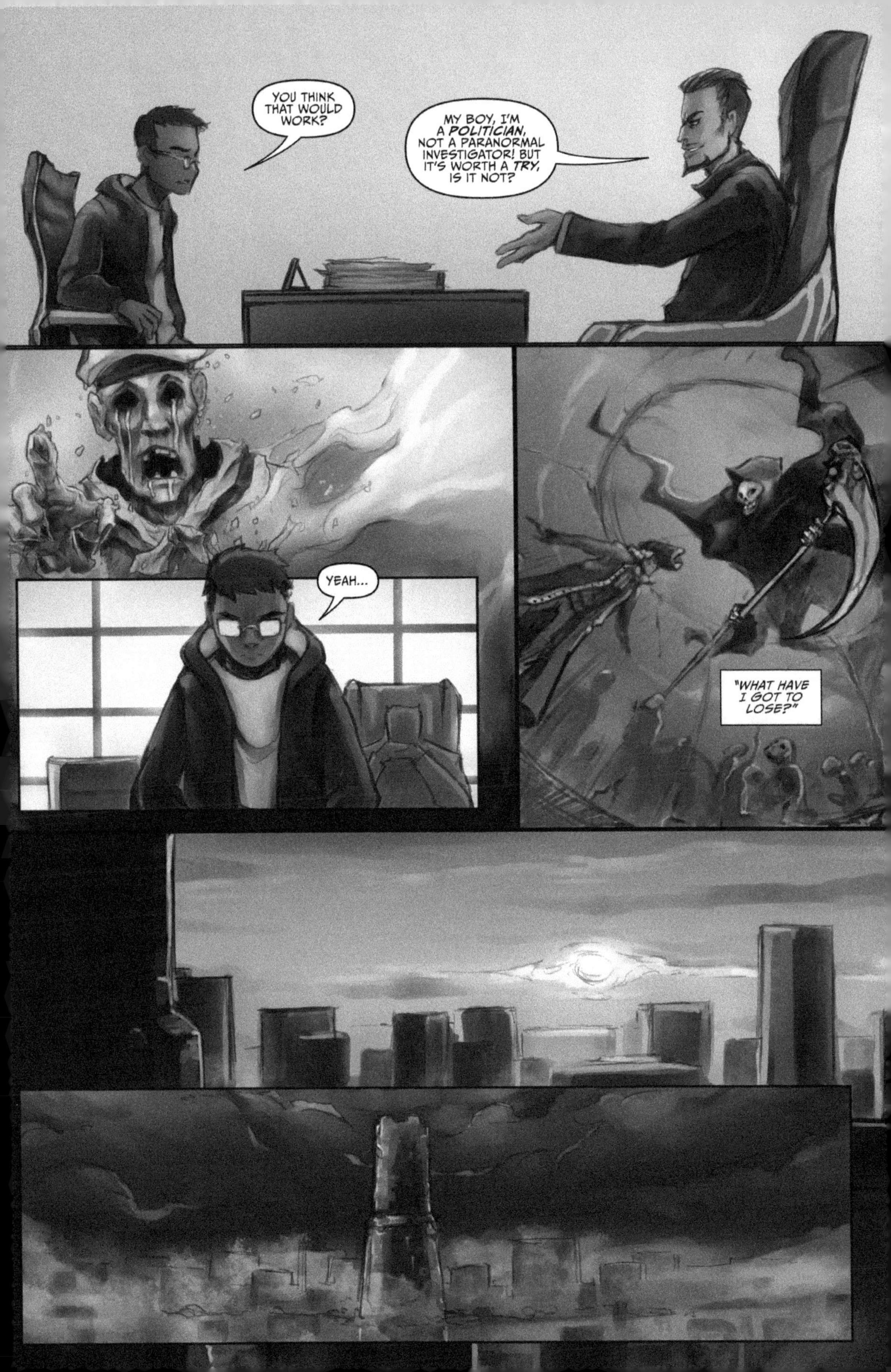
YOU THINK THAT WOULD WORK?
MY BOY, I'M A POLITICIAN, NOT A PARANORMAL INVESTIGATOR! BUT IT'S WORTH A TRY, IS IT NOT?
YEAH...
"WHAT HAVE I GOT TO LOSE?"

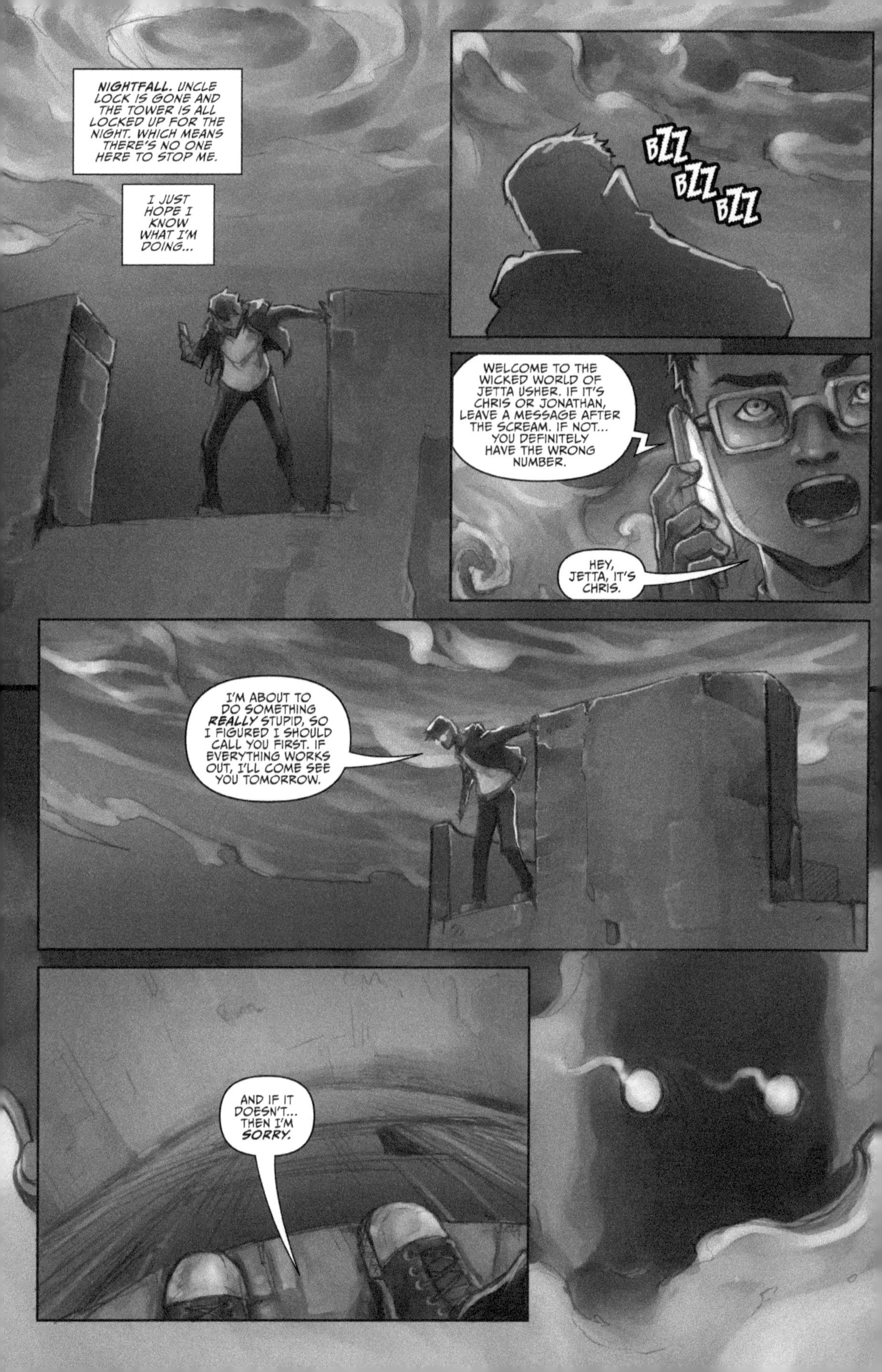
NIGHTFALL. UNCLE LOCK IS GONE AND THE TOWER IS ALL LOCKED UP FOR THE NIGHT. WHICH MEANS THERE'S NO ONE HERE TO STOP ME.
I JUST HOPE I KNOW WHAT I'M DOING...
BZZ BZZ BZZ
WELCOME TO THE WICKED WORLD OF JETTA USHER. IF IT'S CHRIS OR JONATHAN, LEAVE A MESSAGE AFTER THE SCREAM. IF NOT... YOU DEFINITELY HAVE THE WRONG NUMBER.
HEY, JETTA, IT'S CHRIS.
I'M ABOUT TO DO SOMETHING REALLY STUPID, SO I FIGURED I SHOULD CALL YOU FIRST. IF EVERYTHING WORKS OUT, I'LL COME SEE YOU TOMORROW.
AND IF IT DOESN'T... THEN I'M SORRY.

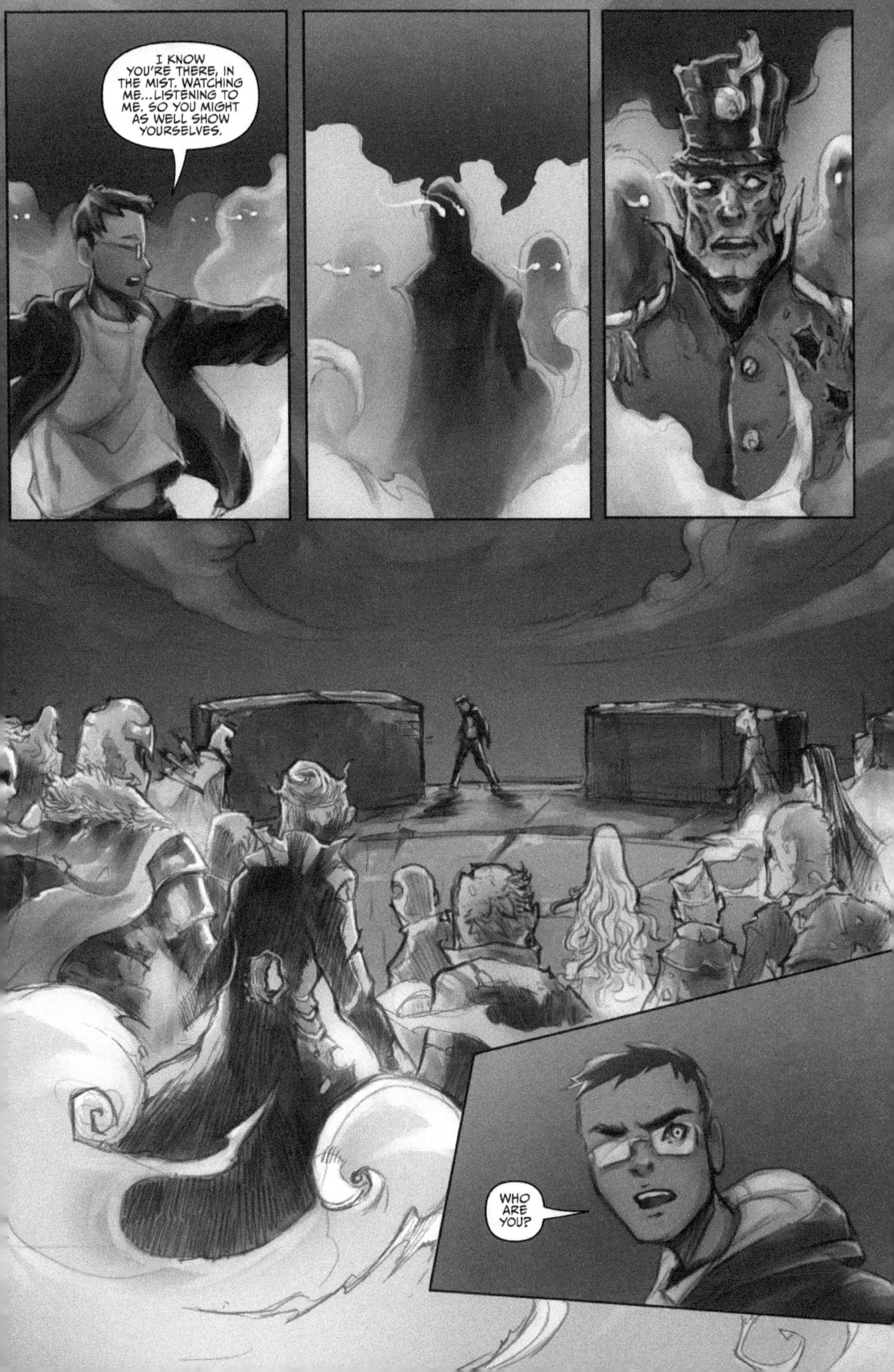
I KNOW YOU'RE THERE, IN THE MIST. WATCHING ME...LISTENING TO ME. SO YOU MIGHT AS WELL SHOW YOURSELVES.
WHO ARE YOU?

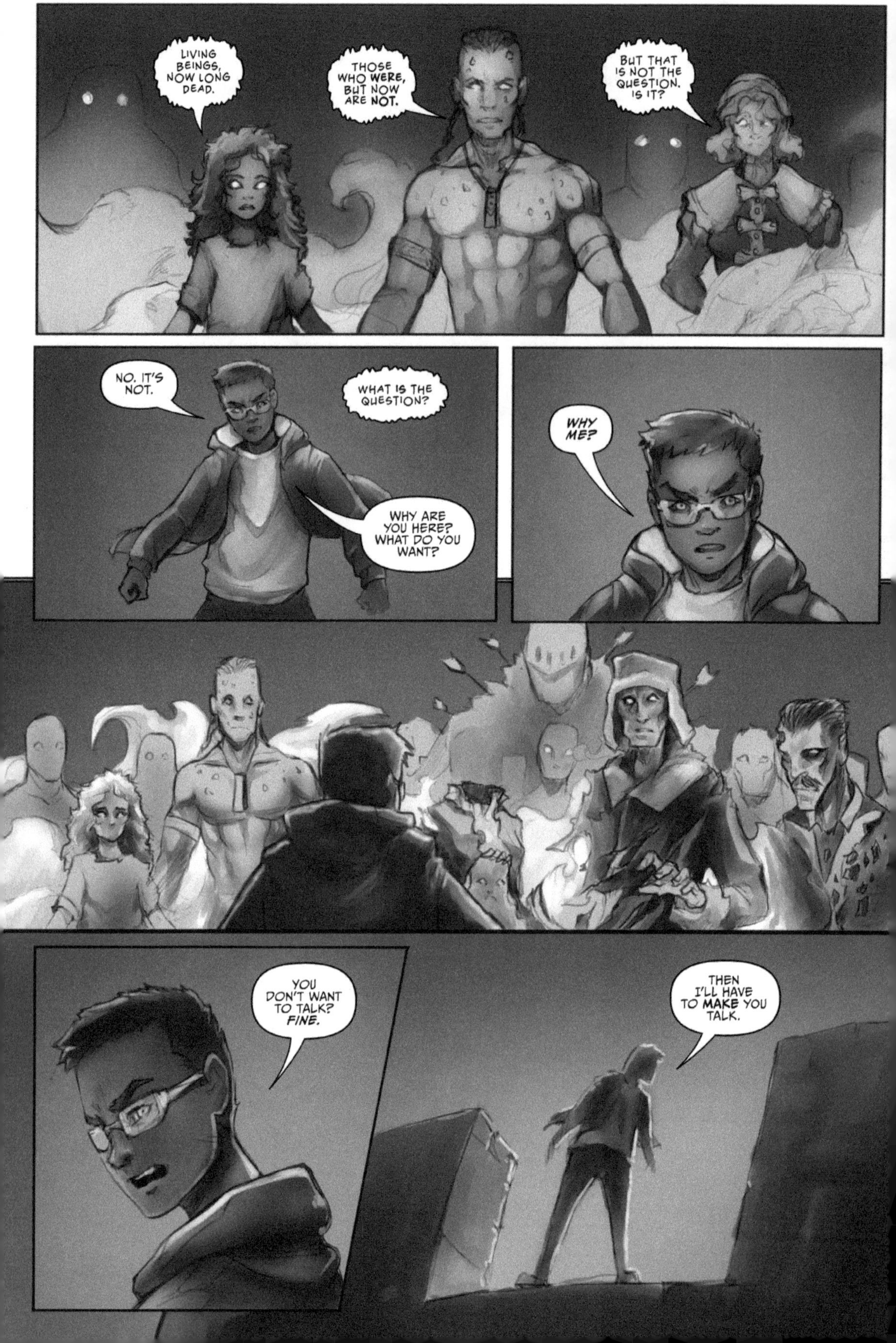
LIVING BEINGS, NOW LONG DEAD.
THOSE WHO **WERE,** BUT NOW ARE **NOT.**
BUT THAT IS NOT THE QUESTION. IS IT?
NO. IT'S NOT.
WHAT **IS** THE QUESTION?
WHY ARE YOU HERE? WHAT DO YOU WANT?
***WHY ME?***
YOU DON'T WANT TO TALK? ***FINE.***
THEN I'LL HAVE TO **MAKE** YOU TALK.

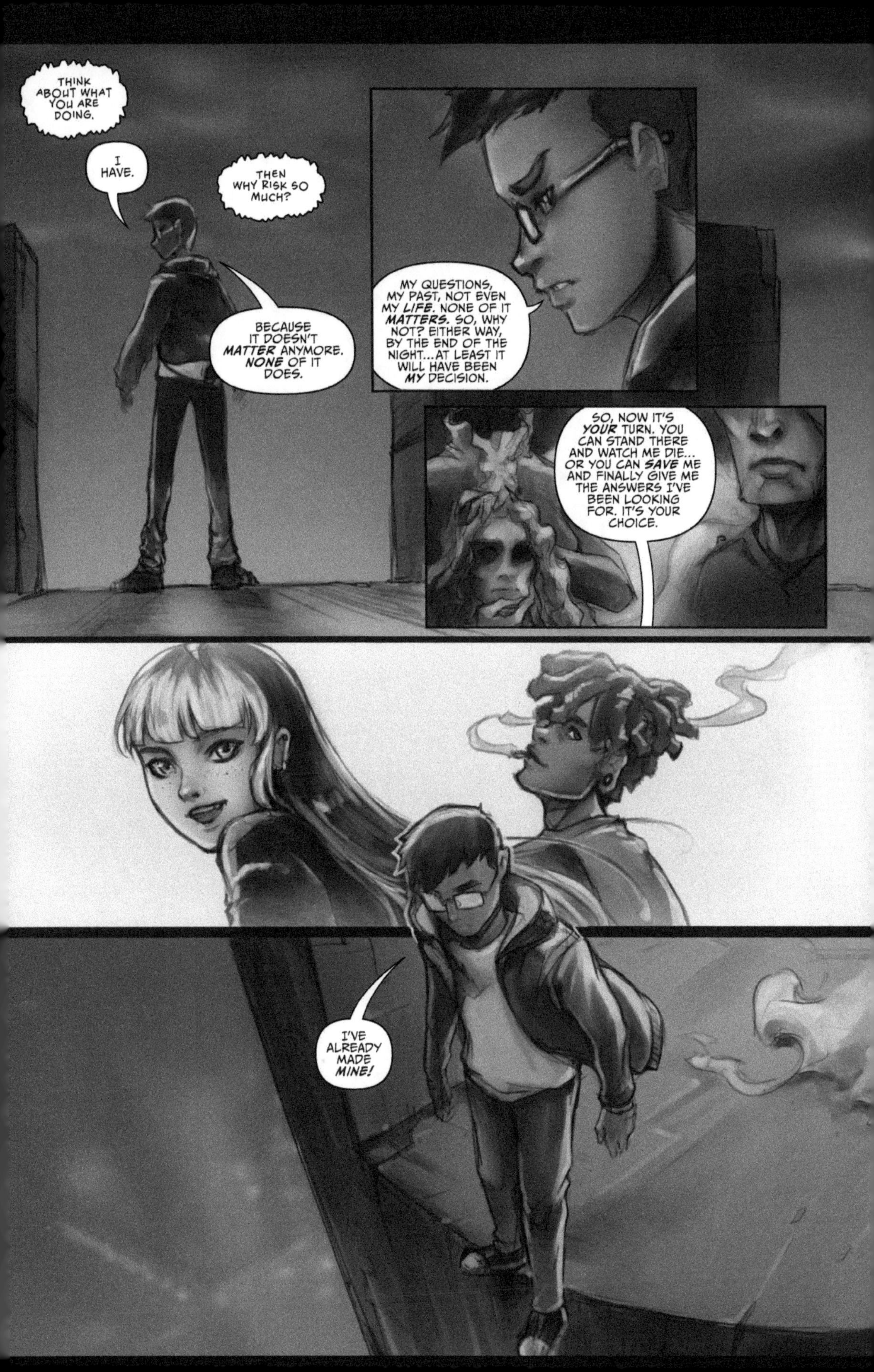
THINK ABOUT WHAT YOU ARE DOING.
I HAVE.
THEN WHY RISK SO MUCH?
BECAUSE IT DOESN'T MATTER ANYMORE. NONE OF IT DOES.
MY QUESTIONS, MY PAST, NOT EVEN MY LIFE. NONE OF IT MATTERS. SO, WHY NOT? EITHER WAY, BY THE END OF THE NIGHT...AT LEAST IT WILL HAVE BEEN MY DECISION.
SO, NOW IT'S YOUR TURN. YOU CAN STAND THERE AND WATCH ME DIE... OR YOU CAN SAVE ME AND FINALLY GIVE ME THE ANSWERS I'VE BEEN LOOKING FOR. IT'S YOUR CHOICE.
I'VE ALREADY MADE MINE!

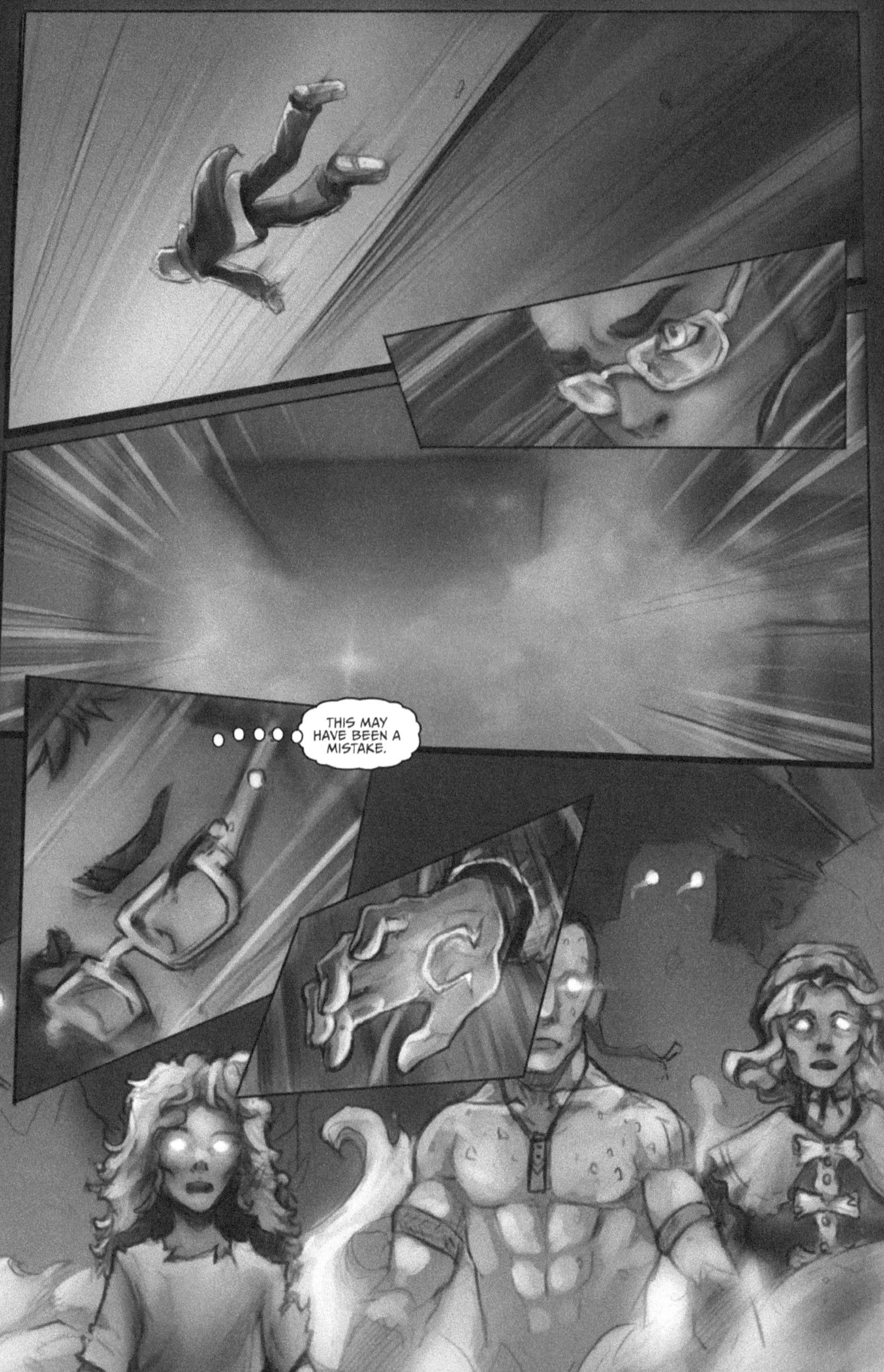
THIS MAY HAVE BEEN A MISTAKE.

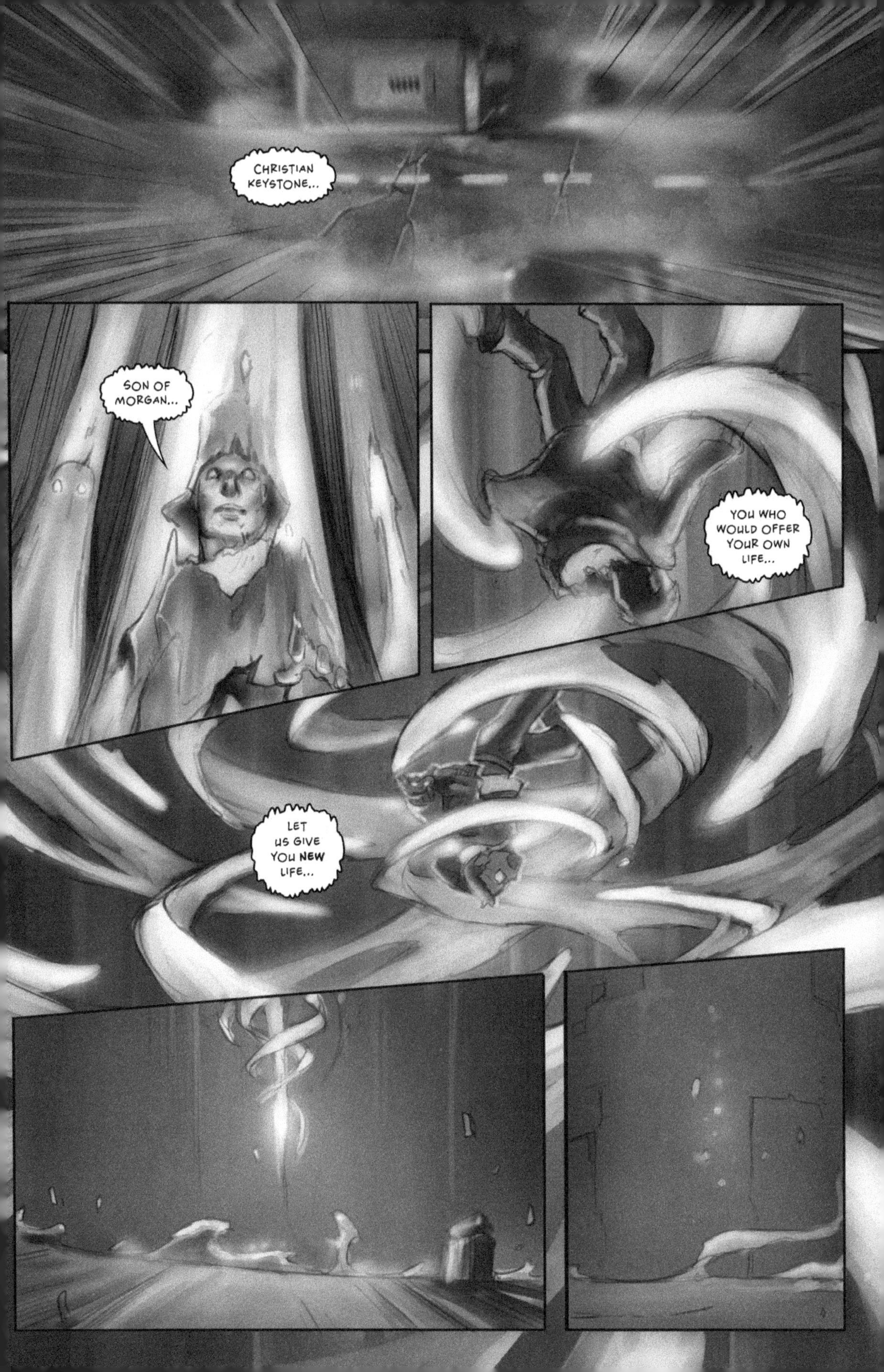
CHRISTIAN KEYSTONE...
SON OF MORGAN...
YOU WHO WOULD OFFER YOUR OWN LIFE...
LET US GIVE YOU NEW LIFE...

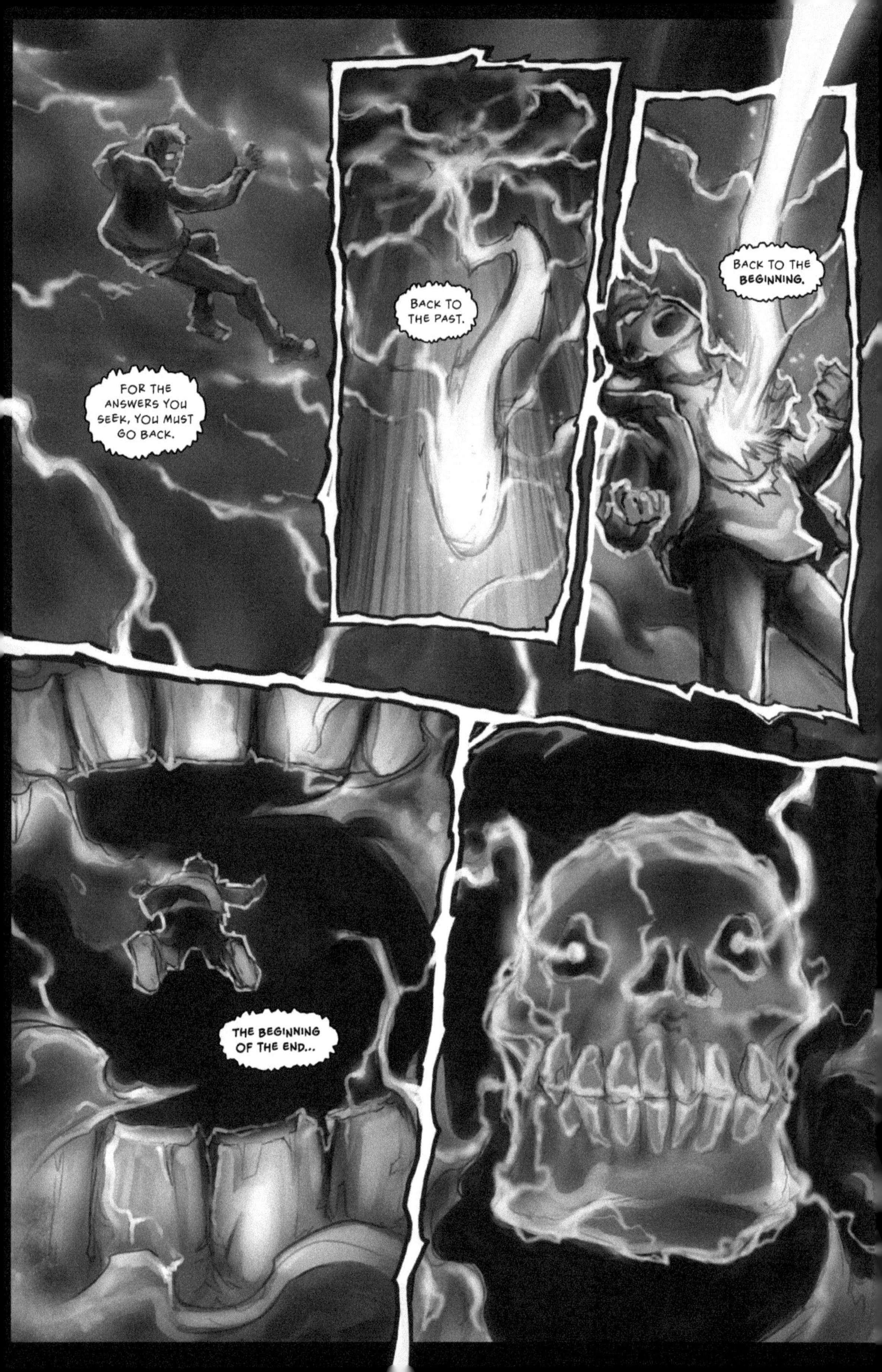
FOR THE ANSWERS YOU SEEK, YOU MUST GO BACK.
BACK TO THE PAST.
BACK TO THE BEGINNING.
THE BEGINNING OF THE END...

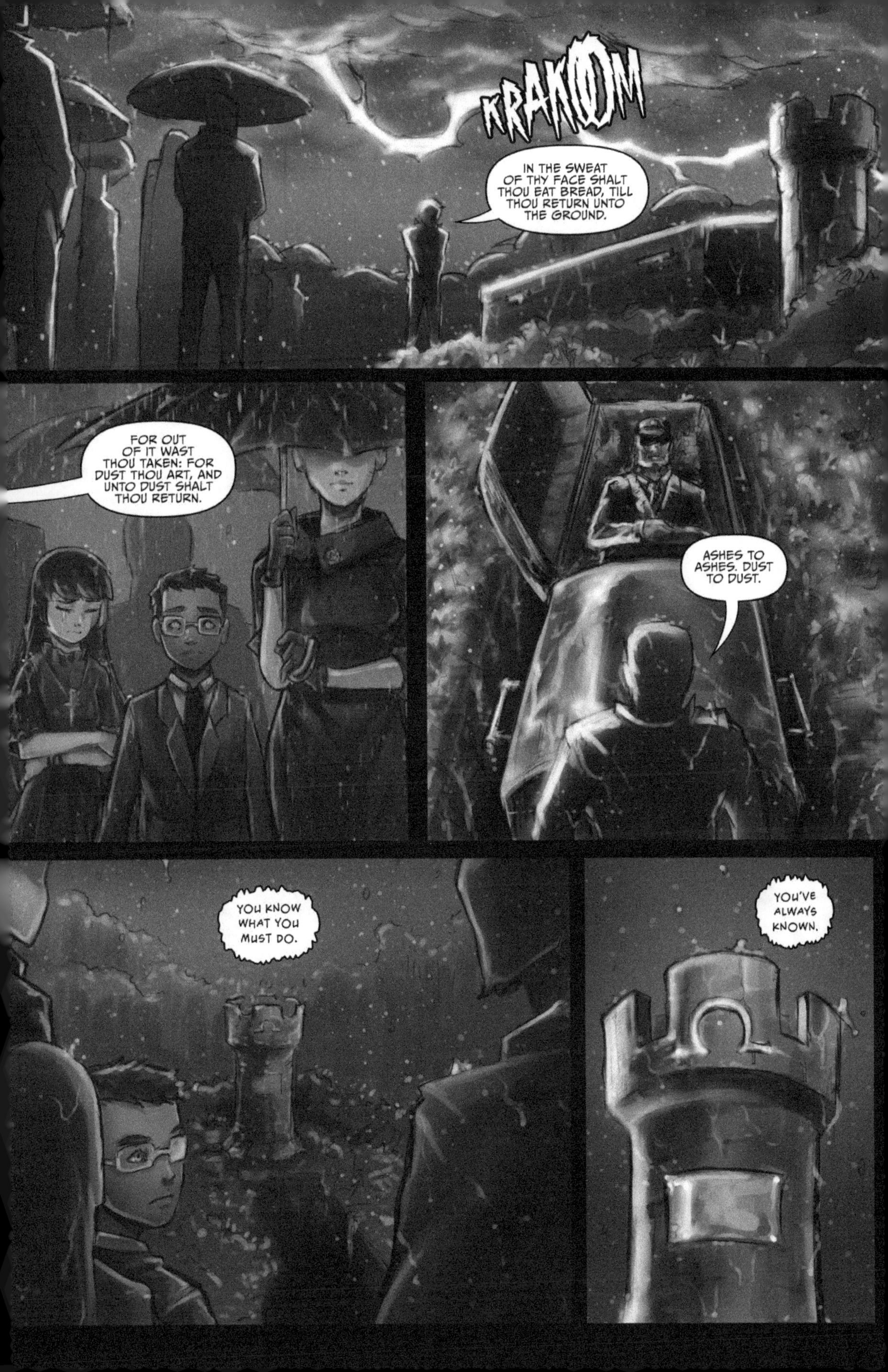
KRAKOOM
IN THE SWEAT OF THY FACE SHALT THOU EAT BREAD, TILL THOU RETURN UNTO THE GROUND.
FOR OUT OF IT WAST THOU TAKEN: FOR DUST THOU ART, AND UNTO DUST SHALT THOU RETURN.
ASHES TO ASHES. DUST TO DUST.
YOU KNOW WHAT YOU MUST DO.
YOU'VE ALWAYS KNOWN.

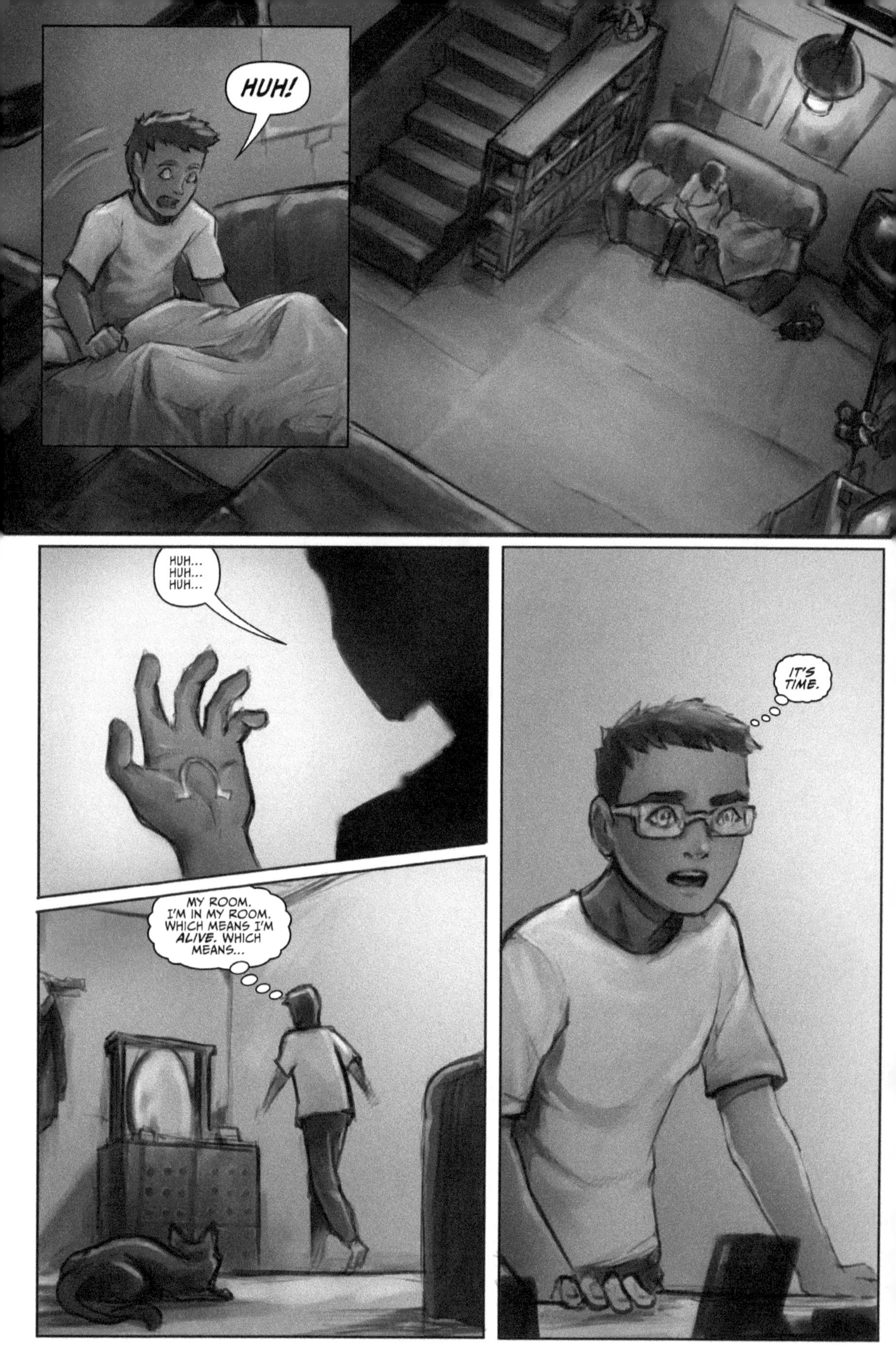
HUH!
HUH...
HUH...
HUH...
MY ROOM.
I'M IN MY ROOM.
WHICH MEANS I'M
ALIVE. WHICH
MEANS...
IT'S TIME.

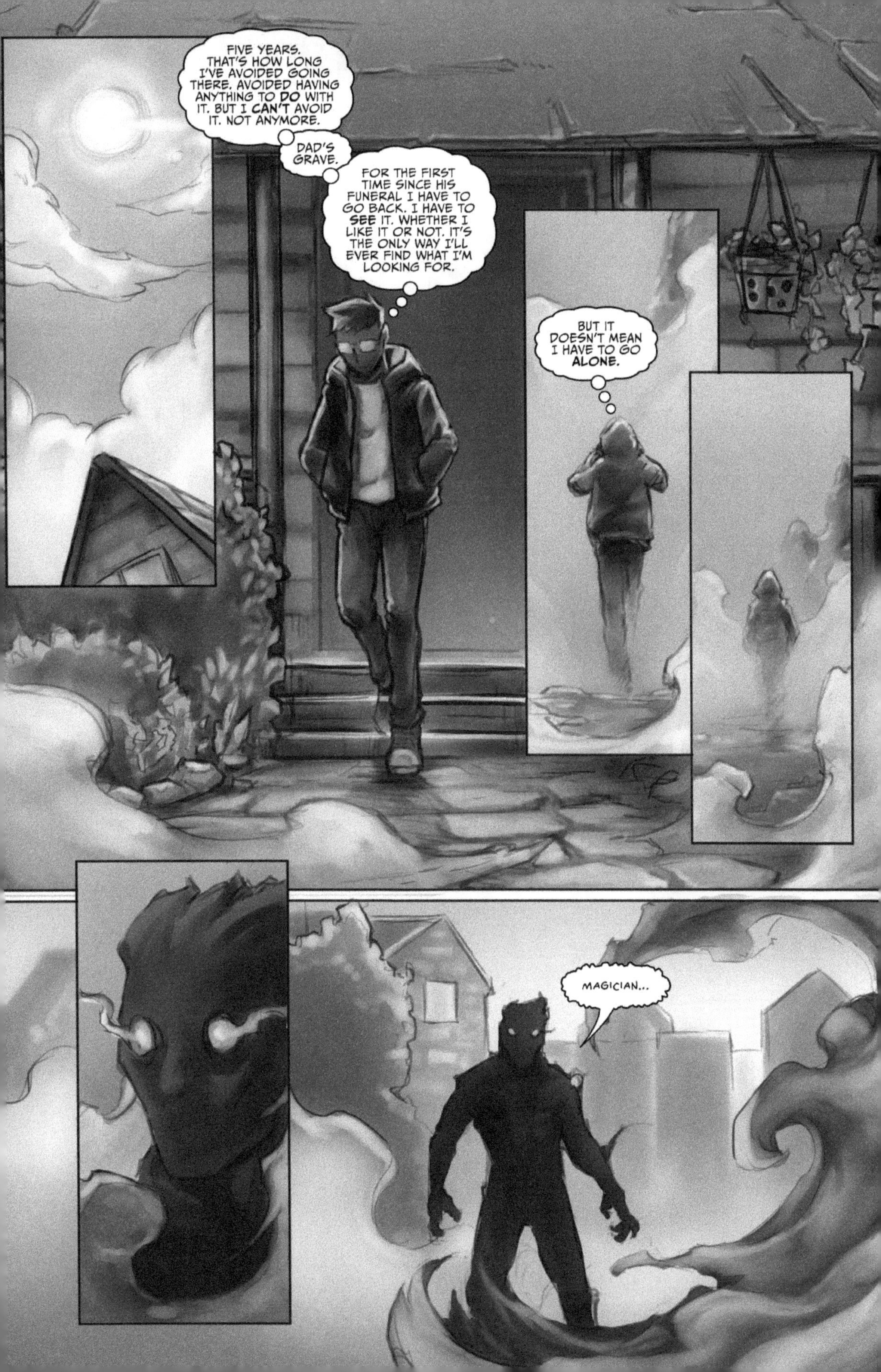
FIVE YEARS. THAT'S HOW LONG I'VE AVOIDED GOING THERE. AVOIDED HAVING ANYTHING TO DO WITH IT. BUT I CAN'T AVOID IT. NOT ANYMORE.
DAD'S GRAVE.
FOR THE FIRST TIME SINCE HIS FUNERAL I HAVE TO GO BACK. I HAVE TO SEE IT. WHETHER I LIKE IT OR NOT. IT'S THE ONLY WAY I'LL EVER FIND WHAT I'M LOOKING FOR.
BUT IT DOESN'T MEAN I HAVE TO GO ALONE.
MAGICIAN...

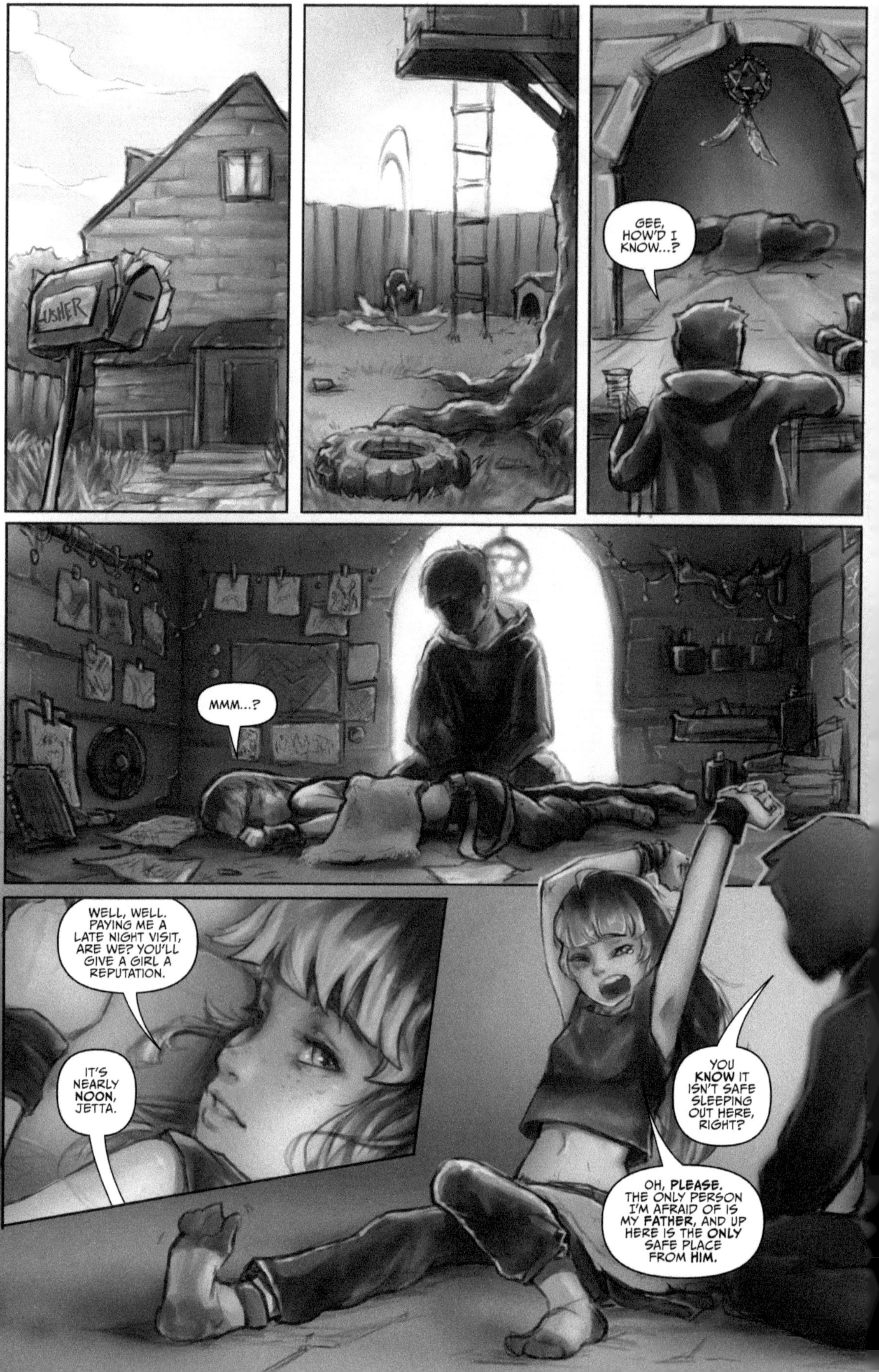
USHER
GEE, HOW'D I KNOW...?
MMM...?
WELL, WELL. PAYING ME A LATE NIGHT VISIT, ARE WE? YOU'LL GIVE A GIRL A REPUTATION.
IT'S NEARLY NOON, JETTA.
YOU KNOW IT ISN'T SAFE SLEEPING OUT HERE, RIGHT?
OH, PLEASE. THE ONLY PERSON I'M AFRAID OF IS MY FATHER, AND UP HERE IS THE ONLY SAFE PLACE FROM HIM.

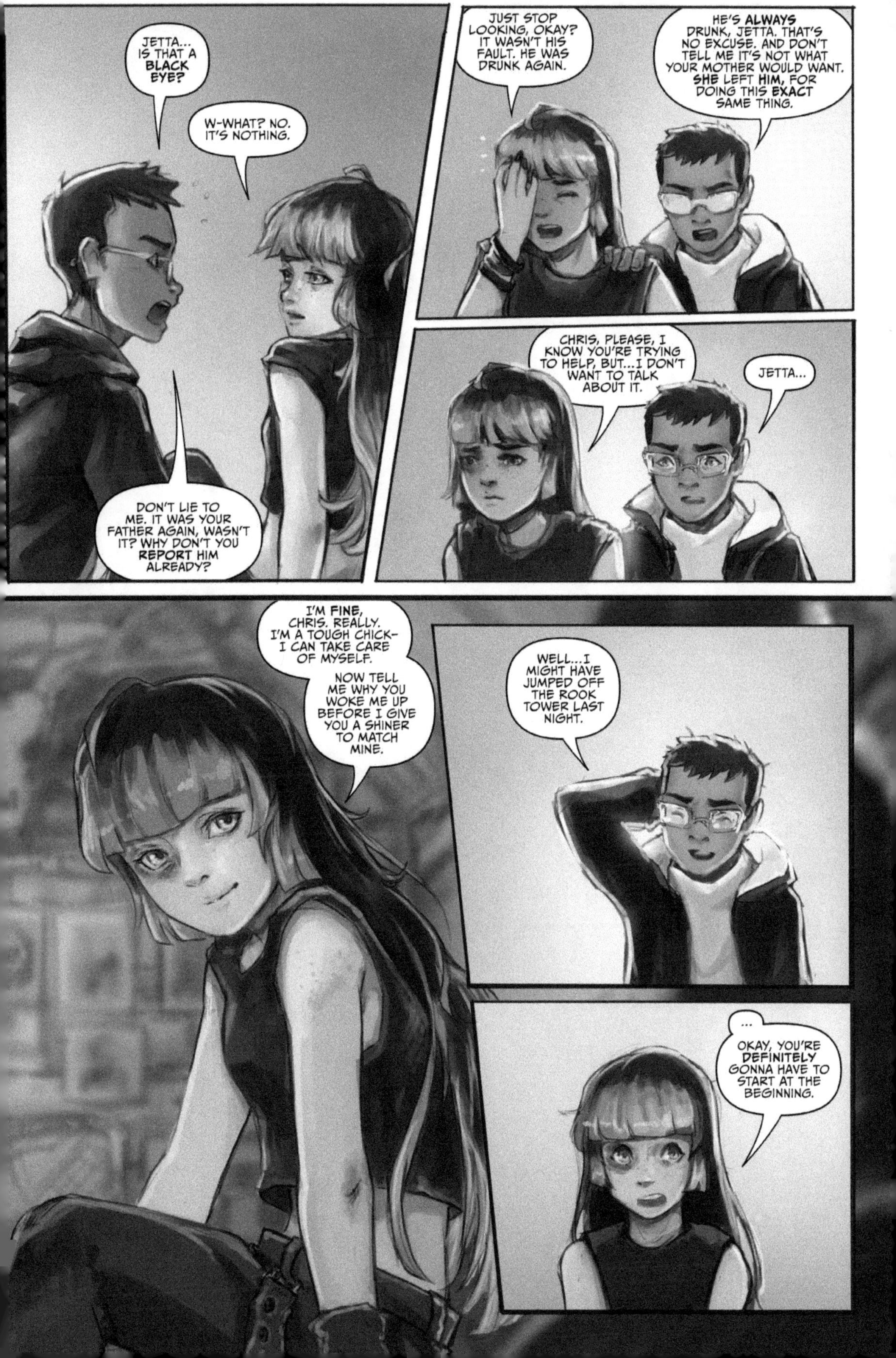
JETTA... IS THAT A BLACK EYE?
W-WHAT? NO. IT'S NOTHING.
DON'T LIE TO ME. IT WAS YOUR FATHER AGAIN, WASN'T IT? WHY DON'T YOU REPORT HIM ALREADY?
JUST STOP LOOKING, OKAY? IT WASN'T HIS FAULT. HE WAS DRUNK AGAIN.
HE'S ALWAYS DRUNK, JETTA. THAT'S NO EXCUSE. AND DON'T TELL ME IT'S NOT WHAT YOUR MOTHER WOULD WANT. SHE LEFT HIM, FOR DOING THIS EXACT SAME THING.
CHRIS, PLEASE, I KNOW YOU'RE TRYING TO HELP, BUT...I DON'T WANT TO TALK ABOUT IT.
JETTA...
I'M FINE, CHRIS. REALLY. I'M A TOUGH CHICK-I CAN TAKE CARE OF MYSELF.
NOW TELL ME WHY YOU WOKE ME UP BEFORE I GIVE YOU A SHINER TO MATCH MINE.
WELL...I MIGHT HAVE JUMPED OFF THE ROOK TOWER LAST NIGHT.
...
OKAY, YOU'RE DEFINITELY GONNA HAVE TO START AT THE BEGINNING.

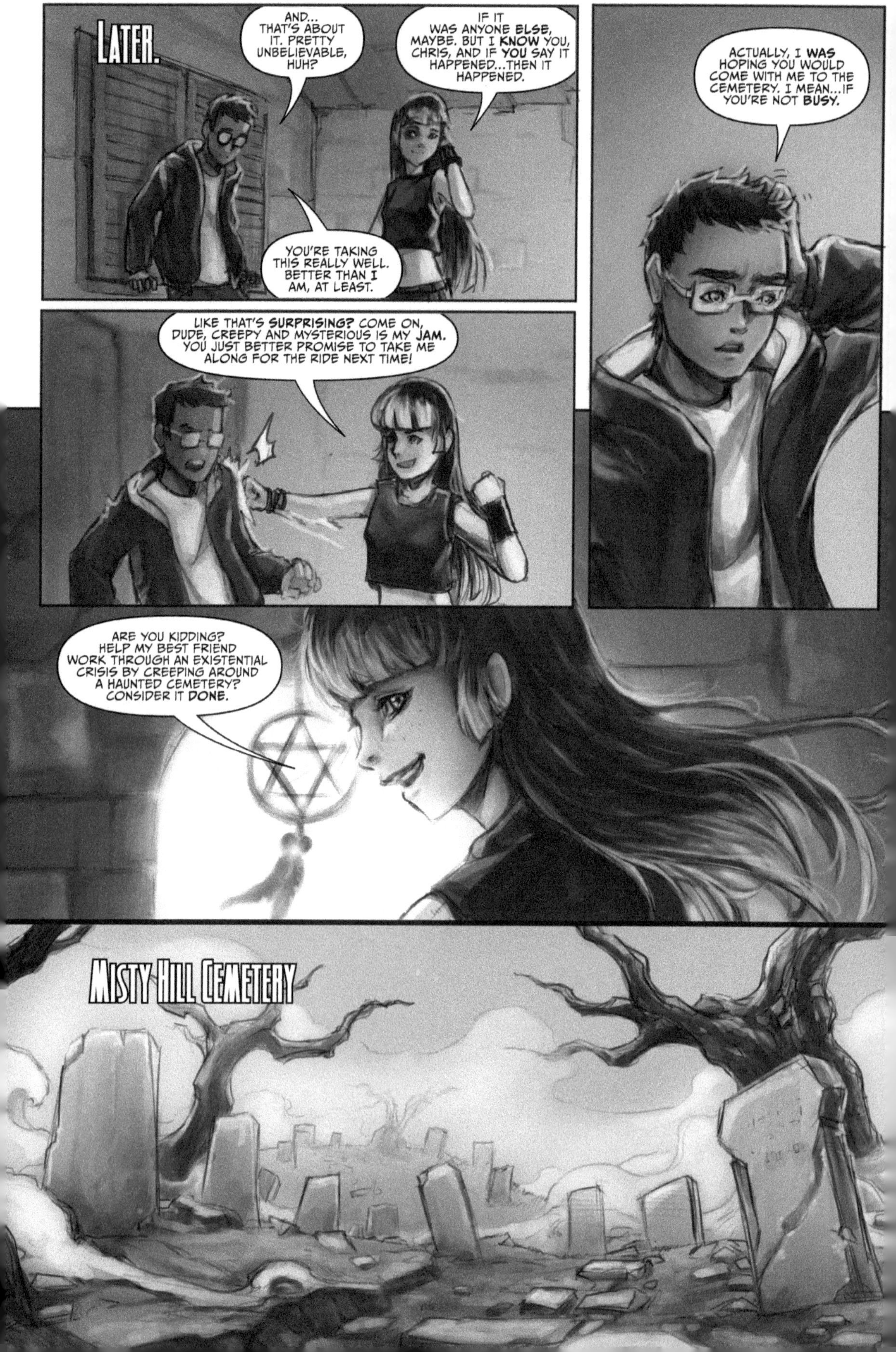
LATER.
AND... THAT'S ABOUT IT. PRETTY UNBELIEVABLE, HUH?
IF IT WAS ANYONE ELSE, MAYBE. BUT I KNOW YOU, CHRIS, AND IF YOU SAY IT HAPPENED...THEN IT HAPPENED.
YOU'RE TAKING THIS REALLY WELL. BETTER THAN I AM, AT LEAST.
LIKE THAT'S SURPRISING? COME ON, DUDE, CREEPY AND MYSTERIOUS IS MY JAM. YOU JUST BETTER PROMISE TO TAKE ME ALONG FOR THE RIDE NEXT TIME!
ACTUALLY, I WAS HOPING YOU WOULD COME WITH ME TO THE CEMETERY. I MEAN...IF YOU'RE NOT BUSY.
ARE YOU KIDDING? HELP MY BEST FRIEND WORK THROUGH AN EXISTENTIAL CRISIS BY CREEPING AROUND A HAUNTED CEMETERY? CONSIDER IT DONE.
MISTY HILL CEMETERY

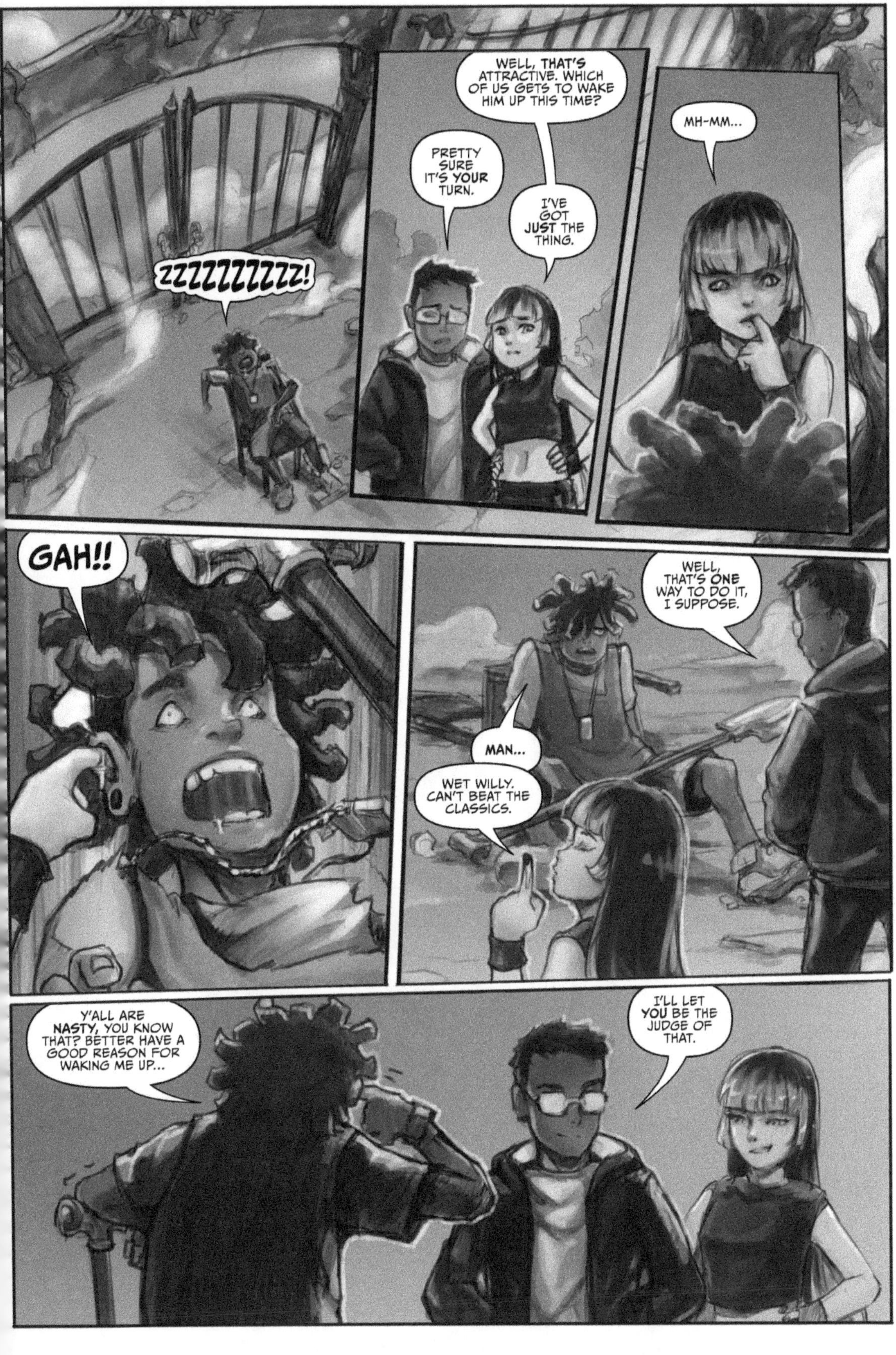
ZZZZZZZZZZ!
WELL, THAT'S ATTRACTIVE. WHICH OF US GETS TO WAKE HIM UP THIS TIME?
PRETTY SURE IT'S YOUR TURN.
I'VE GOT JUST THE THING.
MH-MM...
GAH!!
WELL, THAT'S ONE WAY TO DO IT, I SUPPOSE.
MAN...
WET WILLY. CAN'T BEAT THE CLASSICS.
Y'ALL ARE NASTY, YOU KNOW THAT? BETTER HAVE A GOOD REASON FOR WAKING ME UP...
I'LL LET YOU BE THE JUDGE OF THAT.

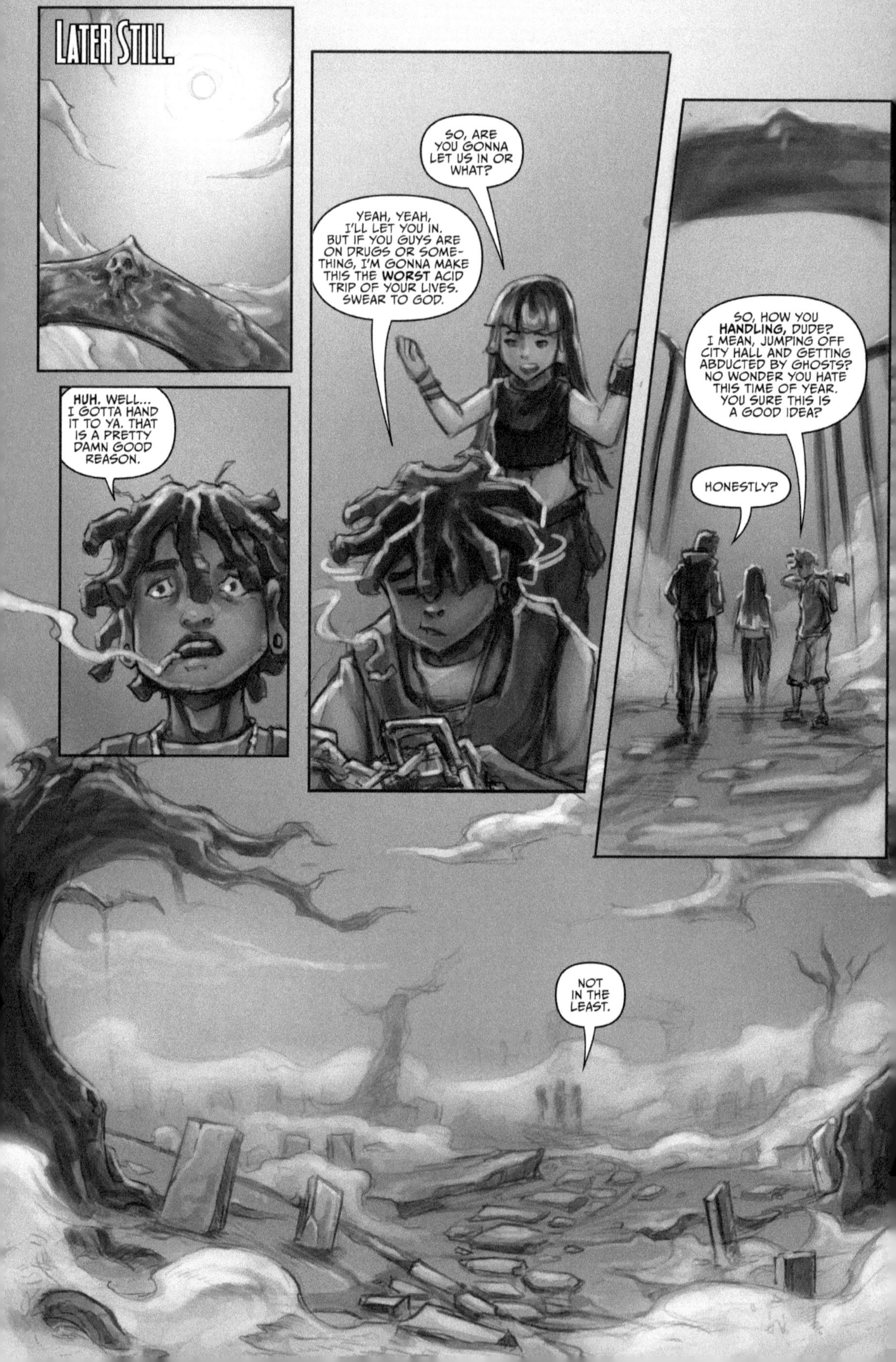
LATER STILL.
SO, ARE YOU GONNA LET US IN OR WHAT?
YEAH, YEAH, I'LL LET YOU IN. BUT IF YOU GUYS ARE ON DRUGS OR SOME-THING, I'M GONNA MAKE THIS THE WORST ACID TRIP OF YOUR LIVES. SWEAR TO GOD.
SO, HOW YOU HANDLING, DUDE? I MEAN, JUMPING OFF CITY HALL AND GETTING ABDUCTED BY GHOSTS? NO WONDER YOU HATE THIS TIME OF YEAR. YOU SURE THIS IS A GOOD IDEA?
HONESTLY?
HUH. WELL... I GOTTA HAND IT TO YA. THAT IS A PRETTY DAMN GOOD REASON.
NOT IN THE LEAST.

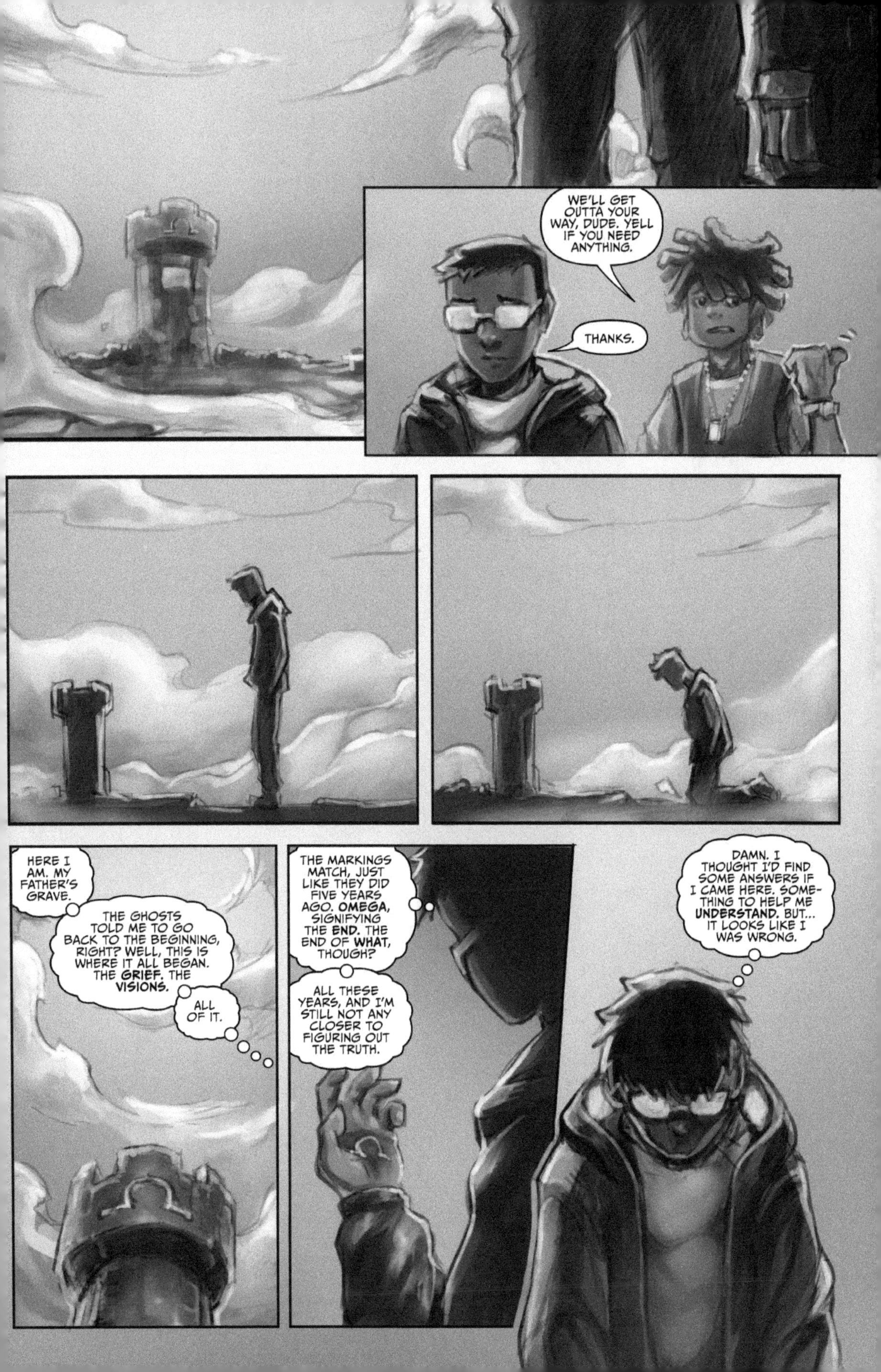
WE'LL GET OUTTA YOUR WAY, DUDE. YELL IF YOU NEED ANYTHING.
THANKS.
HERE I AM. MY FATHER'S GRAVE.
THE GHOSTS TOLD ME TO GO BACK TO THE BEGINNING, RIGHT? WELL, THIS IS WHERE IT ALL BEGAN. THE GRIEF. THE VISIONS.
ALL OF IT.
THE MARKINGS MATCH, JUST LIKE THEY DID FIVE YEARS AGO. OMEGA, SIGNIFYING THE END. THE END OF WHAT, THOUGH?
ALL THESE YEARS, AND I'M STILL NOT ANY CLOSER TO FIGURING OUT THE TRUTH.
DAMN. I THOUGHT I'D FIND SOME ANSWERS IF I CAME HERE. SOMETHING TO HELP ME UNDERSTAND. BUT... IT LOOKS LIKE I WAS WRONG.

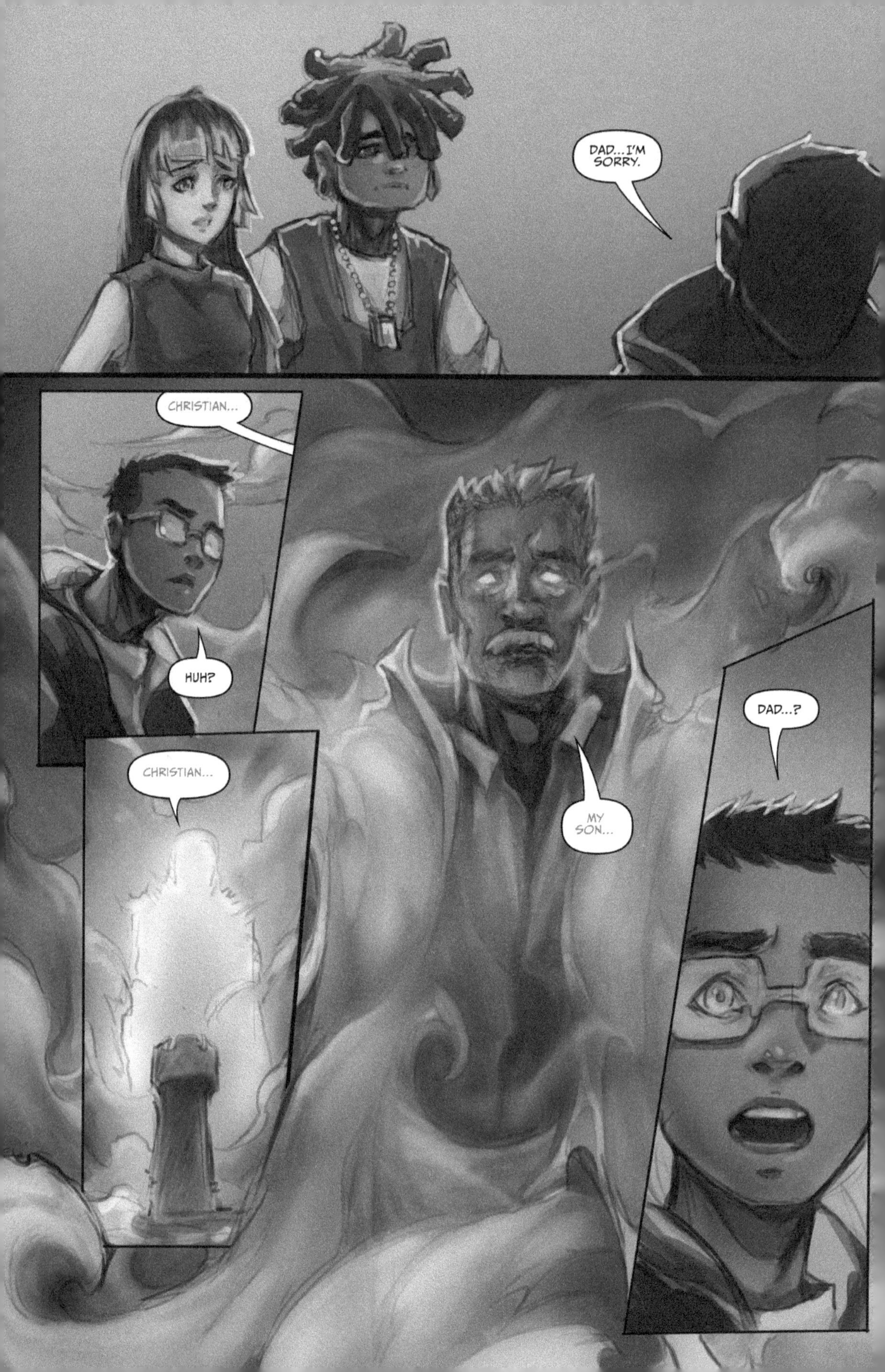
DAD...I'M SORRY.
CHRISTIAN...
HUH?
CHRISTIAN...
MY SON...
DAD...?

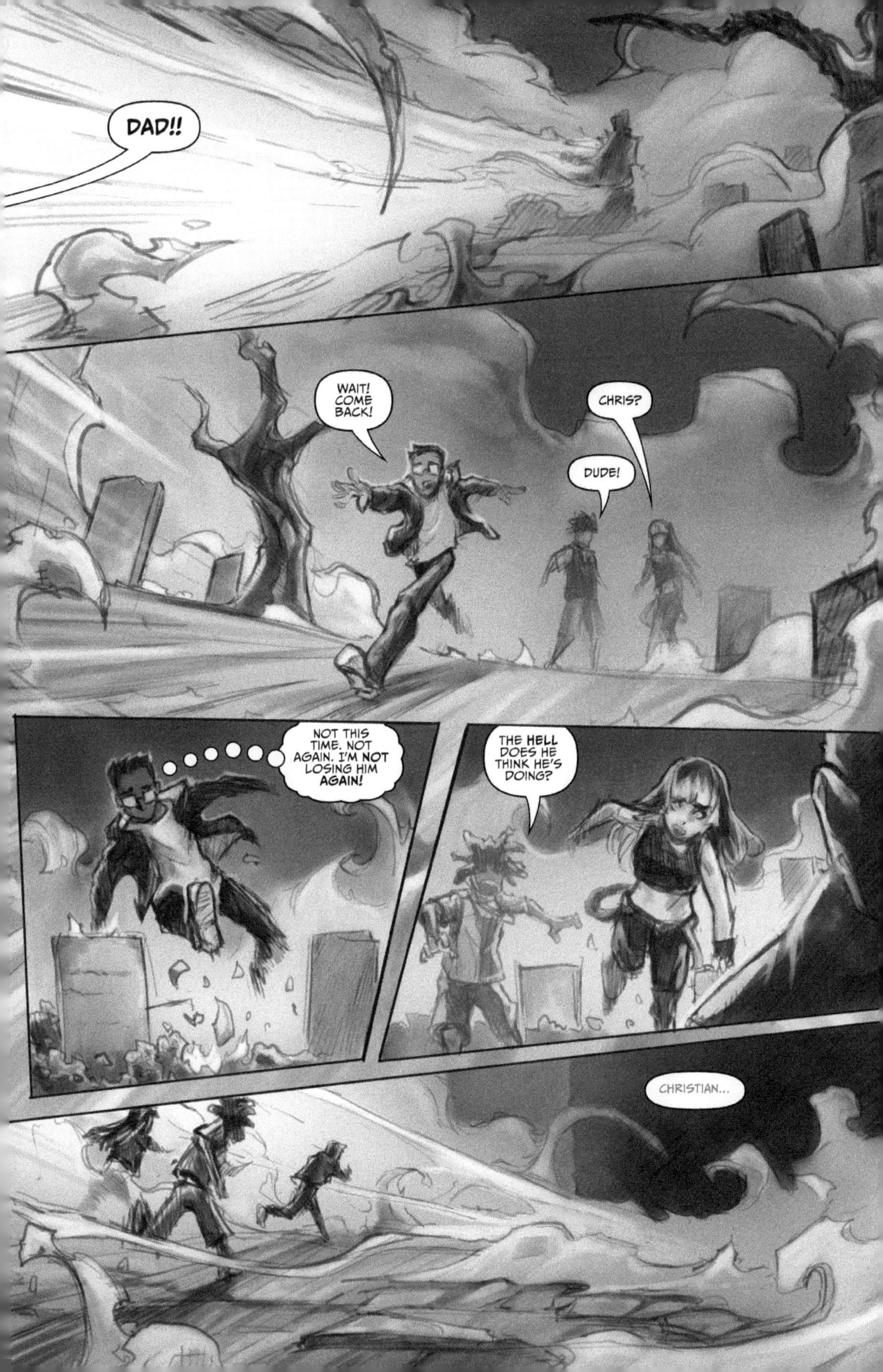
DAD!!
WAIT! COME BACK!
CHRIS?
DUDE!
NOT THIS TIME. NOT AGAIN. I'M NOT LOSING HIM AGAIN!
THE HELL DOES HE THINK HE'S DOING?
CHRISTIAN...

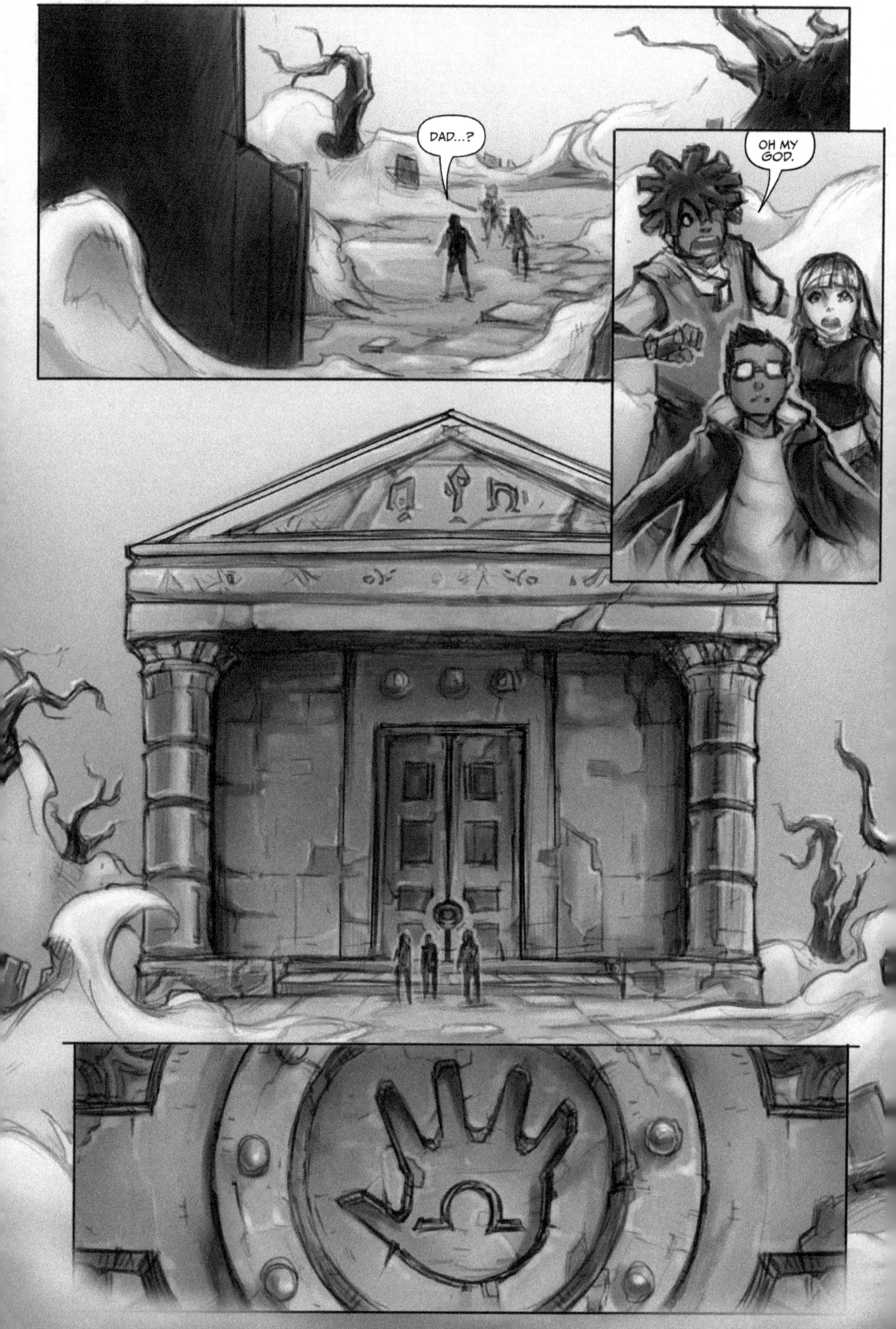
DAD...?
OH MY GOD.

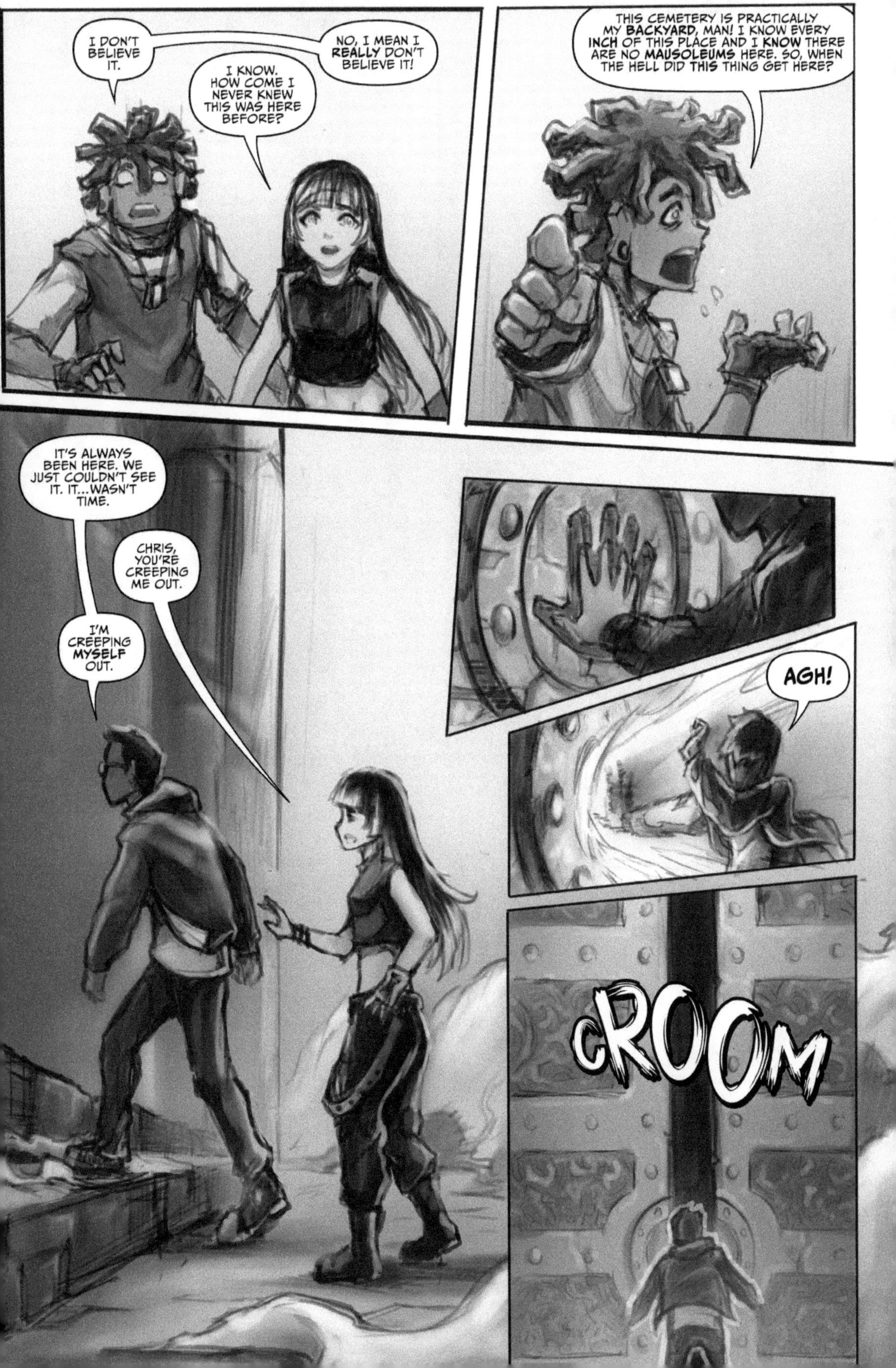
I DON'T BELIEVE IT.
I KNOW. HOW COME I NEVER KNEW THIS WAS HERE BEFORE?
NO, I MEAN I REALLY DON'T BELIEVE IT!
THIS CEMETERY IS PRACTICALLY MY BACKYARD, MAN! I KNOW EVERY INCH OF THIS PLACE AND I KNOW THERE ARE NO MAUSOLEUMS HERE. SO, WHEN THE HELL DID THIS THING GET HERE?
IT'S ALWAYS BEEN HERE. WE JUST COULDN'T SEE IT. IT...WASN'T TIME.
CHRIS, YOU'RE CREEPING ME OUT.
I'M CREEPING MYSELF OUT.
AGH!
cROOm

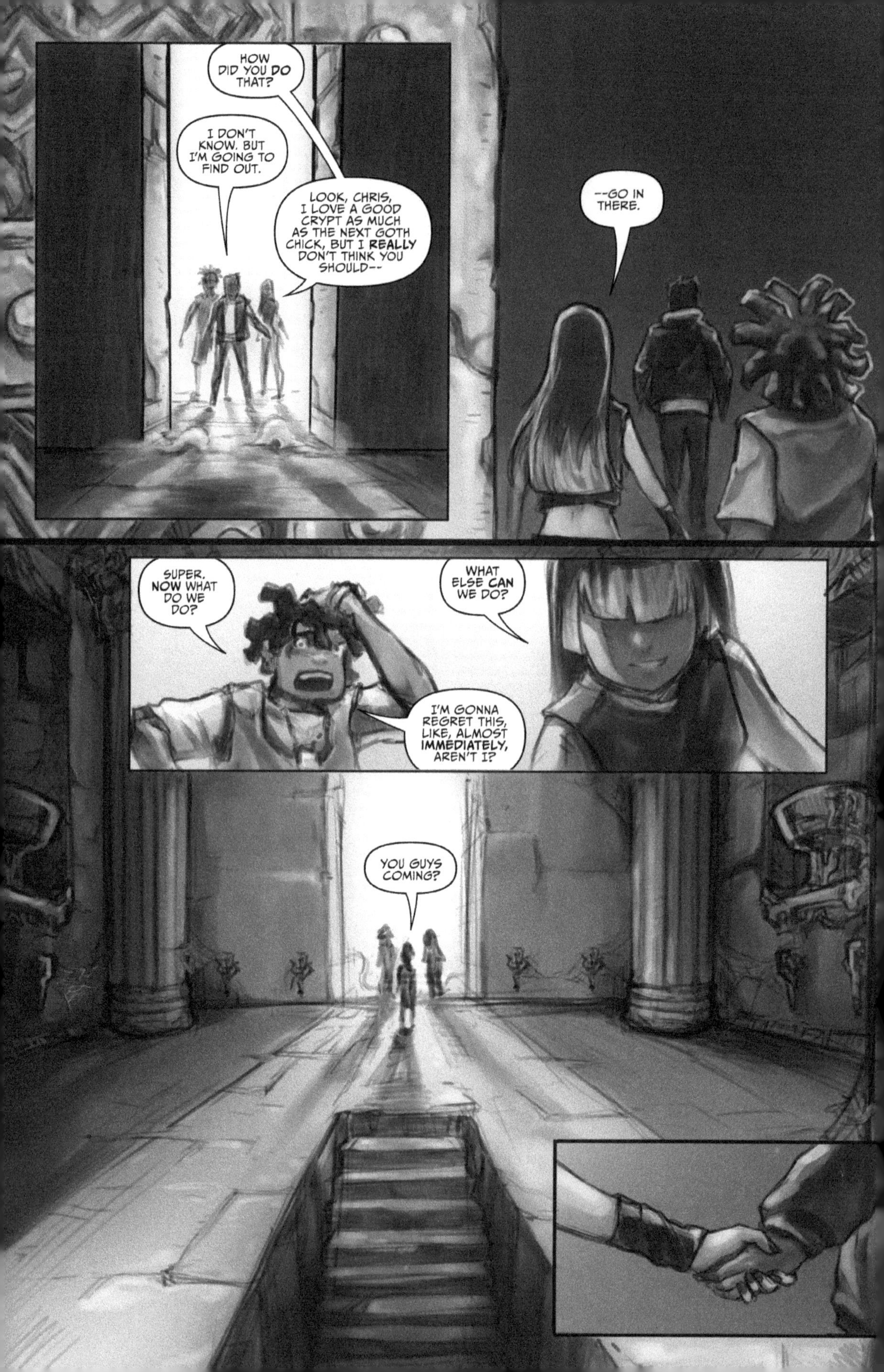
HOW DID YOU DO THAT?
I DON'T KNOW. BUT I'M GOING TO FIND OUT.
LOOK, CHRIS, I LOVE A GOOD CRYPT AS MUCH AS THE NEXT GOTH CHICK, BUT I REALLY DON'T THINK YOU SHOULD--
--GO IN THERE.
SUPER. NOW WHAT DO WE DO?
WHAT ELSE CAN WE DO?
I'M GONNA REGRET THIS, LIKE, ALMOST IMMEDIATELY, AREN'T I?
YOU GUYS COMING?

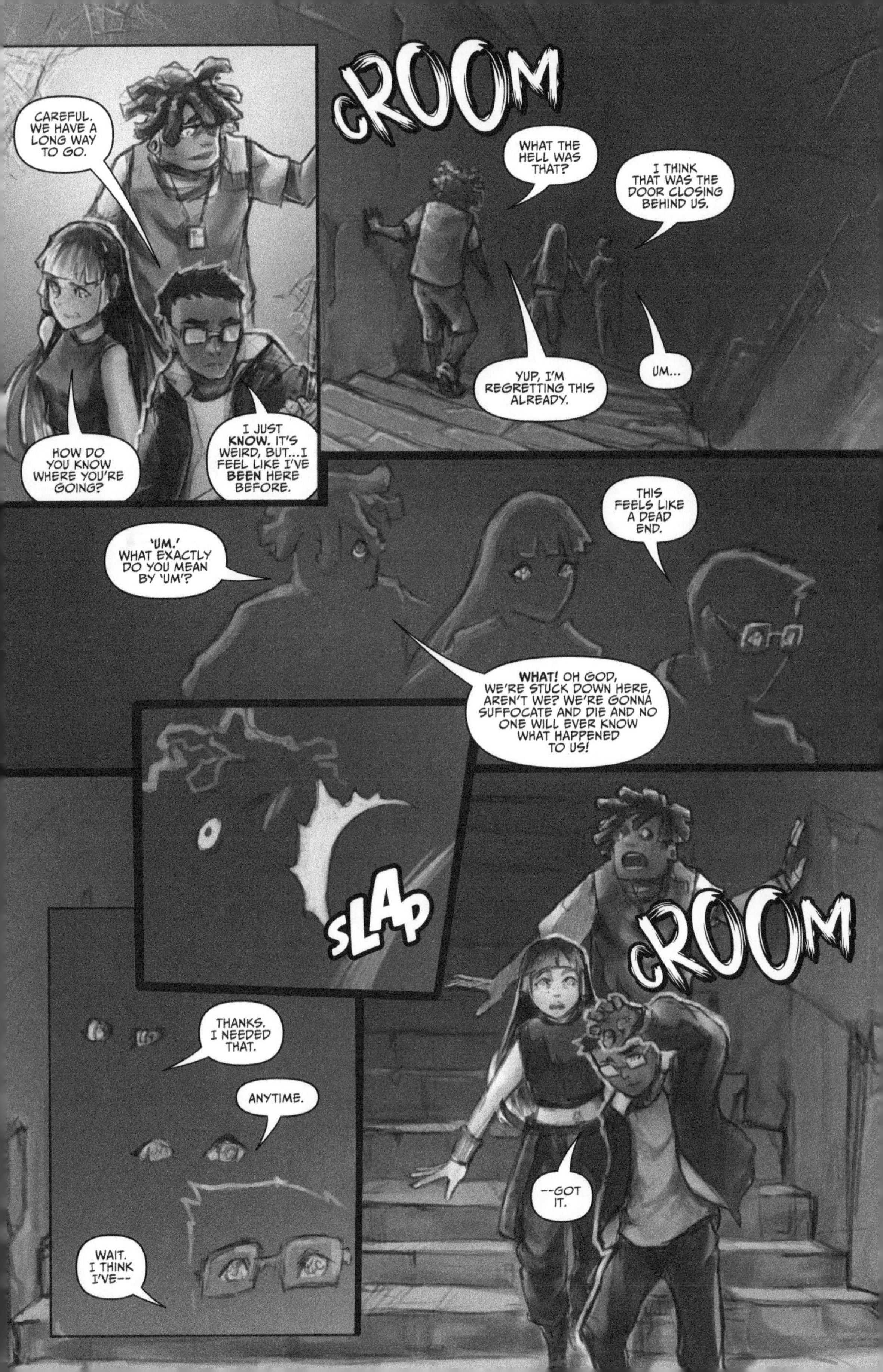

CAREFUL. WE HAVE A LONG WAY TO GO.
HOW DO YOU KNOW WHERE YOU'RE GOING?
I JUST KNOW. IT'S WEIRD, BUT...I FEEL LIKE I'VE BEEN HERE BEFORE.
cROOM
WHAT THE HELL WAS THAT?
I THINK THAT WAS THE DOOR CLOSING BEHIND US.
YUP, I'M REGRETTING THIS ALREADY.
UM...
'UM.' WHAT EXACTLY DO YOU MEAN BY 'UM'?
THIS FEELS LIKE A DEAD END.
WHAT! OH GOD, WE'RE STUCK DOWN HERE, AREN'T WE? WE'RE GONNA SUFFOCATE AND DIE AND NO ONE WILL EVER KNOW WHAT HAPPENED TO US!
sLAp
THANKS. I NEEDED THAT.
ANYTIME.
WAIT. I THINK I'VE--
--GOT IT.
cROOM

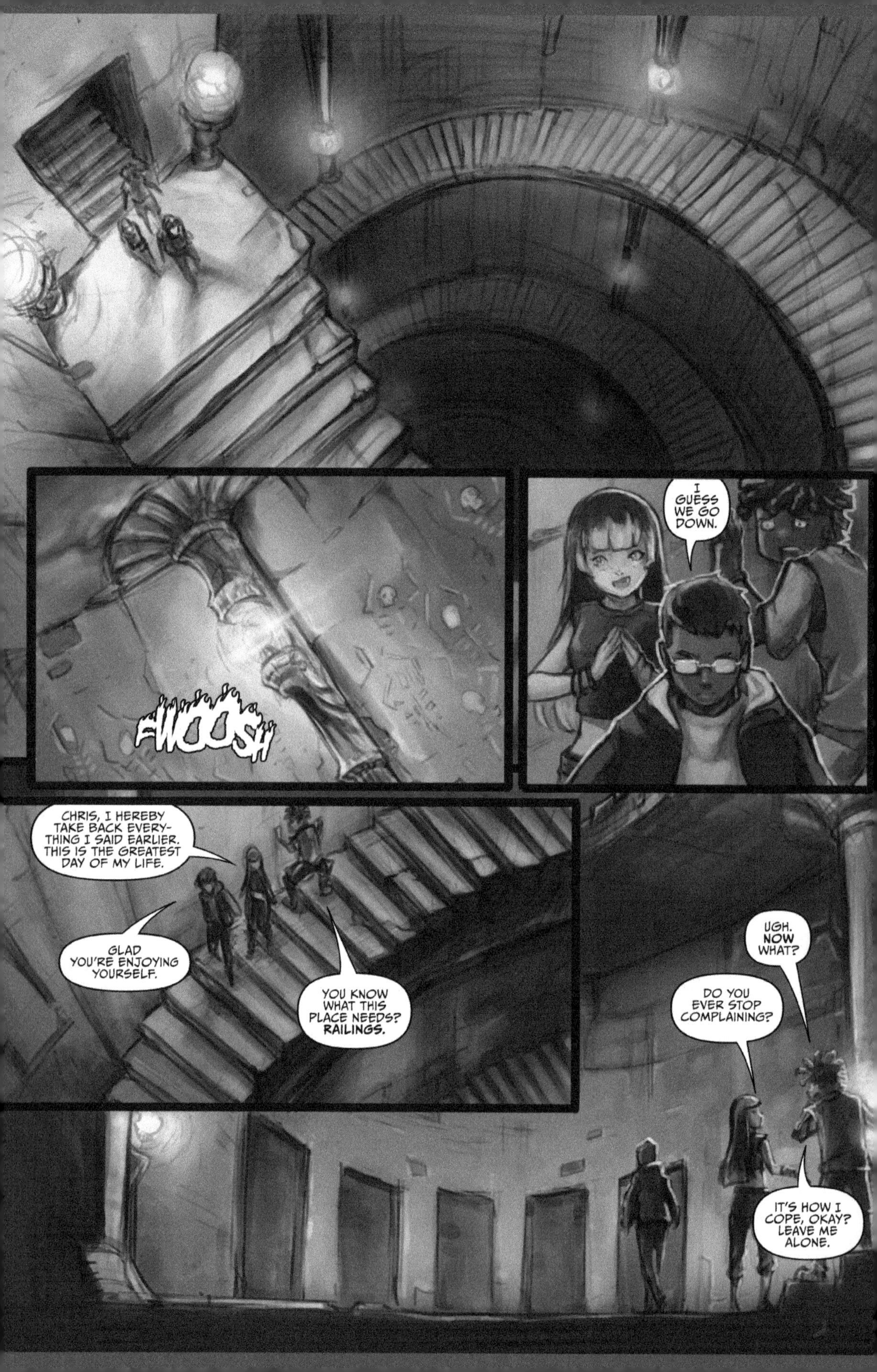
FWOOSH
I GUESS WE GO DOWN.
CHRIS, I HEREBY TAKE BACK EVERY-THING I SAID EARLIER. THIS IS THE GREATEST DAY OF MY LIFE.
GLAD YOU'RE ENJOYING YOURSELF.
YOU KNOW WHAT THIS PLACE NEEDS? **RAILINGS.**
UGH. **NOW** WHAT?
DO YOU EVER STOP COMPLAINING?
IT'S HOW I COPE, OKAY? LEAVE ME ALONE.

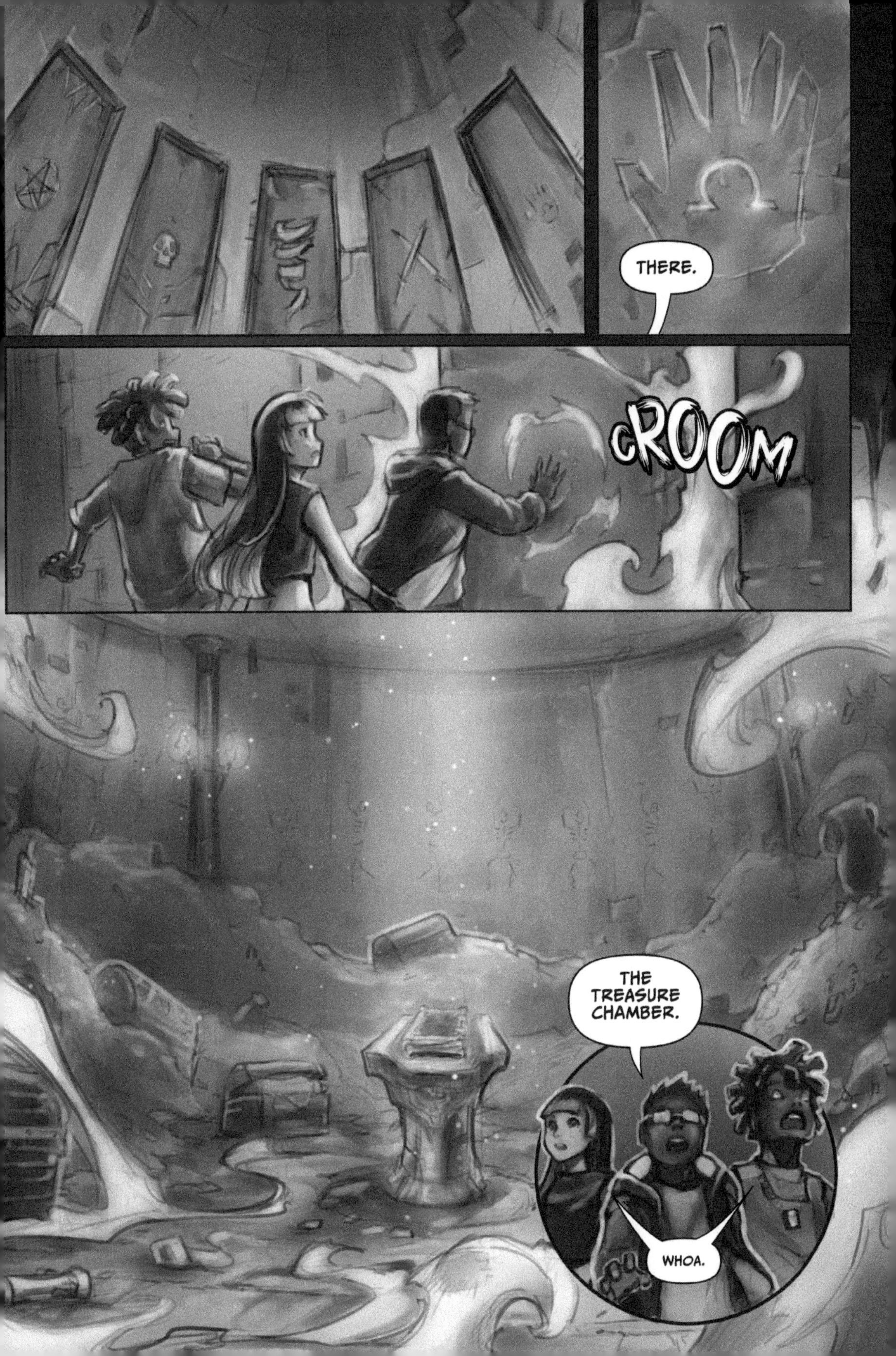
THERE.
CROOM
THE TREASURE CHAMBER.
WHOA.

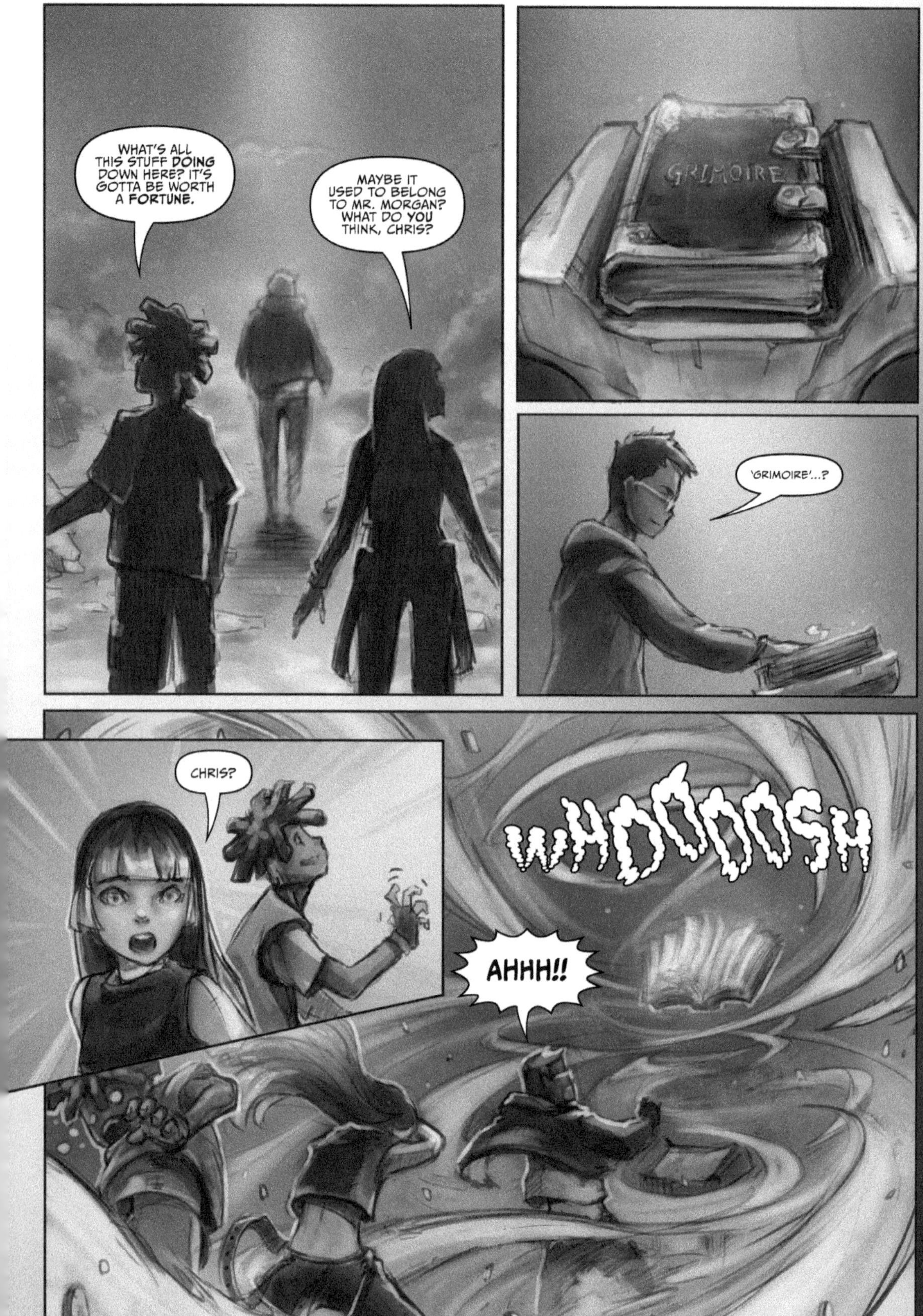
WHAT'S ALL THIS STUFF DOING DOWN HERE? IT'S GOTTA BE WORTH A FORTUNE.
MAYBE IT USED TO BELONG TO MR. MORGAN? WHAT DO YOU THINK, CHRIS?
GRIMOIRE
'GRIMOIRE'...?
CHRIS?
WHOOOOSH
AHHH!!

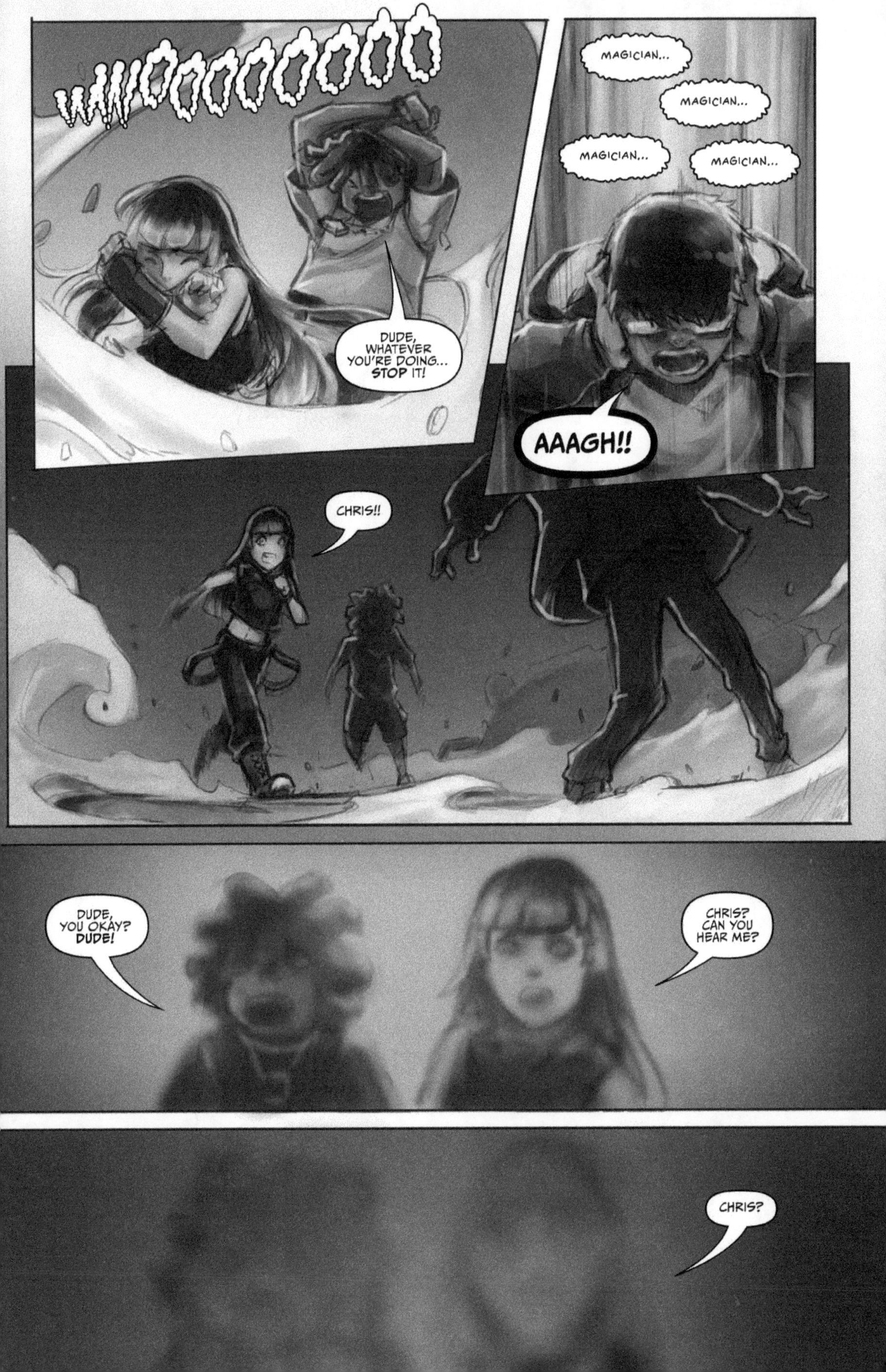
WWOOOOOOOOO
DUDE, WHATEVER YOU'RE DOING... STOP IT!
MAGICIAN...
MAGICIAN...
MAGICIAN...
MAGICIAN...
AAAGH!!
CHRIS!!
DUDE, YOU OKAY? DUDE!
CHRIS? CAN YOU HEAR ME?
CHRIS?

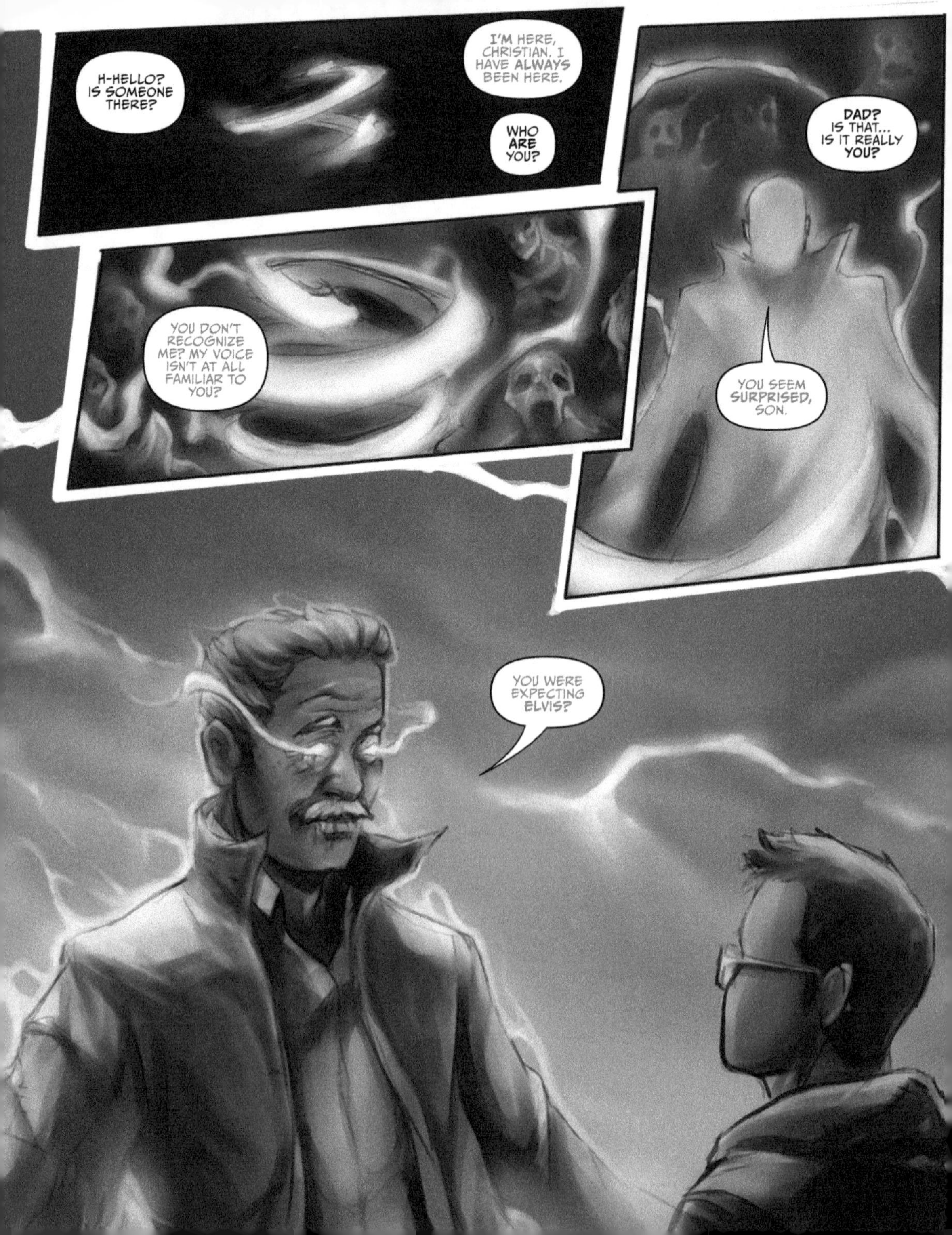
H-HELLO? IS SOMEONE THERE?
I'M HERE, CHRISTIAN. I HAVE ALWAYS BEEN HERE.
WHO ARE YOU?
YOU DON'T RECOGNIZE ME? MY VOICE ISN'T AT ALL FAMILIAR TO YOU?
DAD? IS THAT... IS IT REALLY YOU?
YOU SEEM SURPRISED, SON.
YOU WERE EXPECTING ELVIS?

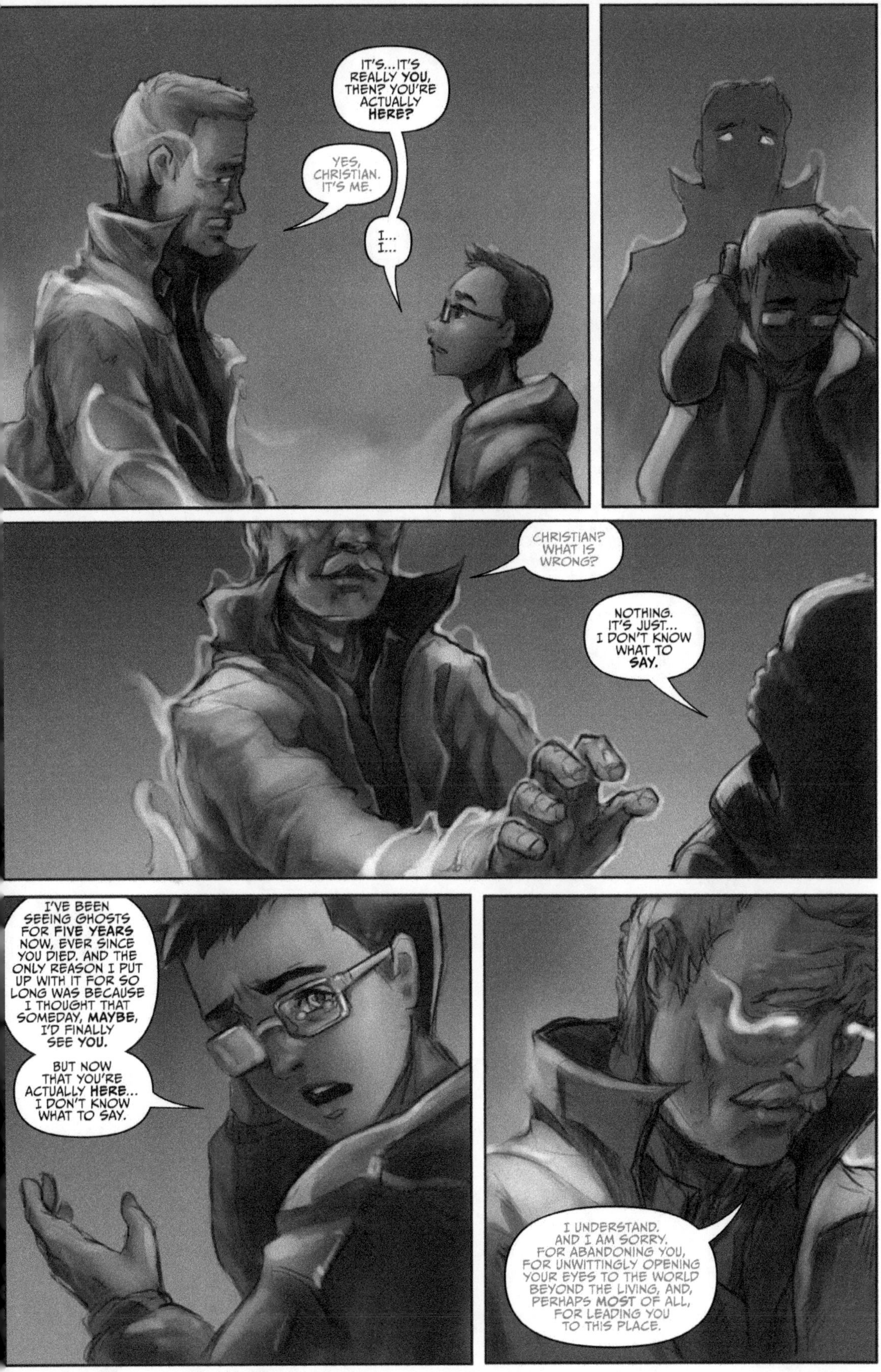
IT'S...IT'S REALLY YOU, THEN? YOU'RE ACTUALLY HERE?
YES, CHRISTIAN. IT'S ME.
I... I...
CHRISTIAN? WHAT IS WRONG?
NOTHING. IT'S JUST... I DON'T KNOW WHAT TO SAY.
I'VE BEEN SEEING GHOSTS FOR FIVE YEARS NOW, EVER SINCE YOU DIED. AND THE ONLY REASON I PUT UP WITH IT FOR SO LONG WAS BECAUSE I THOUGHT THAT SOMEDAY, MAYBE, I'D FINALLY SEE YOU.
BUT NOW THAT YOU'RE ACTUALLY HERE... I DON'T KNOW WHAT TO SAY.
I UNDERSTAND. AND I AM SORRY. FOR ABANDONING YOU, FOR UNWITTINGLY OPENING YOUR EYES TO THE WORLD BEYOND THE LIVING, AND, PERHAPS MOST OF ALL, FOR LEADING YOU TO THIS PLACE.

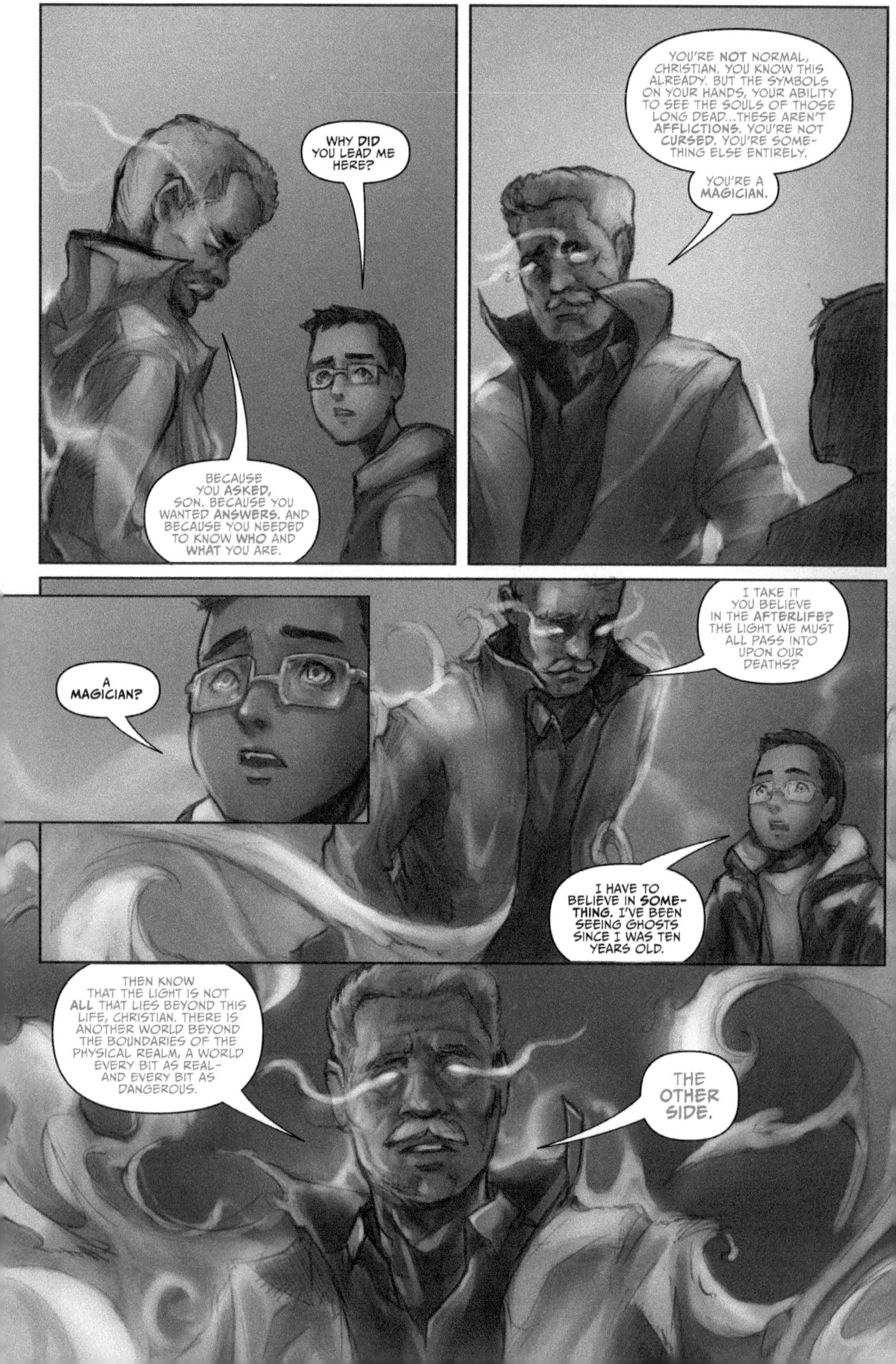
WHY DID YOU LEAD ME HERE?
BECAUSE YOU ASKED, SON. BECAUSE YOU WANTED ANSWERS. AND BECAUSE YOU NEEDED TO KNOW WHO AND WHAT YOU ARE.
YOU'RE NOT NORMAL, CHRISTIAN. YOU KNOW THIS ALREADY. BUT THE SYMBOLS ON YOUR HANDS, YOUR ABILITY TO SEE THE SOULS OF THOSE LONG DEAD...THESE AREN'T AFFLICTIONS. YOU'RE NOT CURSED. YOU'RE SOME-THING ELSE ENTIRELY.
YOU'RE A MAGICIAN.
A MAGICIAN?
I TAKE IT YOU BELIEVE IN THE AFTERLIFE? THE LIGHT WE MUST ALL PASS INTO UPON OUR DEATHS?
I HAVE TO BELIEVE IN SOME-THING. I'VE BEEN SEEING GHOSTS SINCE I WAS TEN YEARS OLD.
THEN KNOW THAT THE LIGHT IS NOT ALL THAT LIES BEYOND THIS LIFE, CHRISTIAN. THERE IS ANOTHER WORLD BEYOND THE BOUNDARIES OF THE PHYSICAL REALM, A WORLD EVERY BIT AS REAL-AND EVERY BIT AS DANGEROUS.
THE OTHER SIDE.

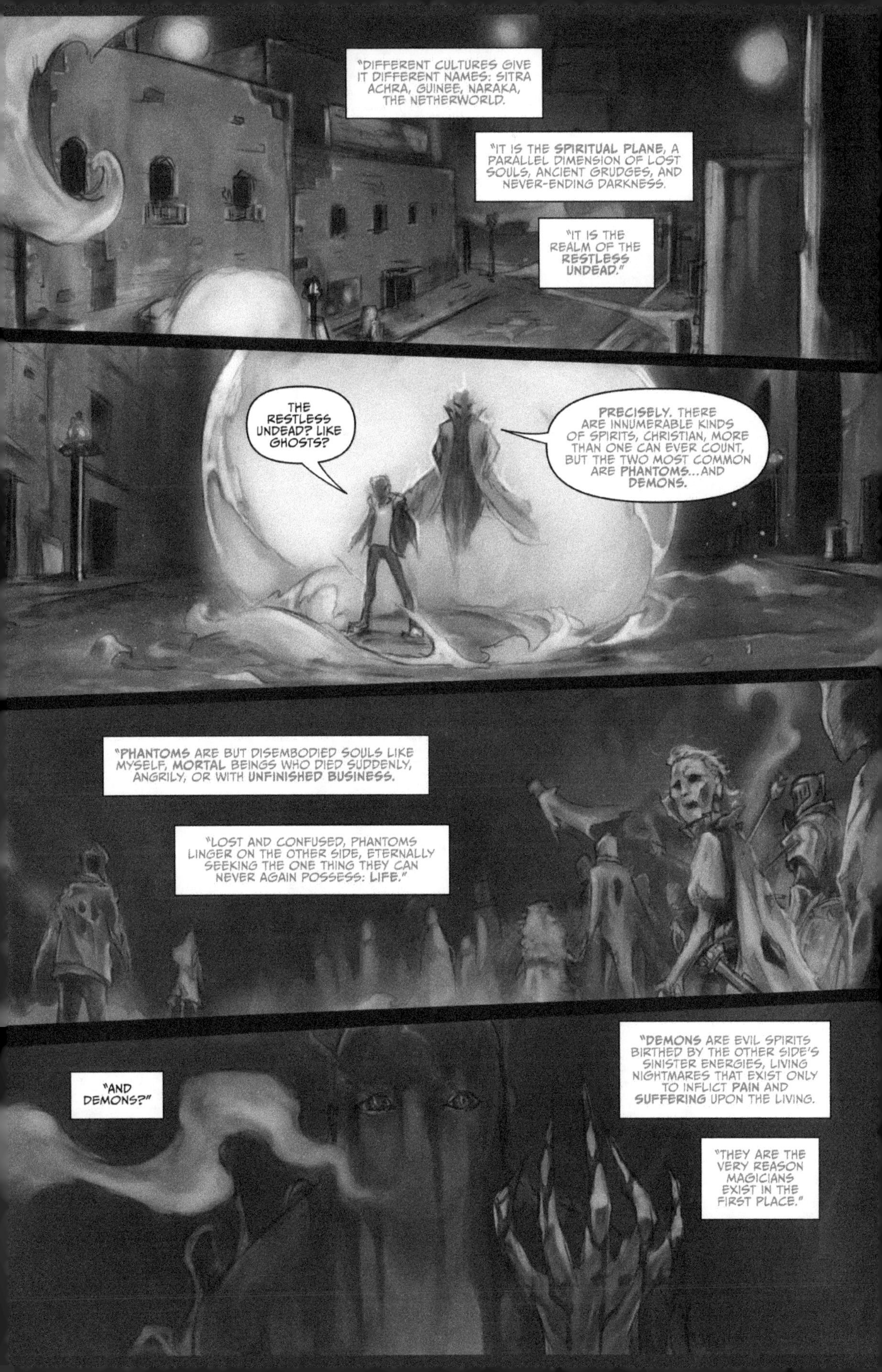
"DIFFERENT CULTURES GIVE IT DIFFERENT NAMES: SITRA ACHRA, GUINEE, NARAKA, THE NETHERWORLD.
"IT IS THE SPIRITUAL PLANE, A PARALLEL DIMENSION OF LOST SOULS, ANCIENT GRUDGES, AND NEVER-ENDING DARKNESS.
"IT IS THE REALM OF THE RESTLESS UNDEAD."
THE RESTLESS UNDEAD? LIKE GHOSTS?
PRECISELY. THERE ARE INNUMERABLE KINDS OF SPIRITS, CHRISTIAN, MORE THAN ONE CAN EVER COUNT, BUT THE TWO MOST COMMON ARE PHANTOMS... AND DEMONS.
"PHANTOMS ARE BUT DISEMBODIED SOULS LIKE MYSELF, MORTAL BEINGS WHO DIED SUDDENLY, ANGRILY, OR WITH UNFINISHED BUSINESS.
"LOST AND CONFUSED, PHANTOMS LINGER ON THE OTHER SIDE, ETERNALLY SEEKING THE ONE THING THEY CAN NEVER AGAIN POSSESS: LIFE."
"AND DEMONS?"
"DEMONS ARE EVIL SPIRITS BIRTHED BY THE OTHER SIDE'S SINISTER ENERGIES, LIVING NIGHTMARES THAT EXIST ONLY TO INFLICT PAIN AND SUFFERING UPON THE LIVING.
"THEY ARE THE VERY REASON MAGICIANS EXIST IN THE FIRST PLACE."

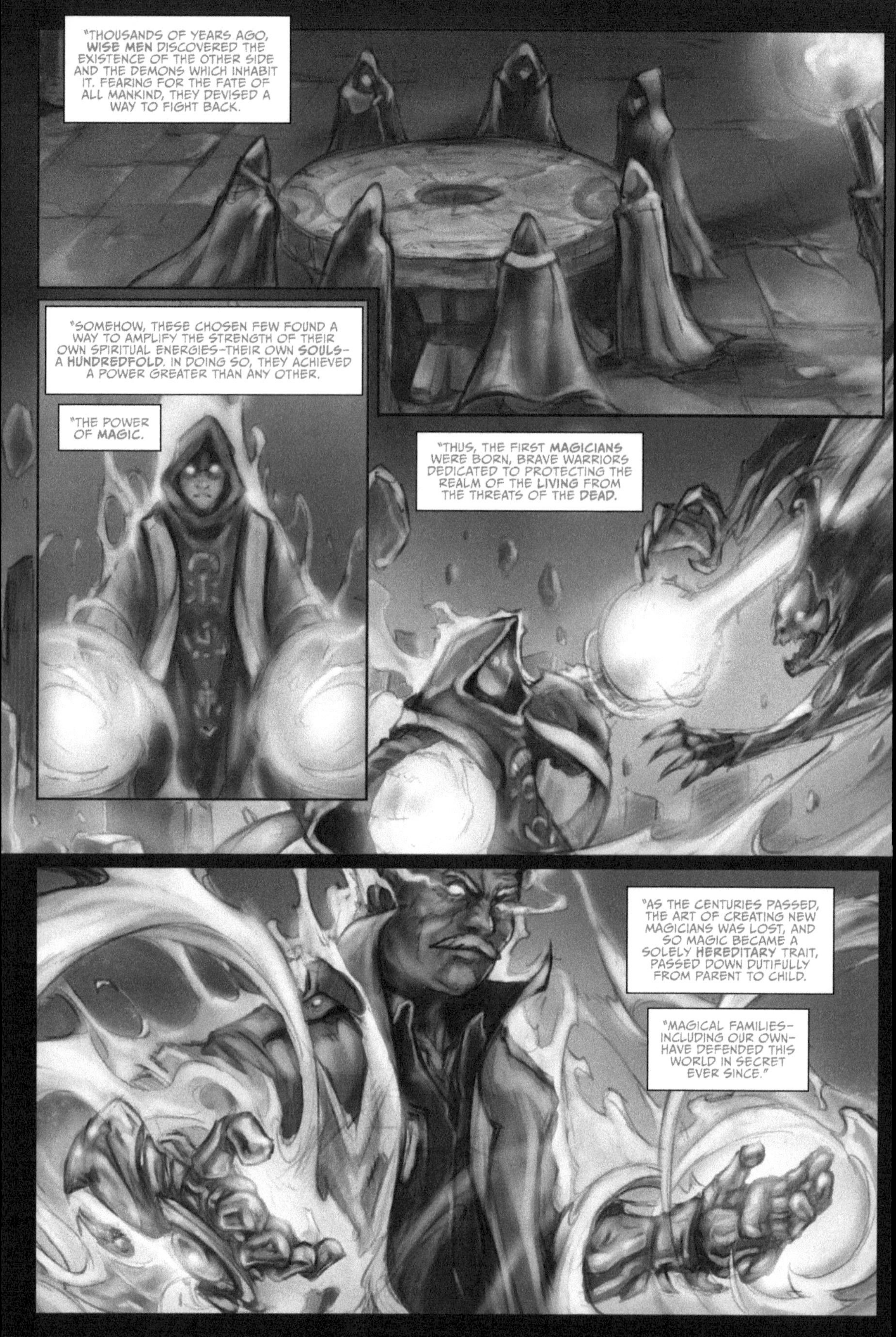
"THOUSANDS OF YEARS AGO, WISE MEN DISCOVERED THE EXISTENCE OF THE OTHER SIDE AND THE DEMONS WHICH INHABIT IT. FEARING FOR THE FATE OF ALL MANKIND, THEY DEVISED A WAY TO FIGHT BACK.
"SOMEHOW, THESE CHOSEN FEW FOUND A WAY TO AMPLIFY THE STRENGTH OF THEIR OWN SPIRITUAL ENERGIES–THEIR OWN SOULS–A HUNDREDFOLD. IN DOING SO, THEY ACHIEVED A POWER GREATER THAN ANY OTHER.
"THE POWER OF MAGIC.
"THUS, THE FIRST MAGICIANS WERE BORN, BRAVE WARRIORS DEDICATED TO PROTECTING THE REALM OF THE LIVING FROM THE THREATS OF THE DEAD.
"AS THE CENTURIES PASSED, THE ART OF CREATING NEW MAGICIANS WAS LOST, AND SO MAGIC BECAME A SOLELY HEREDITARY TRAIT, PASSED DOWN DUTIFULLY FROM PARENT TO CHILD.
"MAGICAL FAMILIES–INCLUDING OUR OWN–HAVE DEFENDED THIS WORLD IN SECRET EVER SINCE."

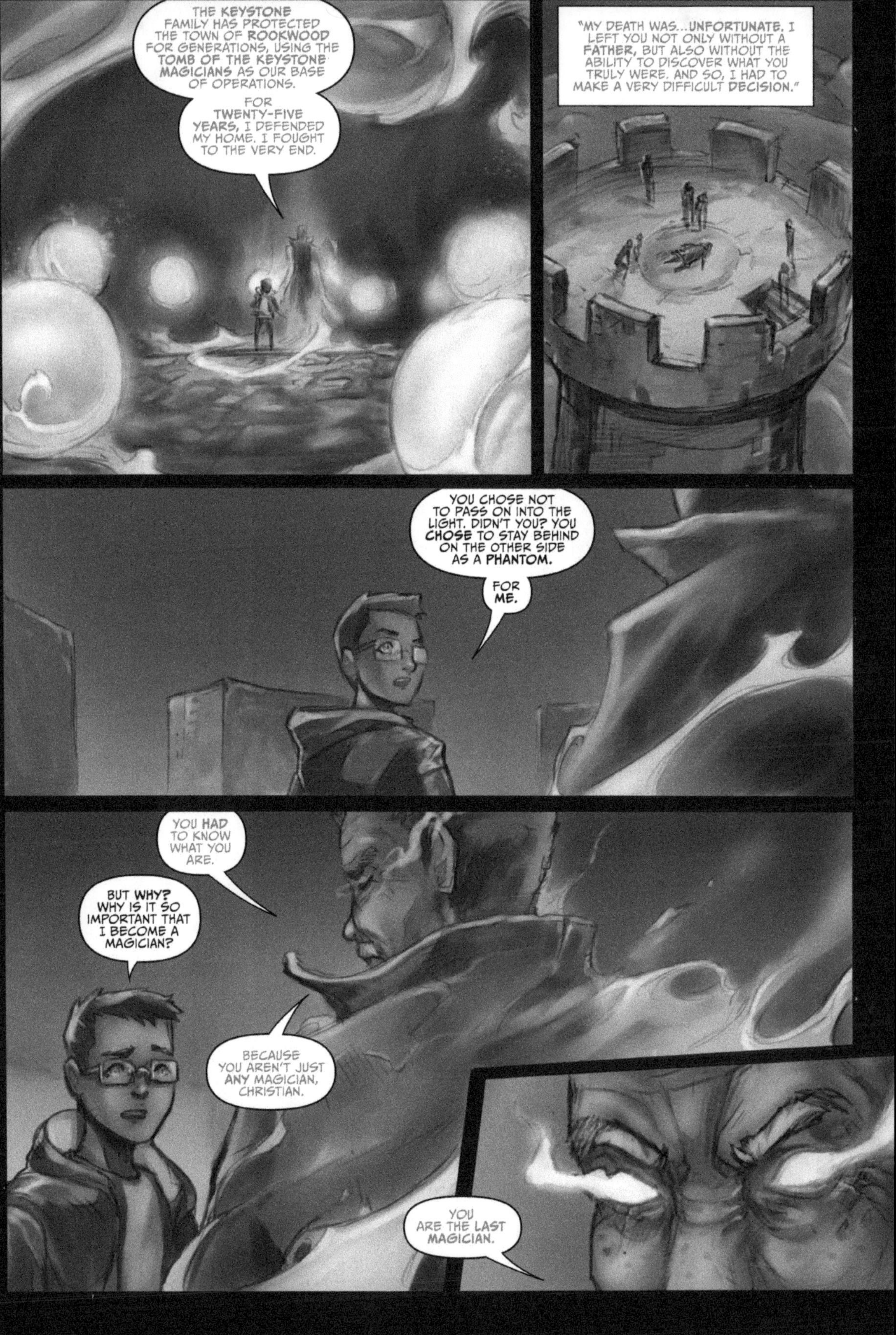
THE KEYSTONE FAMILY HAS PROTECTED THE TOWN OF ROOKWOOD FOR GENERATIONS, USING THE TOMB OF THE KEYSTONE MAGICIANS AS OUR BASE OF OPERATIONS.
FOR TWENTY-FIVE YEARS, I DEFENDED MY HOME. I FOUGHT TO THE VERY END.
"MY DEATH WAS...UNFORTUNATE. I LEFT YOU NOT ONLY WITHOUT A FATHER, BUT ALSO WITHOUT THE ABILITY TO DISCOVER WHAT YOU TRULY WERE. AND SO, I HAD TO MAKE A VERY DIFFICULT DECISION."
YOU CHOSE NOT TO PASS ON INTO THE LIGHT. DIDN'T YOU? YOU CHOSE TO STAY BEHIND ON THE OTHER SIDE AS A PHANTOM.
FOR ME.
YOU HAD TO KNOW WHAT YOU ARE.
BUT WHY? WHY IS IT SO IMPORTANT THAT I BECOME A MAGICIAN?
BECAUSE YOU AREN'T JUST ANY MAGICIAN, CHRISTIAN.
YOU ARE THE LAST MAGICIAN.

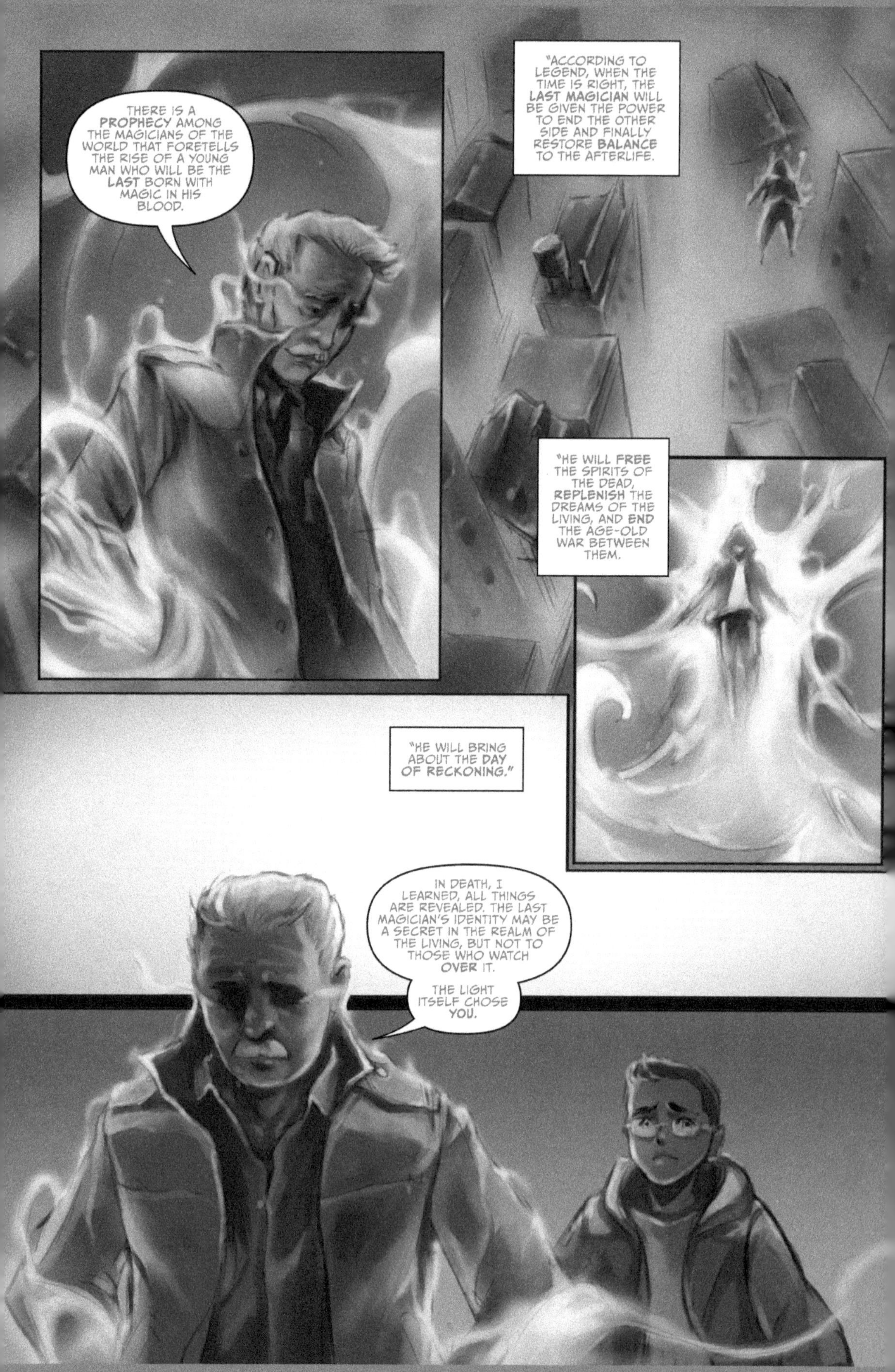
THERE IS A PROPHECY AMONG THE MAGICIANS OF THE WORLD THAT FORETELLS THE RISE OF A YOUNG MAN WHO WILL BE THE LAST BORN WITH MAGIC IN HIS BLOOD.
"ACCORDING TO LEGEND, WHEN THE TIME IS RIGHT, THE LAST MAGICIAN WILL BE GIVEN THE POWER TO END THE OTHER SIDE AND FINALLY RESTORE BALANCE TO THE AFTERLIFE.
"HE WILL FREE THE SPIRITS OF THE DEAD, REPLENISH THE DREAMS OF THE LIVING, AND END THE AGE-OLD WAR BETWEEN THEM.
"HE WILL BRING ABOUT THE DAY OF RECKONING."
IN DEATH, I LEARNED, ALL THINGS ARE REVEALED. THE LAST MAGICIAN'S IDENTITY MAY BE A SECRET IN THE REALM OF THE LIVING, BUT NOT TO THOSE WHO WATCH OVER IT.
THE LIGHT ITSELF CHOSE YOU.

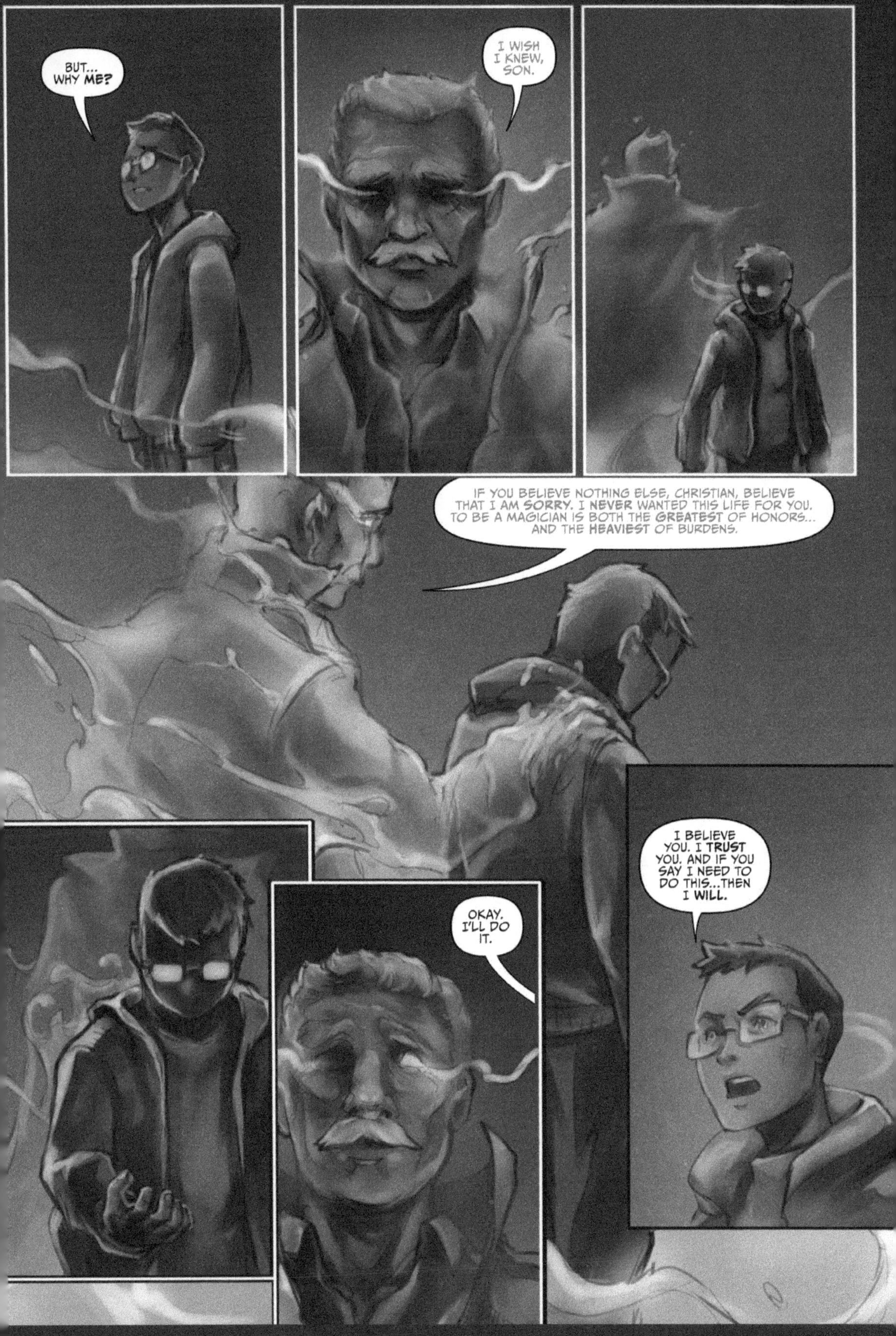
BUT... WHY ME?
I WISH I KNEW, SON.
IF YOU BELIEVE NOTHING ELSE, CHRISTIAN, BELIEVE THAT I AM SORRY. I NEVER WANTED THIS LIFE FOR YOU. TO BE A MAGICIAN IS BOTH THE GREATEST OF HONORS... AND THE HEAVIEST OF BURDENS.
OKAY. I'LL DO IT.
I BELIEVE YOU. I TRUST YOU. AND IF YOU SAY I NEED TO DO THIS...THEN I WILL.

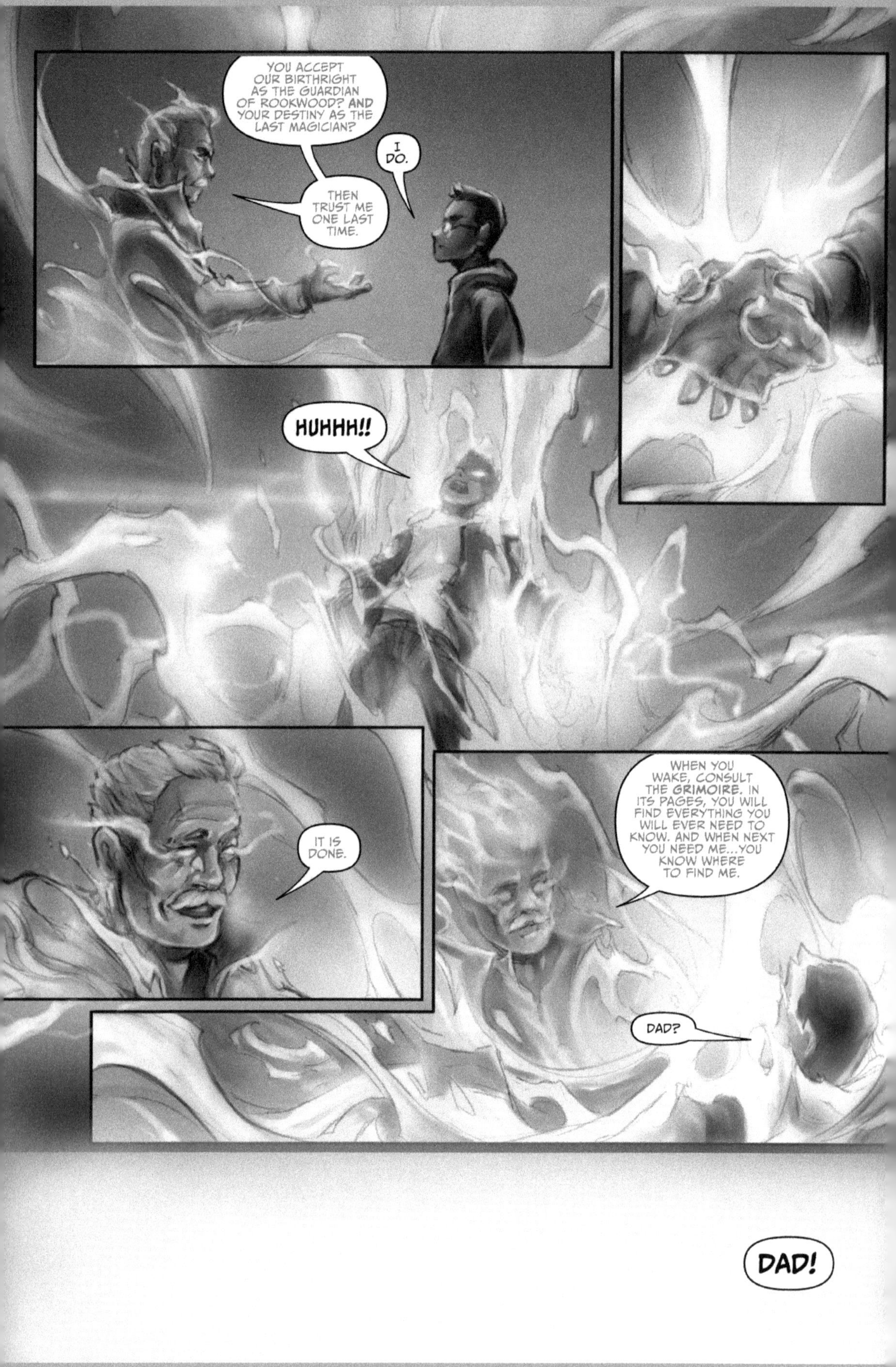

YOU ACCEPT OUR BIRTHRIGHT AS THE GUARDIAN OF ROOKWOOD? AND YOUR DESTINY AS THE LAST MAGICIAN?
I DO.
THEN TRUST ME ONE LAST TIME.
HUHHH!!
IT IS DONE.
WHEN YOU WAKE, CONSULT THE GRIMOIRE. IN ITS PAGES, YOU WILL FIND EVERYTHING YOU WILL EVER NEED TO KNOW. AND WHEN NEXT YOU NEED ME...YOU KNOW WHERE TO FIND ME.
DAD?
DAD!

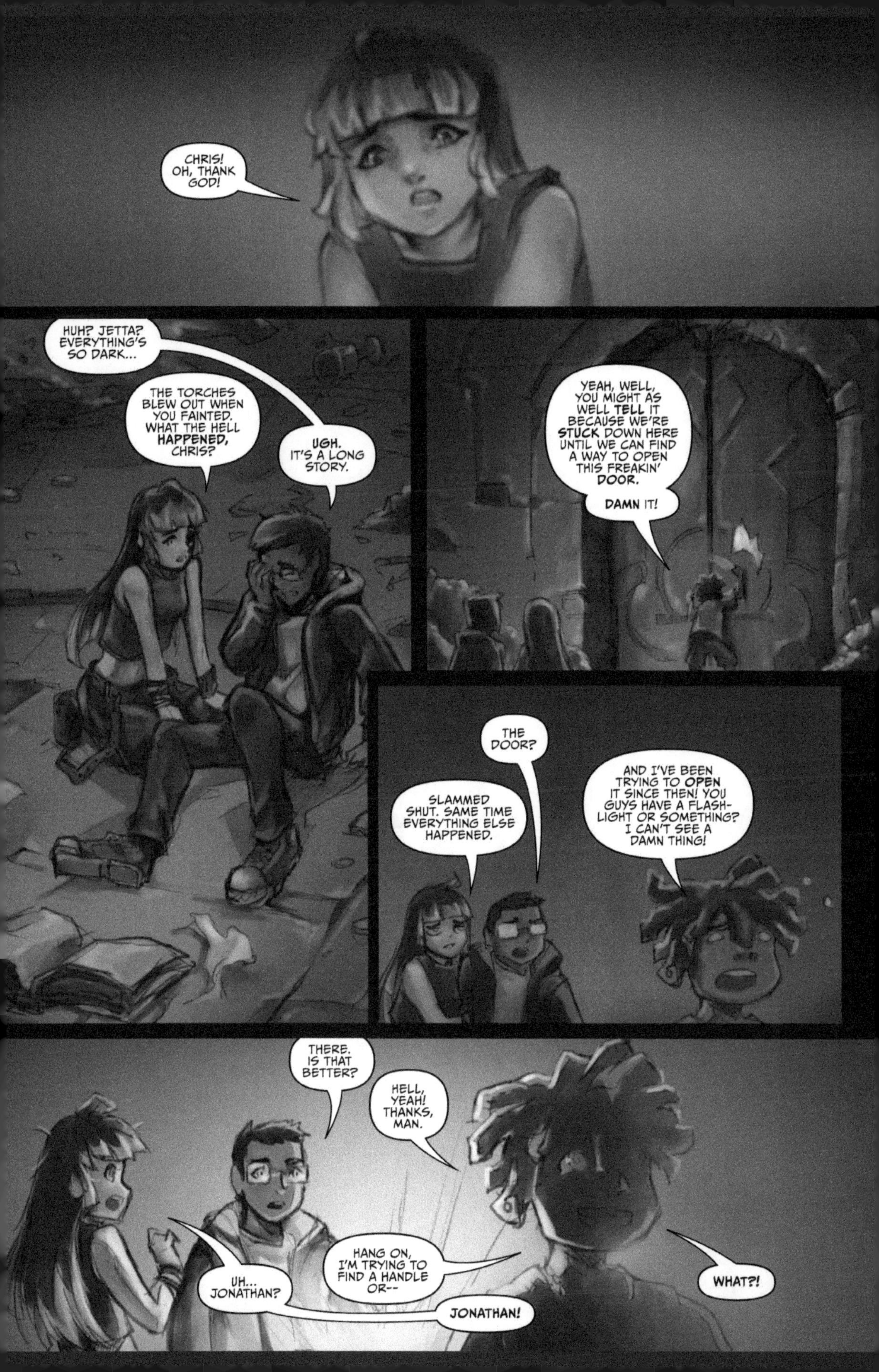
CHRIS! OH, THANK GOD!
HUH? JETTA? EVERYTHING'S SO DARK...
THE TORCHES BLEW OUT WHEN YOU FAINTED. WHAT THE HELL HAPPENED, CHRIS?
UGH. IT'S A LONG STORY.
YEAH, WELL, YOU MIGHT AS WELL TELL IT BECAUSE WE'RE STUCK DOWN HERE UNTIL WE CAN FIND A WAY TO OPEN THIS FREAKIN' DOOR.
DAMN IT!
THE DOOR?
SLAMMED SHUT. SAME TIME EVERYTHING ELSE HAPPENED.
AND I'VE BEEN TRYING TO OPEN IT SINCE THEN! YOU GUYS HAVE A FLASH-LIGHT OR SOMETHING? I CAN'T SEE A DAMN THING!
THERE. IS THAT BETTER?
HELL, YEAH! THANKS, MAN.
HANG ON, I'M TRYING TO FIND A HANDLE OR--
UH... JONATHAN?
JONATHAN!
WHAT?!

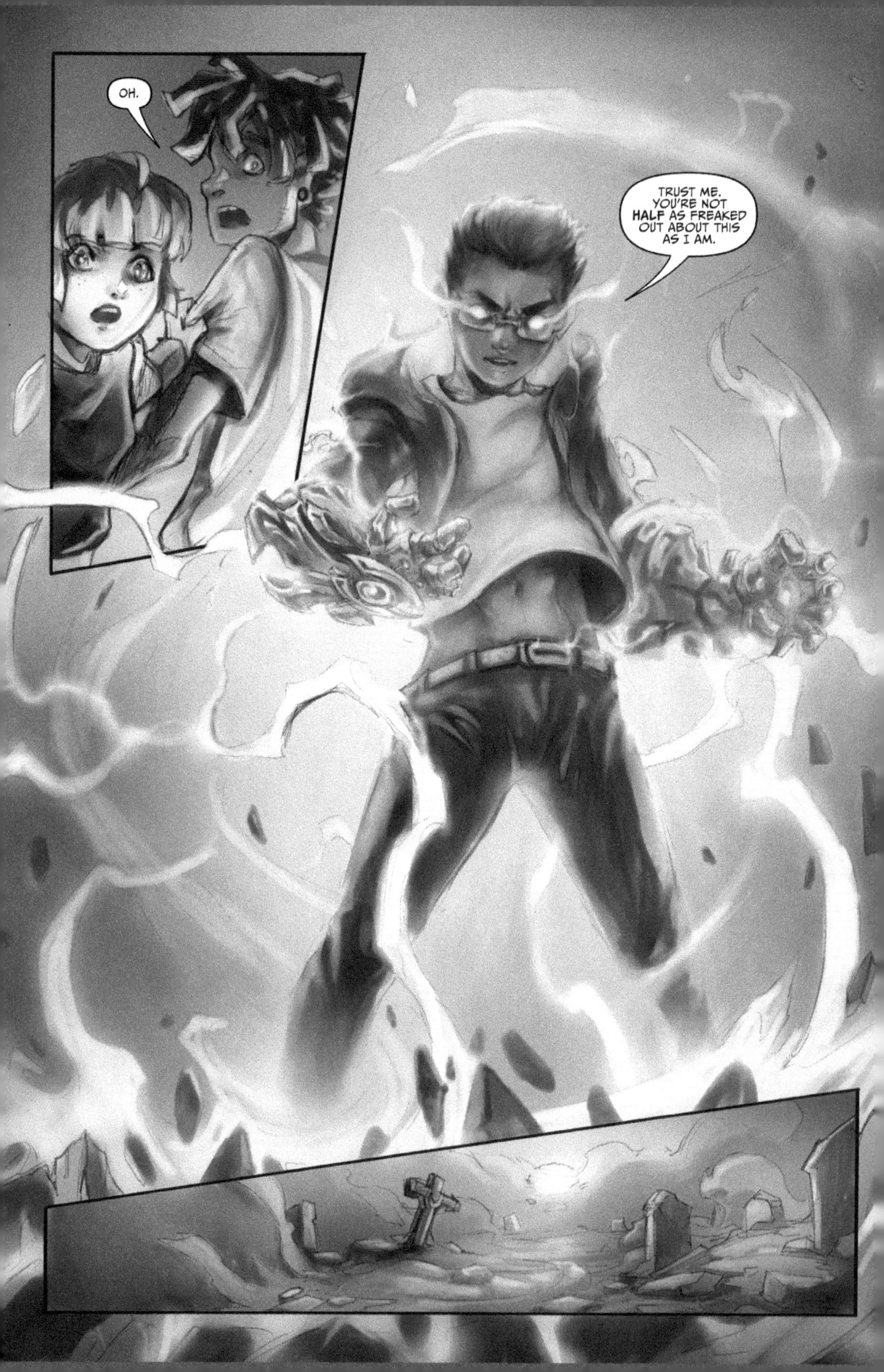
OH.
TRUST ME. YOU'RE NOT **HALF** AS FREAKED OUT ABOUT THIS AS I AM.

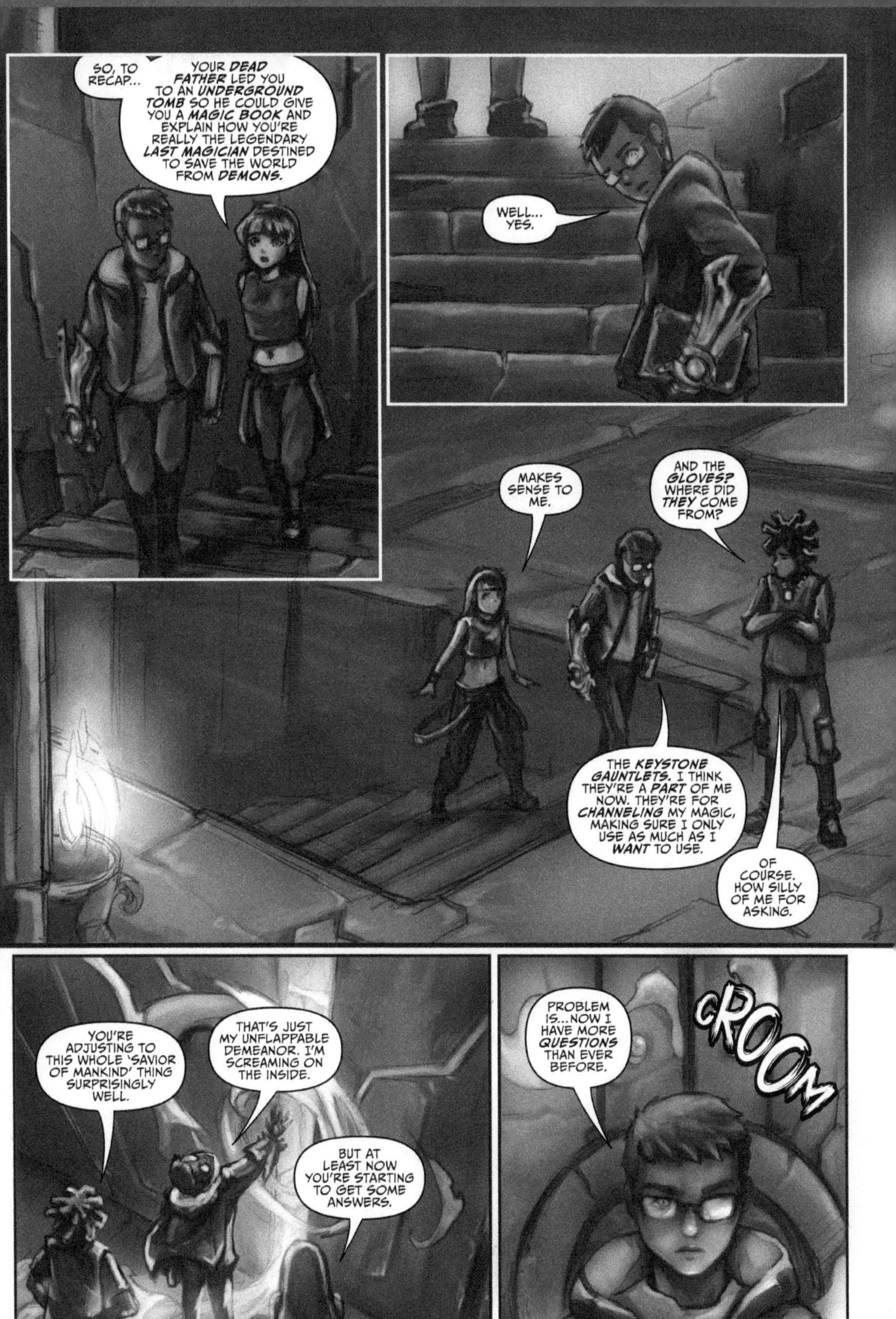
SO, TO RECAP...
YOUR DEAD FATHER LED YOU TO AN UNDERGROUND TOMB SO HE COULD GIVE YOU A MAGIC BOOK AND EXPLAIN HOW YOU'RE REALLY THE LEGENDARY LAST MAGICIAN DESTINED TO SAVE THE WORLD FROM DEMONS.
WELL... YES.
MAKES SENSE TO ME.
AND THE GLOVES? WHERE DID THEY COME FROM?
THE KEYSTONE GAUNTLETS. I THINK THEY'RE A PART OF ME NOW. THEY'RE FOR CHANNELING MY MAGIC, MAKING SURE I ONLY USE AS MUCH AS I WANT TO USE.
OF COURSE. HOW SILLY OF ME FOR ASKING.
YOU'RE ADJUSTING TO THIS WHOLE 'SAVIOR OF MANKIND' THING SURPRISINGLY WELL.
THAT'S JUST MY UNFLAPPABLE DEMEANOR. I'M SCREAMING ON THE INSIDE.
BUT AT LEAST NOW YOU'RE STARTING TO GET SOME ANSWERS.
PROBLEM IS...NOW I HAVE MORE QUESTIONS THAN EVER BEFORE.
CROOM

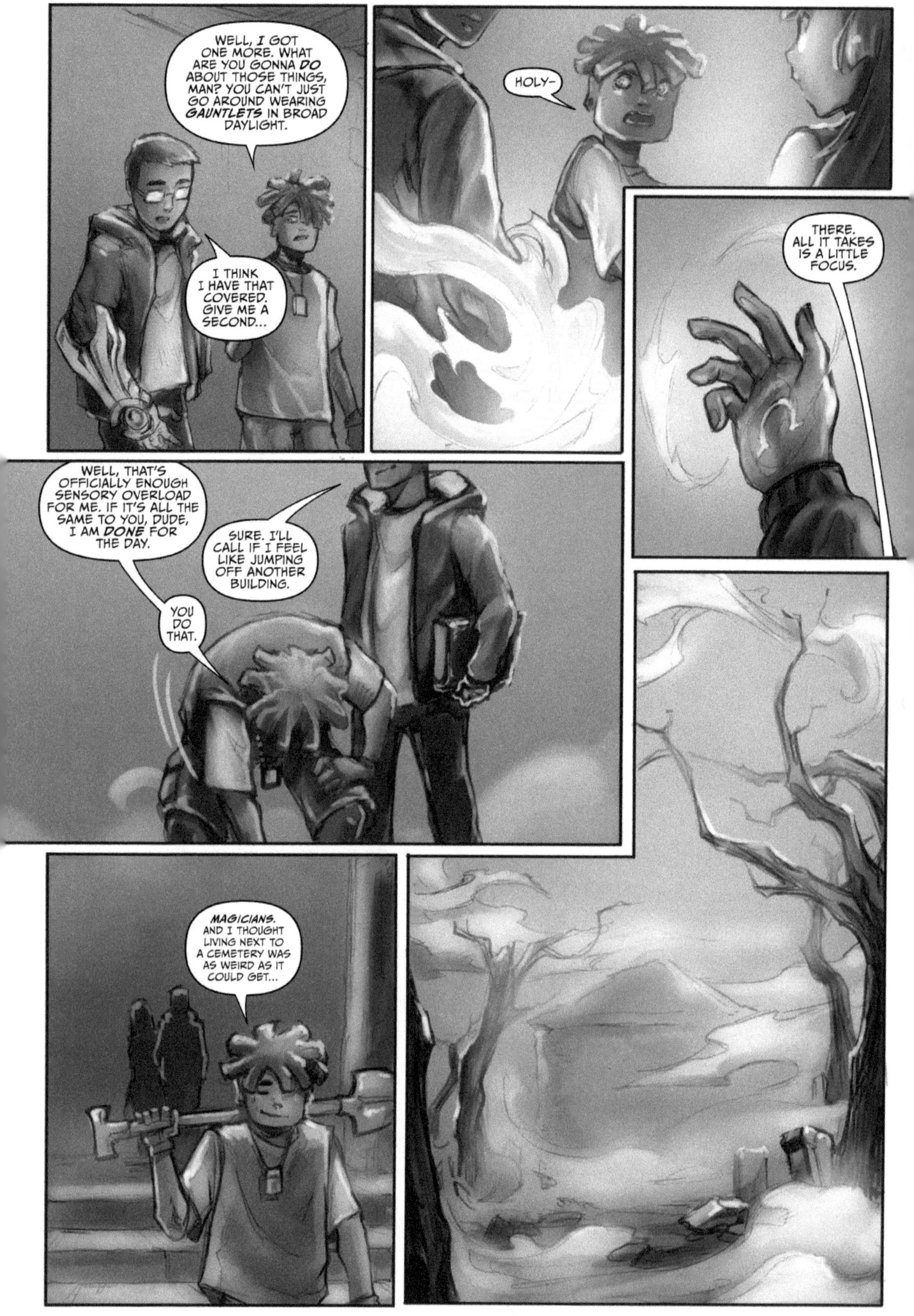
WELL, I GOT ONE MORE. WHAT ARE YOU GONNA DO ABOUT THOSE THINGS, MAN? YOU CAN'T JUST GO AROUND WEARING GAUNTLETS IN BROAD DAYLIGHT.
I THINK I HAVE THAT COVERED. GIVE ME A SECOND...
HOLY-
THERE. ALL IT TAKES IS A LITTLE FOCUS.
WELL, THAT'S OFFICIALLY ENOUGH SENSORY OVERLOAD FOR ME. IF IT'S ALL THE SAME TO YOU, DUDE, I AM DONE FOR THE DAY.
SURE. I'LL CALL IF I FEEL LIKE JUMPING OFF ANOTHER BUILDING.
YOU DO THAT.
MAGICIANS. AND I THOUGHT LIVING NEXT TO A CEMETERY WAS AS WEIRD AS IT COULD GET...

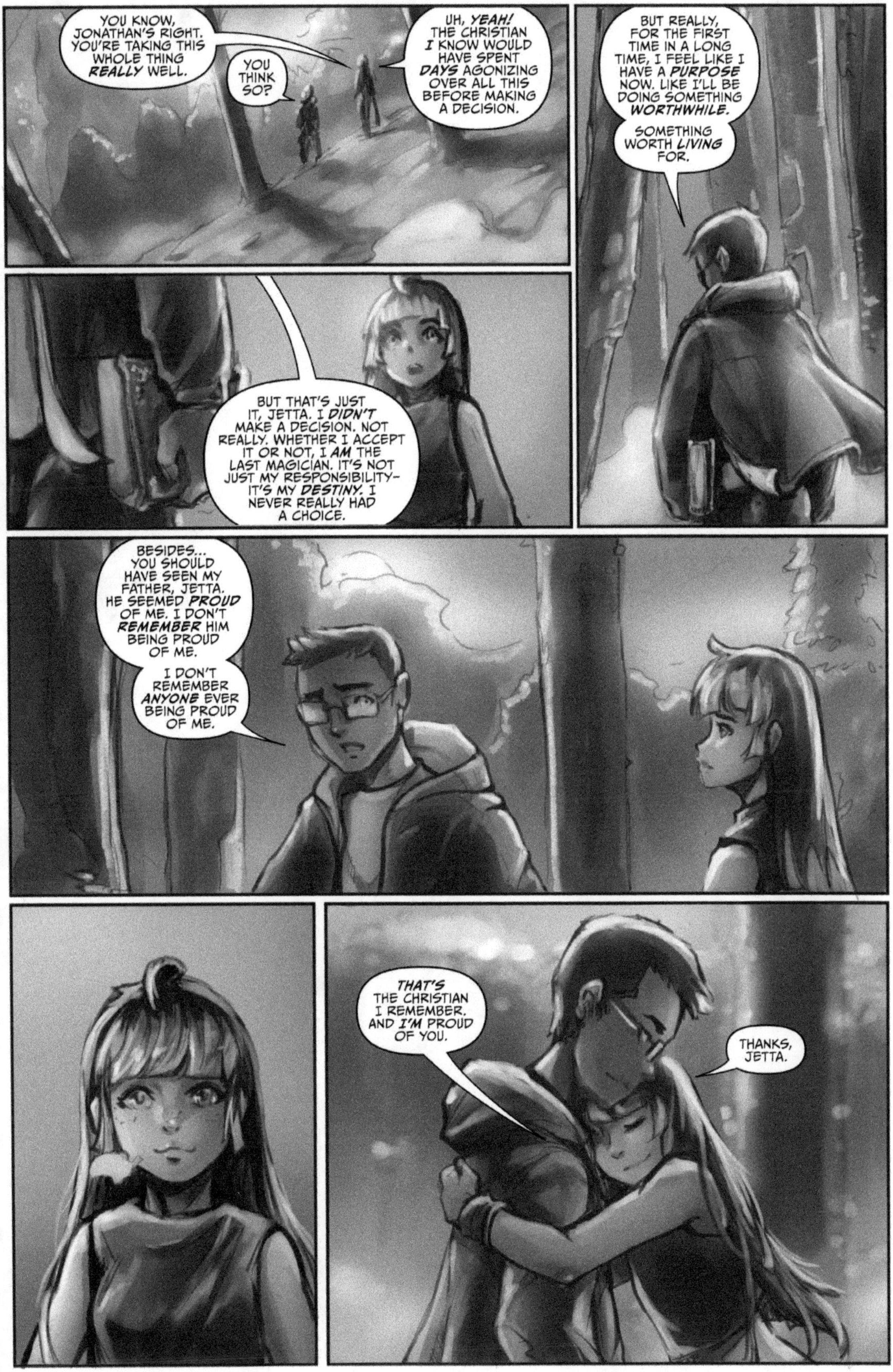
YOU KNOW, JONATHAN'S RIGHT. YOU'RE TAKING THIS WHOLE THING REALLY WELL.
YOU THINK SO?
UH, YEAH! THE CHRISTIAN I KNOW WOULD HAVE SPENT DAYS AGONIZING OVER ALL THIS BEFORE MAKING A DECISION.
BUT THAT'S JUST IT, JETTA. I DIDN'T MAKE A DECISION. NOT REALLY. WHETHER I ACCEPT IT OR NOT, I AM THE LAST MAGICIAN. IT'S NOT JUST MY RESPONSIBILITY– IT'S MY DESTINY. I NEVER REALLY HAD A CHOICE.
BUT REALLY, FOR THE FIRST TIME IN A LONG TIME, I FEEL LIKE I HAVE A PURPOSE NOW. LIKE I'LL BE DOING SOMETHING WORTHWHILE.
SOMETHING WORTH LIVING FOR.
BESIDES... YOU SHOULD HAVE SEEN MY FATHER, JETTA. HE SEEMED PROUD OF ME. I DON'T REMEMBER HIM BEING PROUD OF ME.
I DON'T REMEMBER ANYONE EVER BEING PROUD OF ME.
THAT'S THE CHRISTIAN I REMEMBER. AND I'M PROUD OF YOU.
THANKS, JETTA.

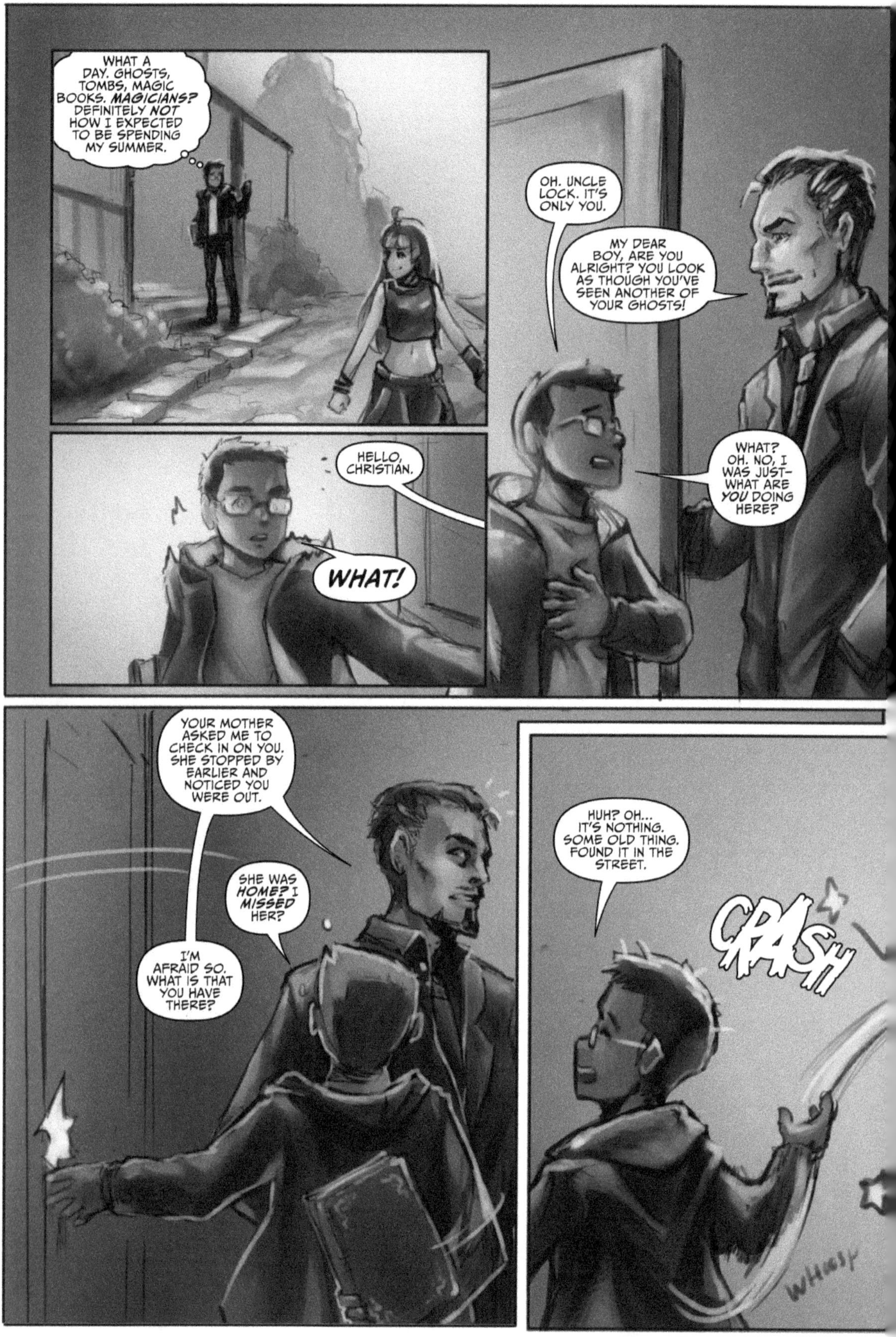

WHAT A DAY. GHOSTS, TOMBS, MAGIC BOOKS. ***MAGICIANS?*** DEFINITELY ***NOT*** HOW I EXPECTED TO BE SPENDING MY SUMMER.
HELLO, CHRISTIAN.
***WHAT!***
OH. UNCLE LOCK. IT'S ONLY YOU.
MY DEAR BOY, ARE YOU ALRIGHT? YOU LOOK AS THOUGH YOU'VE SEEN ANOTHER OF YOUR GHOSTS!
WHAT? OH. NO, I WAS JUST– WHAT ARE ***YOU*** DOING HERE?
YOUR MOTHER ASKED ME TO CHECK IN ON YOU. SHE STOPPED BY EARLIER AND NOTICED YOU WERE OUT.
SHE WAS ***HOME?*** I ***MISSED*** HER?
I'M AFRAID SO. WHAT IS THAT YOU HAVE THERE?
HUH? OH... IT'S NOTHING. SOME OLD THING. FOUND IT IN THE STREET.
CRASH

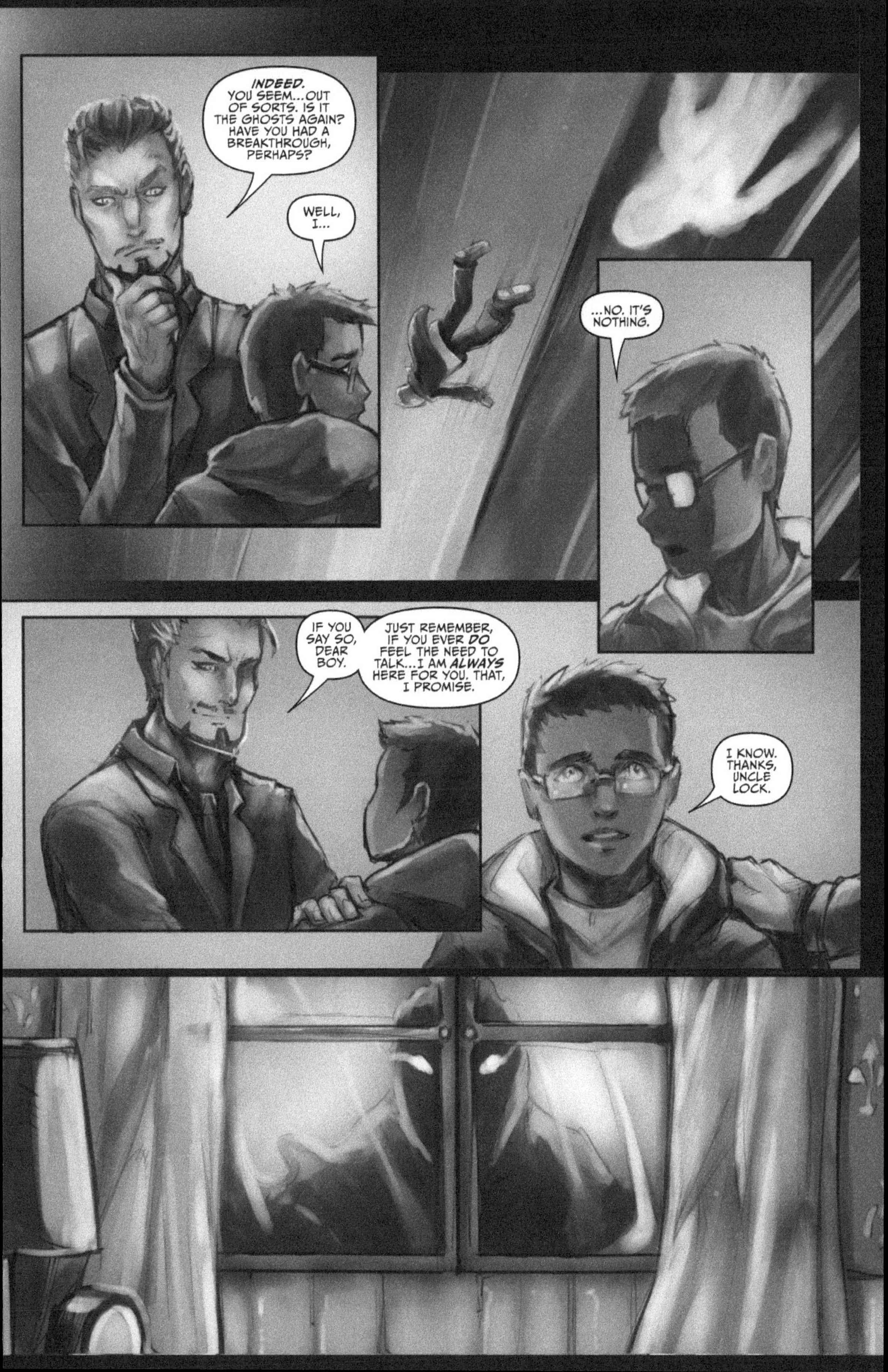
INDEED. YOU SEEM...OUT OF SORTS. IS IT THE GHOSTS AGAIN? HAVE YOU HAD A BREAKTHROUGH, PERHAPS?
WELL, I...
...NO. IT'S NOTHING.
IF YOU SAY SO, DEAR BOY.
JUST REMEMBER, IF YOU EVER DO FEEL THE NEED TO TALK...I AM ALWAYS HERE FOR YOU. THAT, I PROMISE.
I KNOW. THANKS, UNCLE LOCK.

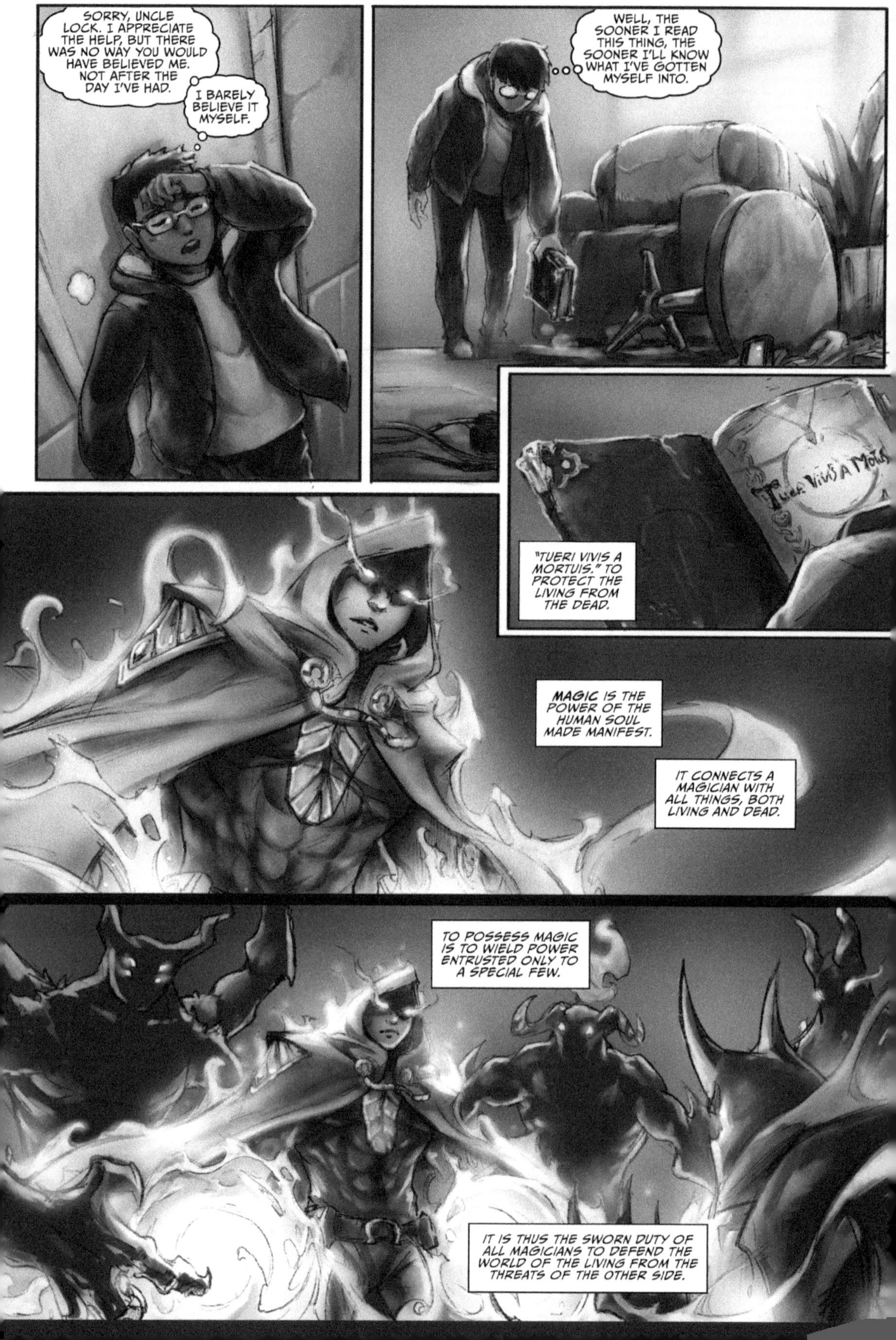

SORRY, UNCLE LOCK. I APPRECIATE THE HELP, BUT THERE WAS NO WAY YOU WOULD HAVE BELIEVED ME. NOT AFTER THE DAY I'VE HAD.
I BARELY BELIEVE IT MYSELF.
WELL, THE SOONER I READ THIS THING, THE SOONER I'LL KNOW WHAT I'VE GOTTEN MYSELF INTO.
"TUERI VIVIS A MORTUIS." TO PROTECT THE LIVING FROM THE DEAD.
MAGIC IS THE POWER OF THE HUMAN SOUL MADE MANIFEST.
IT CONNECTS A MAGICIAN WITH ALL THINGS, BOTH LIVING AND DEAD.
TO POSSESS MAGIC IS TO WIELD POWER ENTRUSTED ONLY TO A SPECIAL FEW.
IT IS THUS THE SWORN DUTY OF ALL MAGICIANS TO DEFEND THE WORLD OF THE LIVING FROM THE THREATS OF THE OTHER SIDE.

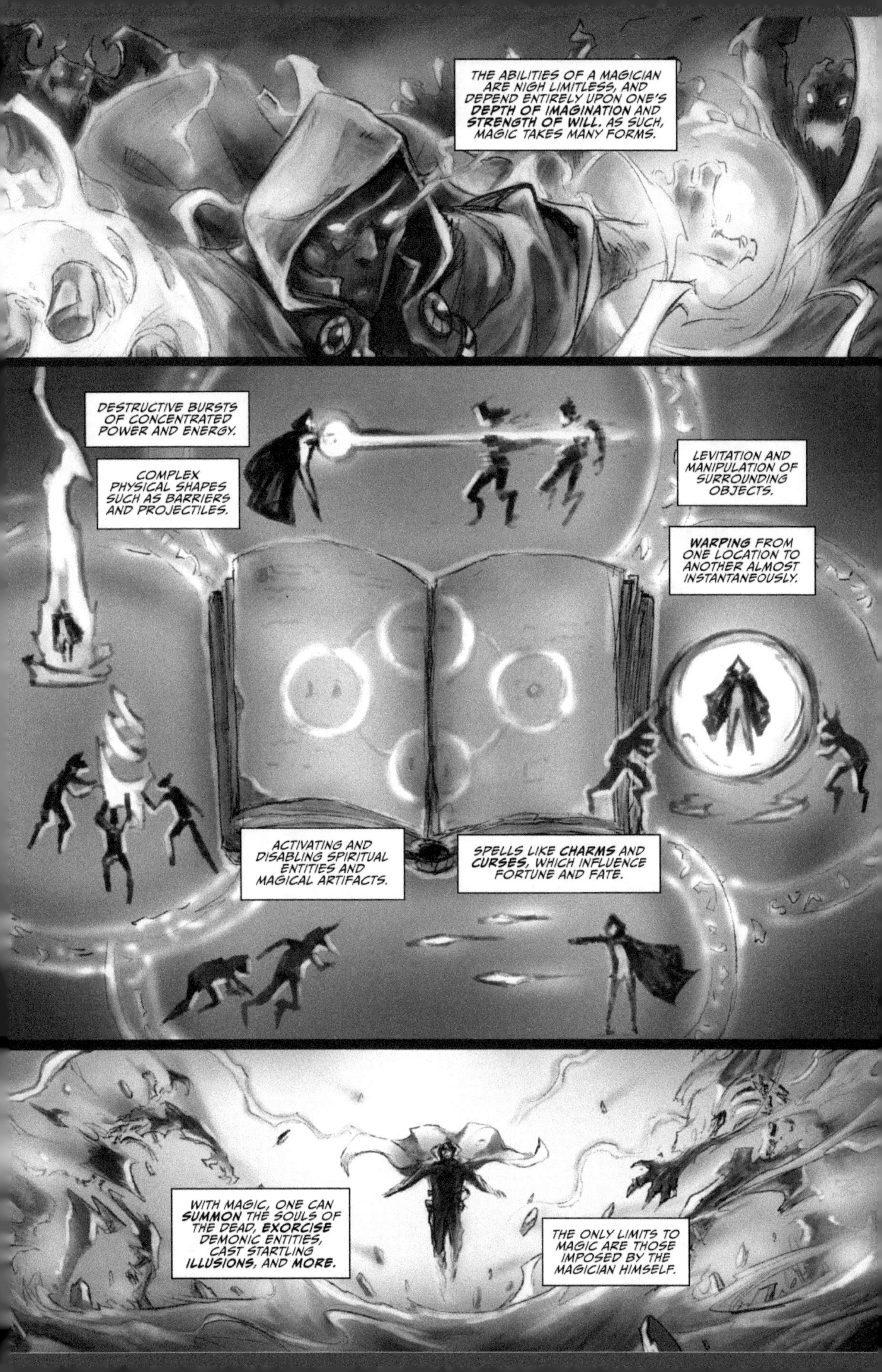
THE ABILITIES OF A MAGICIAN ARE NIGH LIMITLESS, AND DEPEND ENTIRELY UPON ONE'S **DEPTH OF IMAGINATION** AND **STRENGTH OF WILL.** AS SUCH, MAGIC TAKES MANY FORMS.
DESTRUCTIVE BURSTS OF CONCENTRATED POWER AND ENERGY.
COMPLEX PHYSICAL SHAPES SUCH AS BARRIERS AND PROJECTILES.
LEVITATION AND MANIPULATION OF SURROUNDING OBJECTS.
**WARPING** FROM ONE LOCATION TO ANOTHER ALMOST INSTANTANEOUSLY.
ACTIVATING AND DISABLING SPIRITUAL ENTITIES AND MAGICAL ARTIFACTS.
SPELLS LIKE **CHARMS** AND **CURSES**, WHICH INFLUENCE FORTUNE AND FATE.
WITH MAGIC, ONE CAN **SUMMON** THE SOULS OF THE DEAD, **EXORCISE** DEMONIC ENTITIES, CAST STARTLING **ILLUSIONS**, AND **MORE.**
THE ONLY LIMITS TO MAGIC ARE THOSE IMPOSED BY THE MAGICIAN HIMSELF.

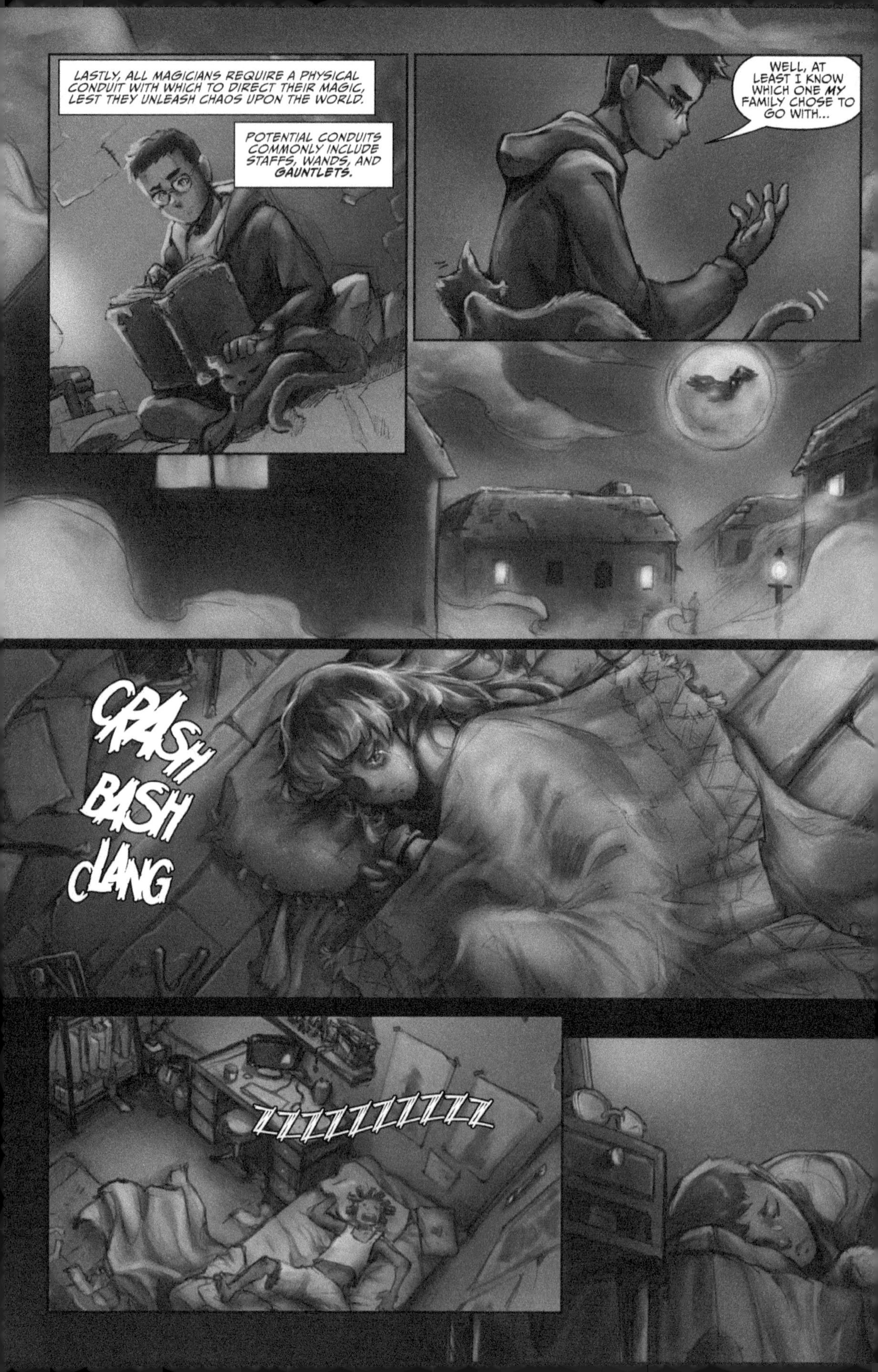

LASTLY, ALL MAGICIANS REQUIRE A PHYSICAL CONDUIT WITH WHICH TO DIRECT THEIR MAGIC, LEST THEY UNLEASH CHAOS UPON THE WORLD.
POTENTIAL CONDUITS COMMONLY INCLUDE STAFFS, WANDS, AND GAUNTLETS.
WELL, AT LEAST I KNOW WHICH ONE MY FAMILY CHOSE TO GO WITH...
CRASH
BASH
CLANG
ZZZZZZZZZZZZ

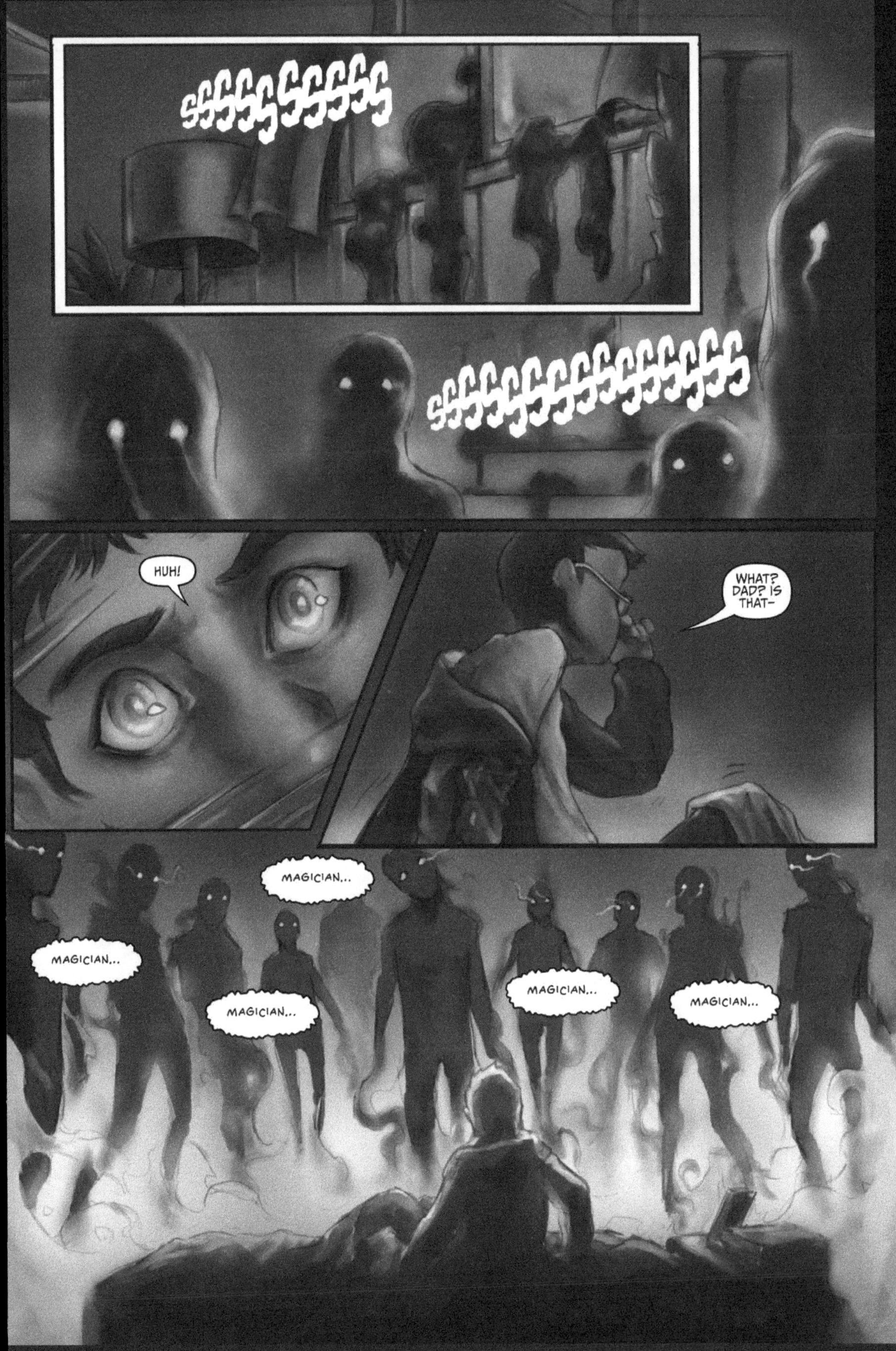
SSSSSSSSSSS
SSSSSSSSSSSSSSSSS
HUH!
WHAT? DAD? IS THAT–
MAGICIAN...
MAGICIAN...
MAGICIAN...
MAGICIAN...
MAGICIAN...

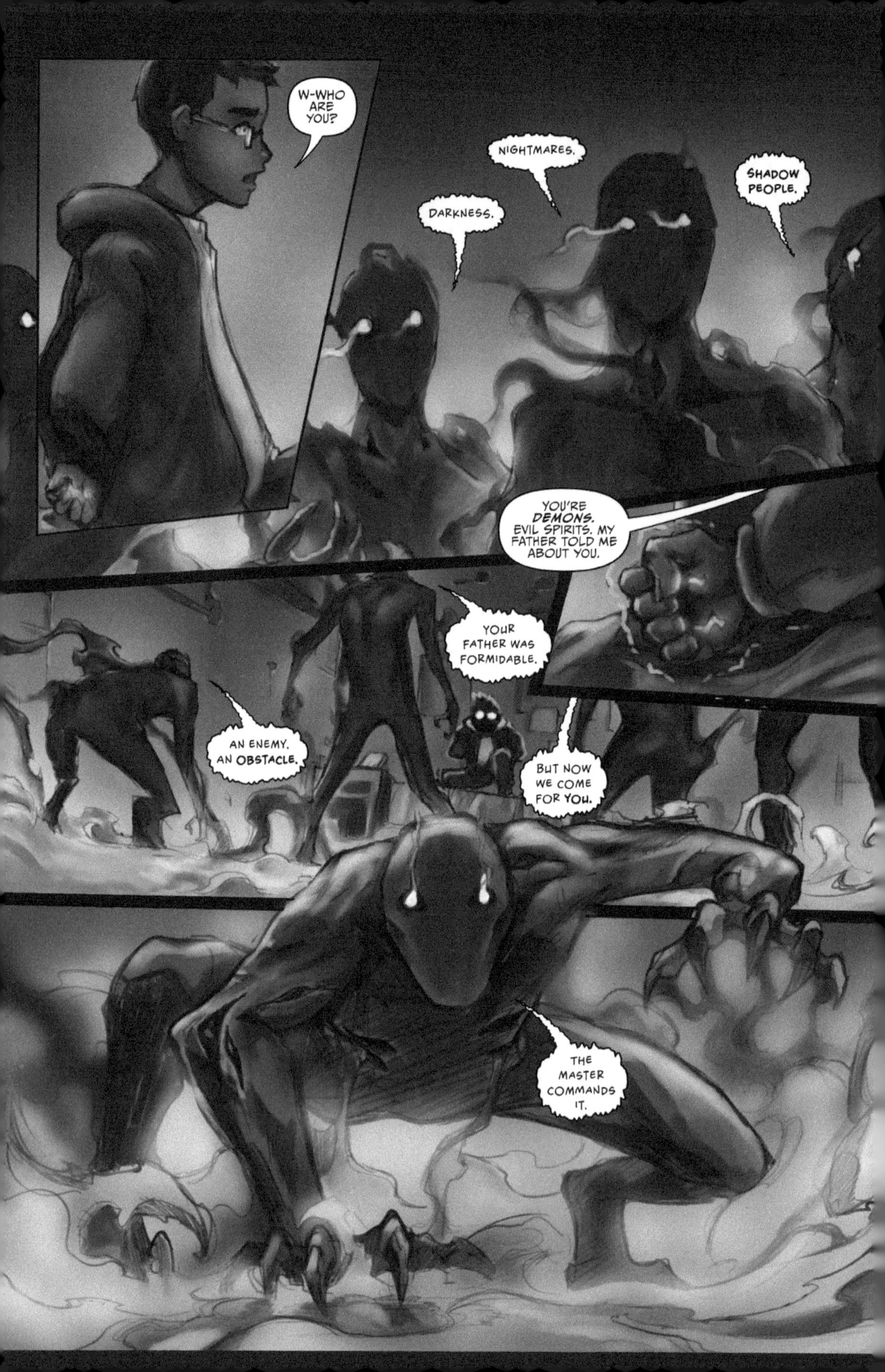
W-WHO ARE YOU?
NIGHTMARES.
DARKNESS.
SHADOW PEOPLE.
YOU'RE *DEMONS.* EVIL SPIRITS. MY FATHER TOLD ME ABOUT YOU.
YOUR FATHER WAS FORMIDABLE.
AN ENEMY. AN **OBSTACLE.**
BUT NOW WE COME FOR **YOU.**
THE MASTER COMMANDS IT.

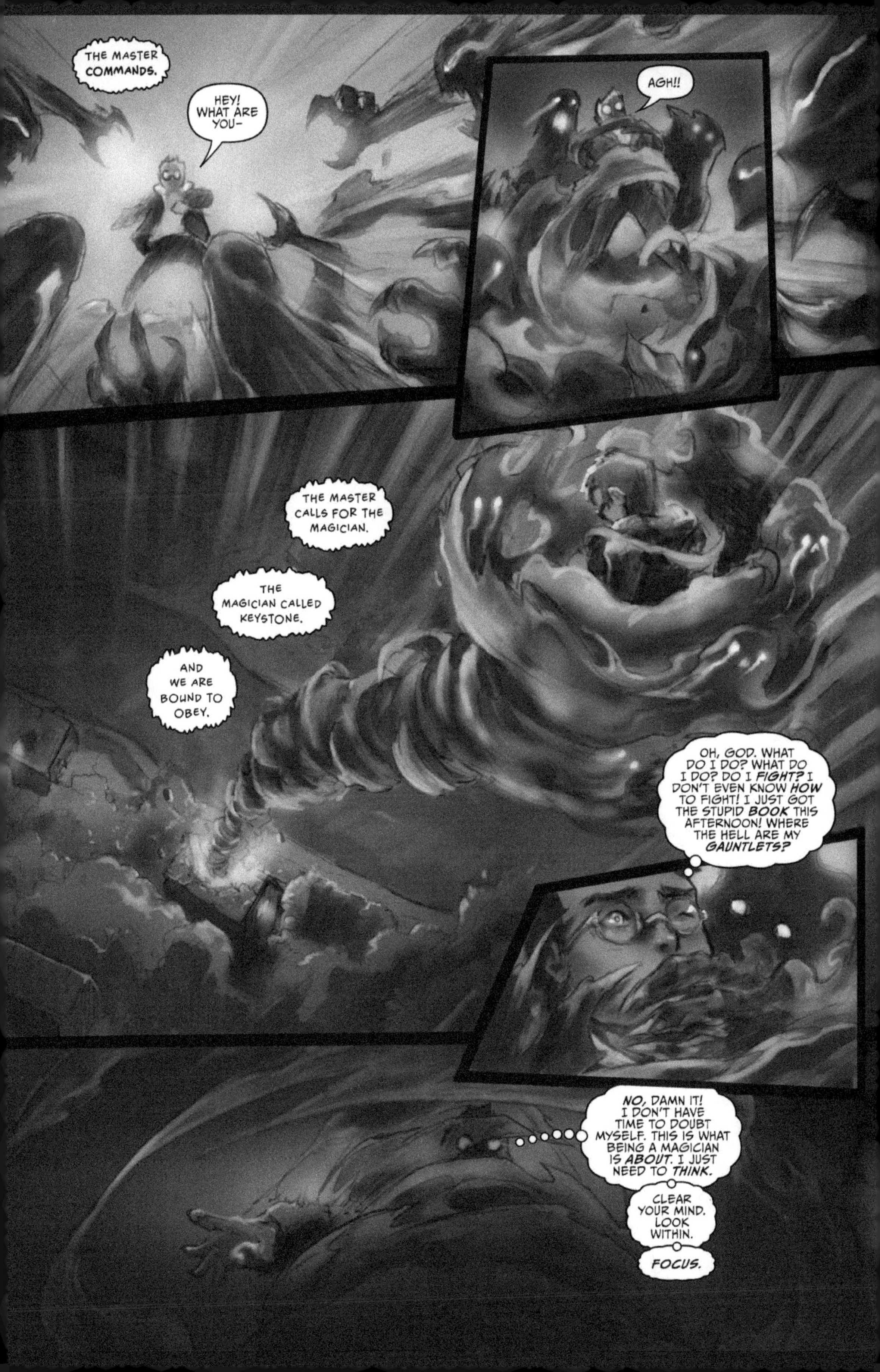
THE MASTER COMMANDS.
HEY! WHAT ARE YOU-
AGH!!
THE MASTER CALLS FOR THE MAGICIAN.
THE MAGICIAN CALLED KEYSTONE.
AND WE ARE BOUND TO OBEY.
OH, GOD. WHAT DO I DO? WHAT DO I DO? DO I FIGHT? I DON'T EVEN KNOW HOW TO FIGHT! I JUST GOT THE STUPID BOOK THIS AFTERNOON! WHERE THE HELL ARE MY GAUNTLETS?
NO, DAMN IT! I DON'T HAVE TIME TO DOUBT MYSELF. THIS IS WHAT BEING A MAGICIAN IS ABOUT. I JUST NEED TO THINK.
CLEAR YOUR MIND. LOOK WITHIN.
FOCUS.

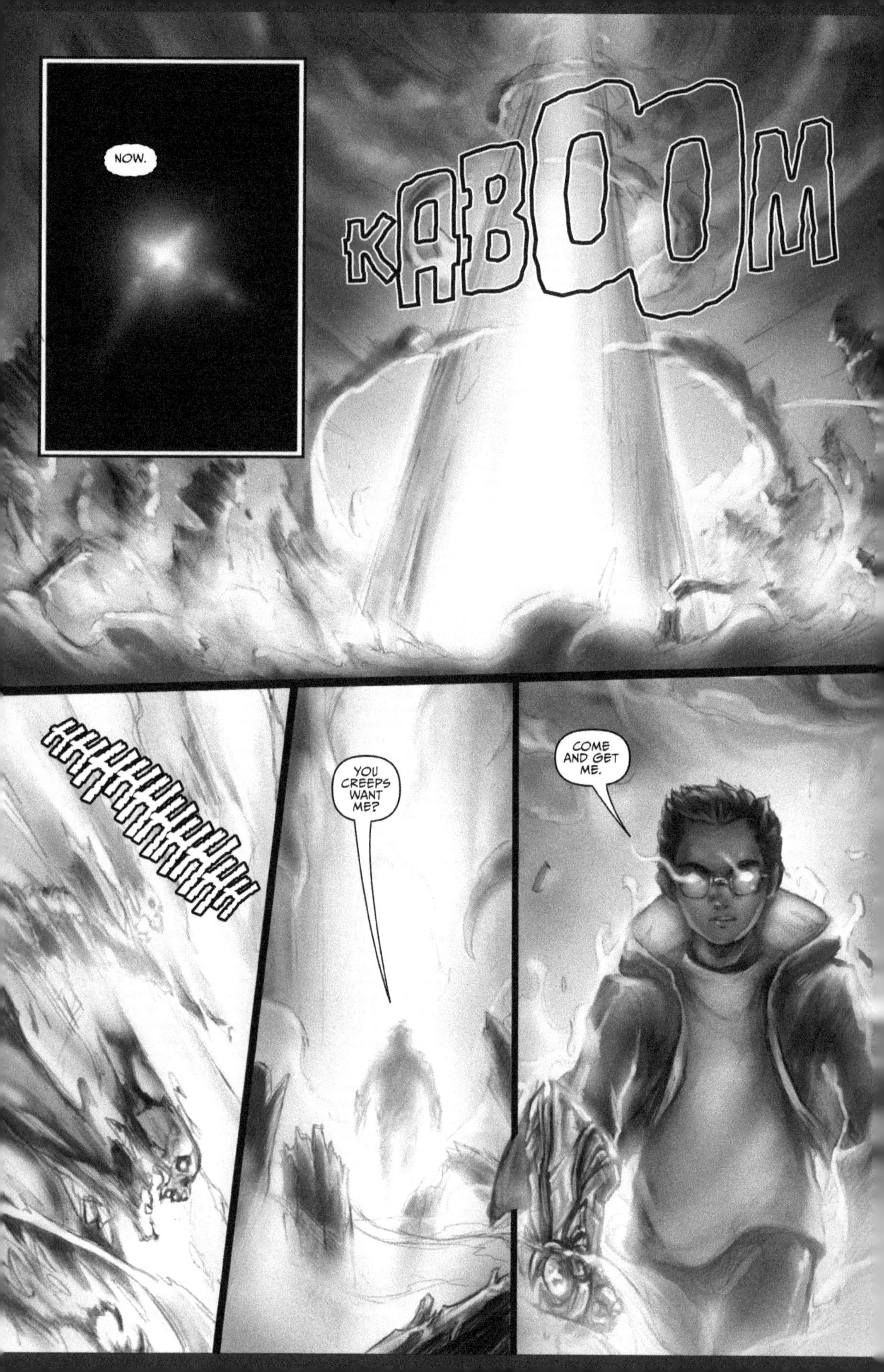
NOW.
KABOOM
YOU CREEPS WANT ME?
COME AND GET ME.

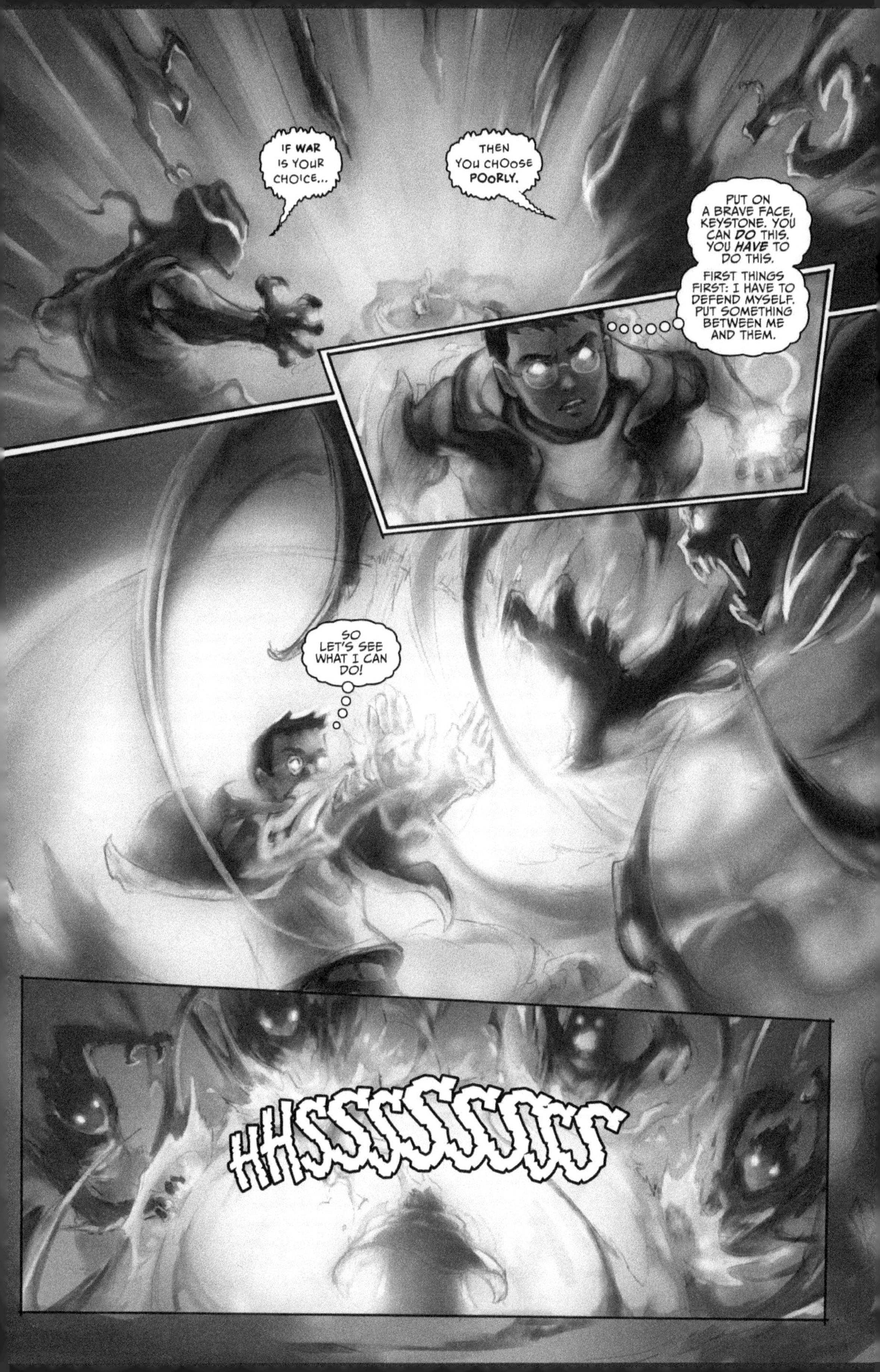
IF WAR IS YOUR CHOICE...
THEN YOU CHOOSE POORLY.
PUT ON A BRAVE FACE, KEYSTONE. YOU CAN DO THIS. YOU HAVE TO DO THIS.
FIRST THINGS FIRST: I HAVE TO DEFEND MYSELF. PUT SOMETHING BETWEEN ME AND THEM.
SO LET'S SEE WHAT I CAN DO!
HHSSSSSSSSS

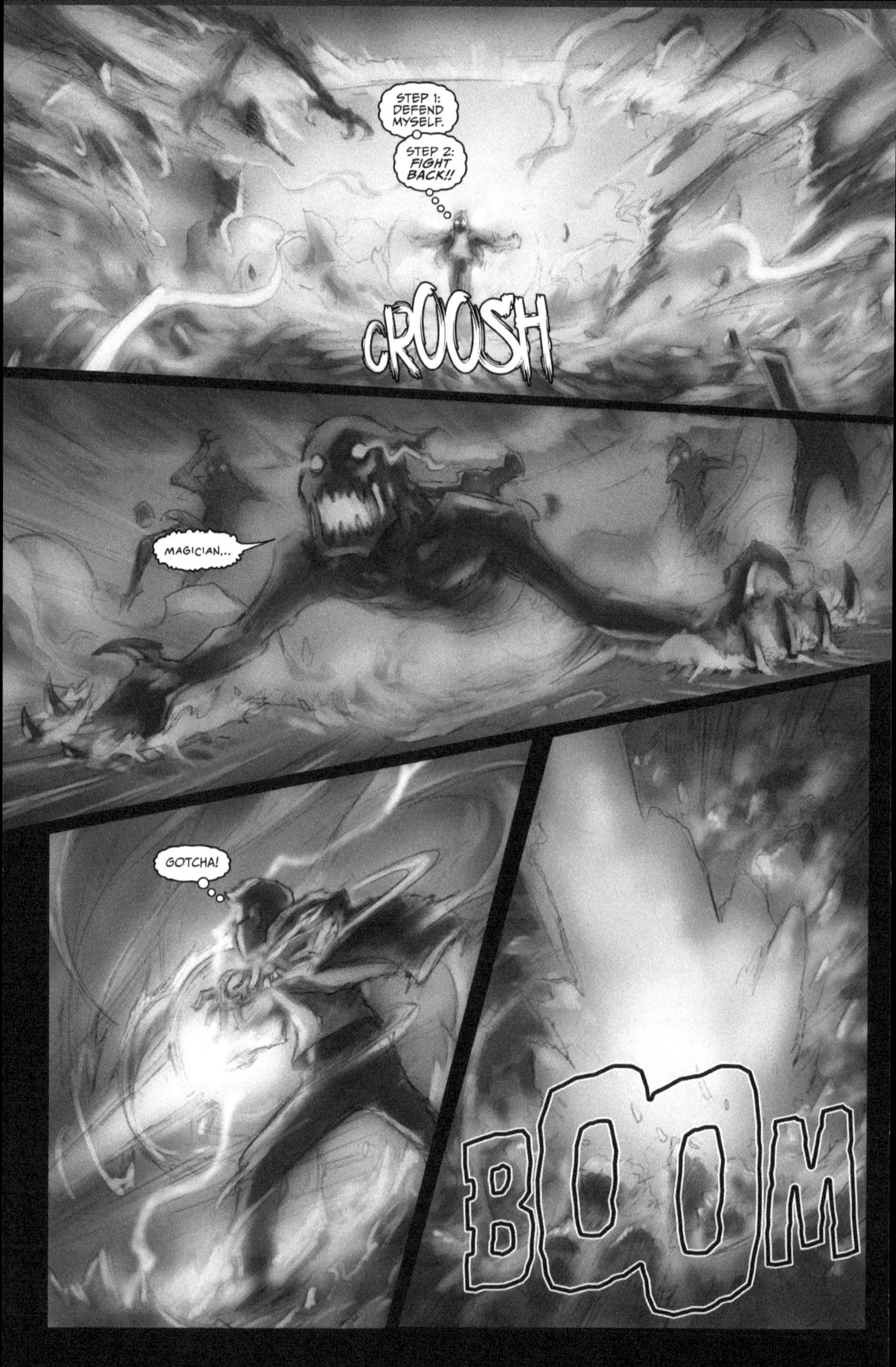
STEP 1: DEFEND MYSELF.
STEP 2: FIGHT BACK!!
CROOSH
MAGICIAN...
GOTCHA!
BOOM

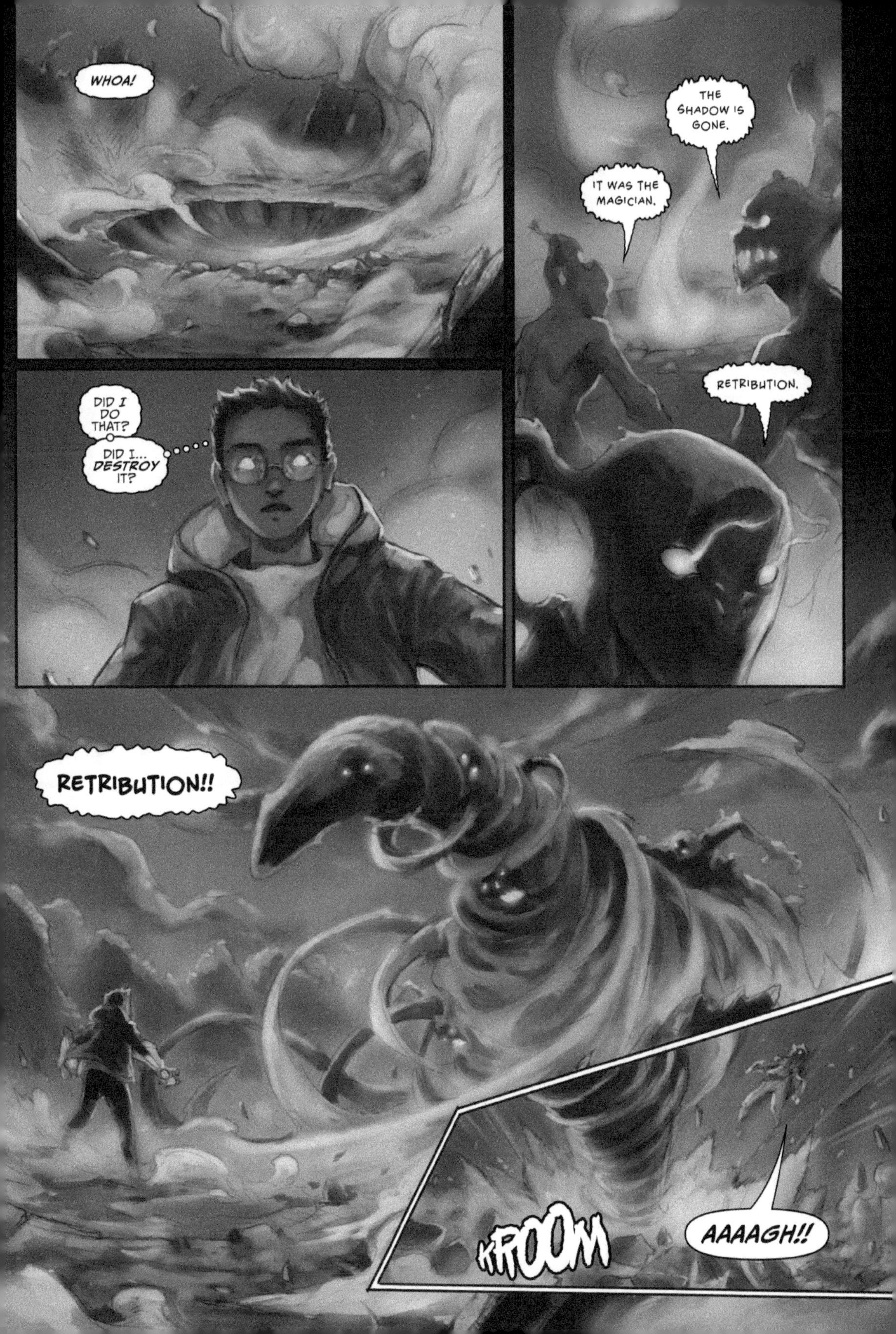
WHOA!
THE SHADOW IS GONE.
IT WAS THE MAGICIAN.
RETRIBUTION.
DID I DO THAT?
DID I... DESTROY IT?
RETRIBUTION!!
KROOM
AAAAGH!!

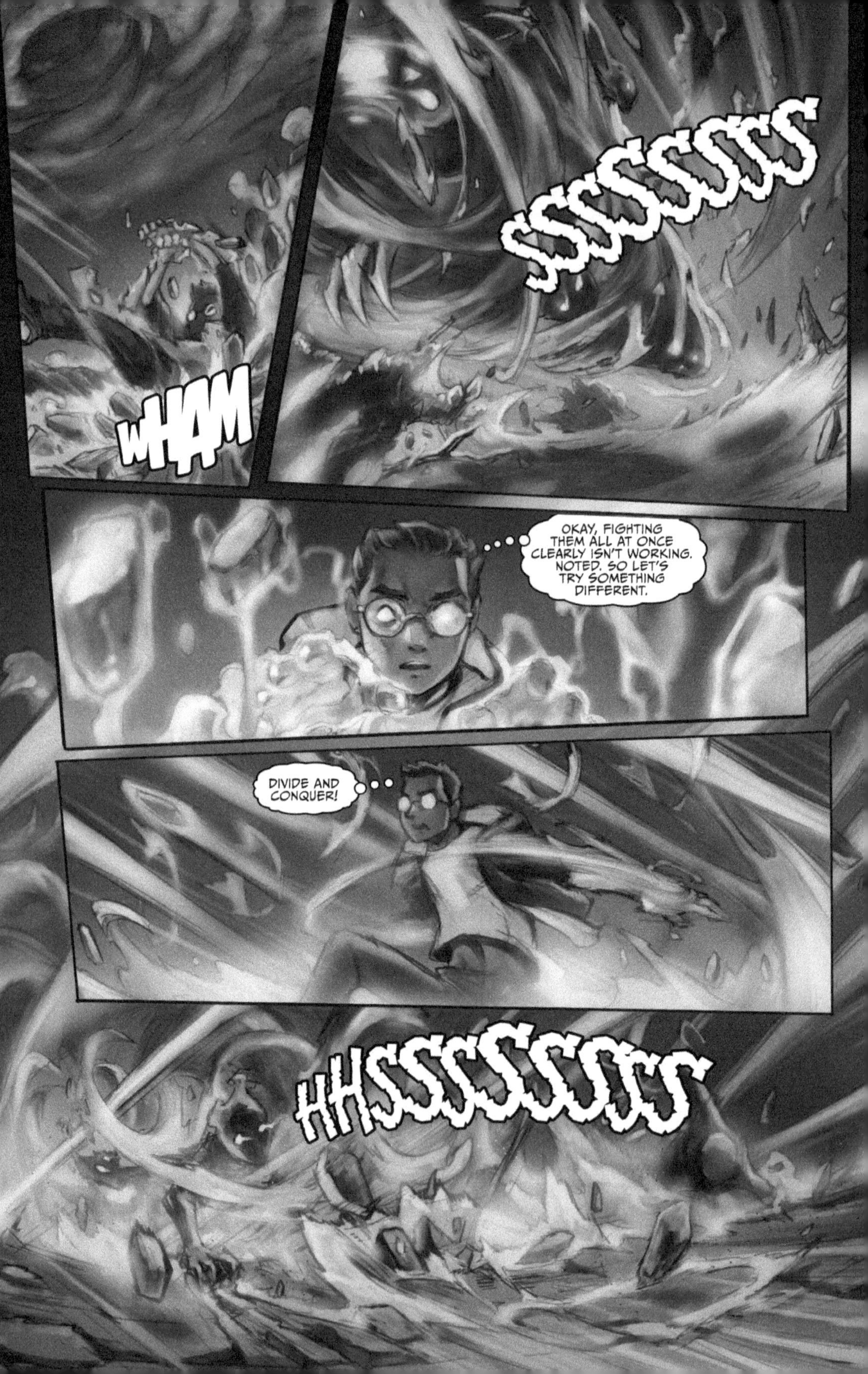
SSSSSSSSS
WHAM
OKAY, FIGHTING THEM ALL AT ONCE CLEARLY ISN'T WORKING. NOTED. SO LET'S TRY SOMETHING DIFFERENT.
DIVIDE AND CONQUER!
HHSSSSSSSSS

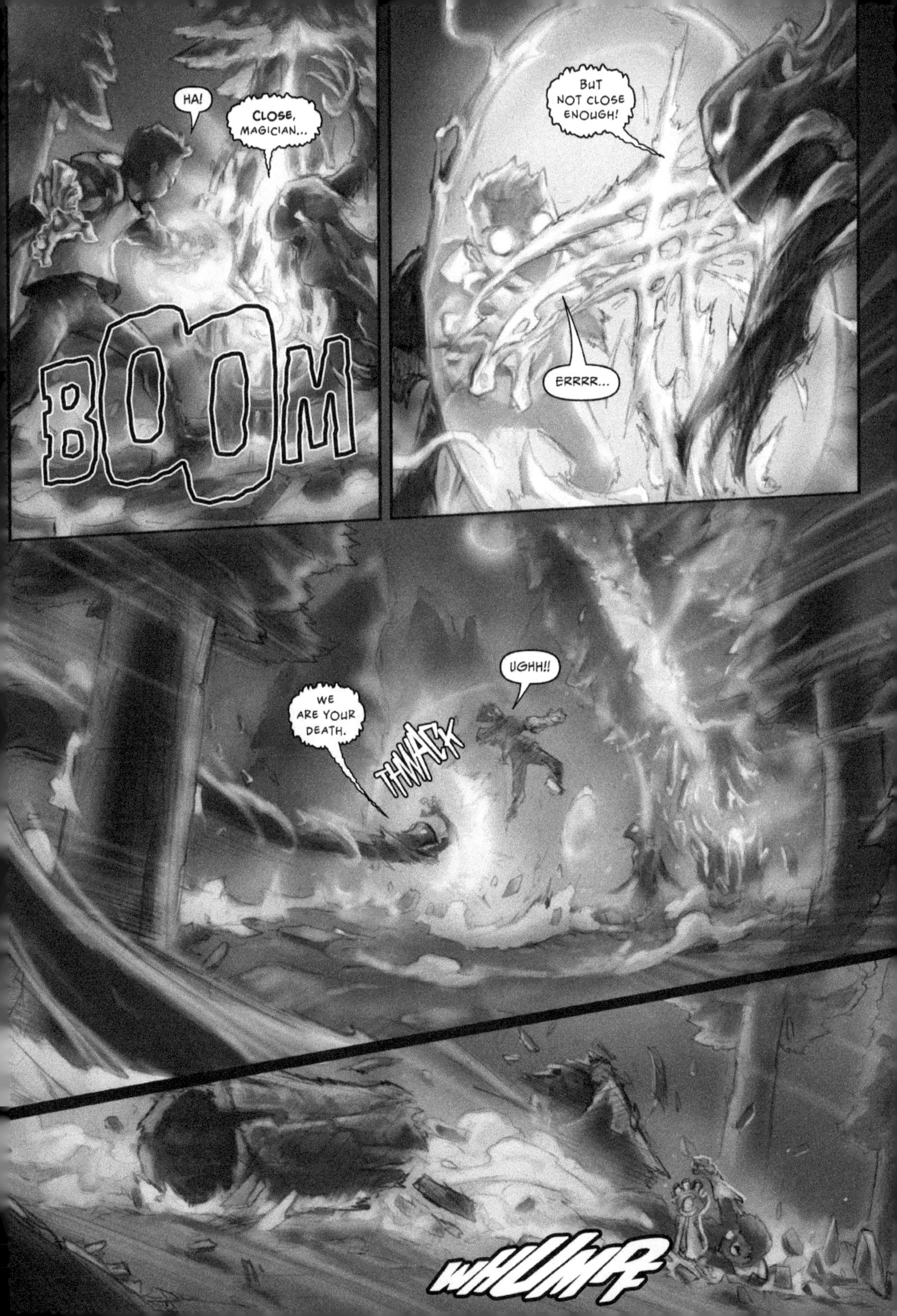
HA!
CLOSE, MAGICIAN...
BOOM
BUT NOT CLOSE ENOUGH!
ERRRR...
UGHH!!
WE ARE YOUR DEATH.
THWACK
WHUMF

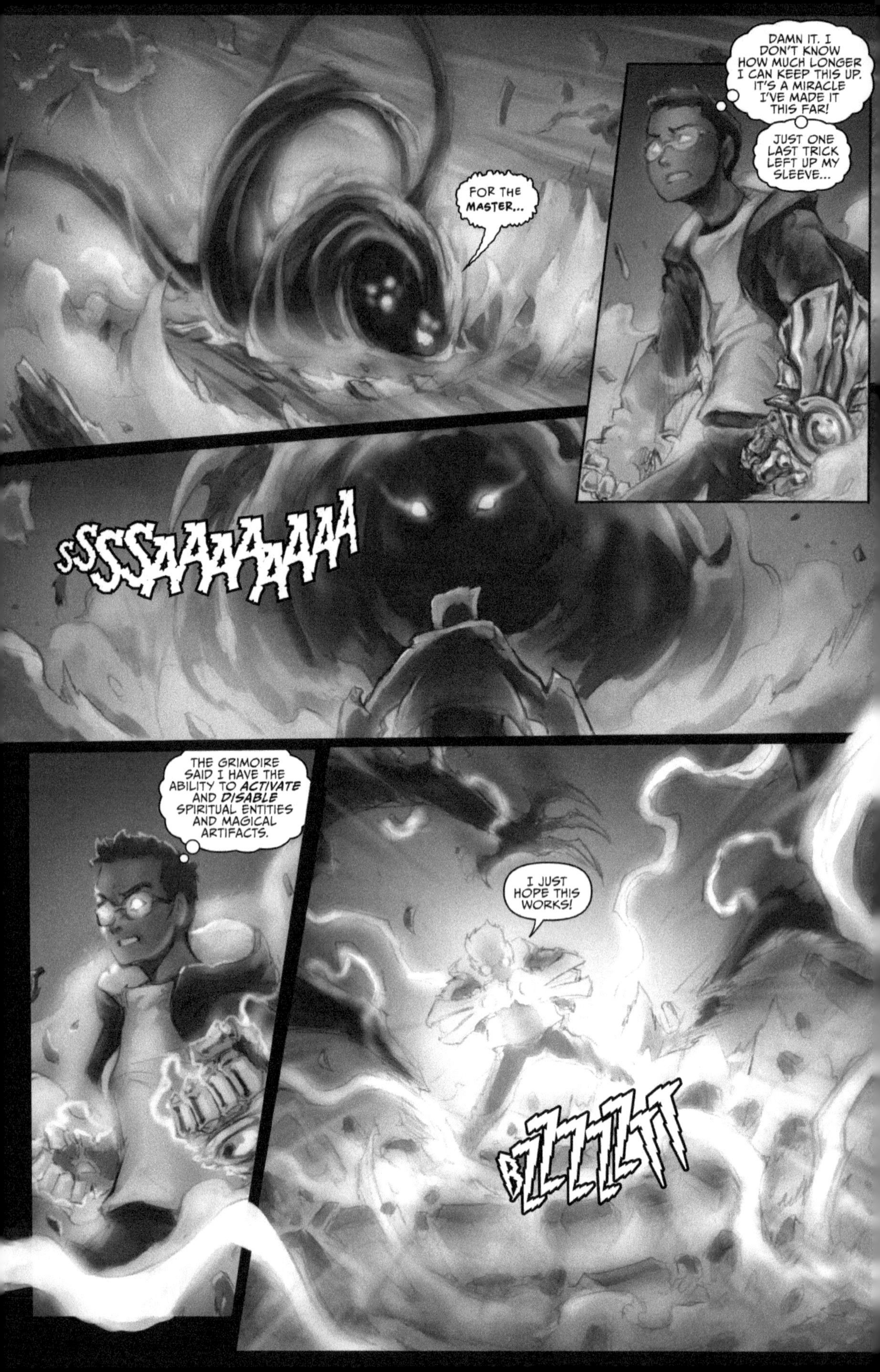
FOR THE MASTER...
DAMN IT. I DON'T KNOW HOW MUCH LONGER I CAN KEEP THIS UP. IT'S A MIRACLE I'VE MADE IT THIS FAR!
JUST ONE LAST TRICK LEFT UP MY SLEEVE...
sSSSAAAAAAAA
THE GRIMOIRE SAID I HAVE THE ABILITY TO ACTIVATE AND DISABLE SPIRITUAL ENTITIES AND MAGICAL ARTIFACTS.
I JUST HOPE THIS WORKS!
BZZZZZTT

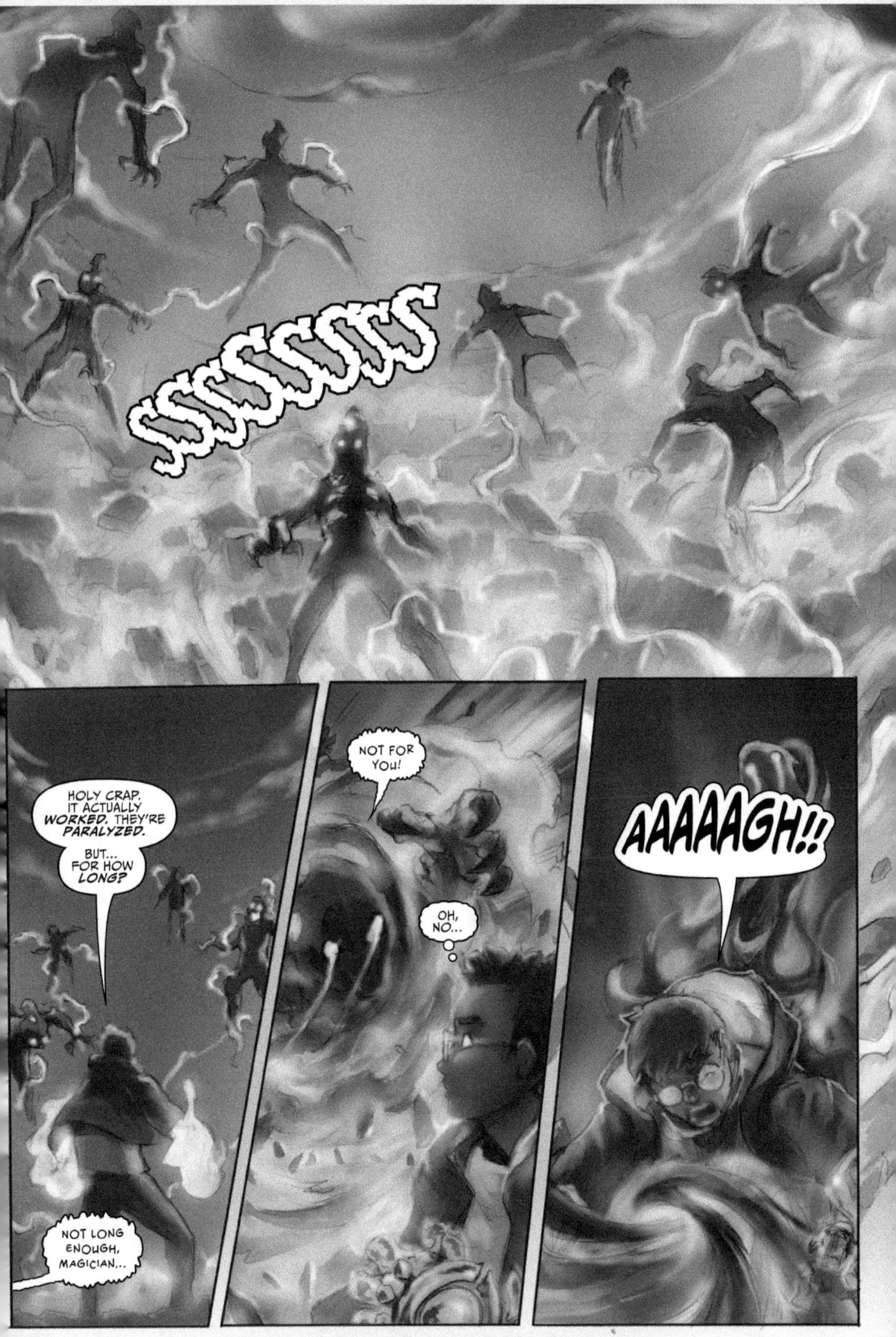
SSSSSSSS
HOLY CRAP. IT ACTUALLY WORKED. THEY'RE PARALYZED.
BUT... FOR HOW LONG?
NOT LONG ENOUGH, MAGICIAN...
NOT FOR YOU!
OH, NO...
AAAAAGH!!

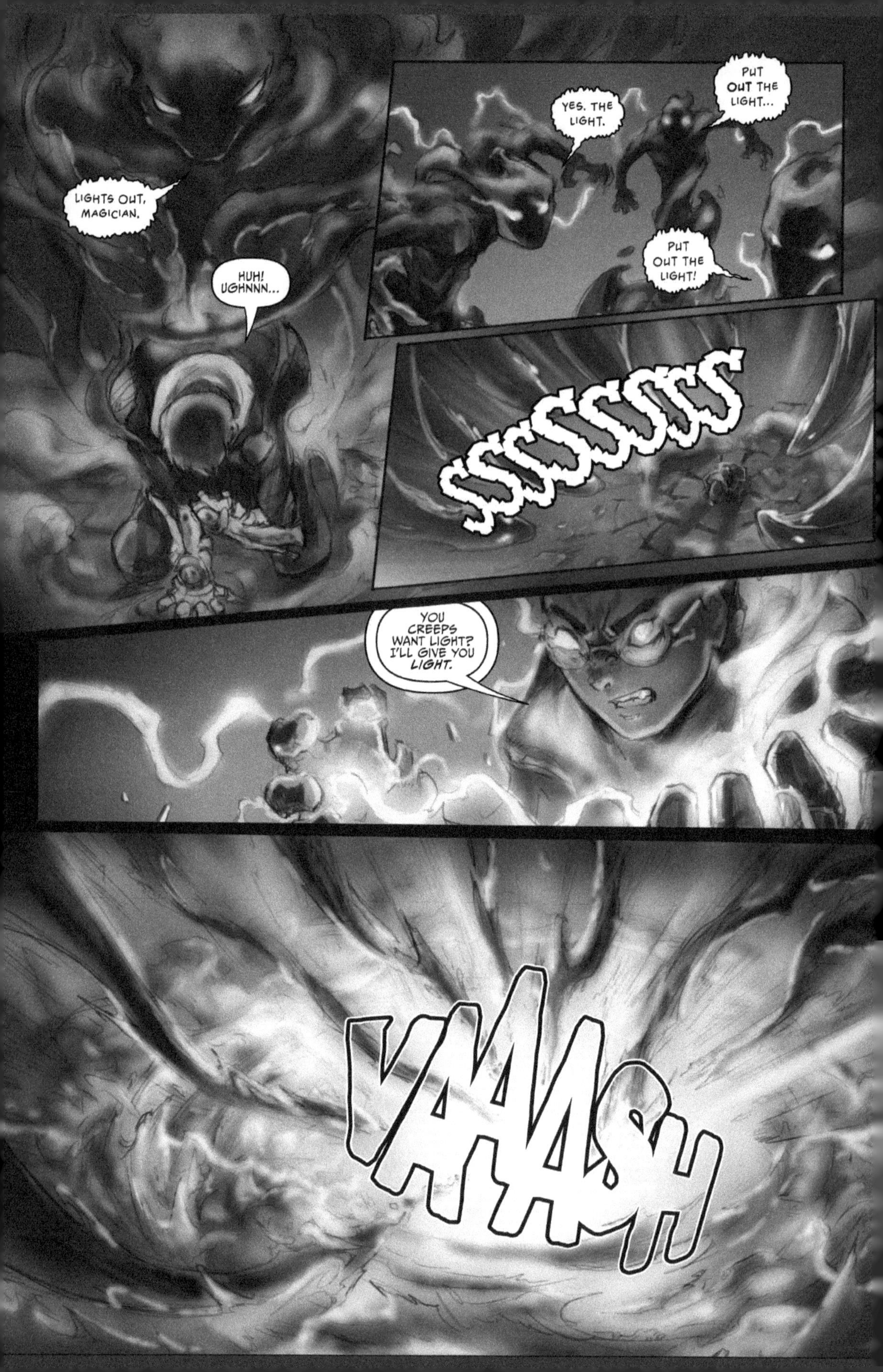
LIGHTS OUT, MAGICIAN.
HUH! UGHNNN...
YES. THE LIGHT.
PUT OUT THE LIGHT...
PUT OUT THE LIGHT!
SSSSSSSSS
YOU CREEPS WANT LIGHT? I'LL GIVE YOU LIGHT.
VAAASH

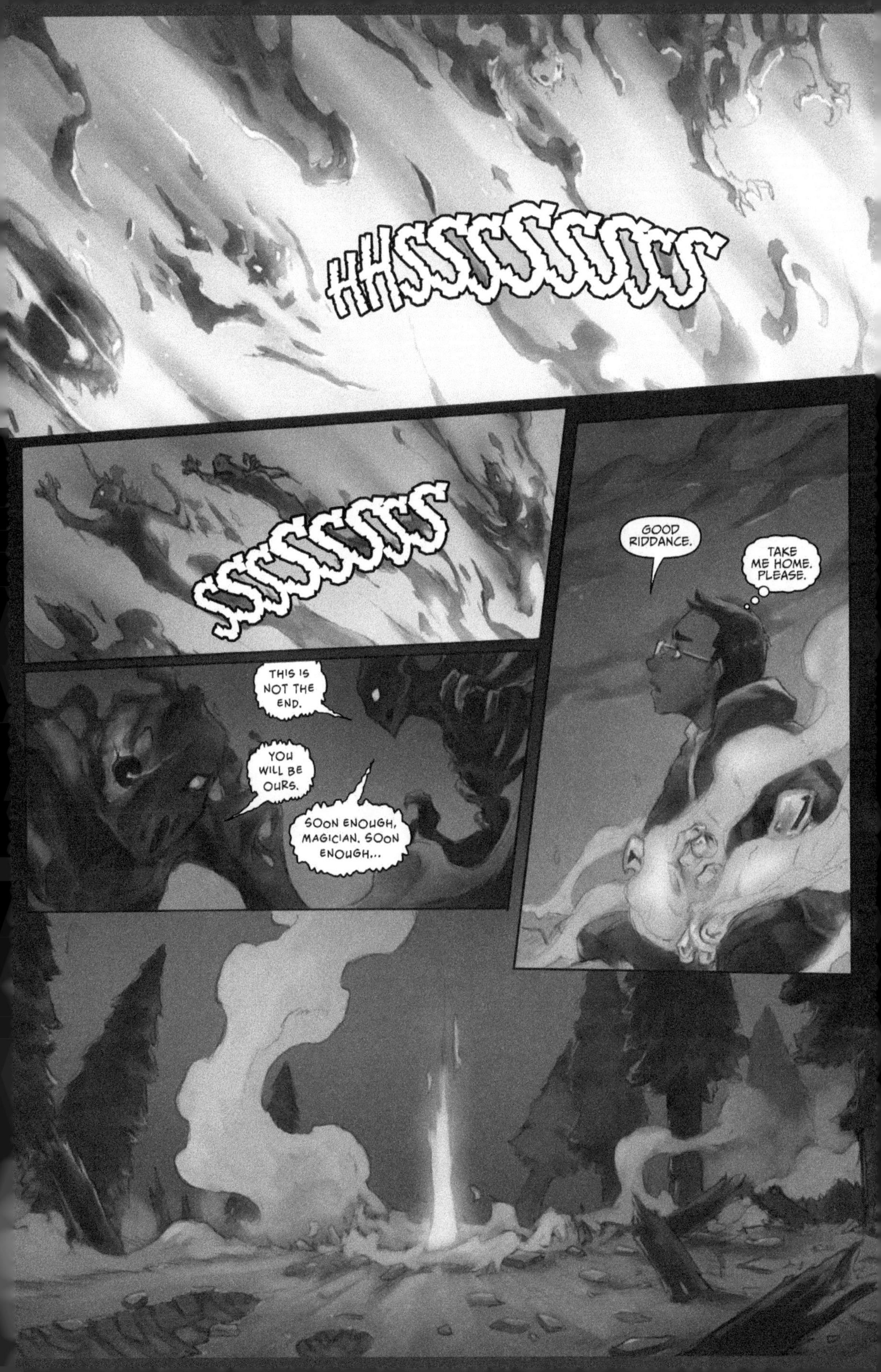
HHSSSSSSSSSSSS
SSSSSSSSSS
GOOD RIDDANCE.
TAKE ME HOME. PLEASE.
THIS IS NOT THE END.
YOU WILL BE OURS.
SOON ENOUGH, MAGICIAN. SOON ENOUGH...

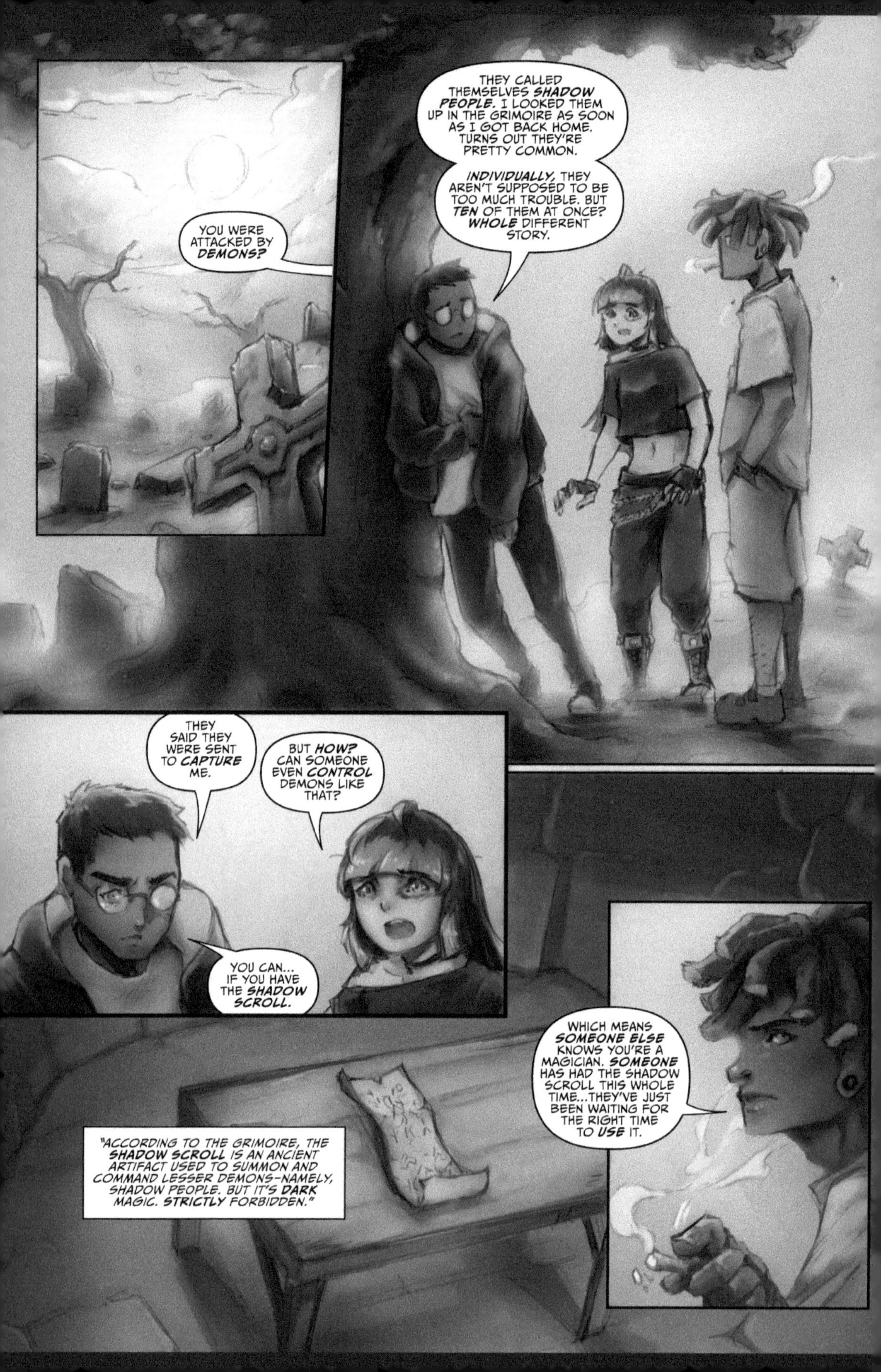
YOU WERE ATTACKED BY DEMONS?
THEY CALLED THEMSELVES SHADOW PEOPLE. I LOOKED THEM UP IN THE GRIMOIRE AS SOON AS I GOT BACK HOME. TURNS OUT THEY'RE PRETTY COMMON.
INDIVIDUALLY, THEY AREN'T SUPPOSED TO BE TOO MUCH TROUBLE. BUT TEN OF THEM AT ONCE? WHOLE DIFFERENT STORY.
THEY SAID THEY WERE SENT TO CAPTURE ME.
BUT HOW? CAN SOMEONE EVEN CONTROL DEMONS LIKE THAT?
YOU CAN... IF YOU HAVE THE SHADOW SCROLL.
"ACCORDING TO THE GRIMOIRE, THE SHADOW SCROLL IS AN ANCIENT ARTIFACT USED TO SUMMON AND COMMAND LESSER DEMONS–NAMELY, SHADOW PEOPLE. BUT IT'S DARK MAGIC. STRICTLY FORBIDDEN."
WHICH MEANS SOMEONE ELSE KNOWS YOU'RE A MAGICIAN. SOMEONE HAS HAD THE SHADOW SCROLL THIS WHOLE TIME...THEY'VE JUST BEEN WAITING FOR THE RIGHT TIME TO USE IT.

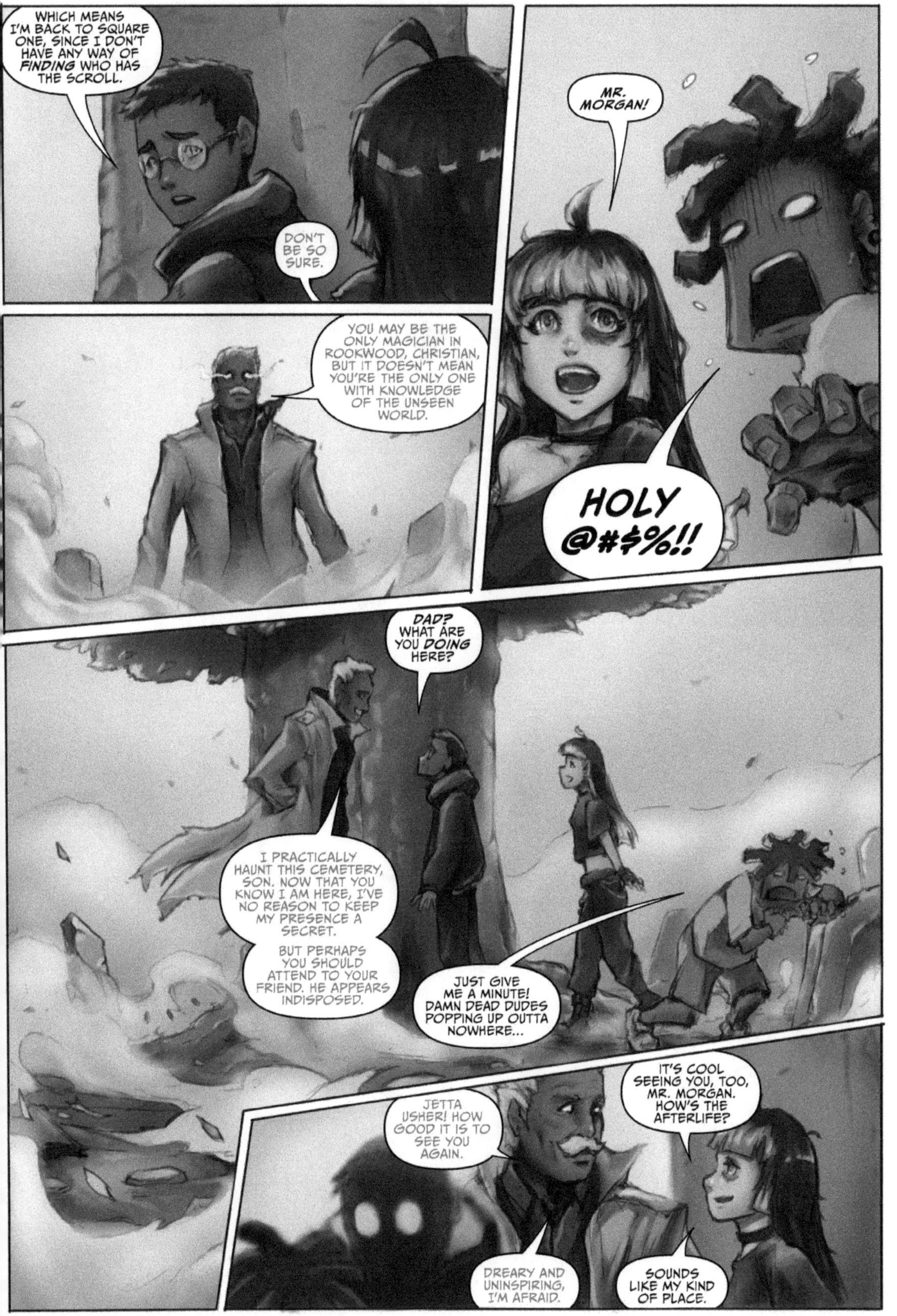
WHICH MEANS I'M BACK TO SQUARE ONE, SINCE I DON'T HAVE ANY WAY OF *FINDING* WHO HAS THE SCROLL.
DON'T BE SO SURE.
YOU MAY BE THE ONLY MAGICIAN IN ROOKWOOD, CHRISTIAN, BUT IT DOESN'T MEAN YOU'RE THE ONLY ONE WITH KNOWLEDGE OF THE UNSEEN WORLD.
MR. MORGAN!
HOLY @#$%!!
*DAD?* WHAT ARE YOU *DOING* HERE?
I PRACTICALLY HAUNT THIS CEMETERY, SON. NOW THAT YOU KNOW I AM HERE, I'VE NO REASON TO KEEP MY PRESENCE A SECRET.
BUT PERHAPS YOU SHOULD ATTEND TO YOUR FRIEND. HE APPEARS INDISPOSED.
JUST GIVE ME A MINUTE! DAMN DEAD DUDES POPPING UP OUTTA NOWHERE...
JETTA USHER! HOW GOOD IT IS TO SEE YOU AGAIN.
IT'S COOL SEEING YOU, TOO, MR. MORGAN. HOW'S THE AFTERLIFE?
DREARY AND UNINSPIRING, I'M AFRAID.
SOUNDS LIKE MY KIND OF PLACE.

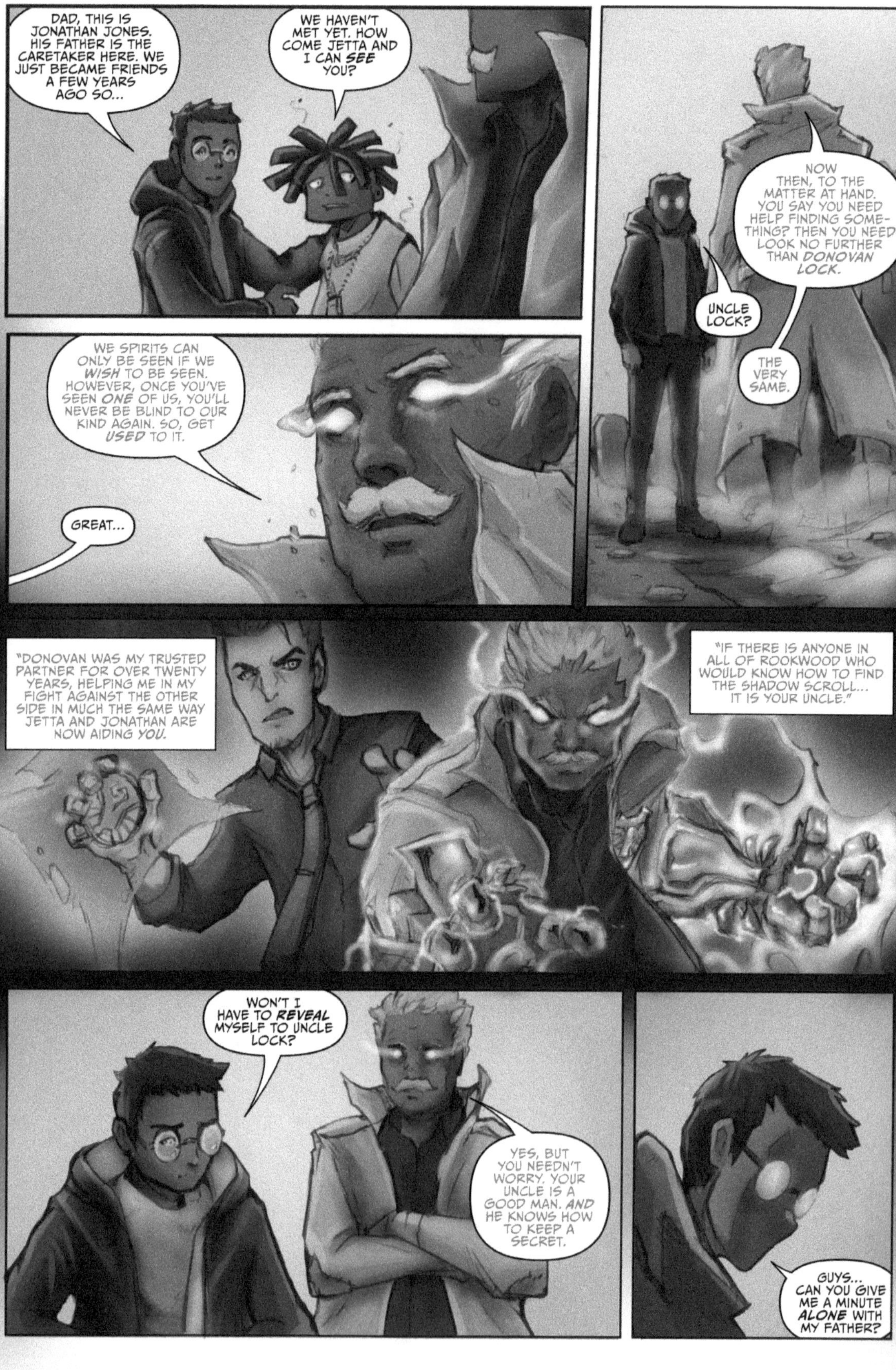
DAD, THIS IS JONATHAN JONES. HIS FATHER IS THE CARETAKER HERE. WE JUST BECAME FRIENDS A FEW YEARS AGO SO...
WE HAVEN'T MET YET. HOW COME JETTA AND I CAN SEE YOU?
WE SPIRITS CAN ONLY BE SEEN IF WE WISH TO BE SEEN. HOWEVER, ONCE YOU'VE SEEN ONE OF US, YOU'LL NEVER BE BLIND TO OUR KIND AGAIN. SO, GET USED TO IT.
GREAT...
NOW THEN, TO THE MATTER AT HAND. YOU SAY YOU NEED HELP FINDING SOME-THING? THEN YOU NEED LOOK NO FURTHER THAN DONOVAN LOCK.
UNCLE LOCK?
THE VERY SAME.
"DONOVAN WAS MY TRUSTED PARTNER FOR OVER TWENTY YEARS, HELPING ME IN MY FIGHT AGAINST THE OTHER SIDE IN MUCH THE SAME WAY JETTA AND JONATHAN ARE NOW AIDING YOU.
"IF THERE IS ANYONE IN ALL OF ROOKWOOD WHO WOULD KNOW HOW TO FIND THE SHADOW SCROLL... IT IS YOUR UNCLE."
WON'T I HAVE TO REVEAL MYSELF TO UNCLE LOCK?
YES, BUT YOU NEEDN'T WORRY. YOUR UNCLE IS A GOOD MAN. AND HE KNOWS HOW TO KEEP A SECRET.
GUYS... CAN YOU GIVE ME A MINUTE ALONE WITH MY FATHER?

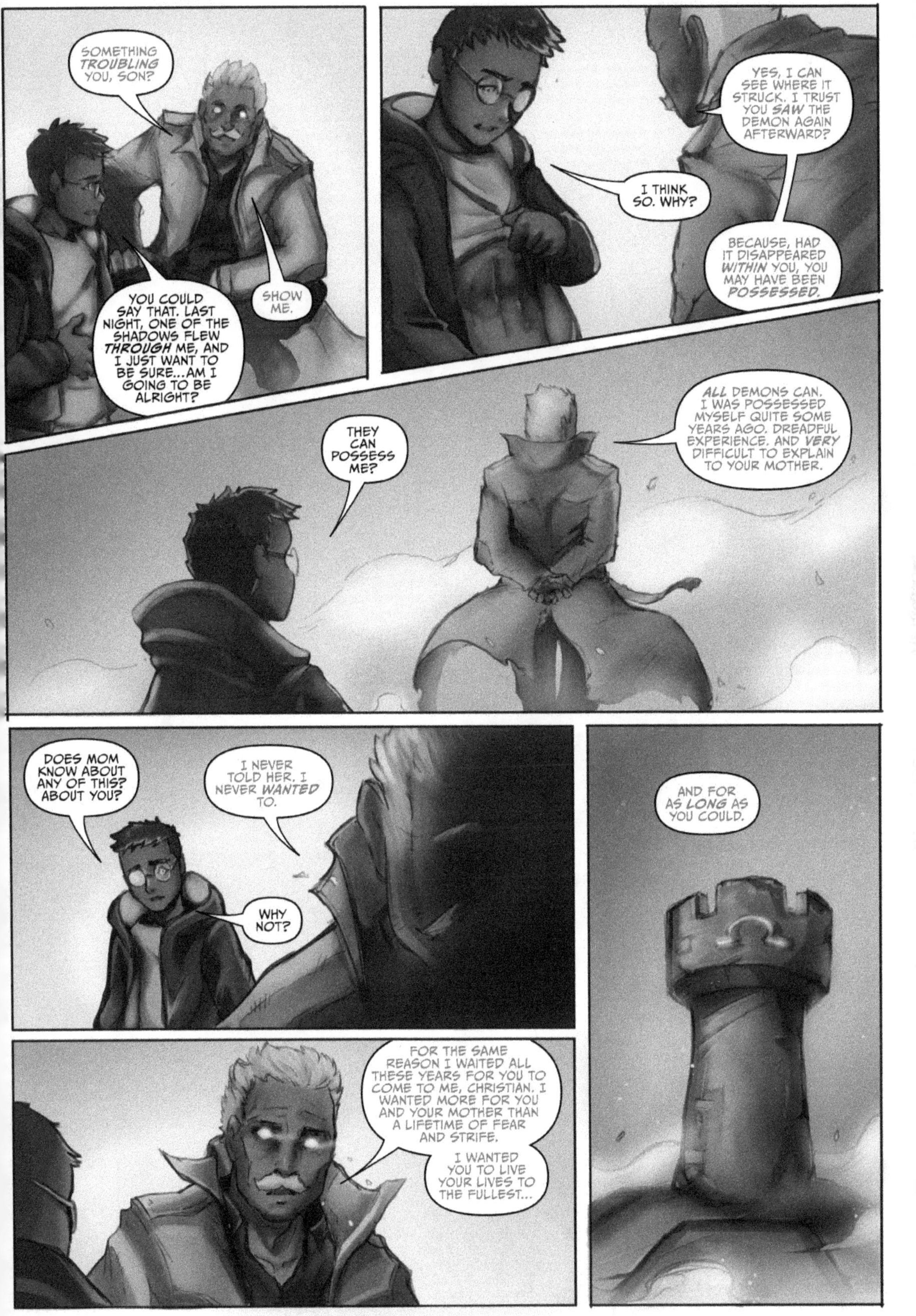
SOMETHING TROUBLING YOU, SON?
YOU COULD SAY THAT. LAST NIGHT, ONE OF THE SHADOWS FLEW THROUGH ME, AND I JUST WANT TO BE SURE...AM I GOING TO BE ALRIGHT?
SHOW ME.
YES, I CAN SEE WHERE IT STRUCK. I TRUST YOU SAW THE DEMON AGAIN AFTERWARD?
I THINK SO. WHY?
BECAUSE, HAD IT DISAPPEARED WITHIN YOU, YOU MAY HAVE BEEN POSSESSED.
THEY CAN POSSESS ME?
ALL DEMONS CAN. I WAS POSSESSED MYSELF QUITE SOME YEARS AGO. DREADFUL EXPERIENCE. AND VERY DIFFICULT TO EXPLAIN TO YOUR MOTHER.
DOES MOM KNOW ABOUT ANY OF THIS? ABOUT YOU?
I NEVER TOLD HER. I NEVER WANTED TO.
WHY NOT?
FOR THE SAME REASON I WAITED ALL THESE YEARS FOR YOU TO COME TO ME, CHRISTIAN. I WANTED MORE FOR YOU AND YOUR MOTHER THAN A LIFETIME OF FEAR AND STRIFE.
I WANTED YOU TO LIVE YOUR LIVES TO THE FULLEST...
AND FOR AS LONG AS YOU COULD.

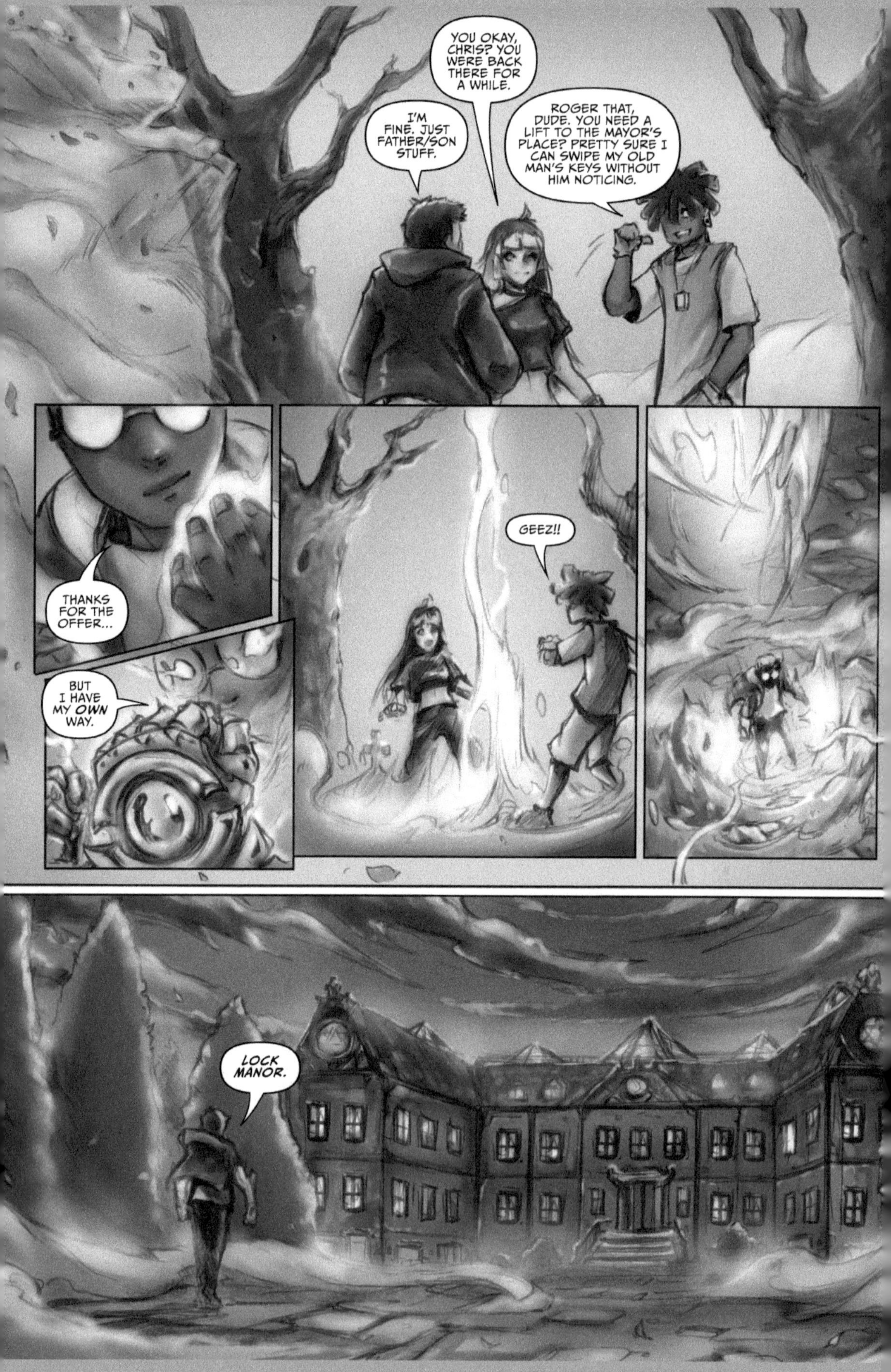
YOU OKAY, CHRIS? YOU WERE BACK THERE FOR A WHILE.
I'M FINE. JUST FATHER/SON STUFF.
ROGER THAT, DUDE. YOU NEED A LIFT TO THE MAYOR'S PLACE? PRETTY SURE I CAN SWIPE MY OLD MAN'S KEYS WITHOUT HIM NOTICING.
THANKS FOR THE OFFER...
BUT I HAVE MY OWN WAY.
GEEZ!!
LOCK MANOR.

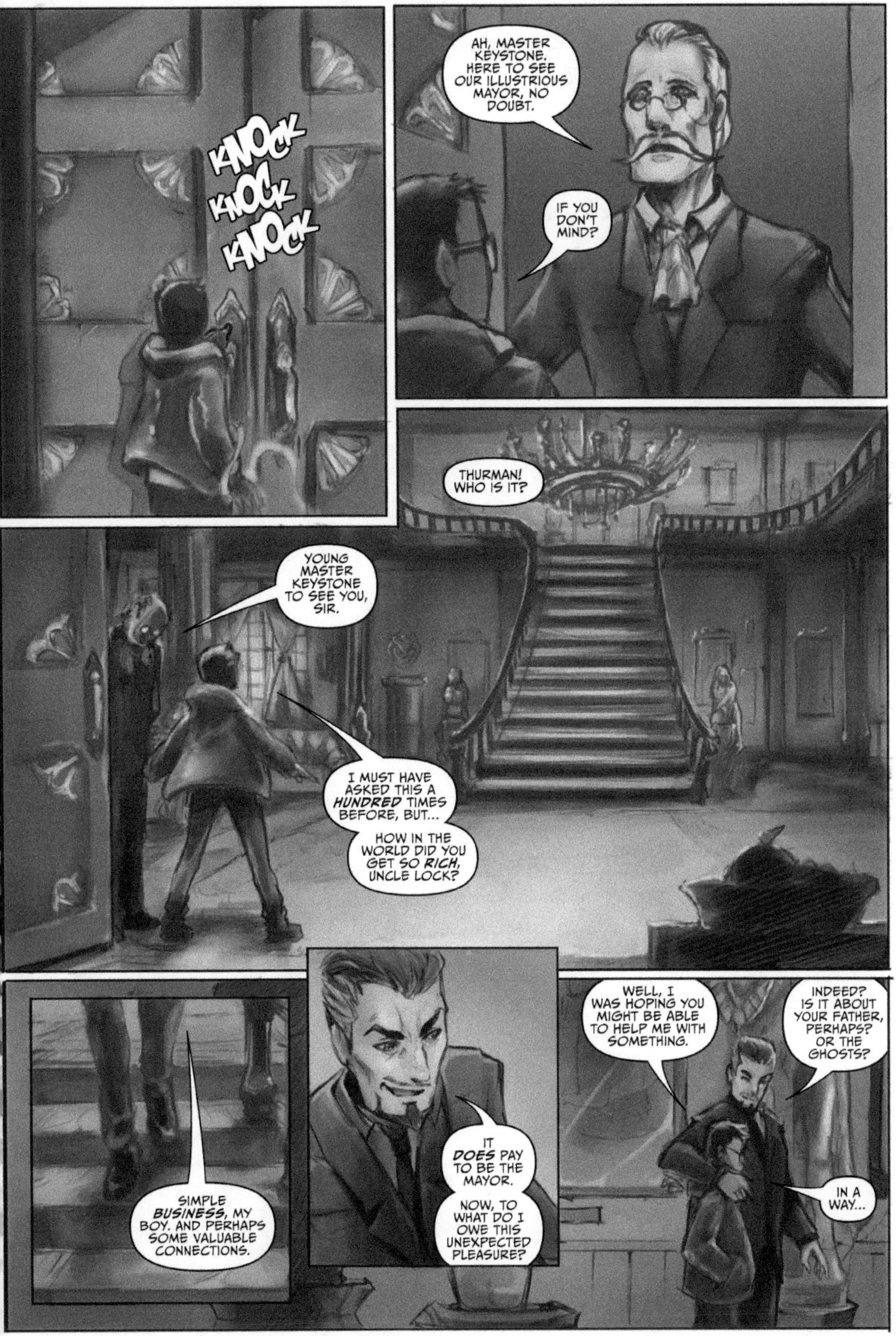
KNOCK KNOCK KNOCK
AH, MASTER KEYSTONE. HERE TO SEE OUR ILLUSTRIOUS MAYOR, NO DOUBT.
IF YOU DON'T MIND?
THURMAN! WHO IS IT?
YOUNG MASTER KEYSTONE TO SEE YOU, SIR.
I MUST HAVE ASKED THIS A *HUNDRED* TIMES BEFORE, BUT...
HOW IN THE WORLD DID YOU GET SO *RICH*, UNCLE LOCK?
SIMPLE *BUSINESS*, MY BOY. AND PERHAPS SOME VALUABLE CONNECTIONS.
IT *DOES* PAY TO BE THE MAYOR.
NOW, TO WHAT DO I OWE THIS UNEXPECTED PLEASURE?
WELL, I WAS HOPING YOU MIGHT BE ABLE TO HELP ME WITH SOMETHING.
INDEED? IS IT ABOUT YOUR FATHER, PERHAPS? OR THE GHOSTS?
IN A WAY...

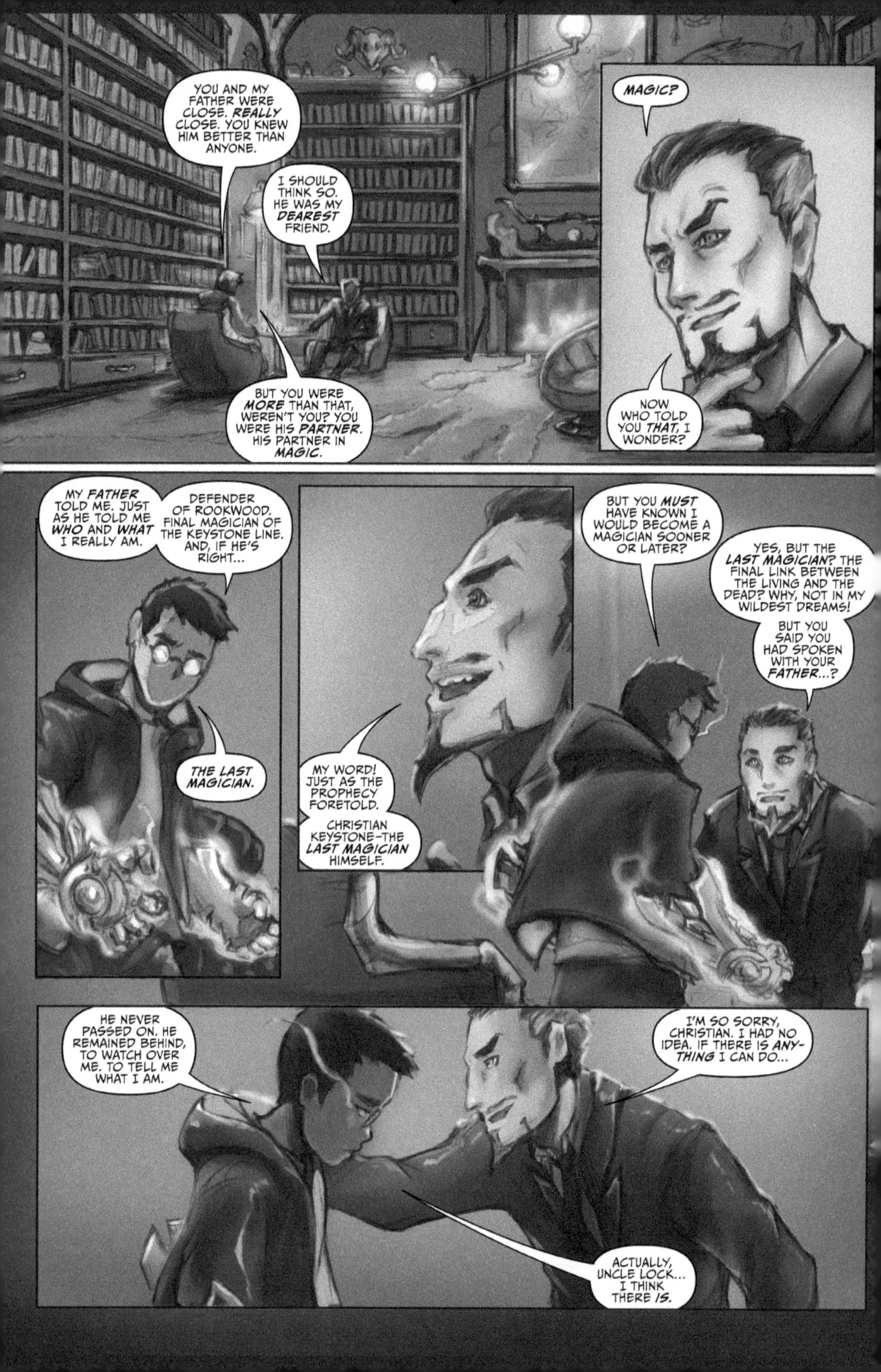
YOU AND MY FATHER WERE CLOSE. REALLY CLOSE. YOU KNEW HIM BETTER THAN ANYONE.
I SHOULD THINK SO. HE WAS MY DEAREST FRIEND.
BUT YOU WERE MORE THAN THAT, WEREN'T YOU? YOU WERE HIS PARTNER. HIS PARTNER IN MAGIC.
MAGIC?
NOW WHO TOLD YOU THAT, I WONDER?
MY FATHER TOLD ME. JUST AS HE TOLD ME WHO AND WHAT I REALLY AM.
DEFENDER OF ROOKWOOD. FINAL MAGICIAN OF THE KEYSTONE LINE. AND, IF HE'S RIGHT...
THE LAST MAGICIAN.
MY WORD! JUST AS THE PROPHECY FORETOLD.
CHRISTIAN KEYSTONE–THE LAST MAGICIAN HIMSELF.
BUT YOU MUST HAVE KNOWN I WOULD BECOME A MAGICIAN SOONER OR LATER?
YES, BUT THE LAST MAGICIAN? THE FINAL LINK BETWEEN THE LIVING AND THE DEAD? WHY, NOT IN MY WILDEST DREAMS!
BUT YOU SAID YOU HAD SPOKEN WITH YOUR FATHER...?
HE NEVER PASSED ON. HE REMAINED BEHIND, TO WATCH OVER ME. TO TELL ME WHAT I AM.
I'M SO SORRY, CHRISTIAN. I HAD NO IDEA. IF THERE IS ANY-THING I CAN DO...
ACTUALLY, UNCLE LOCK... I THINK THERE IS.

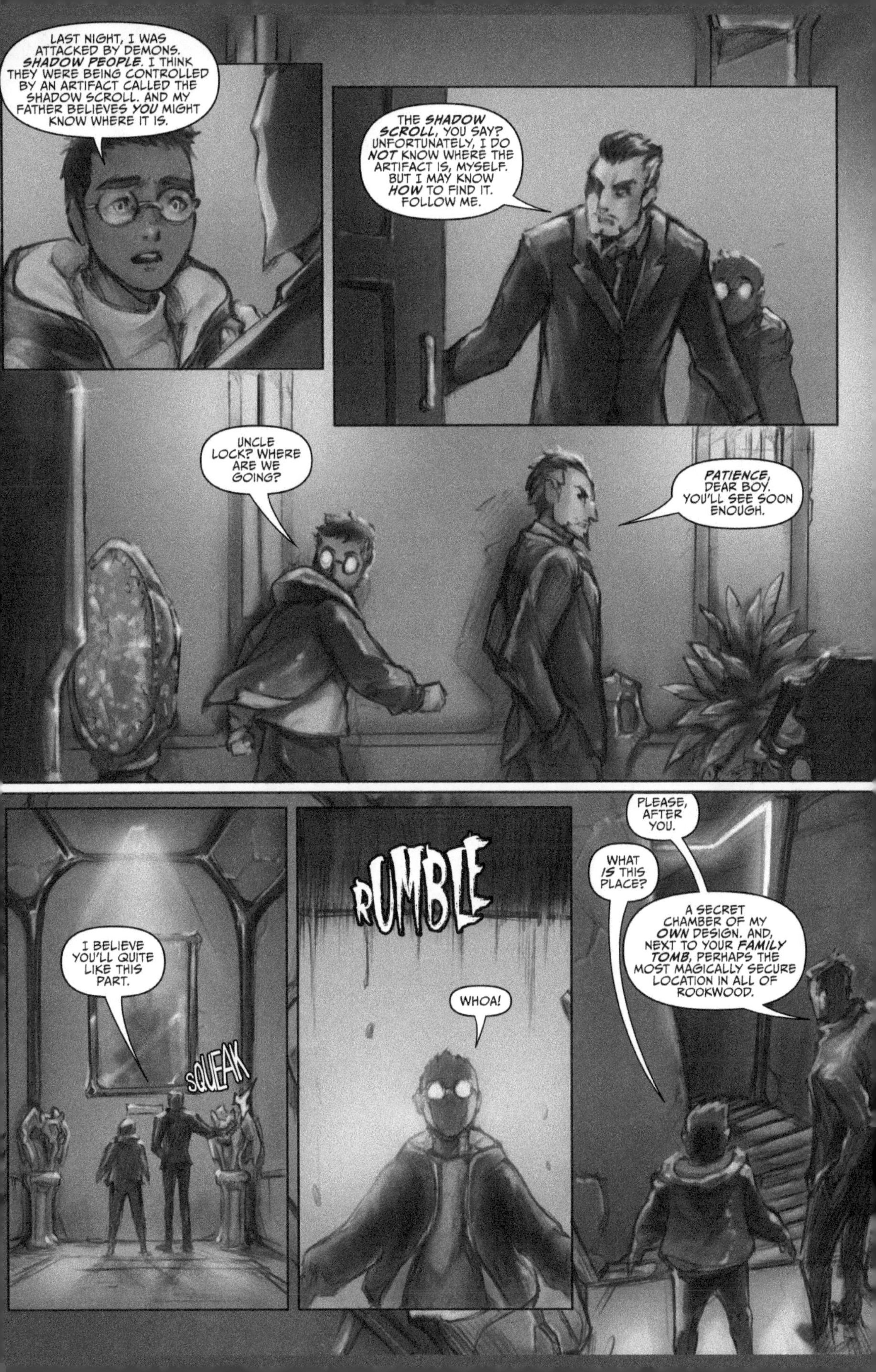
LAST NIGHT, I WAS ATTACKED BY DEMONS. SHADOW PEOPLE. I THINK THEY WERE BEING CONTROLLED BY AN ARTIFACT CALLED THE SHADOW SCROLL. AND MY FATHER BELIEVES YOU MIGHT KNOW WHERE IT IS.
THE SHADOW SCROLL, YOU SAY? UNFORTUNATELY, I DO NOT KNOW WHERE THE ARTIFACT IS, MYSELF. BUT I MAY KNOW HOW TO FIND IT. FOLLOW ME.
UNCLE LOCK? WHERE ARE WE GOING?
PATIENCE, DEAR BOY. YOU'LL SEE SOON ENOUGH.
I BELIEVE YOU'LL QUITE LIKE THIS PART.
SQUEAK
RUMBLE
WHOA!
PLEASE, AFTER YOU.
WHAT IS THIS PLACE?
A SECRET CHAMBER OF MY OWN DESIGN. AND, NEXT TO YOUR FAMILY TOMB, PERHAPS THE MOST MAGICALLY SECURE LOCATION IN ALL OF ROOKWOOD.

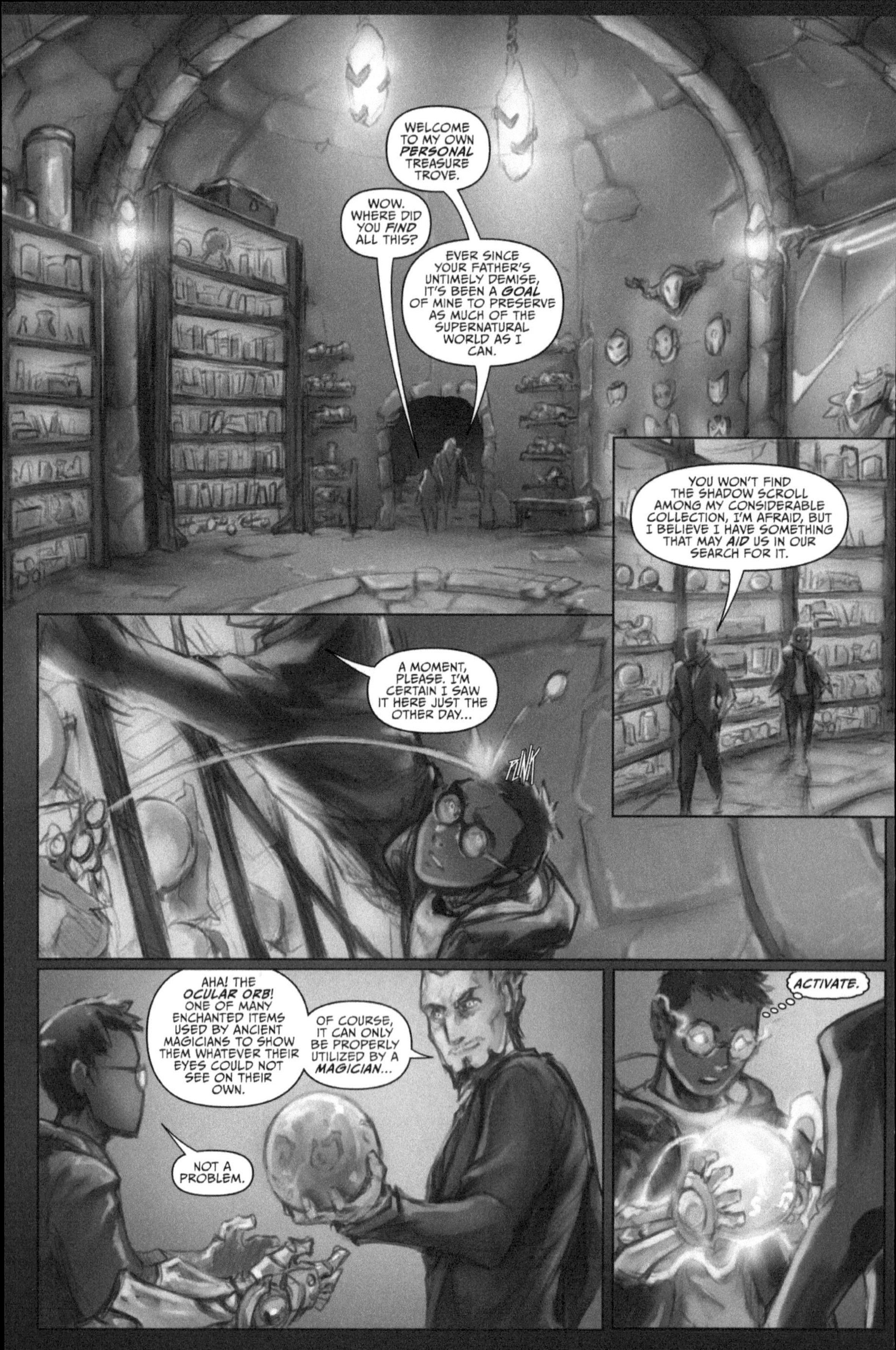
WELCOME TO MY OWN PERSONAL TREASURE TROVE.
WOW. WHERE DID YOU FIND ALL THIS?
EVER SINCE YOUR FATHER'S UNTIMELY DEMISE, IT'S BEEN A GOAL OF MINE TO PRESERVE AS MUCH OF THE SUPERNATURAL WORLD AS I CAN.
YOU WON'T FIND THE SHADOW SCROLL AMONG MY CONSIDERABLE COLLECTION, I'M AFRAID, BUT I BELIEVE I HAVE SOMETHING THAT MAY AID US IN OUR SEARCH FOR IT.
A MOMENT, PLEASE. I'M CERTAIN I SAW IT HERE JUST THE OTHER DAY...
PLINK
AHA! THE OCULAR ORB! ONE OF MANY ENCHANTED ITEMS USED BY ANCIENT MAGICIANS TO SHOW THEM WHATEVER THEIR EYES COULD NOT SEE ON THEIR OWN.
OF COURSE, IT CAN ONLY BE PROPERLY UTILIZED BY A MAGICIAN...
NOT A PROBLEM.
ACTIVATE.

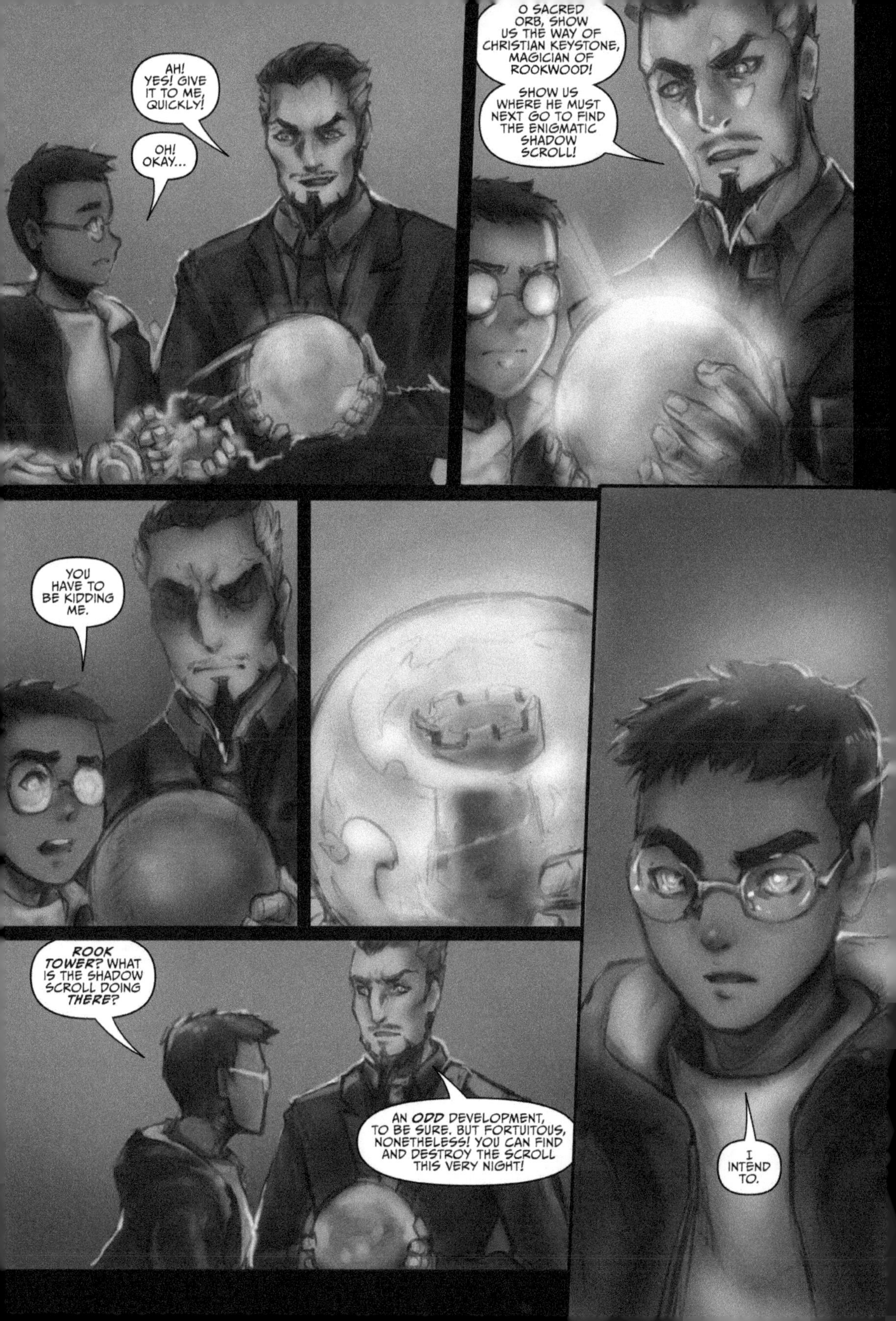
AH! YES! GIVE IT TO ME, QUICKLY!
OH! OKAY...
O SACRED ORB, SHOW US THE WAY OF CHRISTIAN KEYSTONE, MAGICIAN OF ROOKWOOD!
SHOW US WHERE HE MUST NEXT GO TO FIND THE ENIGMATIC SHADOW SCROLL!
YOU HAVE TO BE KIDDING ME.
ROOK TOWER? WHAT IS THE SHADOW SCROLL DOING THERE?
AN ODD DEVELOPMENT, TO BE SURE. BUT FORTUITOUS, NONETHELESS! YOU CAN FIND AND DESTROY THE SCROLL THIS VERY NIGHT!
I INTEND TO.

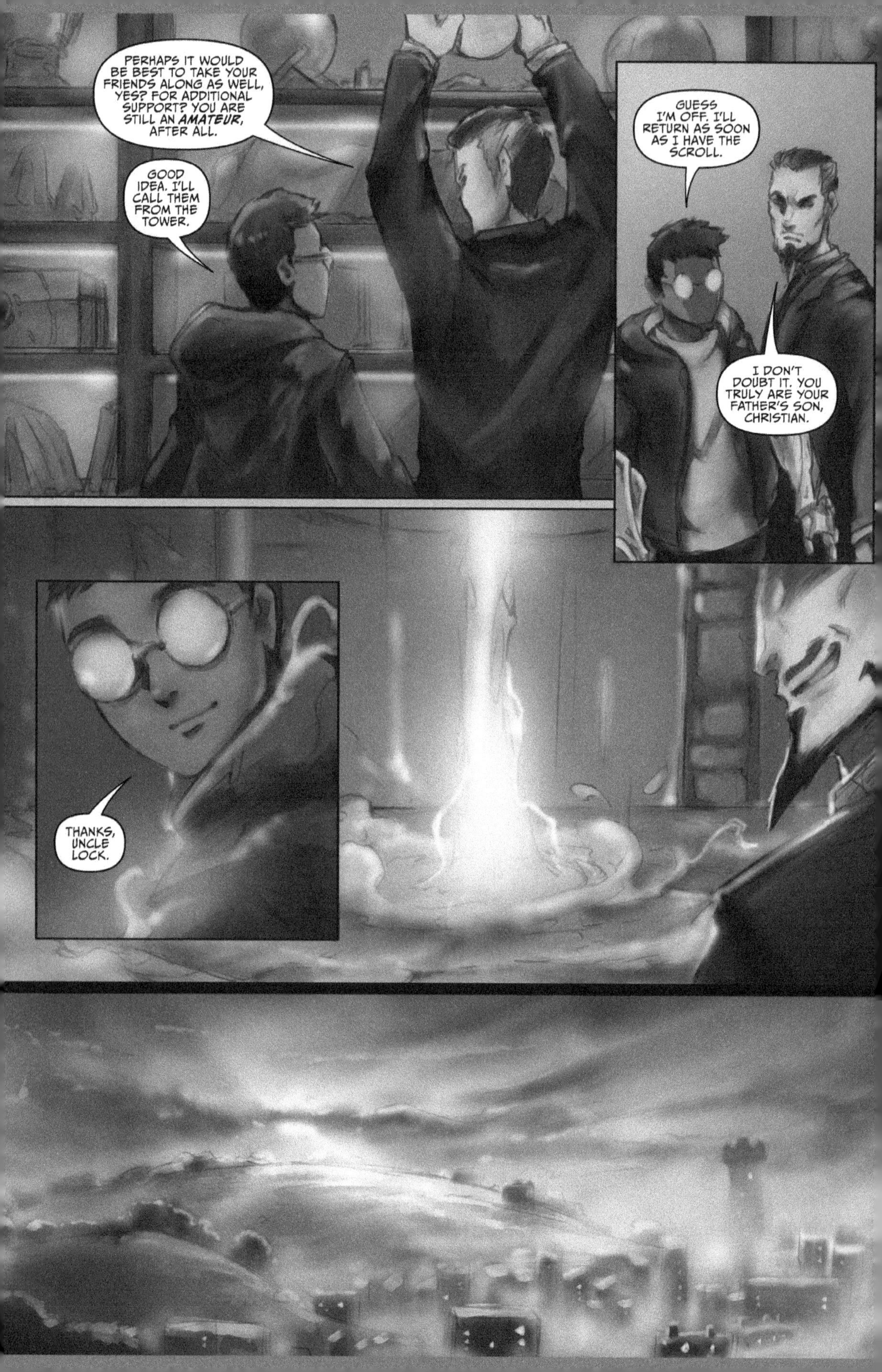
PERHAPS IT WOULD BE BEST TO TAKE YOUR FRIENDS ALONG AS WELL, YES? FOR ADDITIONAL SUPPORT? YOU ARE STILL AN *AMATEUR*, AFTER ALL.
GOOD IDEA. I'LL CALL THEM FROM THE TOWER.
GUESS I'M OFF. I'LL RETURN AS SOON AS I HAVE THE SCROLL.
I DON'T DOUBT IT. YOU TRULY ARE YOUR FATHER'S SON, CHRISTIAN.
THANKS, UNCLE LOCK.

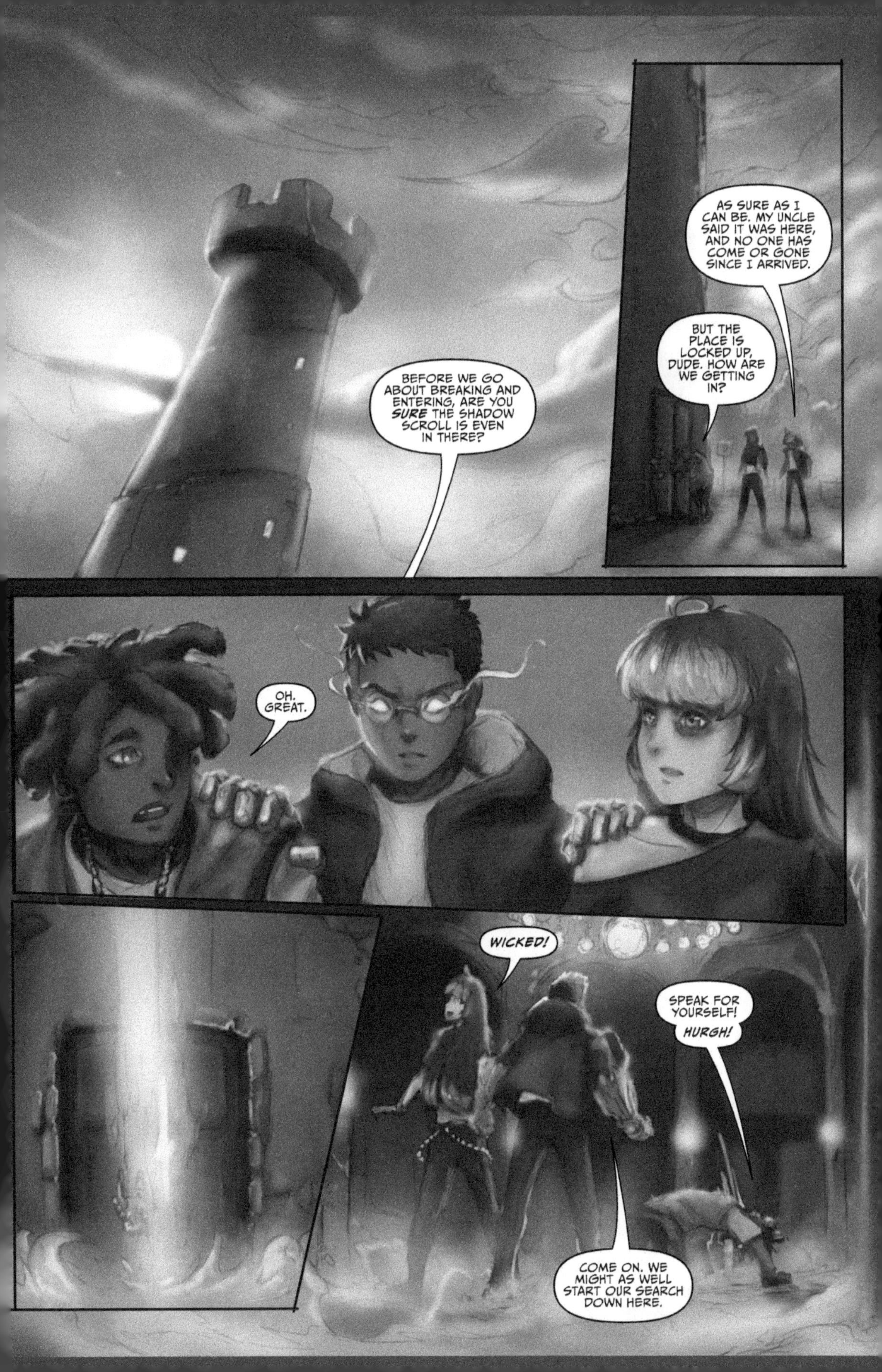
BEFORE WE GO ABOUT BREAKING AND ENTERING, ARE YOU *SURE* THE SHADOW SCROLL IS EVEN IN THERE?
AS SURE AS I CAN BE. MY UNCLE SAID IT WAS HERE, AND NO ONE HAS COME OR GONE SINCE I ARRIVED.
BUT THE PLACE IS LOCKED UP, DUDE. HOW ARE WE GETTING IN?
OH. GREAT.
*WICKED!*
SPEAK FOR YOURSELF! *HURGH!*
COME ON. WE MIGHT AS WELL START OUR SEARCH DOWN HERE.

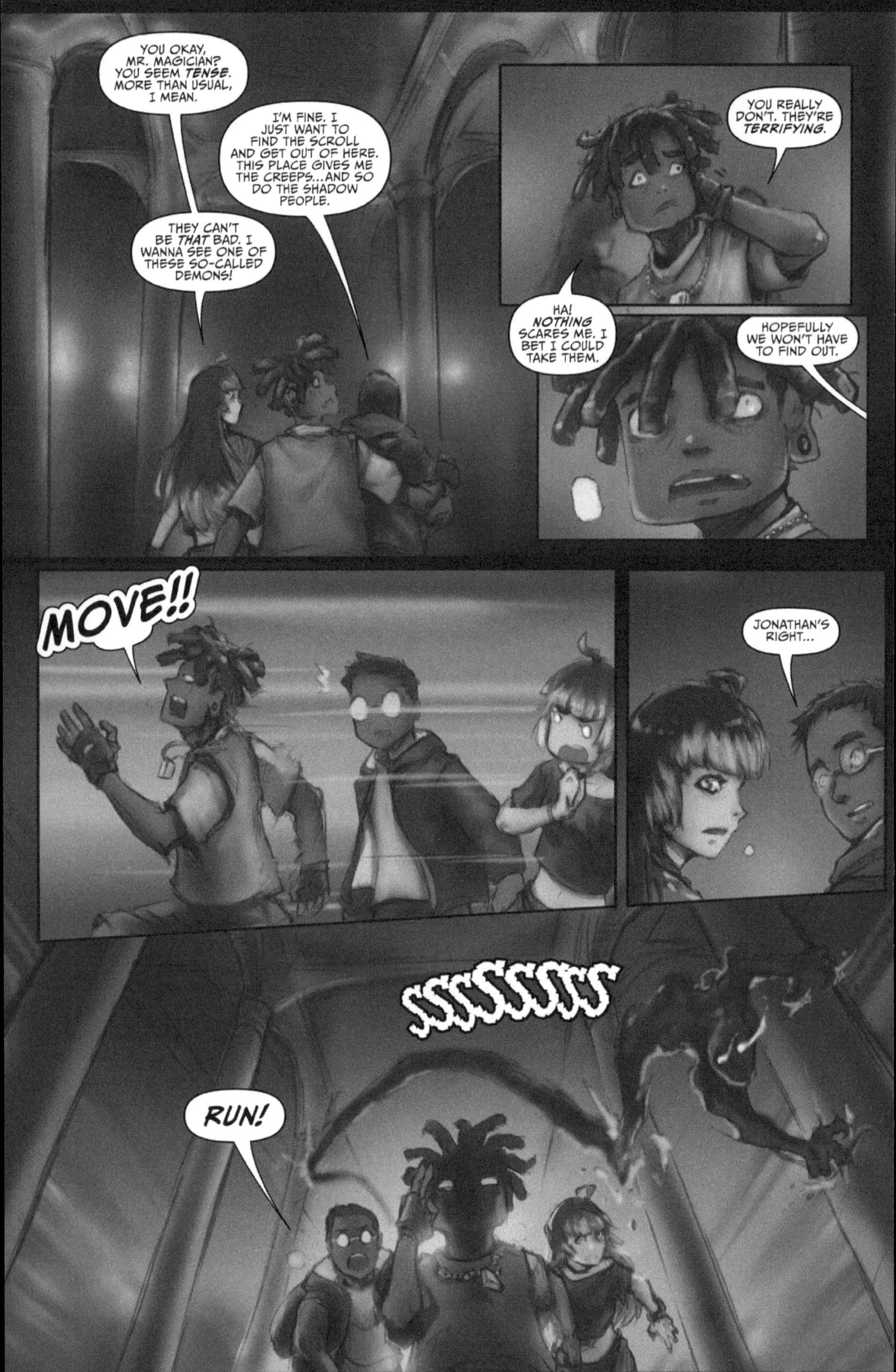
YOU OKAY, MR. MAGICIAN? YOU SEEM *TENSE*. MORE THAN USUAL, I MEAN.
I'M FINE. I JUST WANT TO FIND THE SCROLL AND GET OUT OF HERE. THIS PLACE GIVES ME THE CREEPS...AND SO DO THE SHADOW PEOPLE.
THEY CAN'T BE *THAT* BAD. I WANNA SEE ONE OF THESE SO-CALLED DEMONS!
YOU REALLY DON'T. THEY'RE *TERRIFYING*.
HA! *NOTHING* SCARES ME. I BET I COULD TAKE THEM.
HOPEFULLY WE WON'T HAVE TO FIND OUT.
MOVE!!
JONATHAN'S RIGHT...
SSSSSSSSS
RUN!

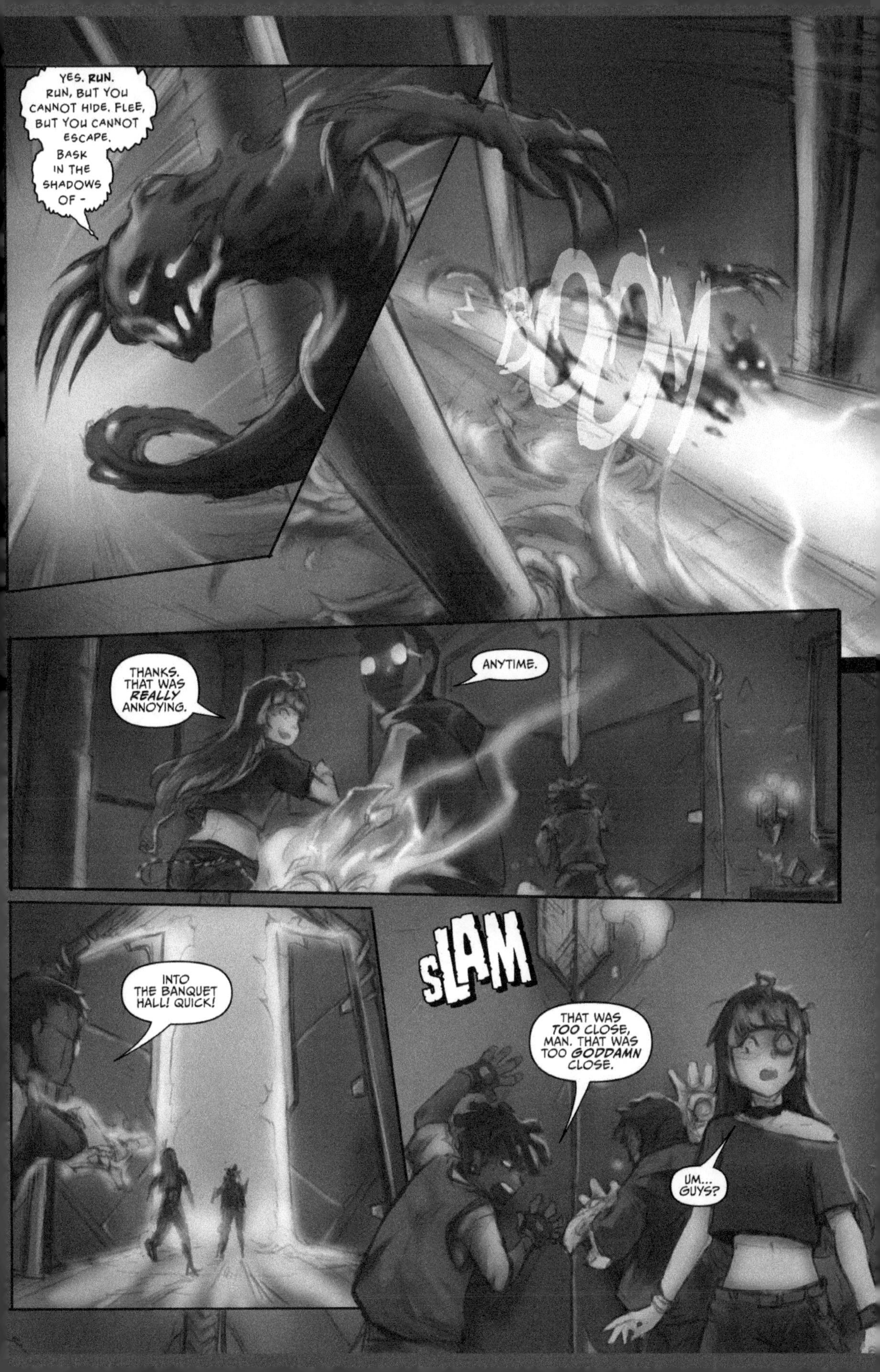
YES. RUN. RUN, BUT YOU CANNOT HIDE. FLEE, BUT YOU CANNOT ESCAPE. BASK IN THE SHADOWS OF -
BOOM
THANKS. THAT WAS REALLY ANNOYING.
ANYTIME.
INTO THE BANQUET HALL! QUICK!
SLAM
THAT WAS TOO CLOSE, MAN. THAT WAS TOO GODDAMN CLOSE.
UM... GUYS?

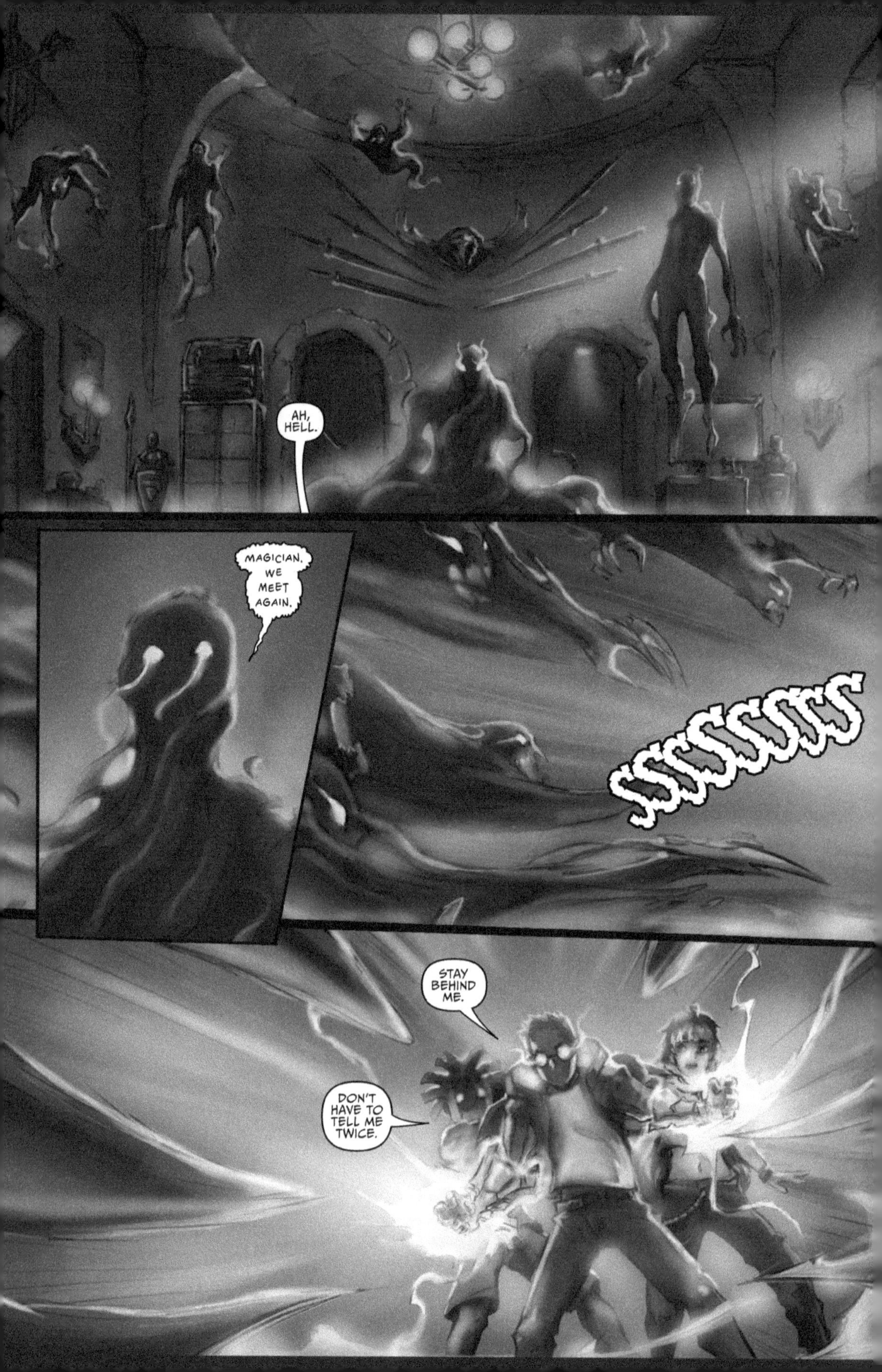
AH, HELL.
MAGICIAN. WE MEET AGAIN.
SSSSSSSS
STAY BEHIND ME.
DON'T HAVE TO TELL ME TWICE.

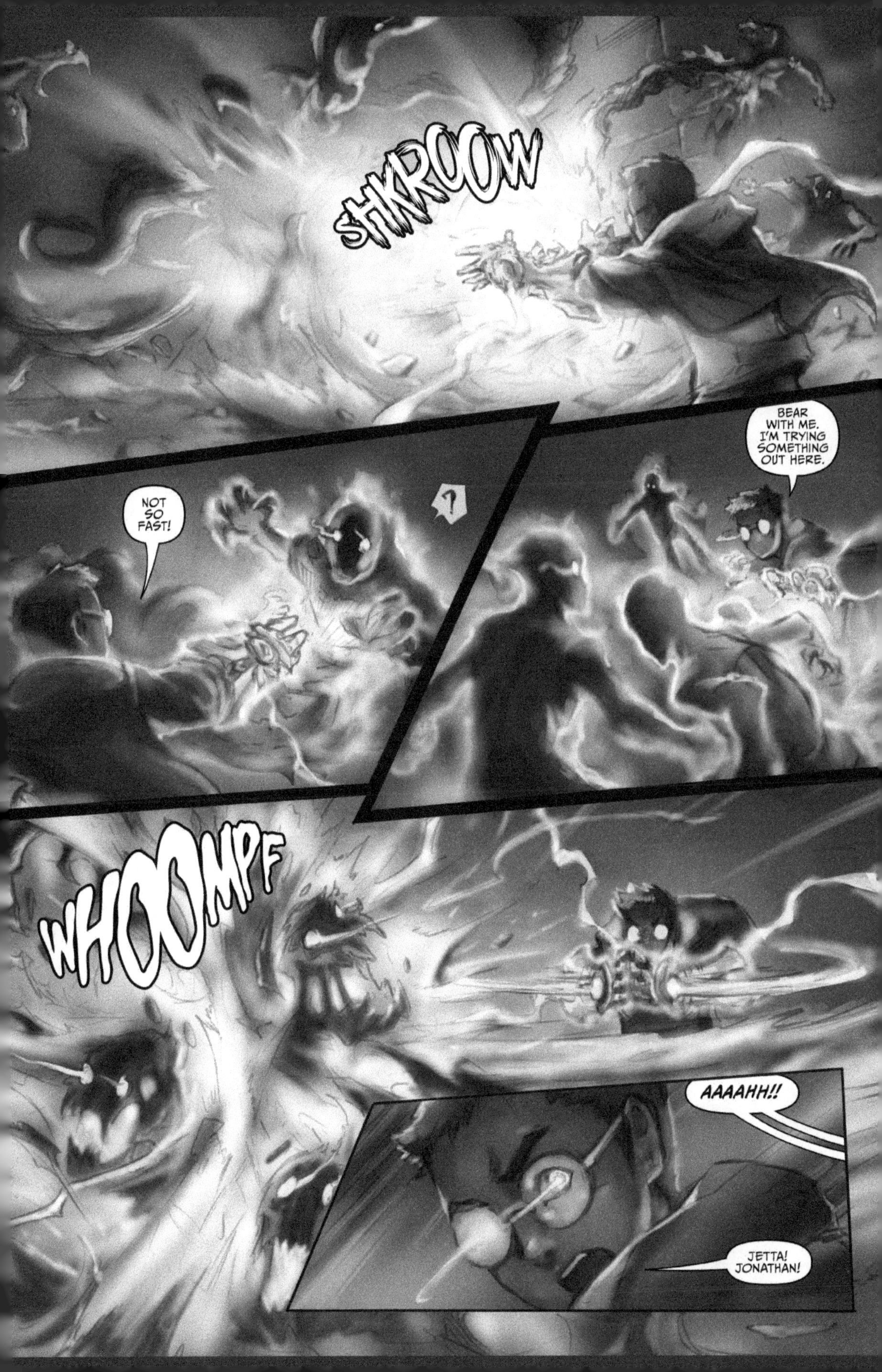
SHKROOW
NOT SO FAST!
?
BEAR WITH ME. I'M TRYING SOMETHING OUT HERE.
WHOOMPF
AAAAHH!!
JETTA! JONATHAN!

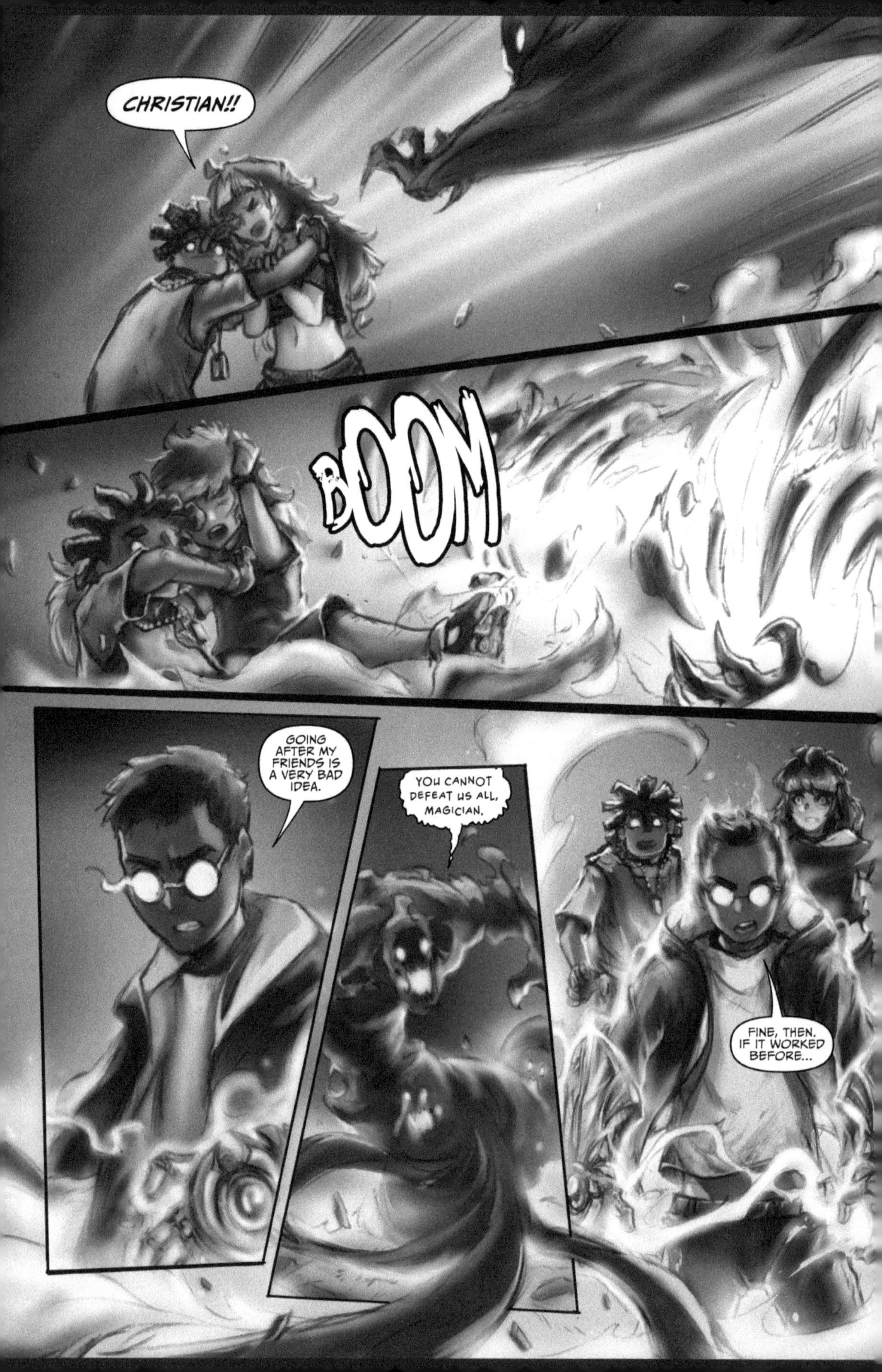
CHRISTIAN!!
BOOM
GOING AFTER MY FRIENDS IS A VERY BAD IDEA.
YOU CANNOT DEFEAT US ALL, MAGICIAN.
FINE, THEN. IF IT WORKED BEFORE...

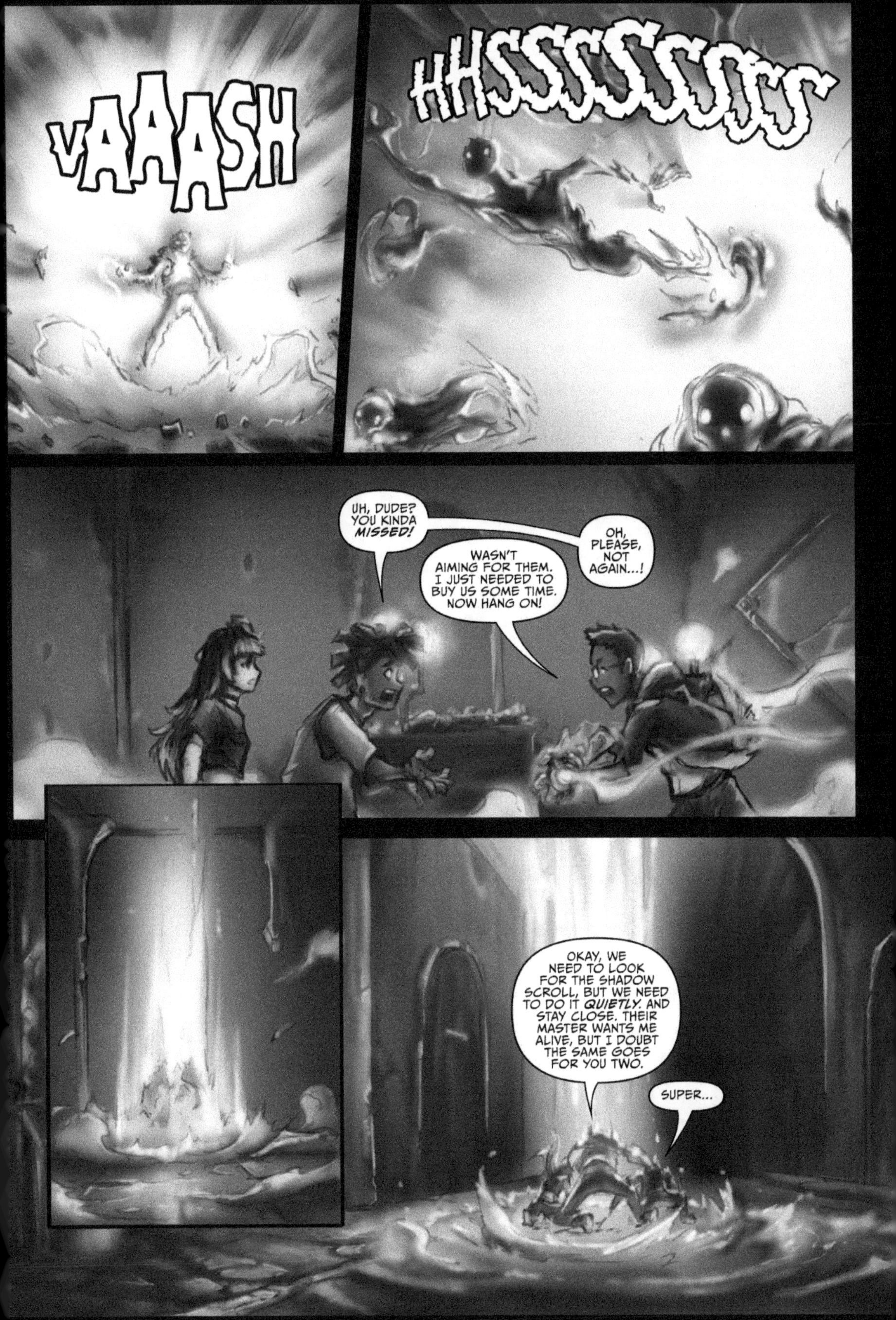
vAAASH
HHSSSSSSSS
UH, DUDE? YOU KINDA *MISSED!*
OH, PLEASE, NOT AGAIN...!
WASN'T AIMING FOR THEM. I JUST NEEDED TO BUY US SOME TIME. NOW HANG ON!
OKAY, WE NEED TO LOOK FOR THE SHADOW SCROLL, BUT WE NEED TO DO IT *QUIETLY*. AND STAY CLOSE. THEIR MASTER WANTS ME ALIVE, BUT I DOUBT THE SAME GOES FOR YOU TWO.
SUPER...

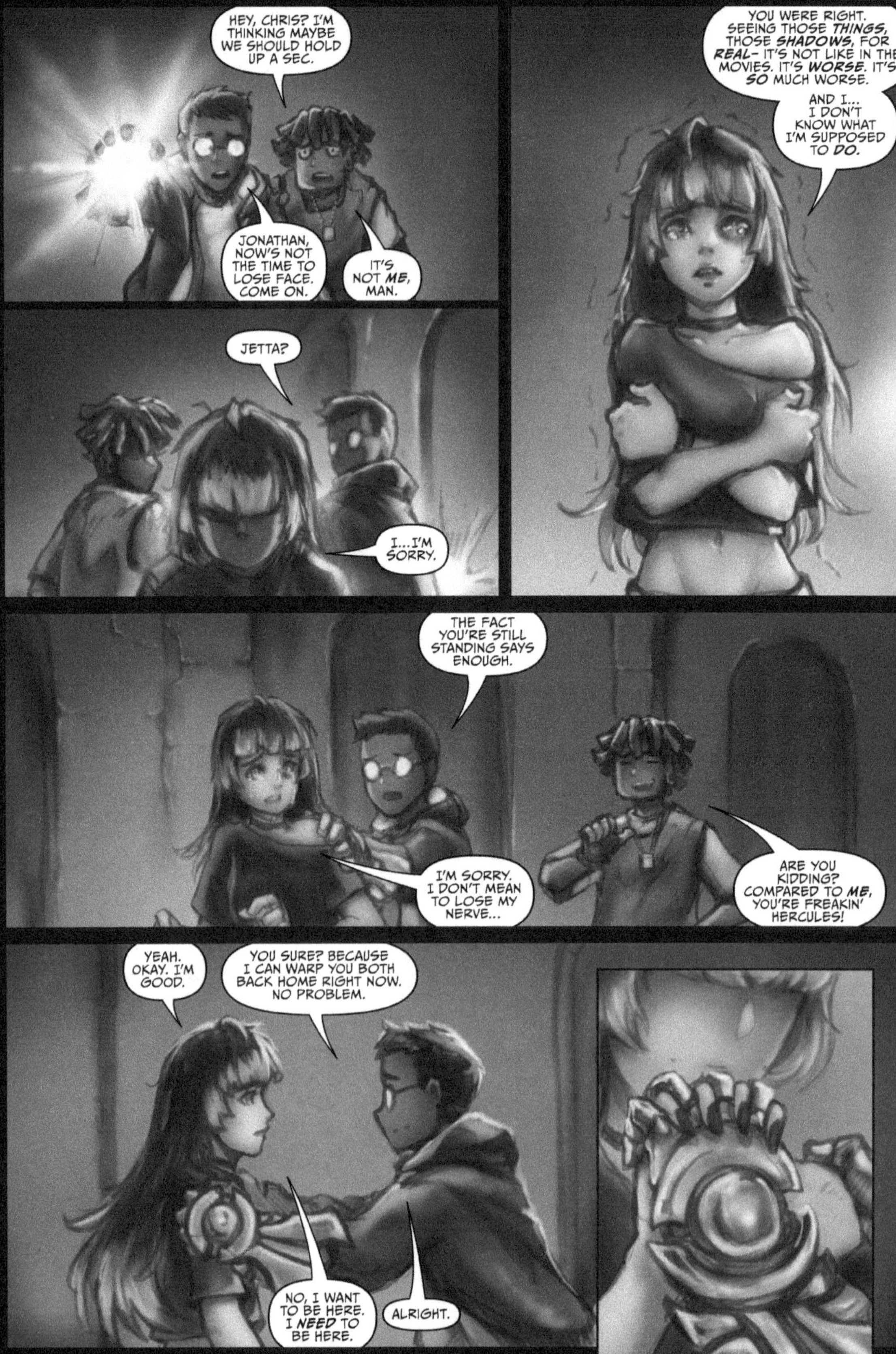
HEY, CHRIS? I'M THINKING MAYBE WE SHOULD HOLD UP A SEC.
JONATHAN, NOW'S NOT THE TIME TO LOSE FACE. COME ON.
IT'S NOT *ME*, MAN.
JETTA?
I...I'M SORRY.
YOU WERE RIGHT. SEEING THOSE *THINGS*, THOSE *SHADOWS*, FOR *REAL*- IT'S NOT LIKE IN THE MOVIES. IT'S *WORSE*. IT'S *SO* MUCH WORSE.
AND I... I DON'T KNOW WHAT I'M SUPPOSED TO *DO*.
THE FACT YOU'RE STILL STANDING SAYS ENOUGH.
I'M SORRY. I DON'T MEAN TO LOSE MY NERVE...
ARE YOU KIDDING? COMPARED TO *ME*, YOU'RE FREAKIN' HERCULES!
YEAH. OKAY. I'M GOOD.
YOU SURE? BECAUSE I CAN WARP YOU BOTH BACK HOME RIGHT NOW. NO PROBLEM.
NO, I WANT TO BE HERE. I *NEED* TO BE HERE.
ALRIGHT.

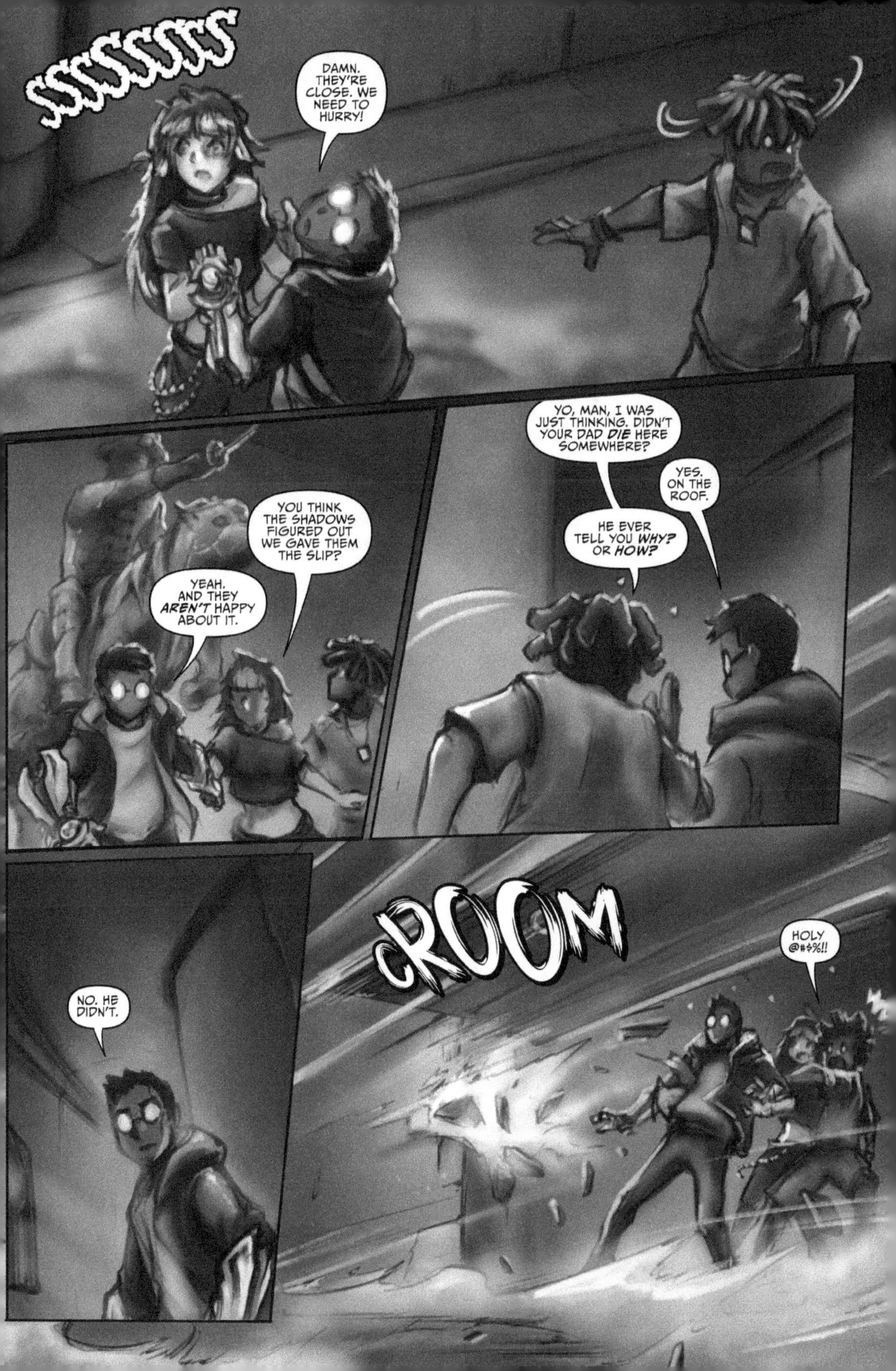
SSSSSSSS
DAMN. THEY'RE CLOSE. WE NEED TO HURRY!
YOU THINK THE SHADOWS FIGURED OUT WE GAVE THEM THE SLIP?
YEAH. AND THEY *AREN'T* HAPPY ABOUT IT.
YO, MAN, I WAS JUST THINKING. DIDN'T YOUR DAD *DIE* HERE SOMEWHERE?
YES. ON THE ROOF.
HE EVER TELL YOU *WHY?* OR *HOW?*
NO. HE DIDN'T.
CROOM
HOLY @#$%!!

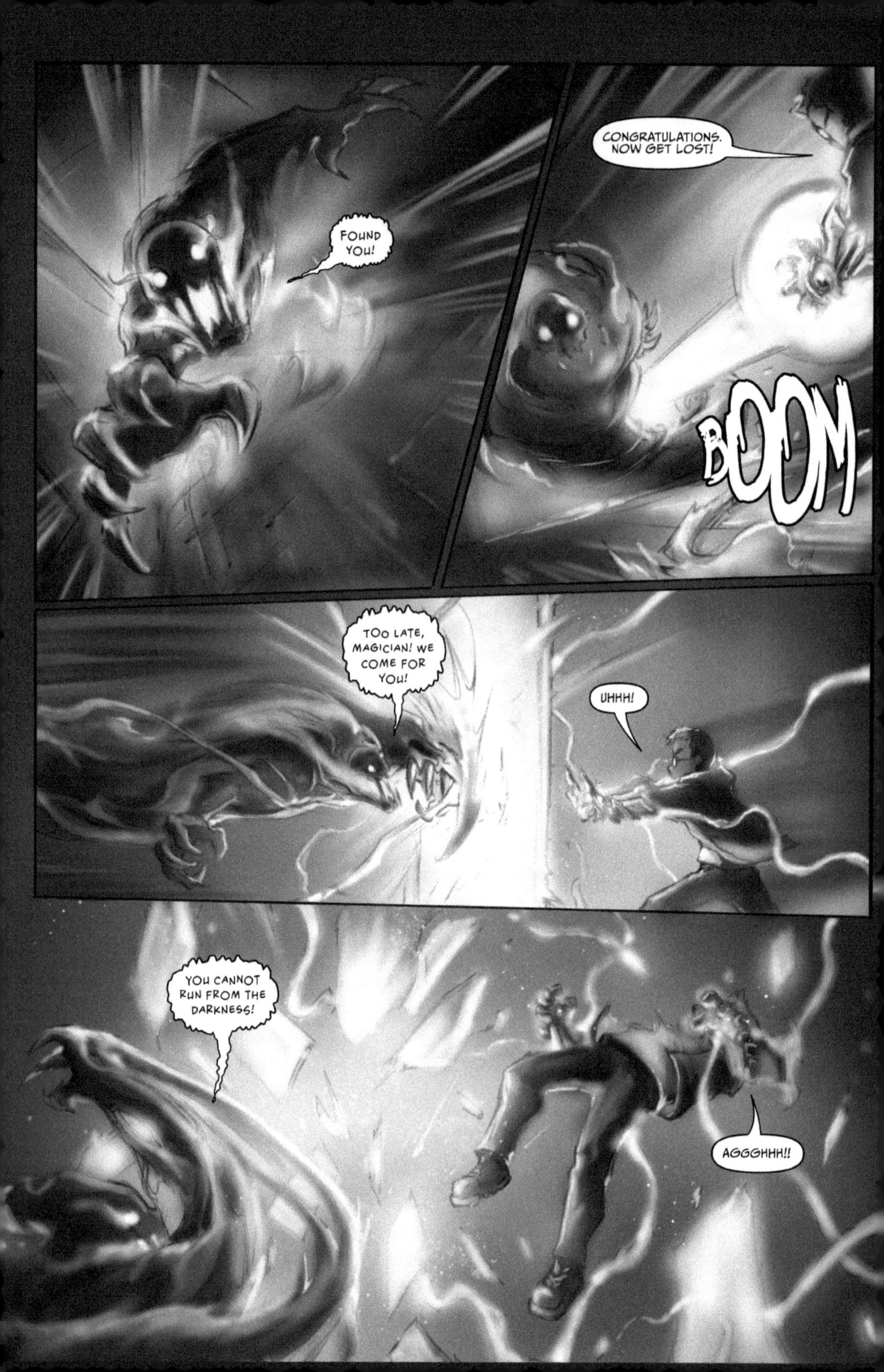

FOUND YOU!
CONGRATULATIONS. NOW GET LOST!
BOOM
TOO LATE, MAGICIAN! WE COME FOR YOU!
UHHH!
YOU CANNOT RUN FROM THE DARKNESS!
AGGGHHH!!

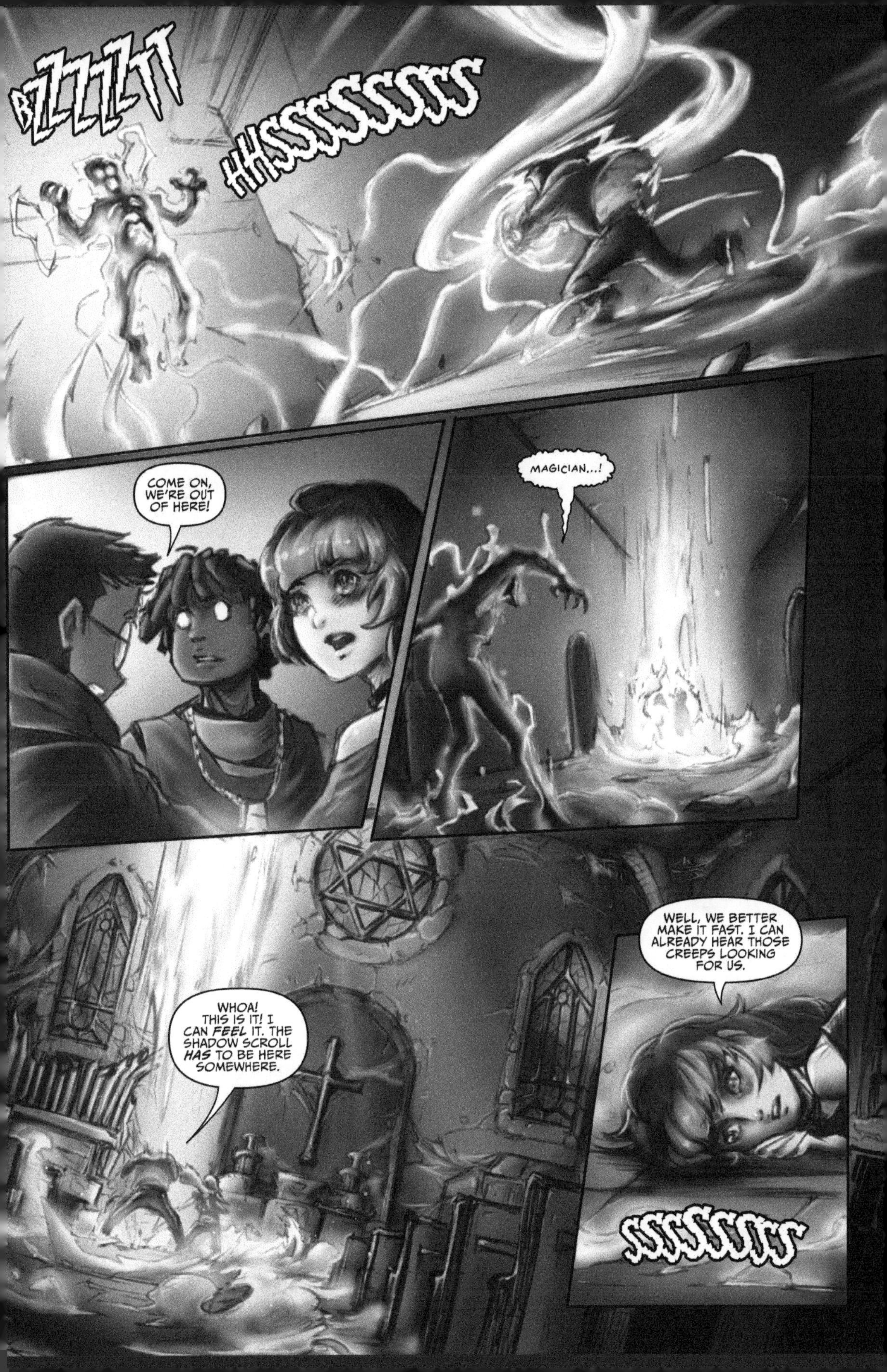
BZZZZZTT
HHSSSSSSSSSS
COME ON, WE'RE OUT OF HERE!
MAGICIAN...!
WHOA! THIS IS IT! I CAN *FEEL* IT. THE SHADOW SCROLL *HAS* TO BE HERE SOMEWHERE.
WELL, WE BETTER MAKE IT FAST. I CAN ALREADY HEAR THOSE CREEPS LOOKING FOR US.
SSSSSSSSS

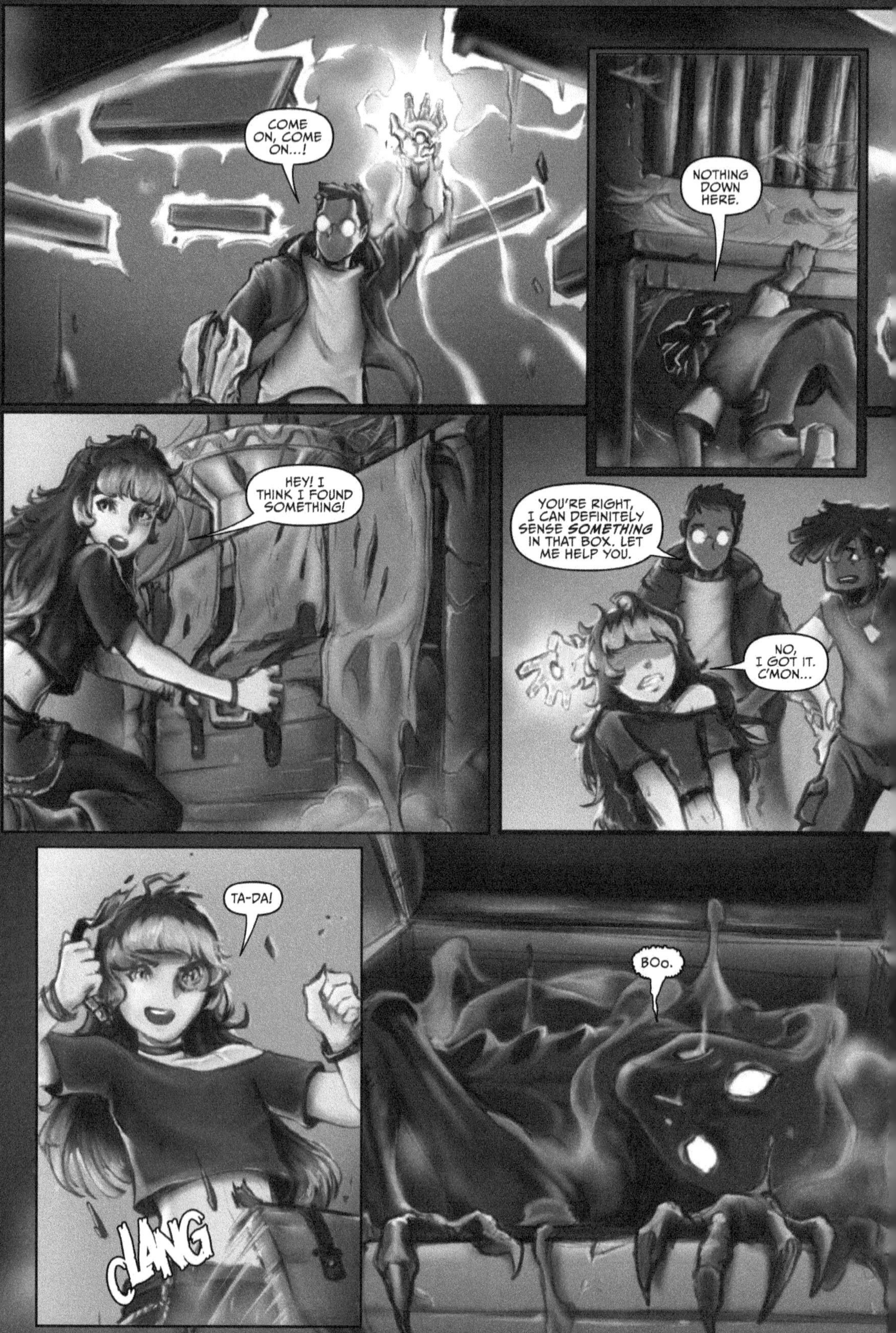
COME ON, COME ON...!
NOTHING DOWN HERE.
HEY! I THINK I FOUND SOMETHING!
YOU'RE RIGHT, I CAN DEFINITELY SENSE *SOMETHING* IN THAT BOX. LET ME HELP YOU.
NO, I GOT IT. C'MON...
TA-DA!
CLANG
BOo.

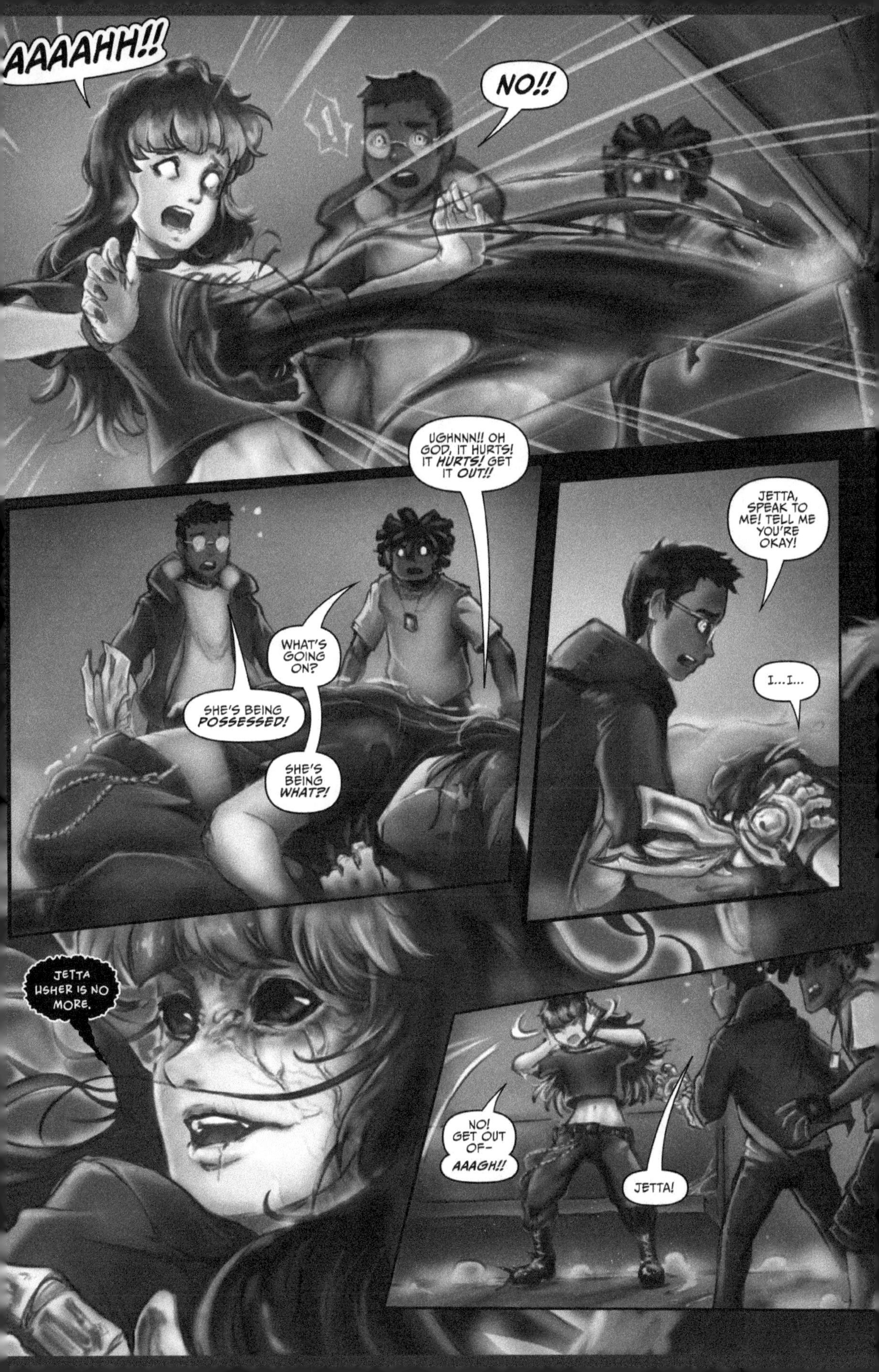
AAAAHH!!
NO!!
UGHNNN!! OH GOD, IT HURTS! IT HURTS! GET IT OUT!!
WHAT'S GOING ON?
SHE'S BEING POSSESSED!
SHE'S BEING WHAT?!
JETTA, SPEAK TO ME! TELL ME YOU'RE OKAY!
I... I...
JETTA USHER IS NO MORE.
NO! GET OUT OF- AAAGH!!
JETTA!

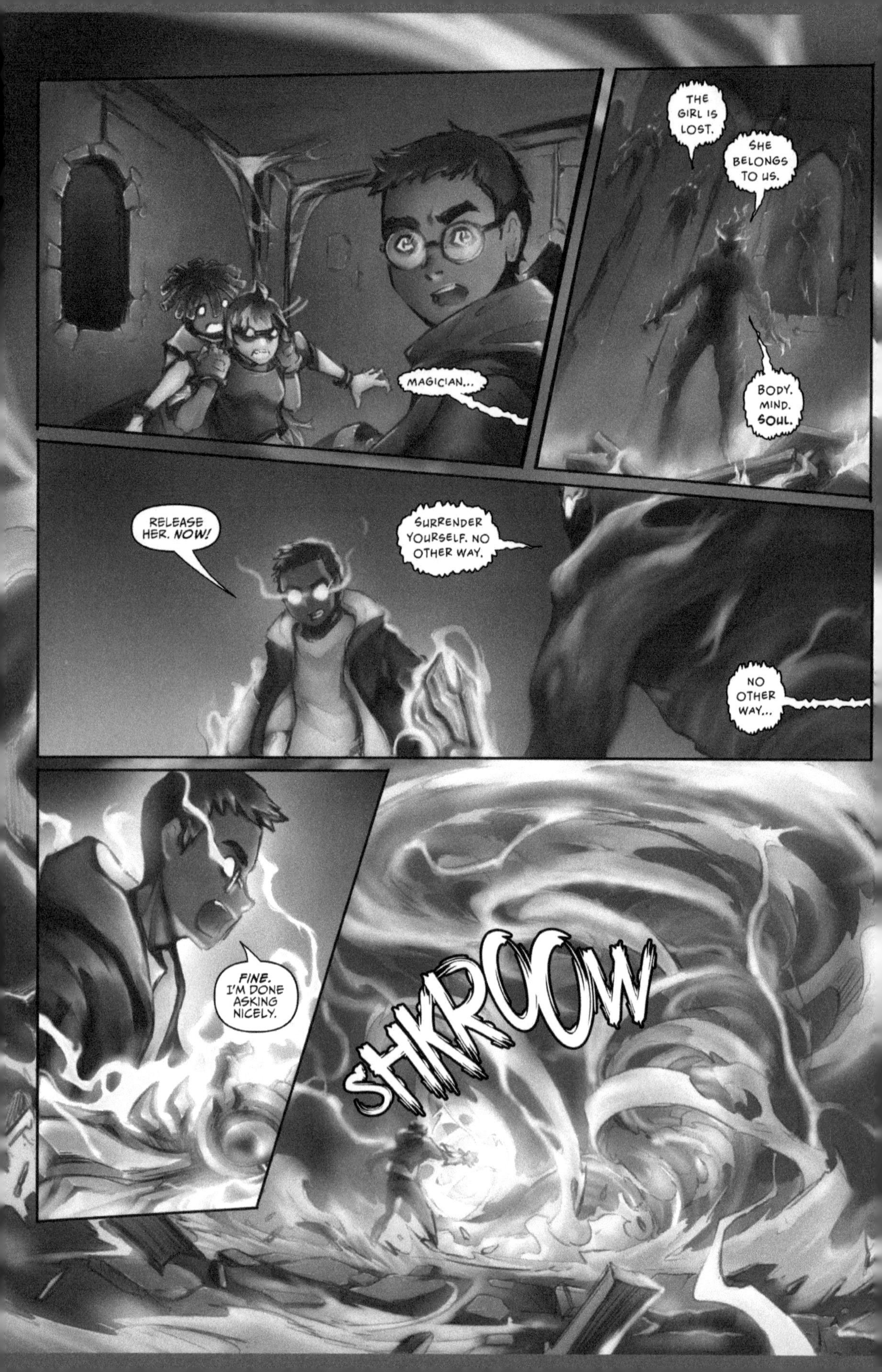
MAGICIAN...
THE GIRL IS LOST.
SHE BELONGS TO US.
BODY. MIND. SOUL.
RELEASE HER. NOW!
SURRENDER YOURSELF. NO OTHER WAY.
NO OTHER WAY...
FINE. I'M DONE ASKING NICELY.
SHKROOOW

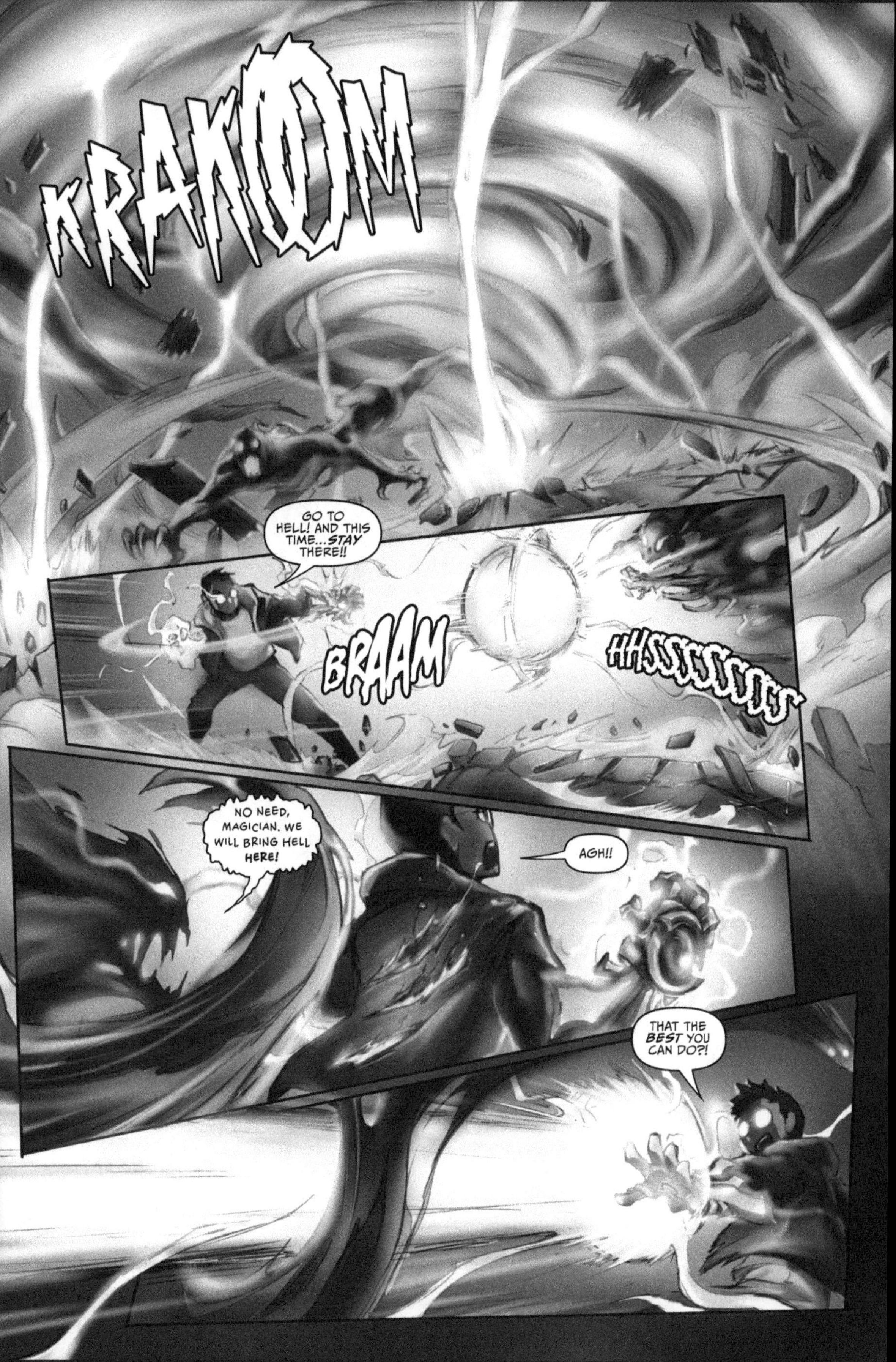
KRAKOOM
GO TO HELL! AND THIS TIME... STAY THERE!!
BRAAM
HHSSSSSSSSSS
NO NEED, MAGICIAN. WE WILL BRING HELL HERE!
AGH!!
THAT THE BEST YOU CAN DO?!

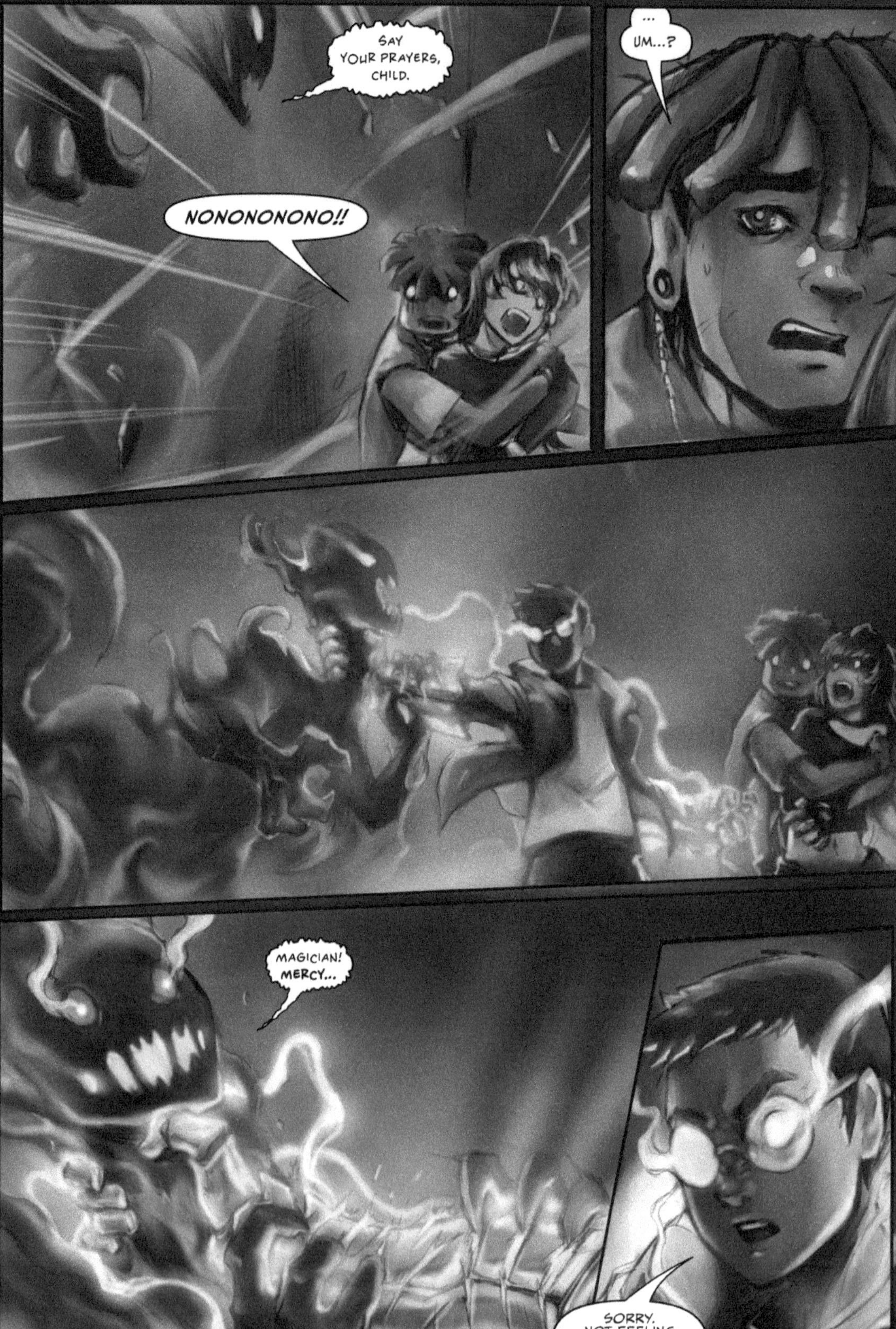

SAY YOUR PRAYERS, CHILD.
NONONONONO!!
... UM...?
MAGICIAN! MERCY...
SORRY. NOT FEELING PARTICULARLY *MERCIFUL* AT THE MOMENT!

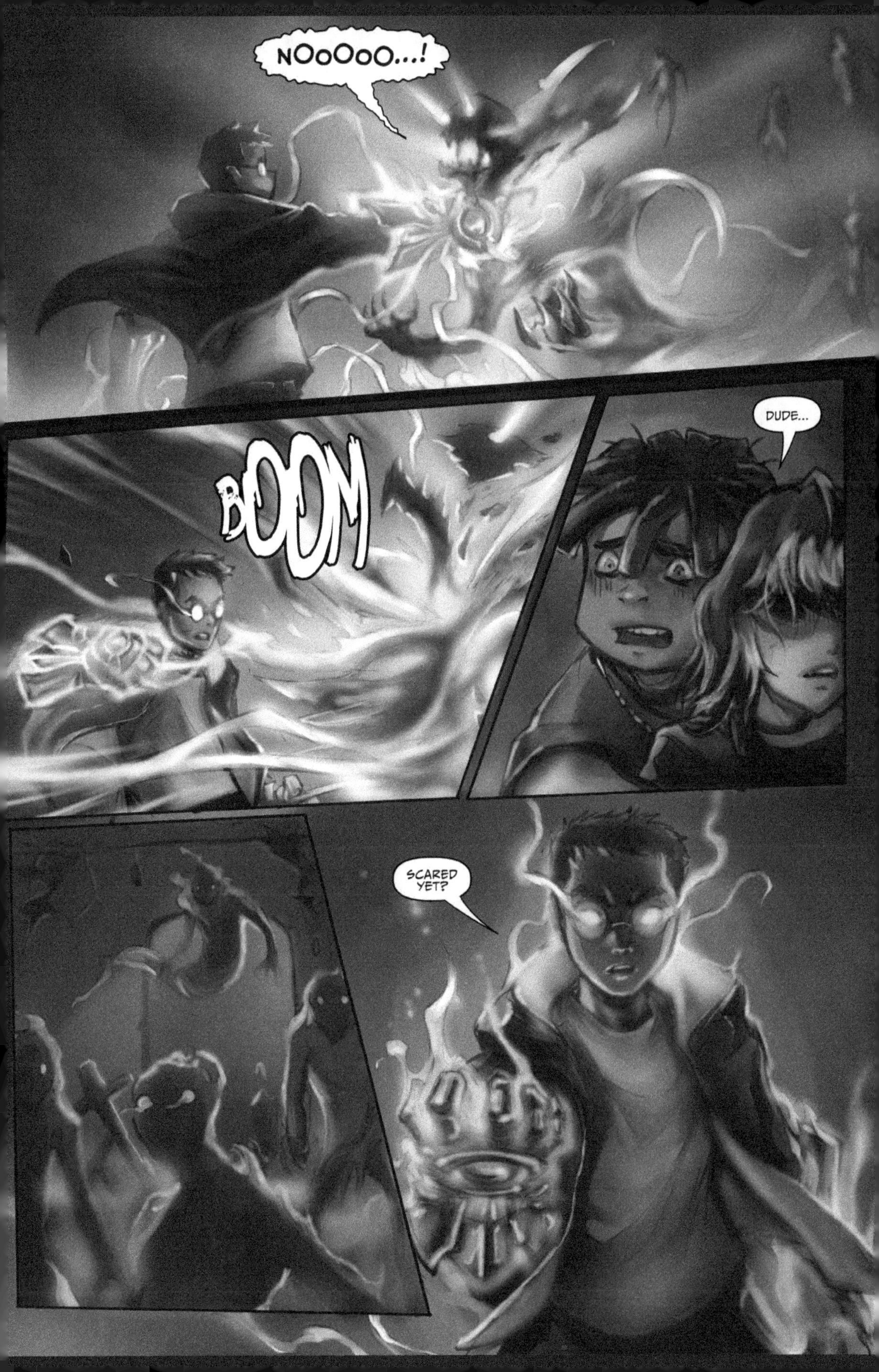
NOOOOO...!
BOOM
DUDE...
SCARED YET?

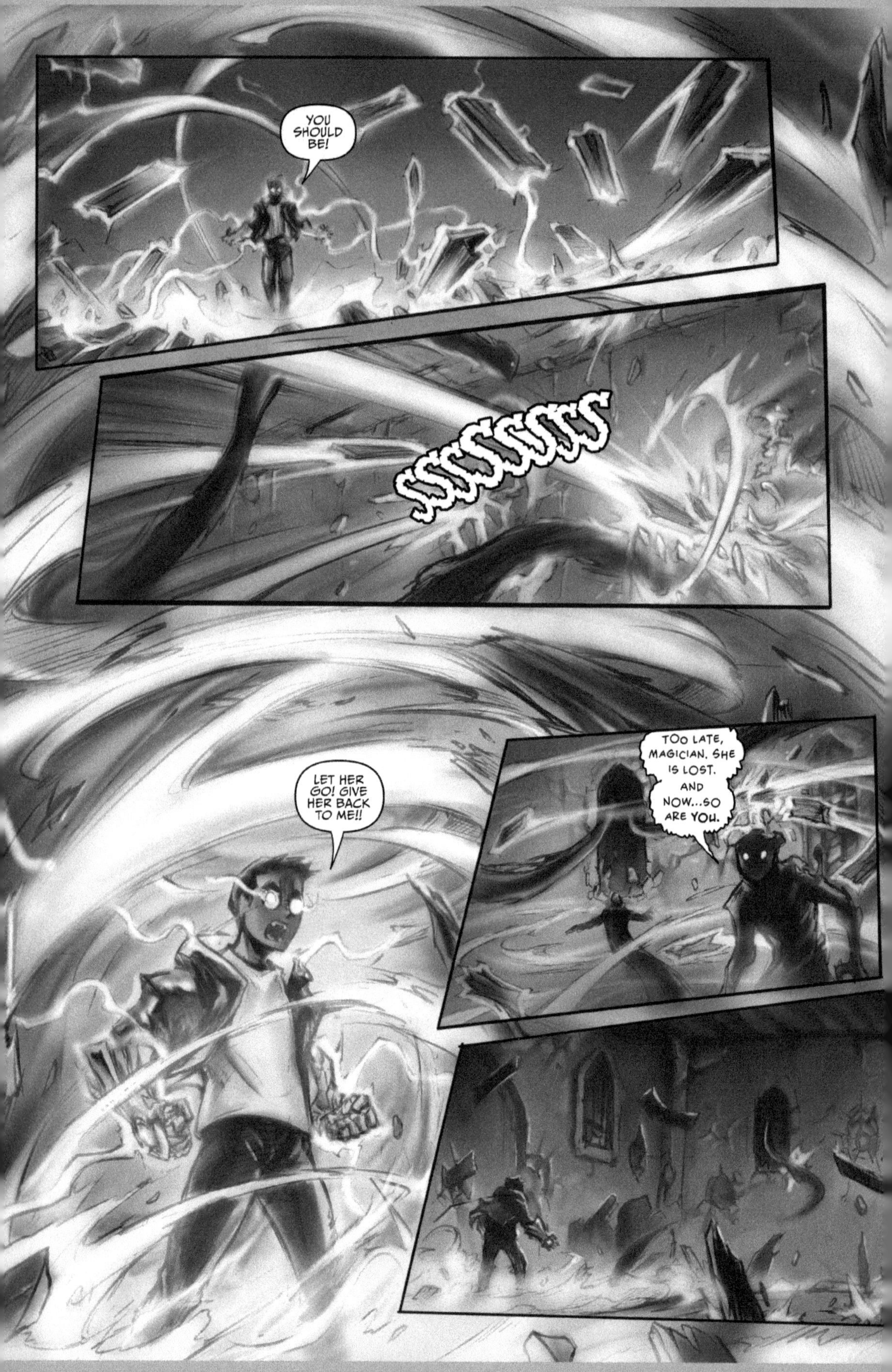
YOU SHOULD BE!
SSSSSSSS
LET HER GO! GIVE HER BACK TO ME!!
TOo LATE, MAGICIAN. SHE IS LOST.
AND NOW...SO ARE YOU.

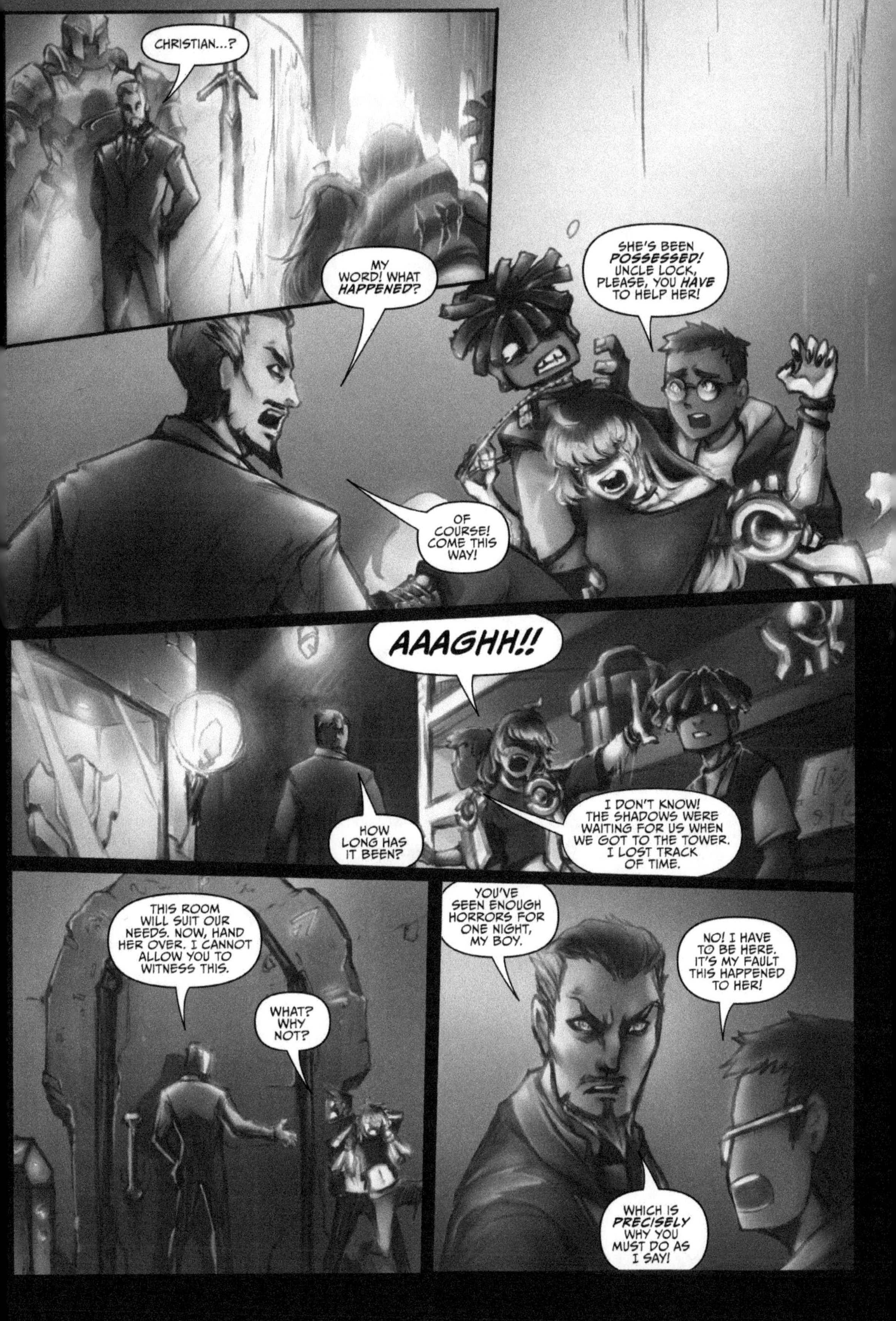
CHRISTIAN...?
MY WORD! WHAT *HAPPENED*?
SHE'S BEEN *POSSESSED!* UNCLE LOCK, PLEASE, YOU *HAVE* TO HELP HER!
OF COURSE! COME THIS WAY!
AAAGHH!!
HOW LONG HAS IT BEEN?
I DON'T KNOW! THE SHADOWS WERE WAITING FOR US WHEN WE GOT TO THE TOWER. I LOST TRACK OF TIME.
THIS ROOM WILL SUIT OUR NEEDS. NOW, HAND HER OVER. I CANNOT ALLOW YOU TO WITNESS THIS.
WHAT? WHY NOT?
YOU'VE SEEN ENOUGH HORRORS FOR ONE NIGHT, MY BOY.
NO! I HAVE TO BE HERE. IT'S MY FAULT THIS HAPPENED TO HER!
WHICH IS *PRECISELY* WHY YOU MUST DO AS I SAY!

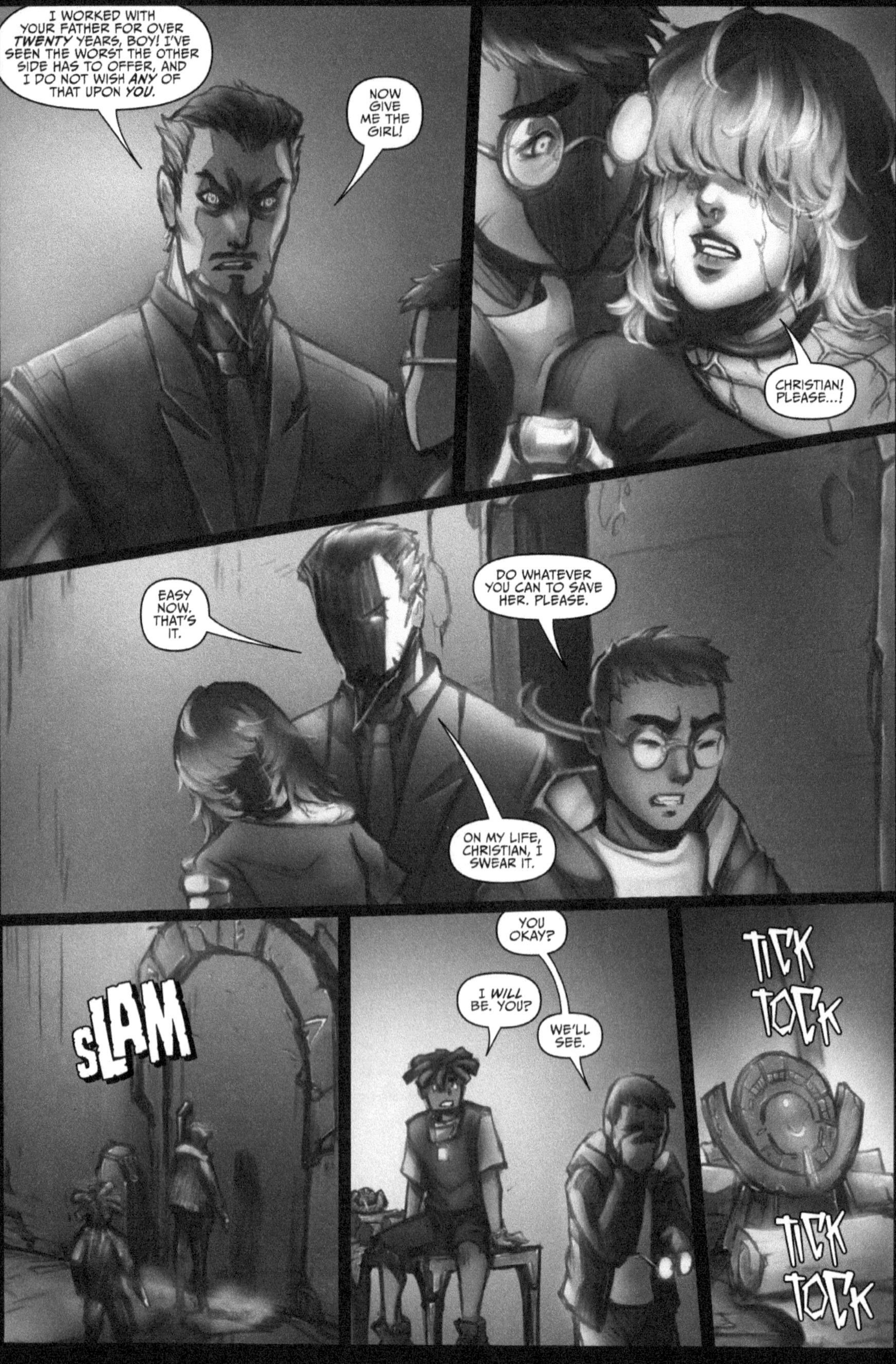
I WORKED WITH YOUR FATHER FOR OVER *TWENTY* YEARS, BOY! I'VE SEEN THE WORST THE OTHER SIDE HAS TO OFFER, AND I DO NOT WISH *ANY* OF THAT UPON *YOU.*
NOW GIVE ME THE GIRL!
CHRISTIAN! PLEASE...!
EASY NOW. THAT'S IT.
DO WHATEVER YOU CAN TO SAVE HER. PLEASE.
ON MY LIFE, CHRISTIAN, I SWEAR IT.
SLAM
YOU OKAY?
I *WILL* BE. YOU?
WE'LL SEE.
TICK TOCK
TICK TOCK

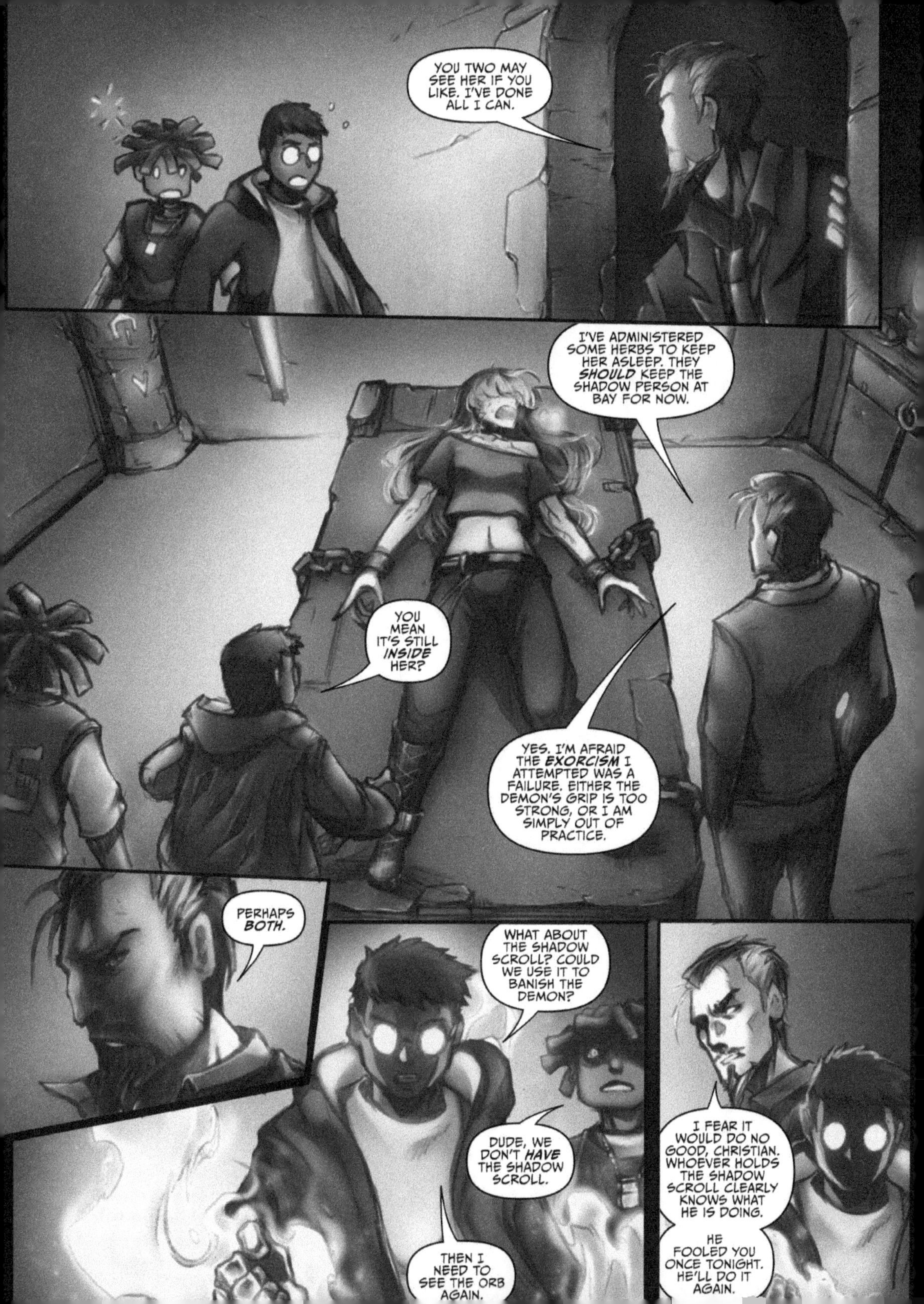
YOU TWO MAY SEE HER IF YOU LIKE. I'VE DONE ALL I CAN.
I'VE ADMINISTERED SOME HERBS TO KEEP HER ASLEEP. THEY *SHOULD* KEEP THE SHADOW PERSON AT BAY FOR NOW.
YOU MEAN IT'S STILL *INSIDE* HER?
YES. I'M AFRAID THE *EXORCISM* I ATTEMPTED WAS A FAILURE. EITHER THE DEMON'S GRIP IS TOO STRONG, OR I AM SIMPLY OUT OF PRACTICE.
PERHAPS *BOTH.*
WHAT ABOUT THE SHADOW SCROLL? COULD WE USE IT TO BANISH THE DEMON?
DUDE, WE DON'T *HAVE* THE SHADOW SCROLL.
I FEAR IT WOULD DO NO GOOD, CHRISTIAN. WHOEVER HOLDS THE SHADOW SCROLL CLEARLY KNOWS WHAT HE IS DOING.
HE FOOLED YOU ONCE TONIGHT. HE'LL DO IT AGAIN.
THEN I NEED TO SEE THE ORB AGAIN.

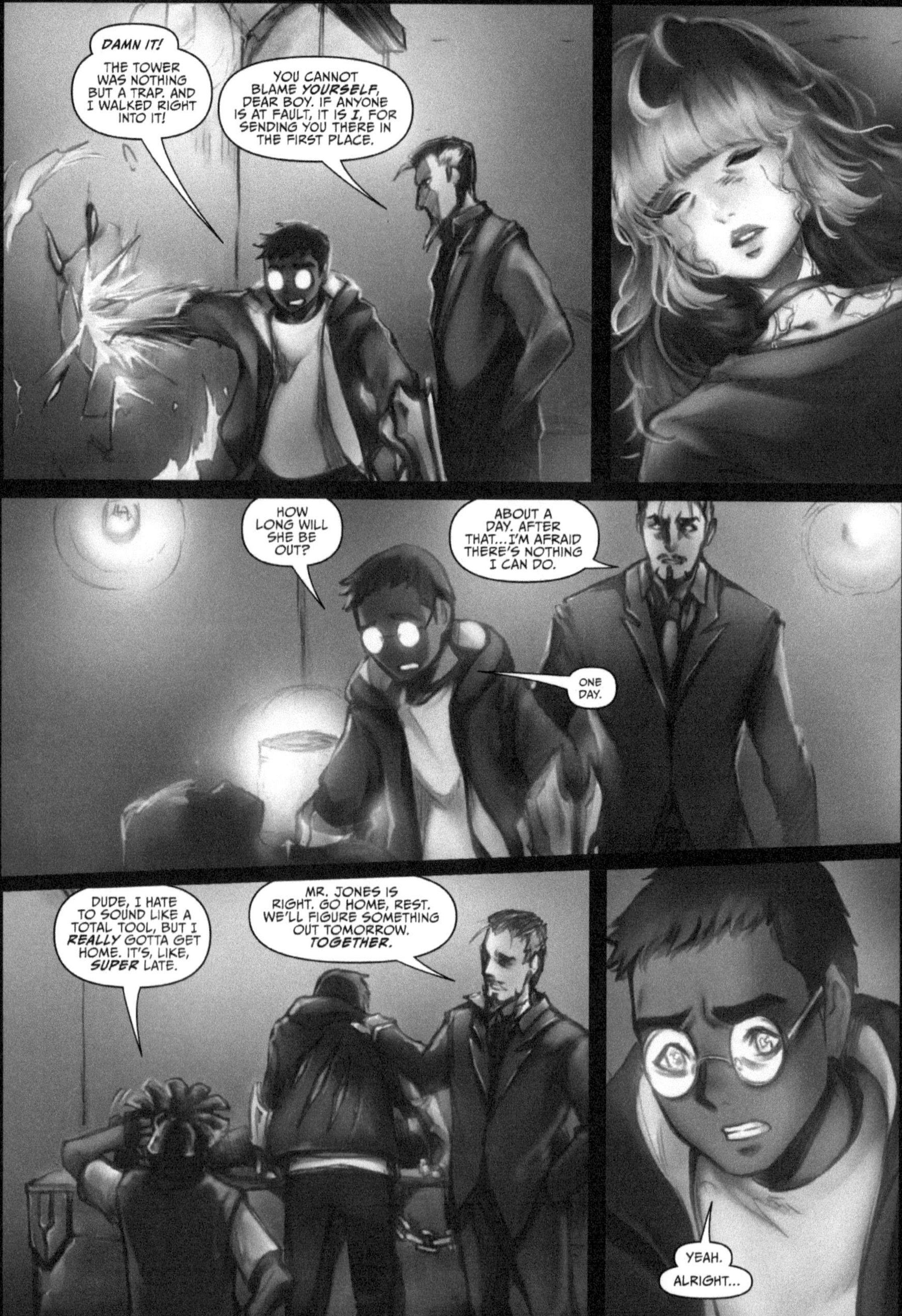
DAMN IT!
THE TOWER WAS NOTHING BUT A TRAP. AND I WALKED RIGHT INTO IT!
YOU CANNOT BLAME YOURSELF, DEAR BOY. IF ANYONE IS AT FAULT, IT IS I, FOR SENDING YOU THERE IN THE FIRST PLACE.
HOW LONG WILL SHE BE OUT?
ABOUT A DAY. AFTER THAT... I'M AFRAID THERE'S NOTHING I CAN DO.
ONE DAY.
DUDE, I HATE TO SOUND LIKE A TOTAL TOOL, BUT I REALLY GOTTA GET HOME. IT'S, LIKE, SUPER LATE.
MR. JONES IS RIGHT. GO HOME, REST. WE'LL FIGURE SOMETHING OUT TOMORROW. TOGETHER.
YEAH. ALRIGHT...

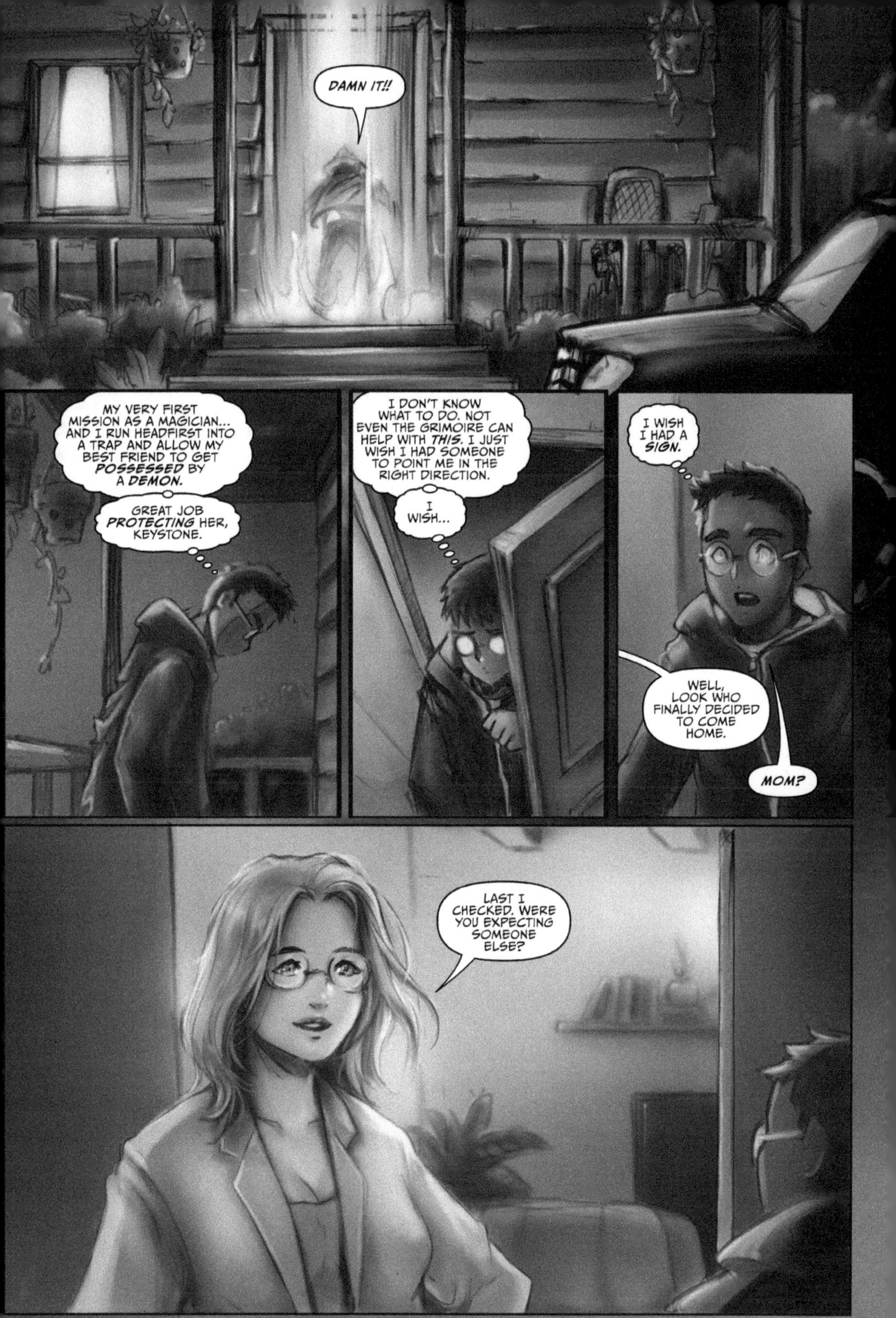
DAMN IT!!
MY VERY FIRST MISSION AS A MAGICIAN... AND I RUN HEADFIRST INTO A TRAP AND ALLOW MY BEST FRIEND TO GET POSSESSED BY A DEMON.
GREAT JOB PROTECTING HER, KEYSTONE.
I DON'T KNOW WHAT TO DO. NOT EVEN THE GRIMOIRE CAN HELP WITH THIS. I JUST WISH I HAD SOMEONE TO POINT ME IN THE RIGHT DIRECTION.
I WISH...
I WISH I HAD A SIGN.
WELL, LOOK WHO FINALLY DECIDED TO COME HOME.
MOM?
LAST I CHECKED. WERE YOU EXPECTING SOMEONE ELSE?

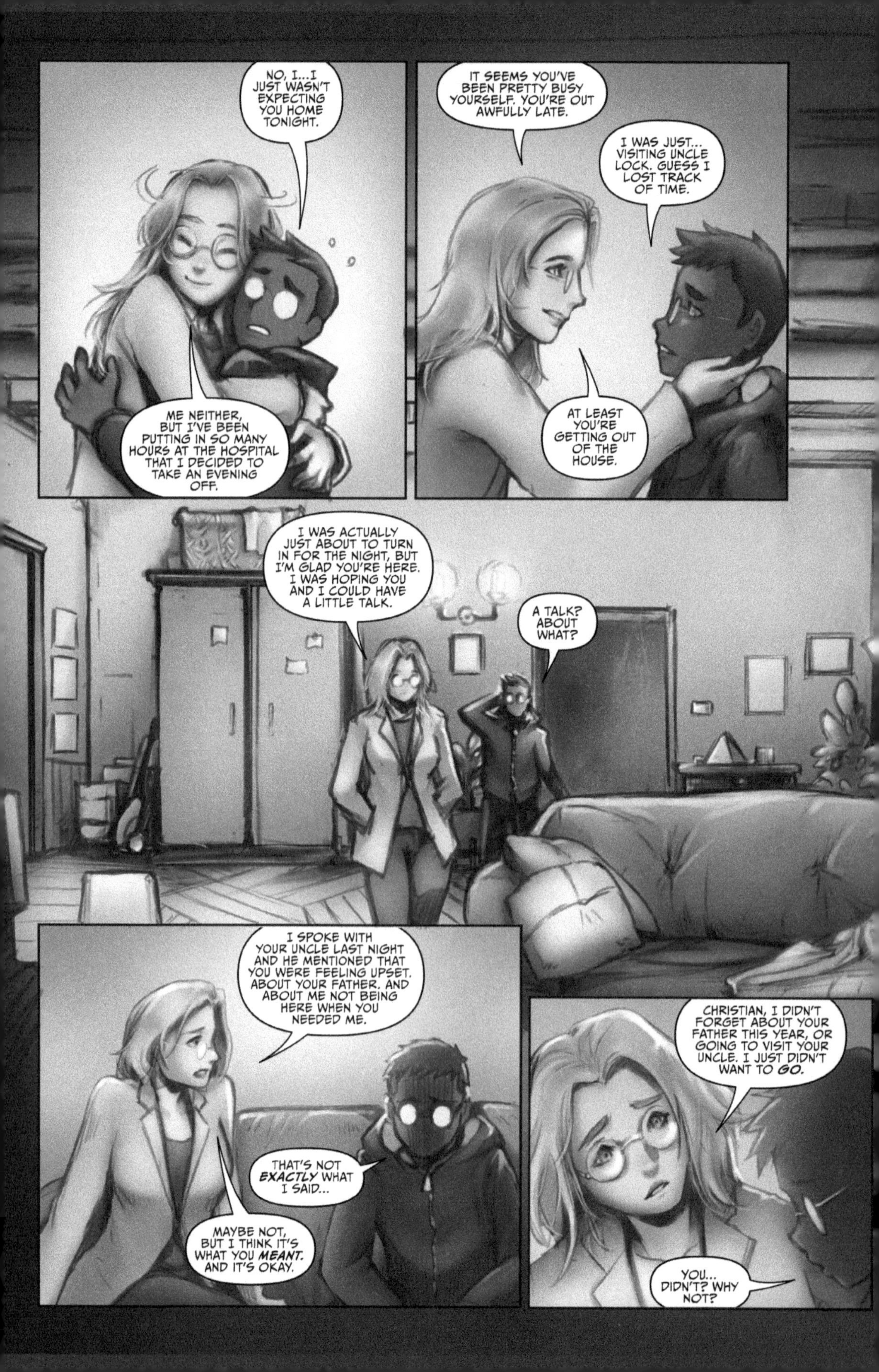
NO, I...I JUST WASN'T EXPECTING YOU HOME TONIGHT.
ME NEITHER, BUT I'VE BEEN PUTTING IN SO MANY HOURS AT THE HOSPITAL THAT I DECIDED TO TAKE AN EVENING OFF.
IT SEEMS YOU'VE BEEN PRETTY BUSY YOURSELF. YOU'RE OUT AWFULLY LATE.
I WAS JUST... VISITING UNCLE LOCK. GUESS I LOST TRACK OF TIME.
AT LEAST YOU'RE GETTING OUT OF THE HOUSE.
I WAS ACTUALLY JUST ABOUT TO TURN IN FOR THE NIGHT, BUT I'M GLAD YOU'RE HERE. I WAS HOPING YOU AND I COULD HAVE A LITTLE TALK.
A TALK? ABOUT WHAT?
I SPOKE WITH YOUR UNCLE LAST NIGHT AND HE MENTIONED THAT YOU WERE FEELING UPSET. ABOUT YOUR FATHER. AND ABOUT ME NOT BEING HERE WHEN YOU NEEDED ME.
THAT'S NOT ***EXACTLY*** WHAT I SAID...
MAYBE NOT, BUT I THINK IT'S WHAT YOU ***MEANT.*** AND IT'S OKAY.
CHRISTIAN, I DIDN'T FORGET ABOUT YOUR FATHER THIS YEAR, OR GOING TO VISIT YOUR UNCLE. I JUST DIDN'T WANT TO ***GO.***
YOU... DIDN'T? WHY NOT?

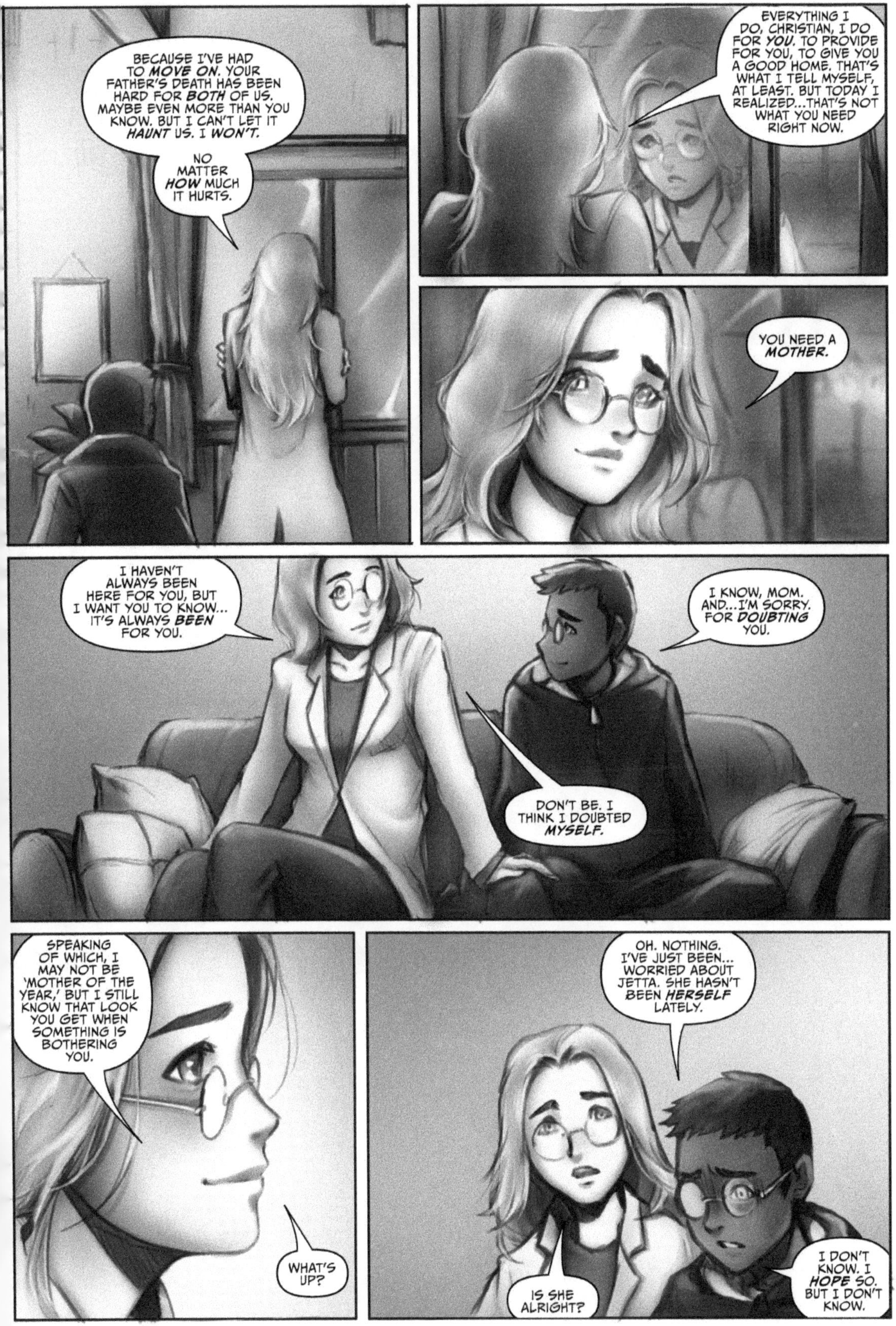
BECAUSE I'VE HAD TO MOVE ON. YOUR FATHER'S DEATH HAS BEEN HARD FOR BOTH OF US. MAYBE EVEN MORE THAN YOU KNOW. BUT I CAN'T LET IT HAUNT US. I WON'T.
NO MATTER HOW MUCH IT HURTS.
EVERYTHING I DO, CHRISTIAN, I DO FOR YOU. TO PROVIDE FOR YOU, TO GIVE YOU A GOOD HOME. THAT'S WHAT I TELL MYSELF, AT LEAST. BUT TODAY I REALIZED...THAT'S NOT WHAT YOU NEED RIGHT NOW.
YOU NEED A MOTHER.
I HAVEN'T ALWAYS BEEN HERE FOR YOU, BUT I WANT YOU TO KNOW... IT'S ALWAYS BEEN FOR YOU.
I KNOW, MOM. AND...I'M SORRY. FOR DOUBTING YOU.
DON'T BE. I THINK I DOUBTED MYSELF.
SPEAKING OF WHICH, I MAY NOT BE 'MOTHER OF THE YEAR,' BUT I STILL KNOW THAT LOOK YOU GET WHEN SOMETHING IS BOTHERING YOU.
WHAT'S UP?
OH. NOTHING. I'VE JUST BEEN... WORRIED ABOUT JETTA. SHE HASN'T BEEN HERSELF LATELY.
IS SHE ALRIGHT?
I DON'T KNOW. I HOPE SO. BUT I DON'T KNOW.

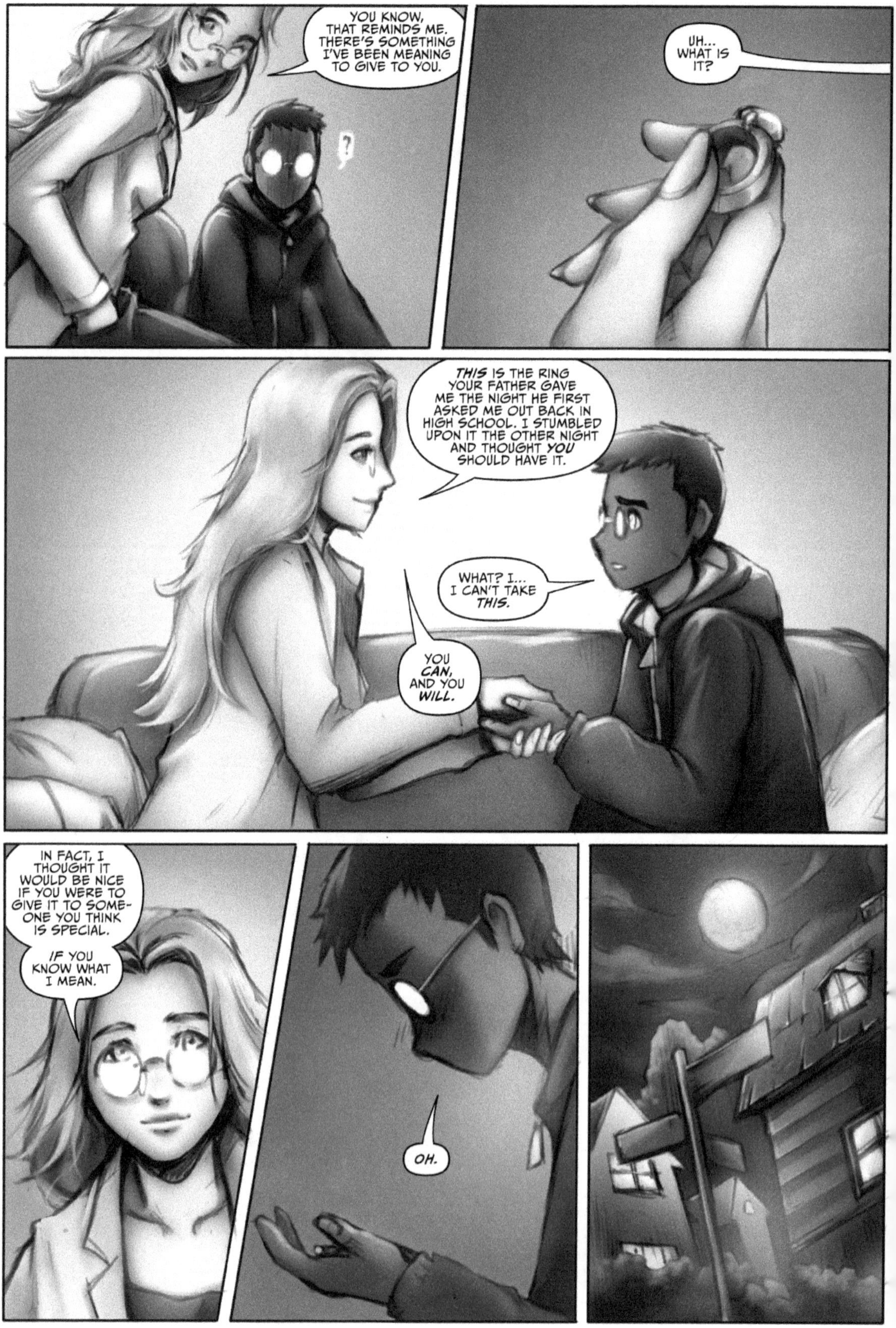
YOU KNOW, THAT REMINDS ME. THERE'S SOMETHING I'VE BEEN MEANING TO GIVE TO YOU.
?
UH... WHAT IS IT?
*THIS* IS THE RING YOUR FATHER GAVE ME THE NIGHT HE FIRST ASKED ME OUT BACK IN HIGH SCHOOL. I STUMBLED UPON IT THE OTHER NIGHT AND THOUGHT *YOU* SHOULD HAVE IT.
WHAT? I... I CAN'T TAKE *THIS*.
YOU *CAN*, AND YOU *WILL*.
IN FACT, I THOUGHT IT WOULD BE NICE IF YOU WERE TO GIVE IT TO SOME-ONE YOU THINK IS SPECIAL.
*IF* YOU KNOW WHAT I MEAN.
*OH*.

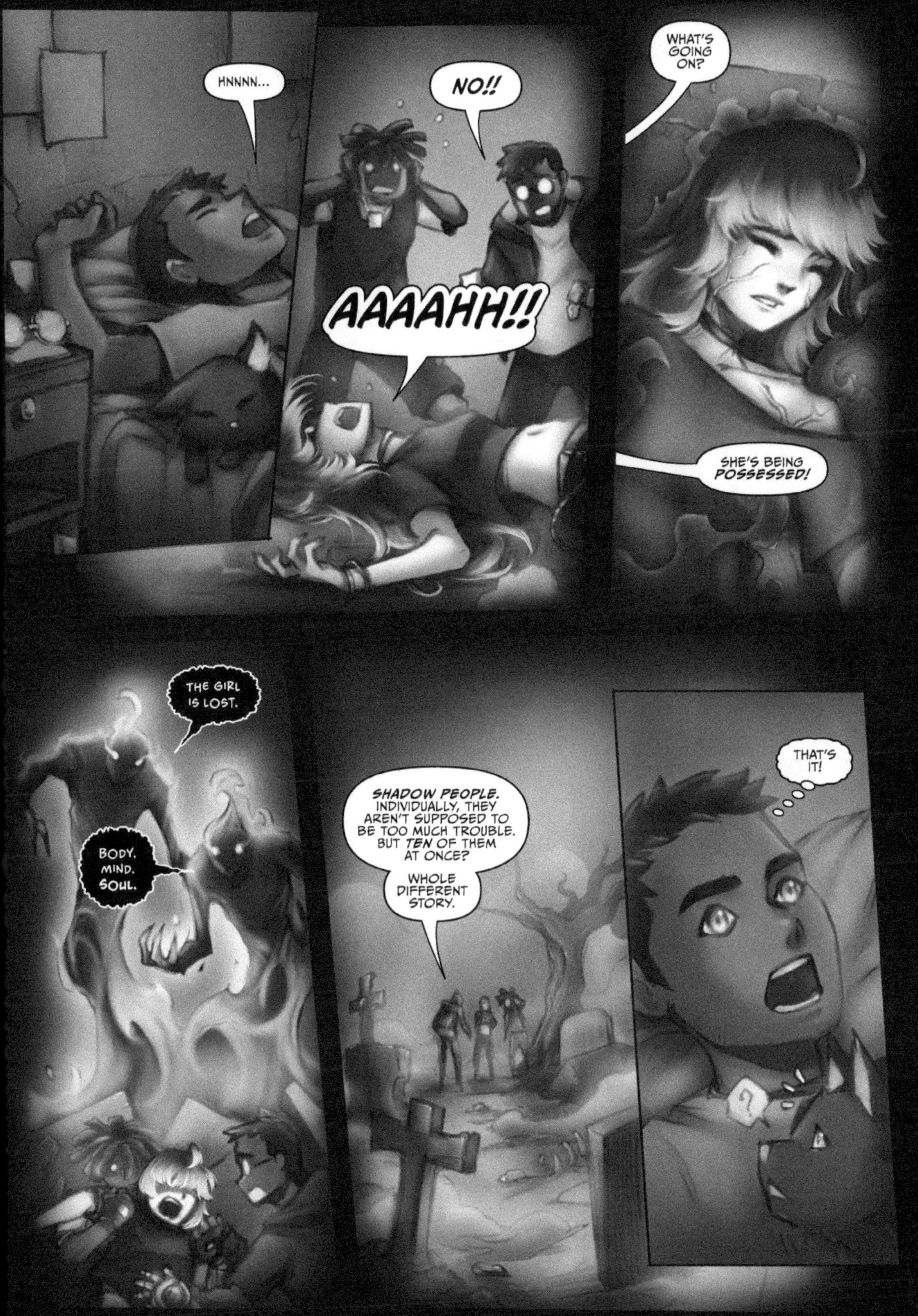
HNNNN...
NO!!
AAAAHH!!
WHAT'S GOING ON?
SHE'S BEING POSSESSED!
THE GIRL IS LOST.
BODY. MIND. SOUL.
SHADOW PEOPLE. INDIVIDUALLY, THEY AREN'T SUPPOSED TO BE TOO MUCH TROUBLE. BUT TEN OF THEM AT ONCE?
WHOLE DIFFERENT STORY.
THAT'S IT!

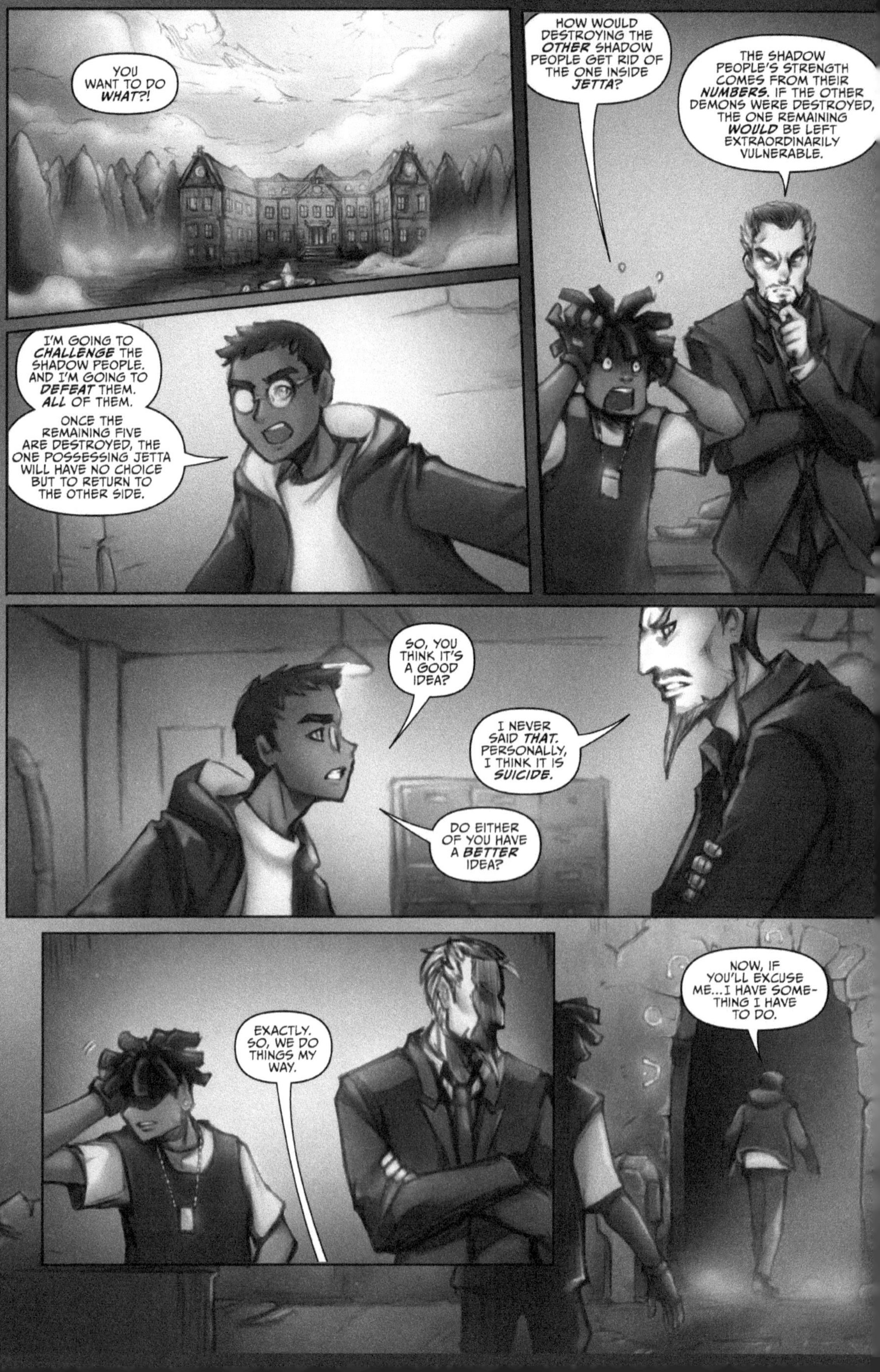
YOU WANT TO DO WHAT?!
HOW WOULD DESTROYING THE OTHER SHADOW PEOPLE GET RID OF THE ONE INSIDE JETTA?
THE SHADOW PEOPLE'S STRENGTH COMES FROM THEIR NUMBERS. IF THE OTHER DEMONS WERE DESTROYED, THE ONE REMAINING WOULD BE LEFT EXTRAORDINARILY VULNERABLE.
I'M GOING TO CHALLENGE THE SHADOW PEOPLE. AND I'M GOING TO DEFEAT THEM. ALL OF THEM.
ONCE THE REMAINING FIVE ARE DESTROYED, THE ONE POSSESSING JETTA WILL HAVE NO CHOICE BUT TO RETURN TO THE OTHER SIDE.
SO, YOU THINK IT'S A GOOD IDEA?
I NEVER SAID THAT. PERSONALLY, I THINK IT IS SUICIDE.
DO EITHER OF YOU HAVE A BETTER IDEA?
EXACTLY. SO, WE DO THINGS MY WAY.
NOW, IF YOU'LL EXCUSE ME...I HAVE SOME-THING I HAVE TO DO.

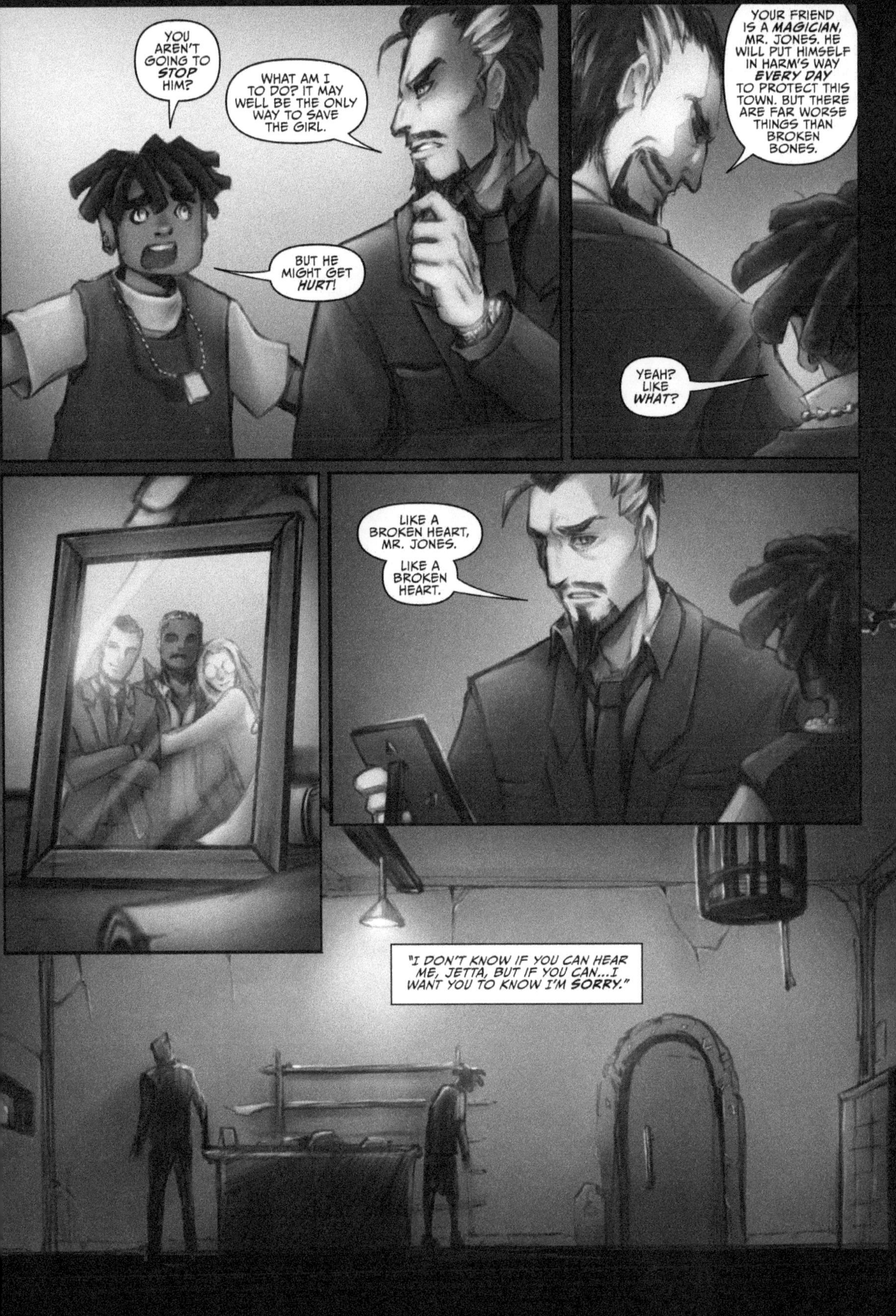
YOU AREN'T GOING TO STOP HIM?
WHAT AM I TO DO? IT MAY WELL BE THE ONLY WAY TO SAVE THE GIRL.
BUT HE MIGHT GET HURT!
YOUR FRIEND IS A MAGICIAN, MR. JONES. HE WILL PUT HIMSELF IN HARM'S WAY EVERY DAY TO PROTECT THIS TOWN. BUT THERE ARE FAR WORSE THINGS THAN BROKEN BONES.
YEAH? LIKE WHAT?
LIKE A BROKEN HEART, MR. JONES.
LIKE A BROKEN HEART.
"I DON'T KNOW IF YOU CAN HEAR ME, JETTA, BUT IF YOU CAN...I WANT YOU TO KNOW I'M SORRY."

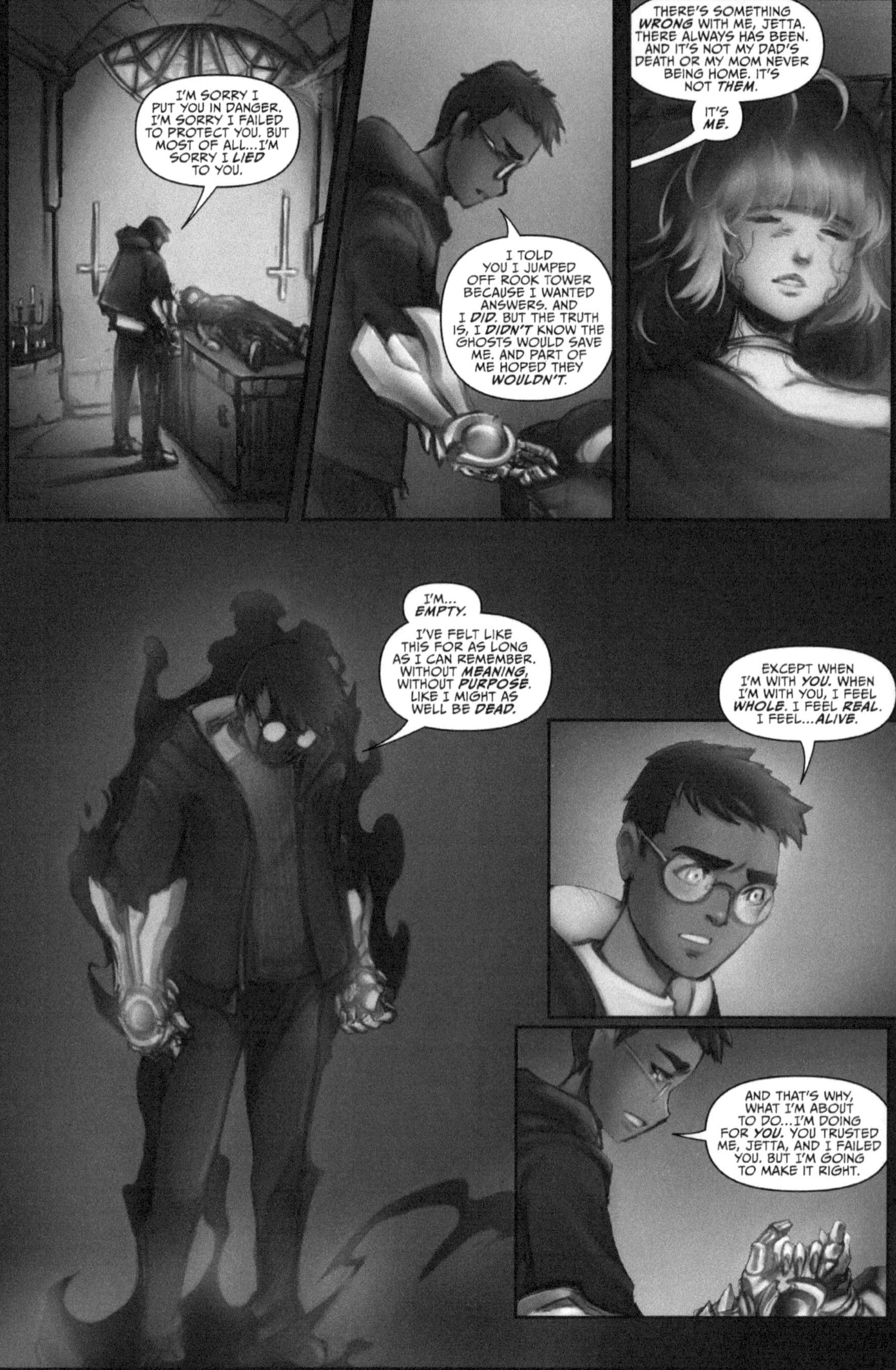
I'M SORRY I PUT YOU IN DANGER. I'M SORRY I FAILED TO PROTECT YOU. BUT MOST OF ALL...I'M SORRY I LIED TO YOU.
I TOLD YOU I JUMPED OFF ROOK TOWER BECAUSE I WANTED ANSWERS. AND I DID. BUT THE TRUTH IS, I DIDN'T KNOW THE GHOSTS WOULD SAVE ME. AND PART OF ME HOPED THEY WOULDN'T.
THERE'S SOMETHING WRONG WITH ME, JETTA. THERE ALWAYS HAS BEEN. AND IT'S NOT MY DAD'S DEATH OR MY MOM NEVER BEING HOME. IT'S NOT THEM.
IT'S ME.
I'M... EMPTY.
I'VE FELT LIKE THIS FOR AS LONG AS I CAN REMEMBER. WITHOUT MEANING, WITHOUT PURPOSE. LIKE I MIGHT AS WELL BE DEAD.
EXCEPT WHEN I'M WITH YOU. WHEN I'M WITH YOU, I FEEL WHOLE. I FEEL REAL. I FEEL...ALIVE.
AND THAT'S WHY, WHAT I'M ABOUT TO DO...I'M DOING FOR YOU. YOU TRUSTED ME, JETTA, AND I FAILED YOU. BUT I'M GOING TO MAKE IT RIGHT.

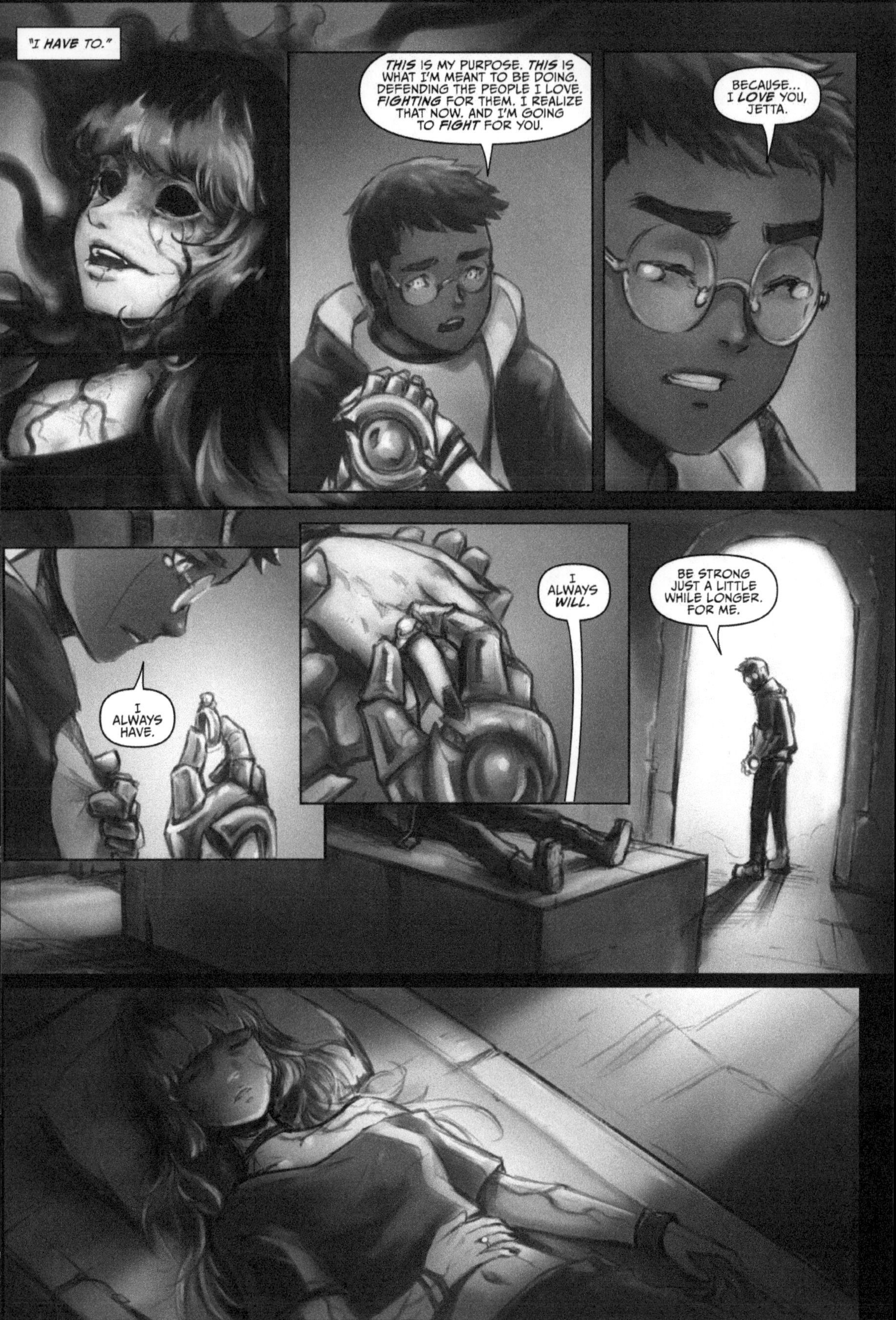
"I HAVE TO."
THIS IS MY PURPOSE. THIS IS WHAT I'M MEANT TO BE DOING. DEFENDING THE PEOPLE I LOVE. FIGHTING FOR THEM. I REALIZE THAT NOW. AND I'M GOING TO FIGHT FOR YOU.
BECAUSE... I LOVE YOU, JETTA.
I ALWAYS HAVE.
I ALWAYS WILL.
BE STRONG JUST A LITTLE WHILE LONGER. FOR ME.

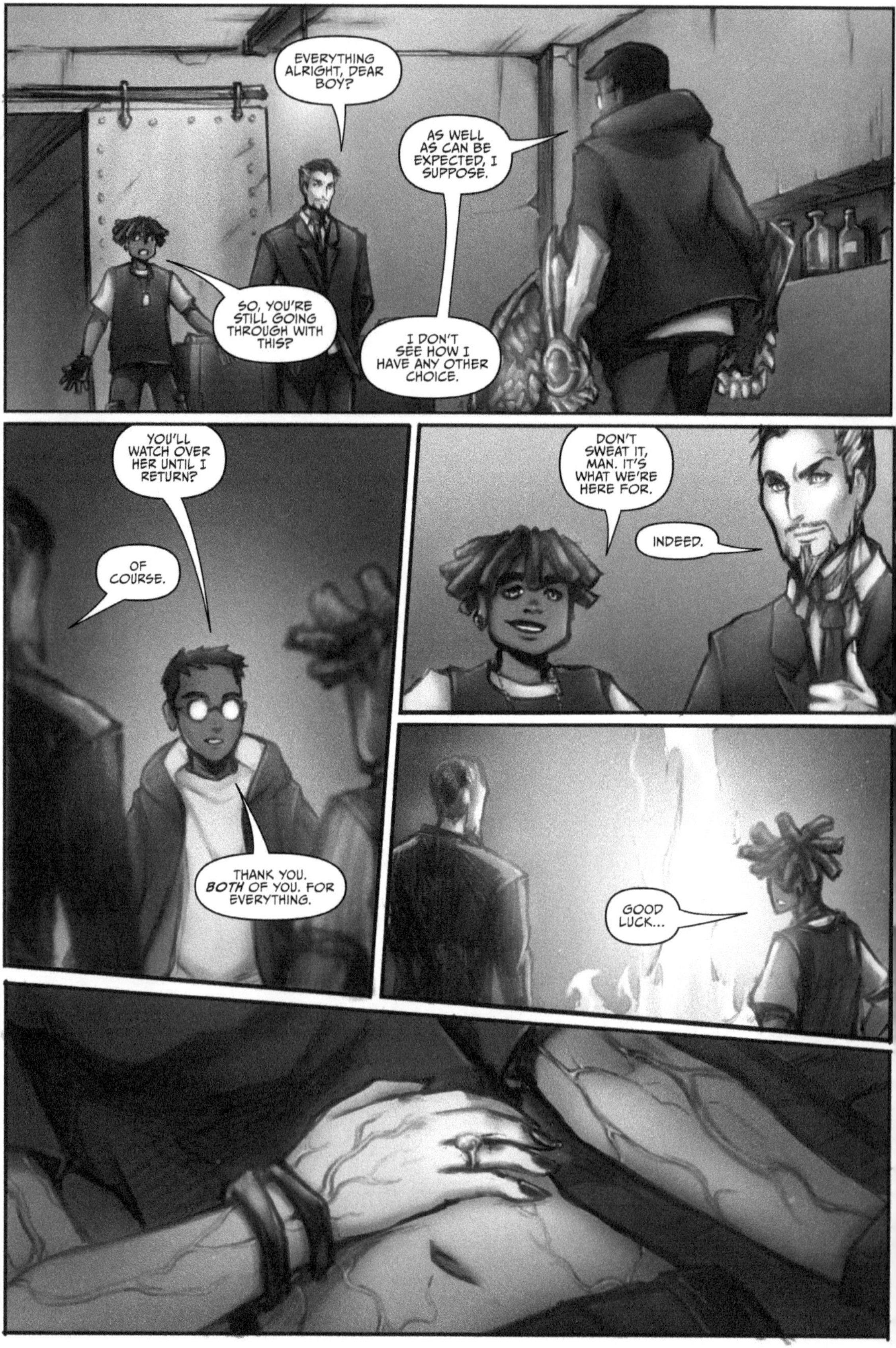
EVERYTHING ALRIGHT, DEAR BOY?
AS WELL AS CAN BE EXPECTED, I SUPPOSE.
SO, YOU'RE STILL GOING THROUGH WITH THIS?
I DON'T SEE HOW I HAVE ANY OTHER CHOICE.
YOU'LL WATCH OVER HER UNTIL I RETURN?
OF COURSE.
THANK YOU. *BOTH* OF YOU. FOR EVERYTHING.
DON'T SWEAT IT, MAN. IT'S WHAT WE'RE HERE FOR.
INDEED.
GOOD LUCK...

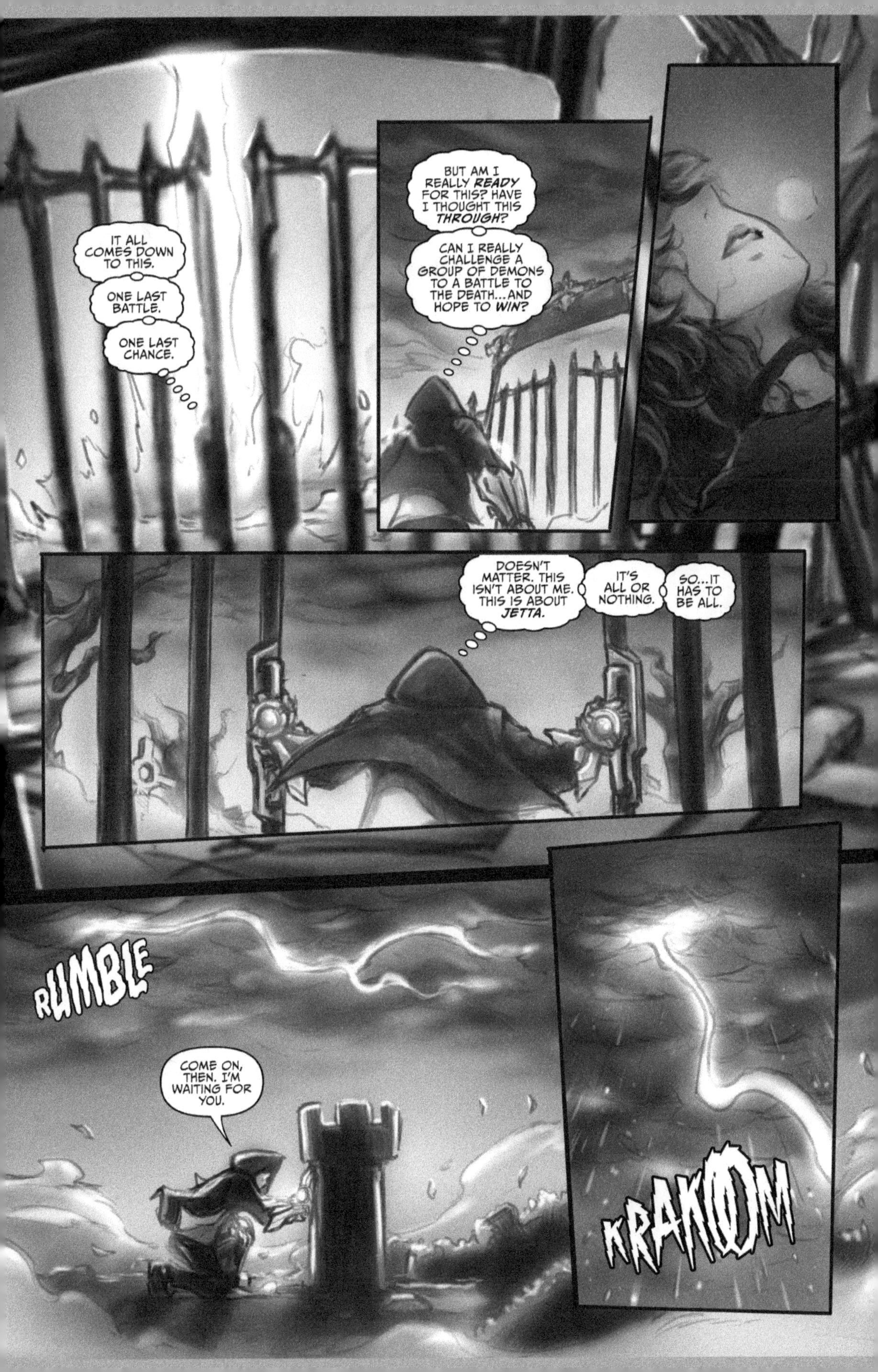
IT ALL COMES DOWN TO THIS.
ONE LAST BATTLE.
ONE LAST CHANCE.
BUT AM I REALLY READY FOR THIS? HAVE I THOUGHT THIS THROUGH?
CAN I REALLY CHALLENGE A GROUP OF DEMONS TO A BATTLE TO THE DEATH...AND HOPE TO WIN?
DOESN'T MATTER. THIS ISN'T ABOUT ME. THIS IS ABOUT JETTA.
IT'S ALL OR NOTHING.
SO...IT HAS TO BE ALL.
RUMBLE
COME ON, THEN. I'M WAITING FOR YOU.
KRAKOOM

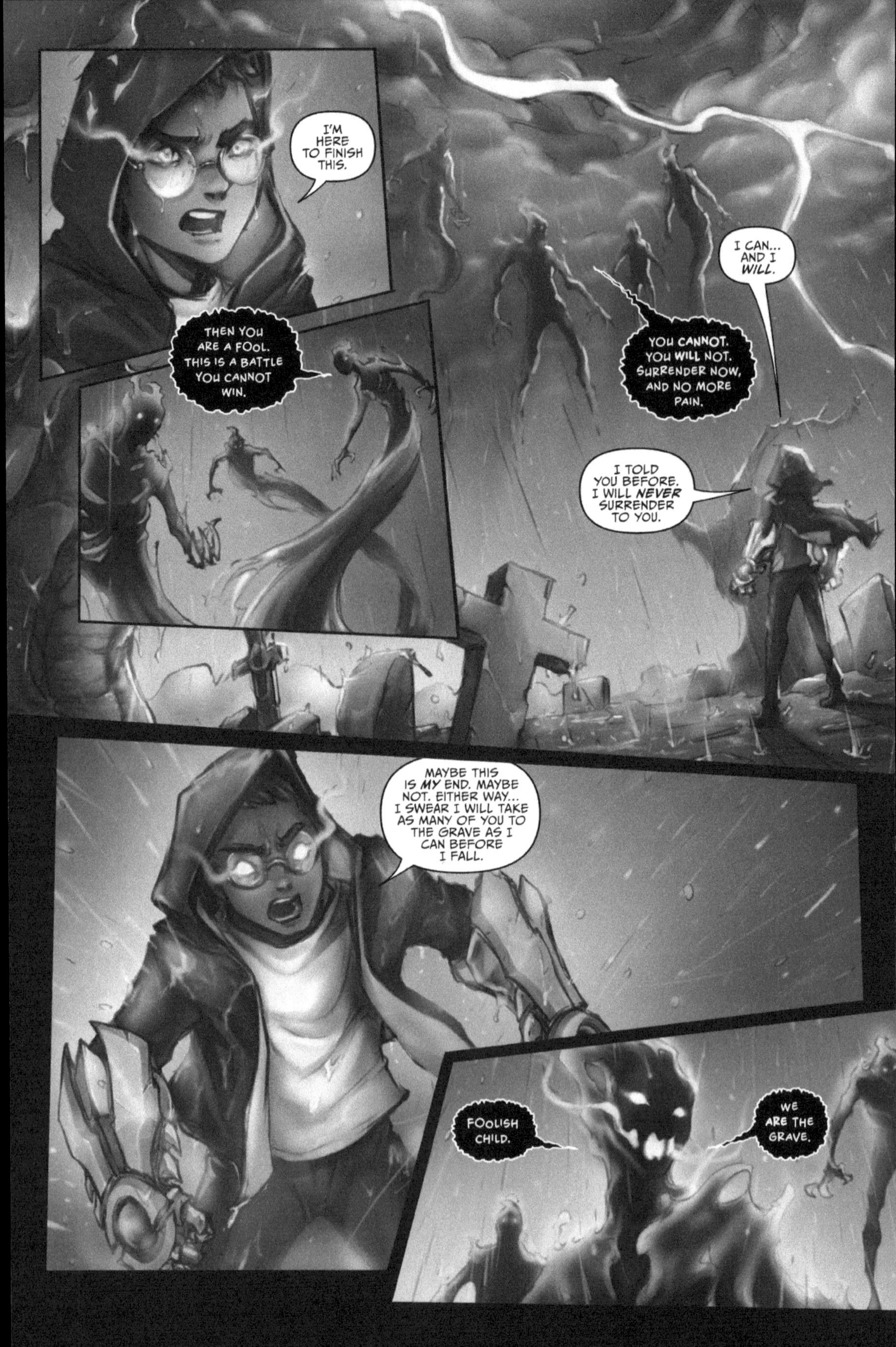
I'M HERE TO FINISH THIS.
THEN YOU ARE A FOOL. THIS IS A BATTLE YOU CANNOT WIN.
I CAN... AND I *WILL*.
YOU CANNOT. YOU WILL NOT. SURRENDER NOW, AND NO MORE PAIN.
I TOLD YOU BEFORE. I WILL *NEVER* SURRENDER TO YOU.
MAYBE THIS IS *MY* END. MAYBE NOT. EITHER WAY... I SWEAR I WILL TAKE AS MANY OF YOU TO THE GRAVE AS I CAN BEFORE I FALL.
FOOLISH CHILD.
WE ARE THE GRAVE.

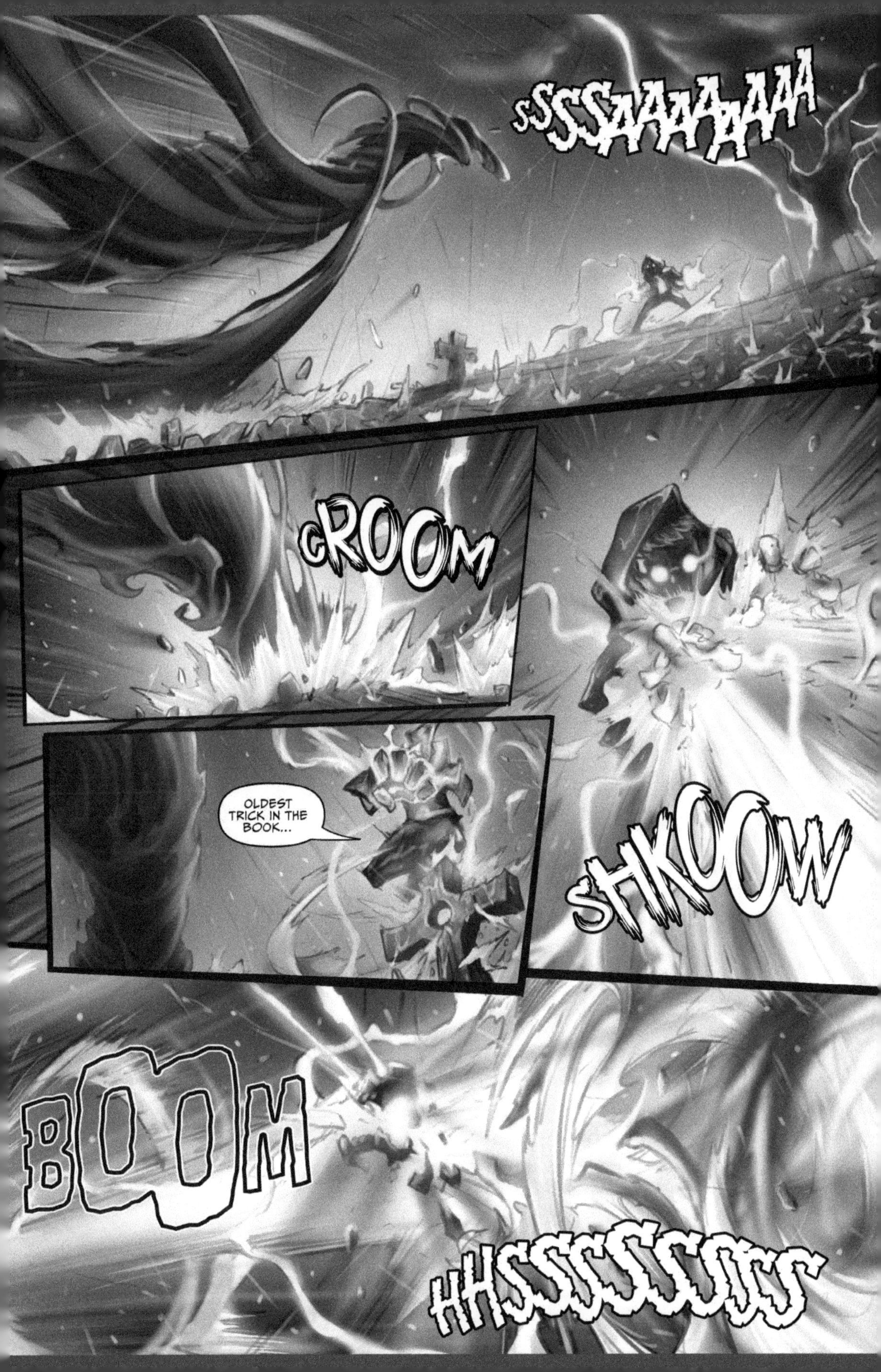
SSSAAAAAAAA
CROOM
OLDEST TRICK IN THE BOOK...
SHKOOOW
BOOM
HHSSSSSSSSS

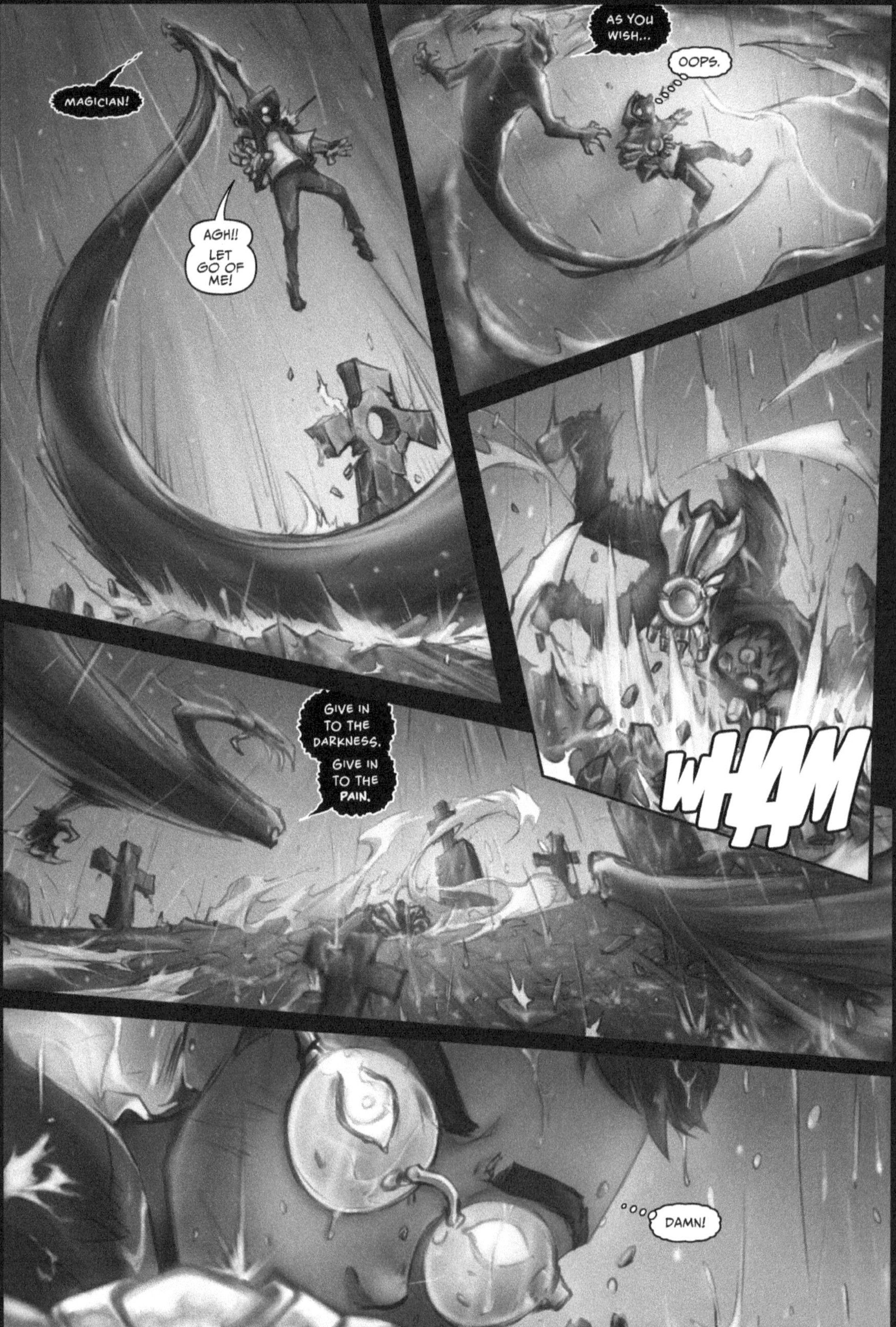
MAGICIAN!
AGH!! LET GO OF ME!
AS YOU WISH...
OOPS.
WHAM
GIVE IN TO THE DARKNESS.
GIVE IN TO THE PAIN.
DAMN!

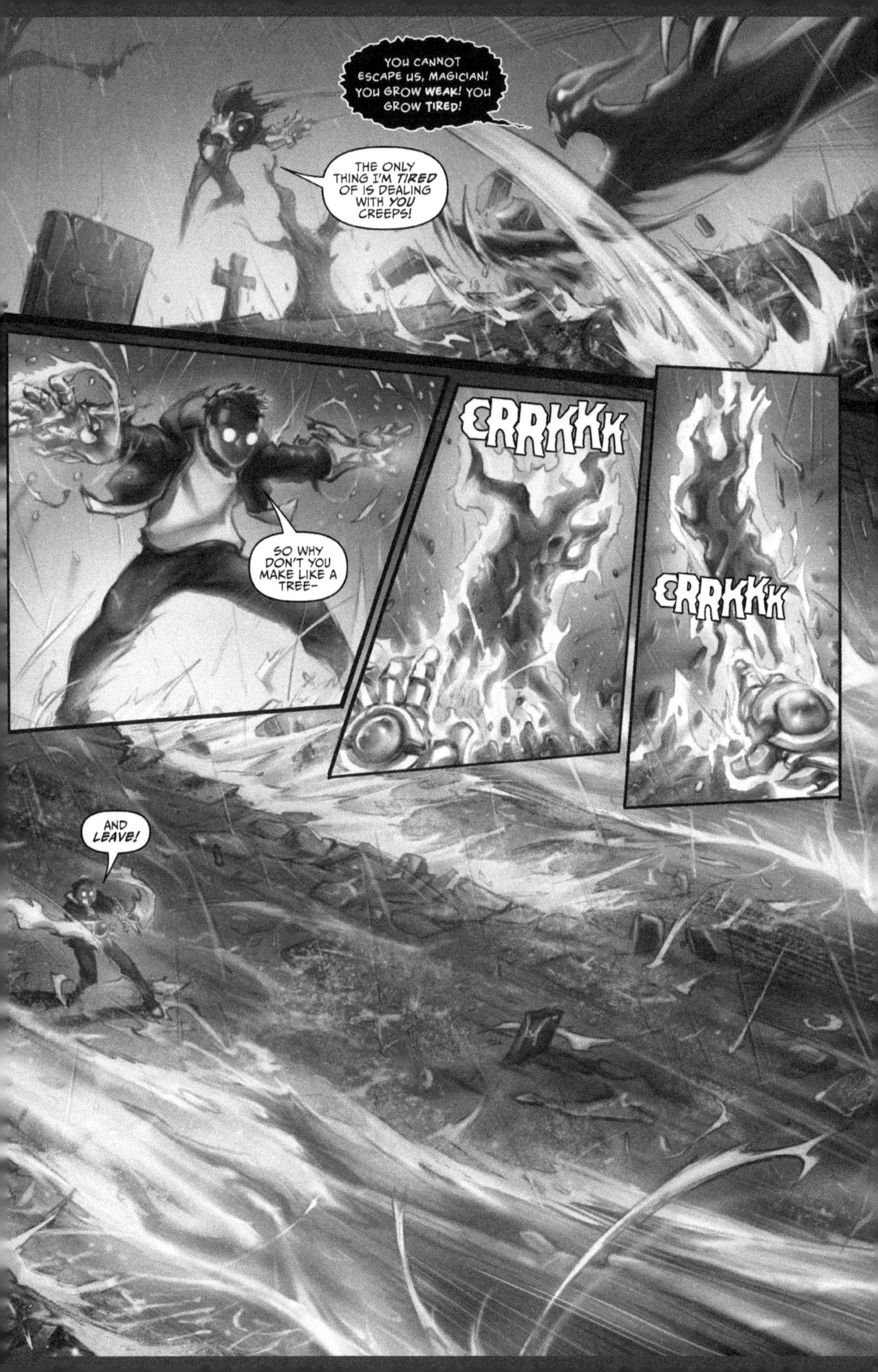
YOU CANNOT ESCAPE US, MAGICIAN! YOU GROW WEAK! YOU GROW TIRED!
THE ONLY THING I'M TIRED OF IS DEALING WITH YOU CREEPS!
SO WHY DON'T YOU MAKE LIKE A TREE-
CRRKKK
CRRKKK
AND LEAVE!

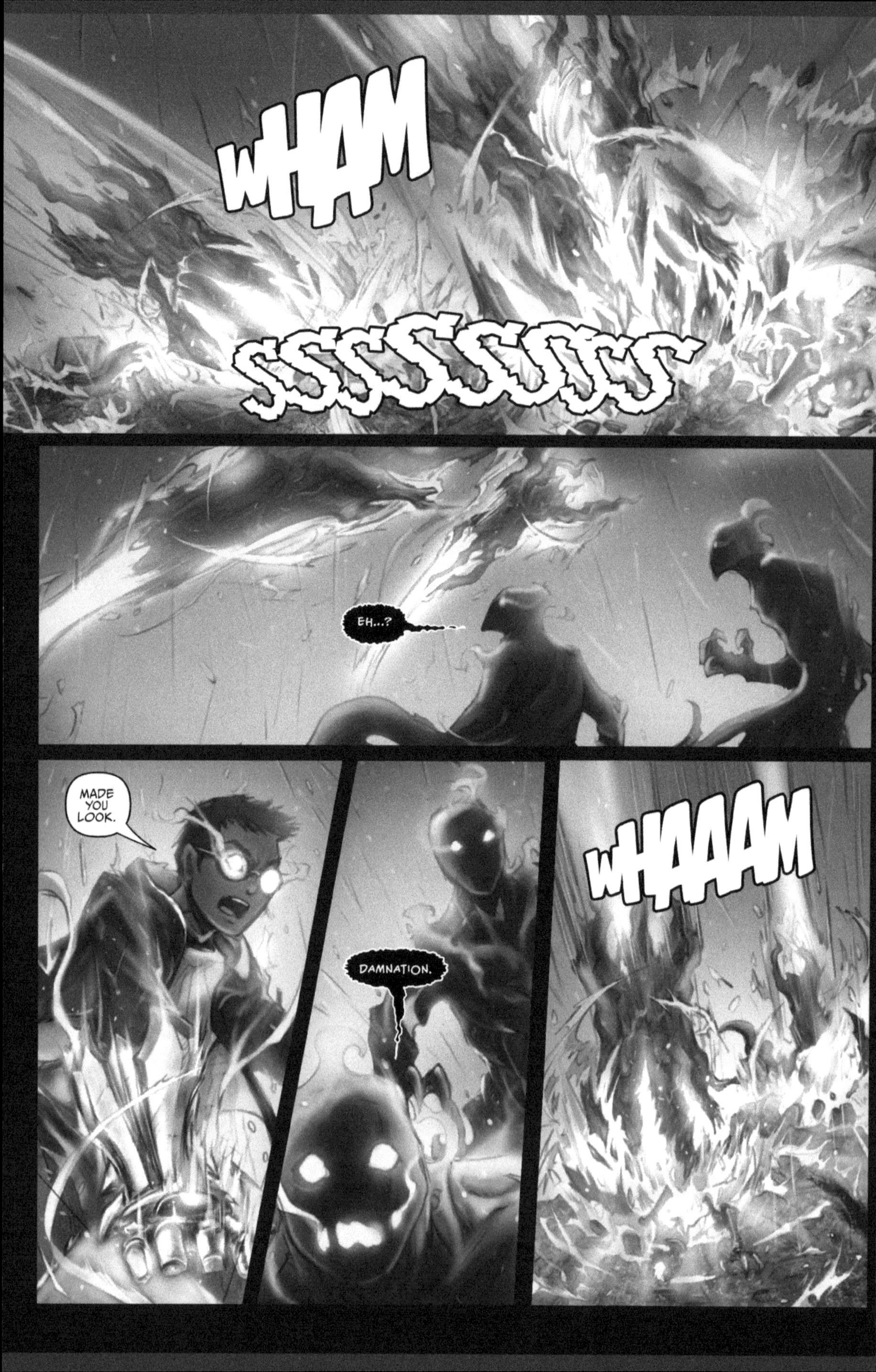
wHAM
SSSSSSSSSSSSSSS
EH...?
MADE YOU LOOK.
DAMNATION.
wHAAAM

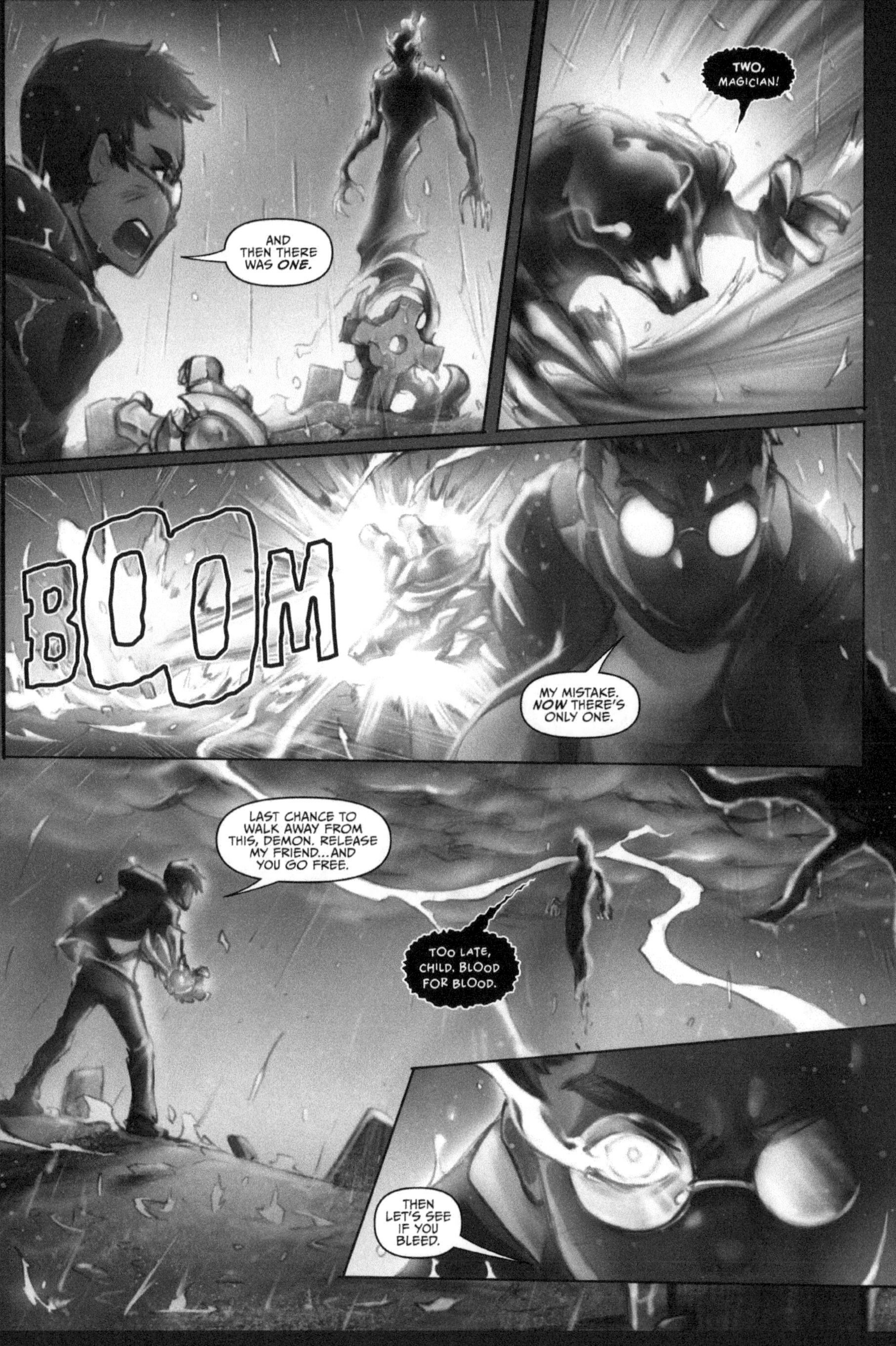
AND THEN THERE WAS ONE.
TWO, MAGICIAN!
BOOM
MY MISTAKE. NOW THERE'S ONLY ONE.
LAST CHANCE TO WALK AWAY FROM THIS, DEMON. RELEASE MY FRIEND...AND YOU GO FREE.
TOO LATE, CHILD. BLOOD FOR BLOOD.
THEN LET'S SEE IF YOU BLEED.

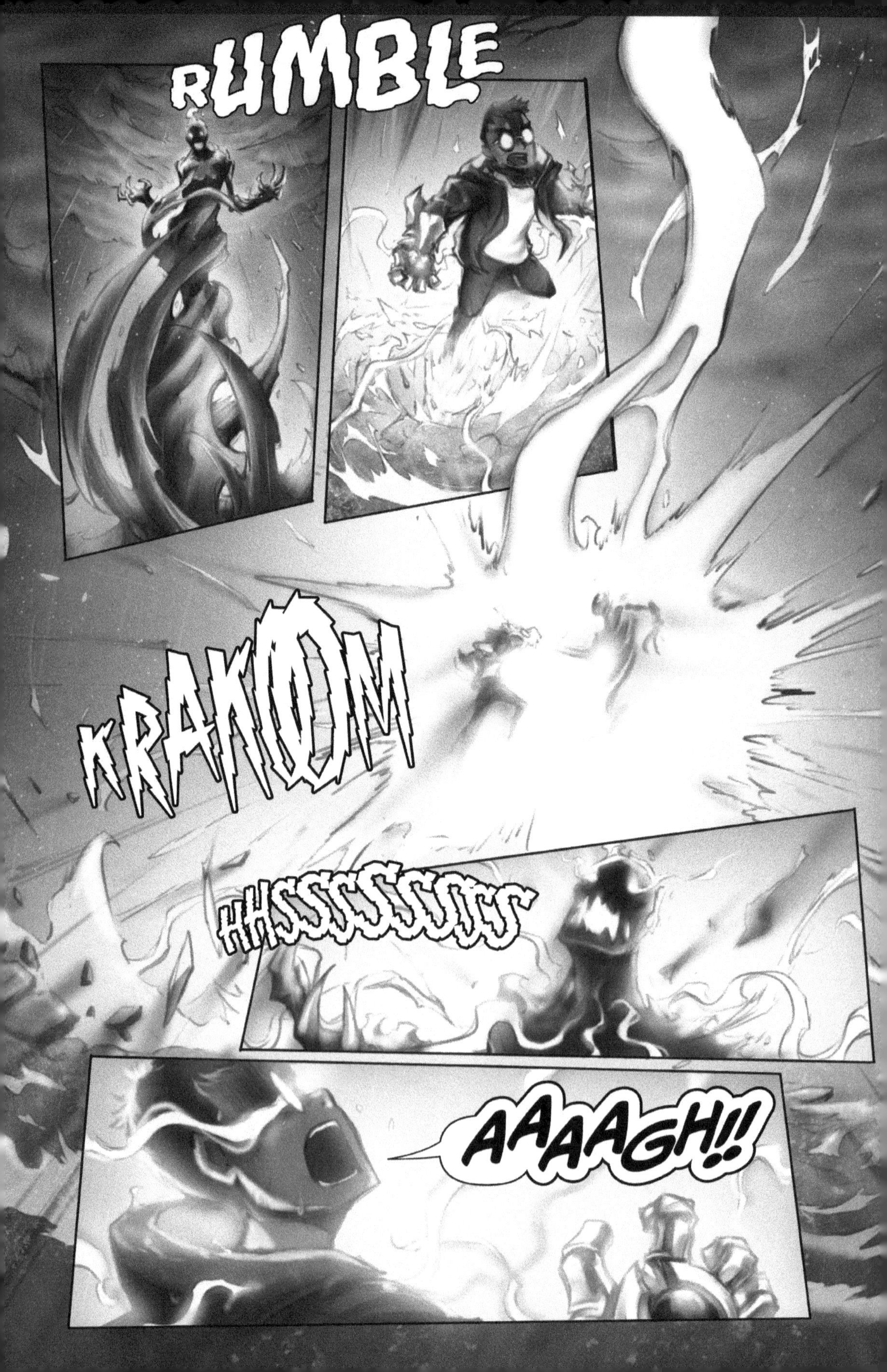
RUMBLE
KRAKOOM
HHSSSSSSSSSSS
AAAAGH!!

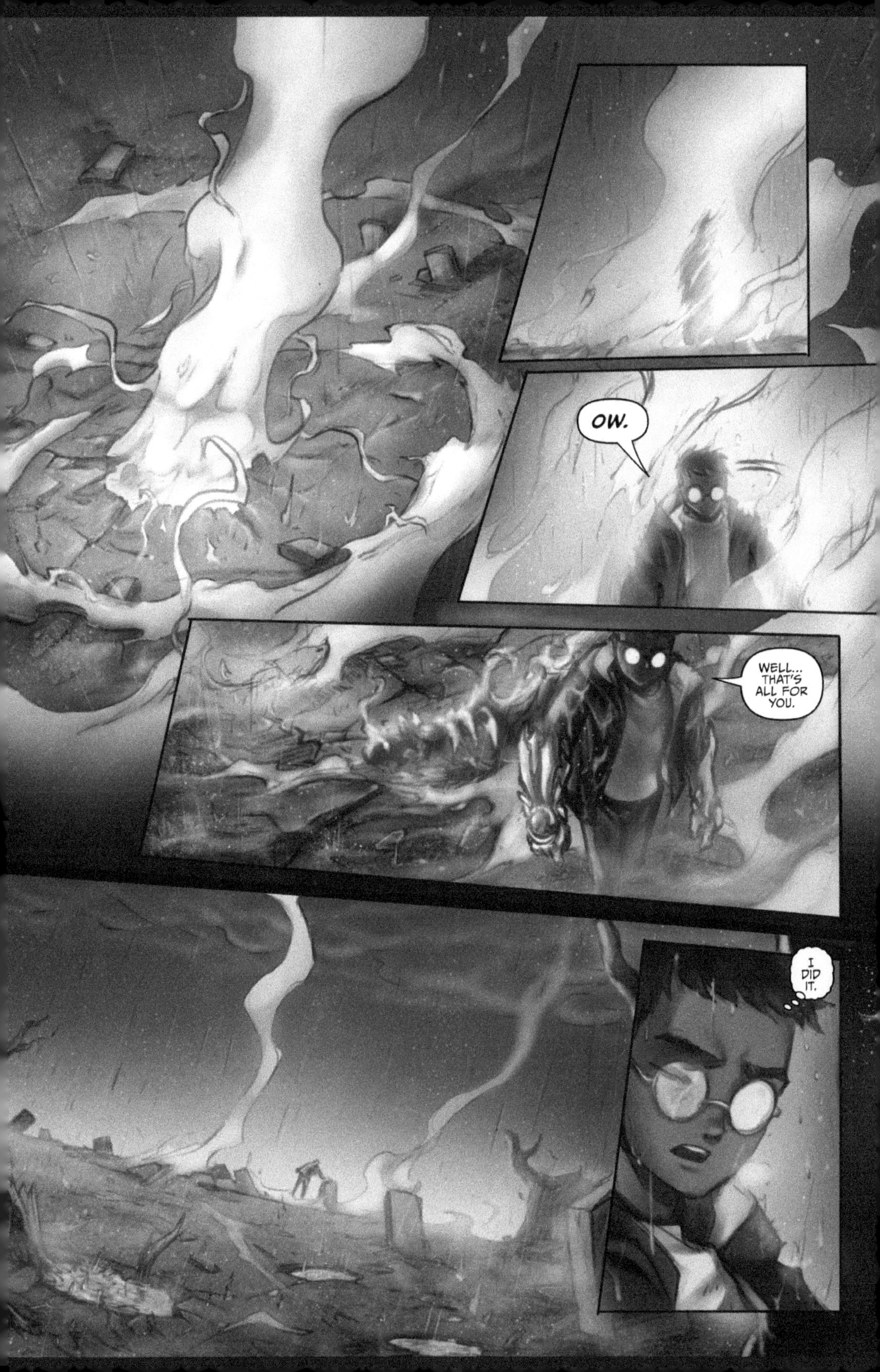
OW.
WELL... THAT'S ALL FOR YOU.
I DID IT.

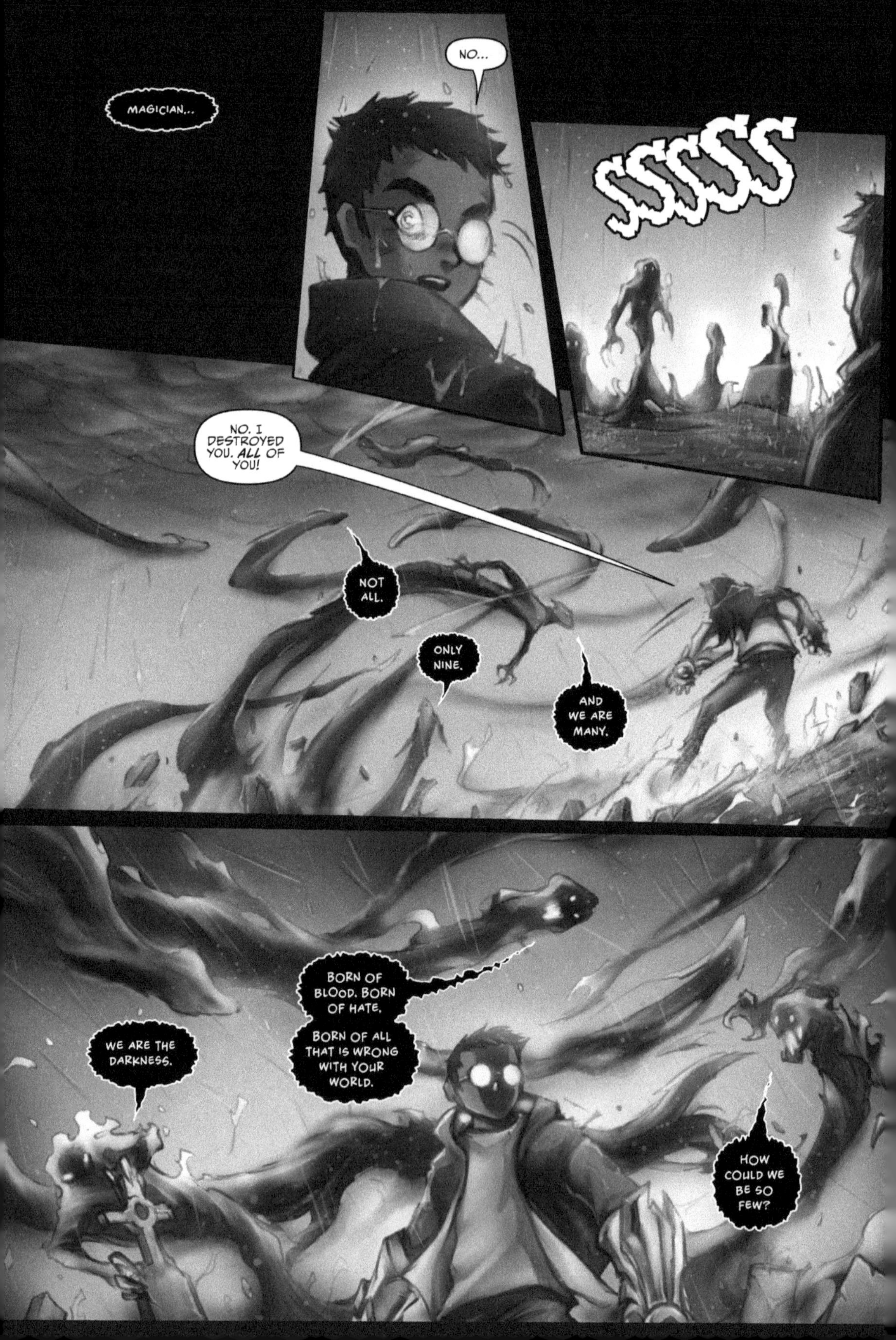
MAGICIAN...
NO...
SSSSSS
NO. I DESTROYED YOU. *ALL* OF YOU!
NOT ALL.
ONLY NINE.
AND WE ARE MANY.
WE ARE THE DARKNESS.
BORN OF BLOOD. BORN OF HATE.
BORN OF ALL THAT IS WRONG WITH YOUR WORLD.
HOW COULD WE BE SO FEW?

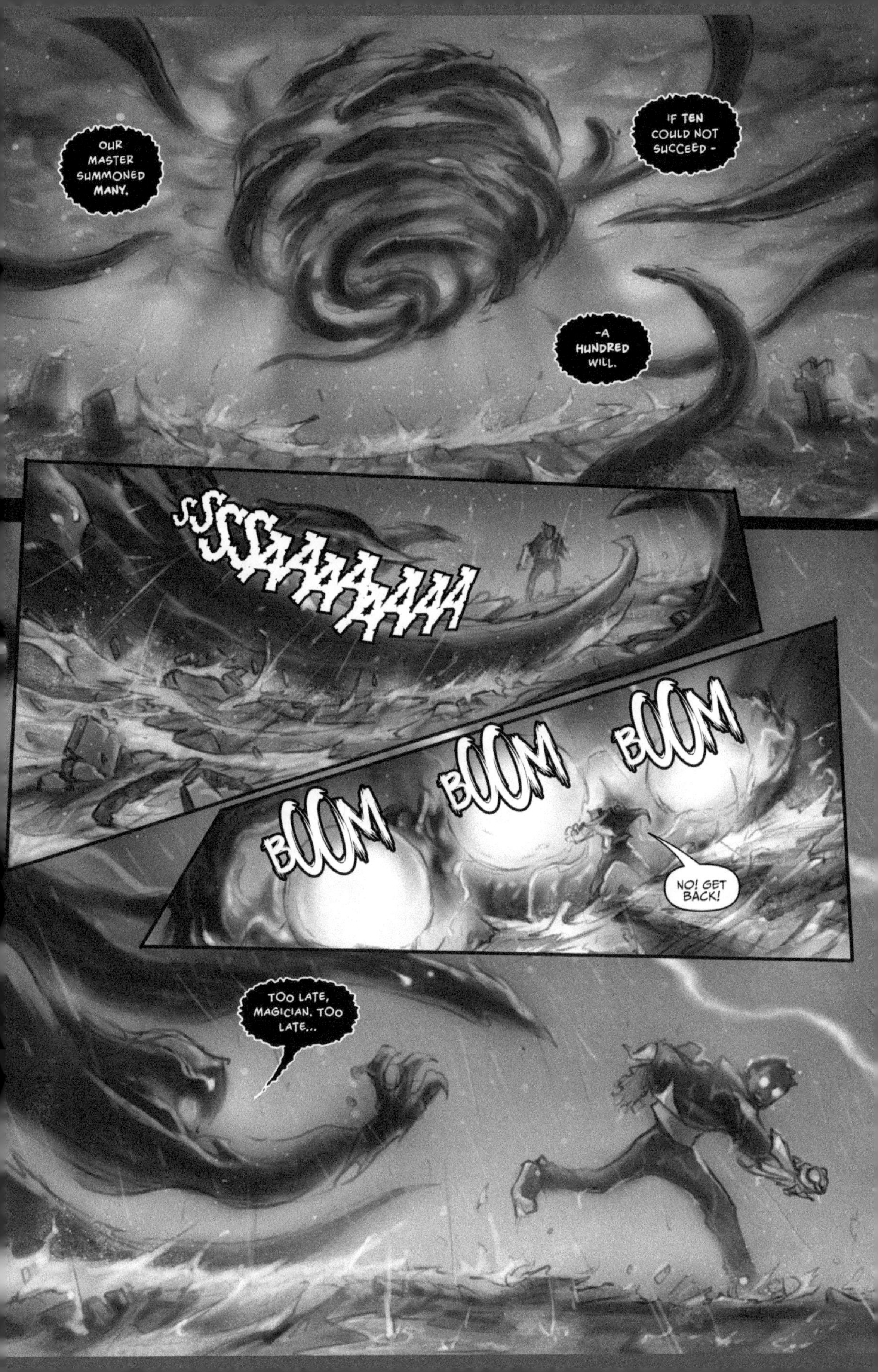
OUR MASTER SUMMONED MANY.
IF TEN COULD NOT SUCCEED -
-A HUNDRED WILL.
SSCRAAAAAAAA
BOOM
BOOM
BOOM
NO! GET BACK!
TOO LATE, MAGICIAN. TOO LATE...

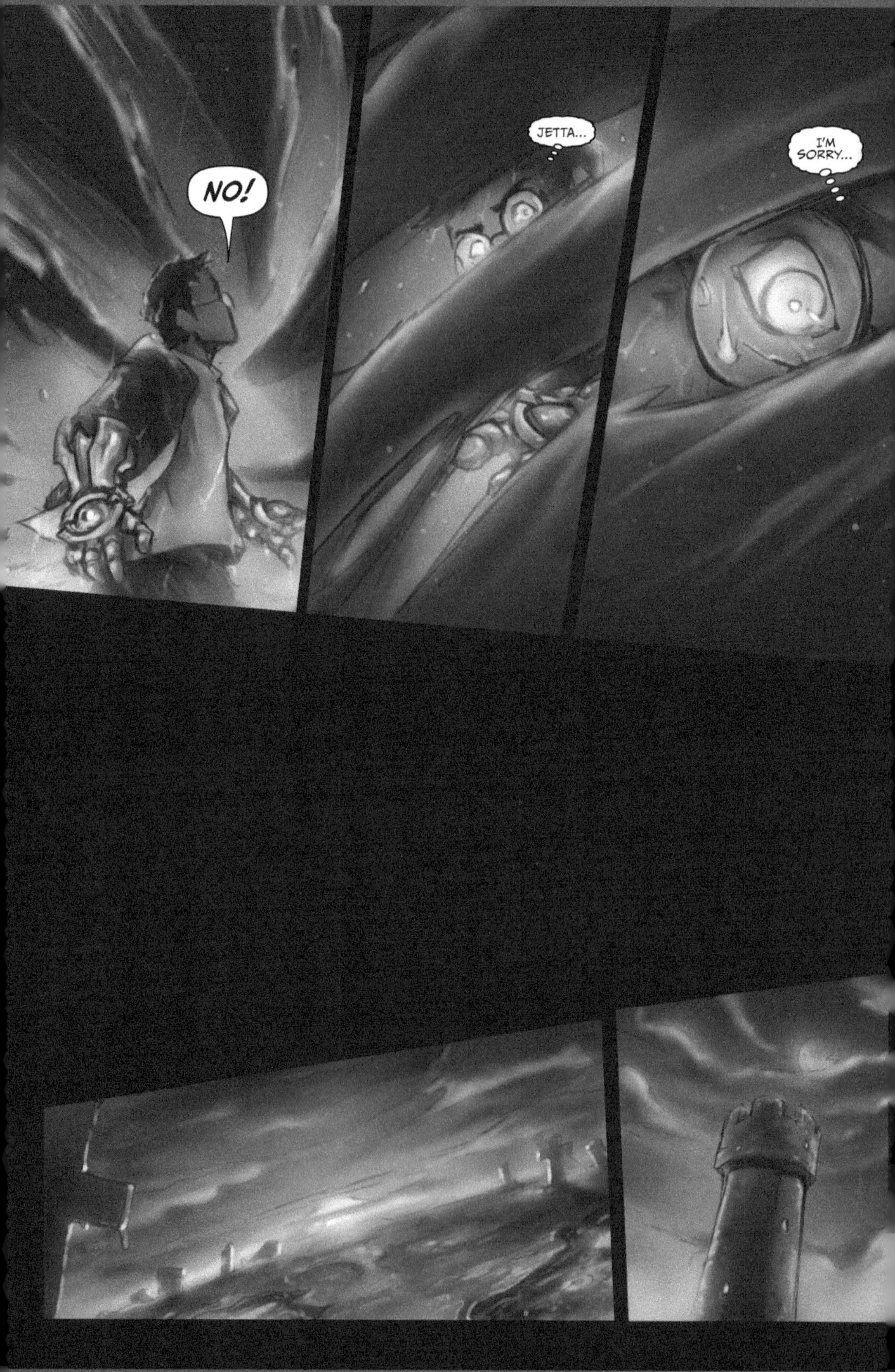
NO!
JETTA...
I'M SORRY...

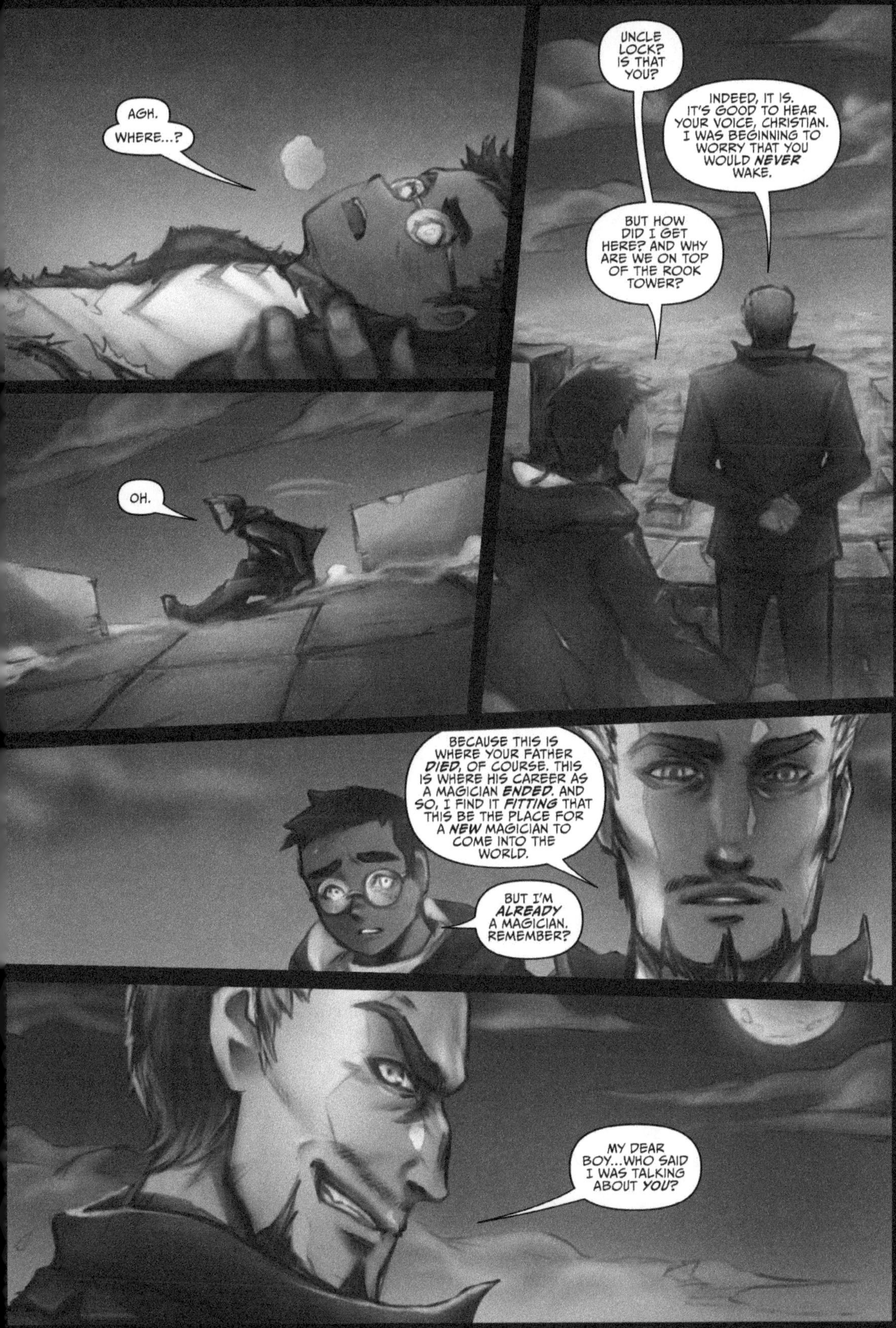
AGH.
WHERE...?
UNCLE LOCK? IS THAT YOU?
INDEED, IT IS. IT'S GOOD TO HEAR YOUR VOICE, CHRISTIAN. I WAS BEGINNING TO WORRY THAT YOU WOULD NEVER WAKE.
OH.
BUT HOW DID I GET HERE? AND WHY ARE WE ON TOP OF THE ROOK TOWER?
BECAUSE THIS IS WHERE YOUR FATHER DIED, OF COURSE. THIS IS WHERE HIS CAREER AS A MAGICIAN ENDED. AND SO, I FIND IT FITTING THAT THIS BE THE PLACE FOR A NEW MAGICIAN TO COME INTO THE WORLD.
BUT I'M ALREADY A MAGICIAN. REMEMBER?
MY DEAR BOY...WHO SAID I WAS TALKING ABOUT YOU?

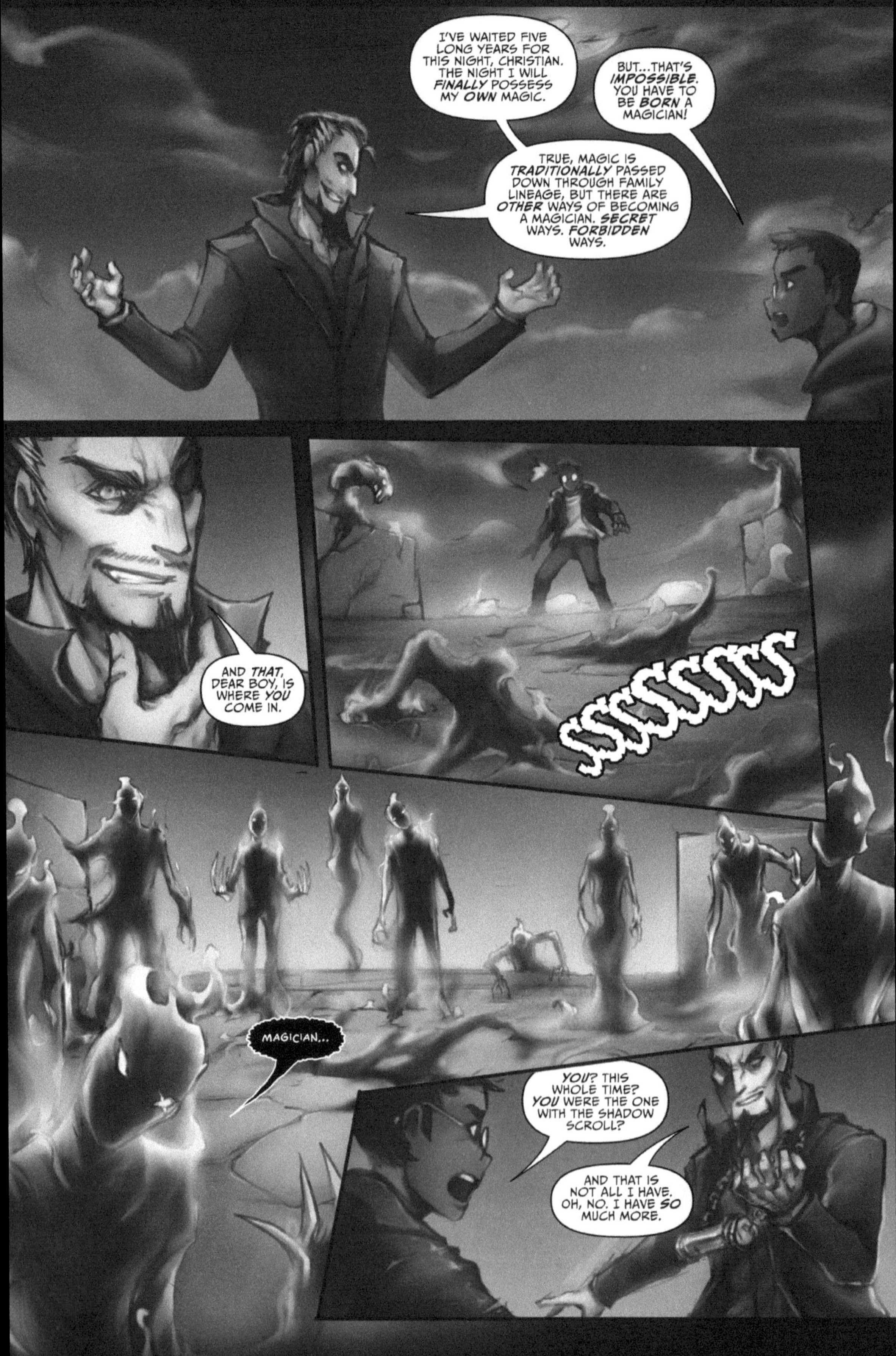
I'VE WAITED FIVE LONG YEARS FOR THIS NIGHT, CHRISTIAN. THE NIGHT I WILL FINALLY POSSESS MY OWN MAGIC.
BUT...THAT'S IMPOSSIBLE. YOU HAVE TO BE BORN A MAGICIAN!
TRUE, MAGIC IS TRADITIONALLY PASSED DOWN THROUGH FAMILY LINEAGE, BUT THERE ARE OTHER WAYS OF BECOMING A MAGICIAN. SECRET WAYS. FORBIDDEN WAYS.
AND THAT, DEAR BOY, IS WHERE YOU COME IN.
SSSSSSSS
MAGICIAN...
YOU? THIS WHOLE TIME? YOU WERE THE ONE WITH THE SHADOW SCROLL?
AND THAT IS NOT ALL I HAVE. OH, NO. I HAVE SO MUCH MORE.

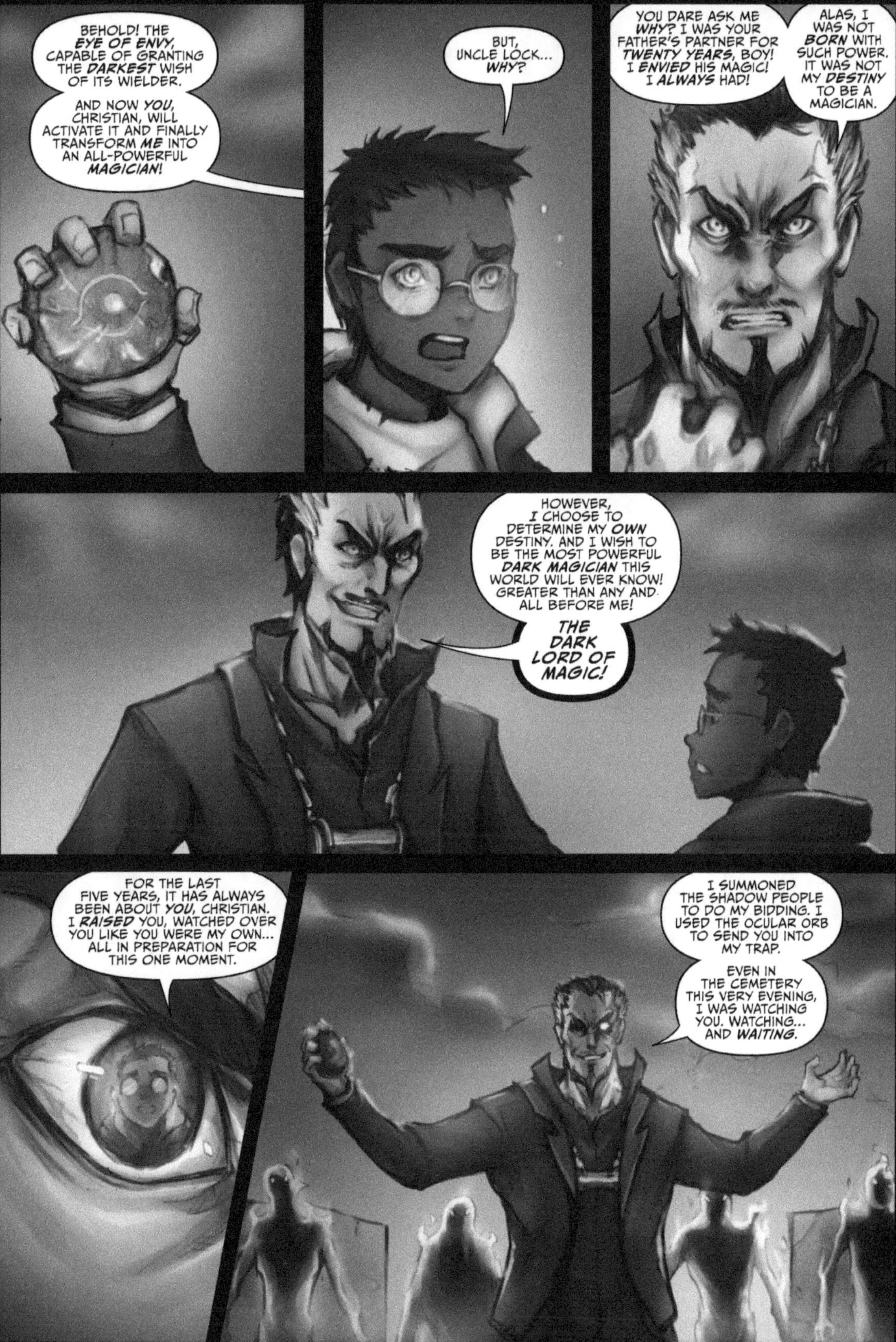
BEHOLD! THE EYE OF ENVY, CAPABLE OF GRANTING THE DARKEST WISH OF ITS WIELDER.
AND NOW YOU, CHRISTIAN, WILL ACTIVATE IT AND FINALLY TRANSFORM ME INTO AN ALL-POWERFUL MAGICIAN!
BUT, UNCLE LOCK... WHY?
YOU DARE ASK ME WHY? I WAS YOUR FATHER'S PARTNER FOR TWENTY YEARS, BOY! I ENVIED HIS MAGIC! I ALWAYS HAD!
ALAS, I WAS NOT BORN WITH SUCH POWER. IT WAS NOT MY DESTINY TO BE A MAGICIAN.
HOWEVER, I CHOOSE TO DETERMINE MY OWN DESTINY. AND I WISH TO BE THE MOST POWERFUL DARK MAGICIAN THIS WORLD WILL EVER KNOW! GREATER THAN ANY AND ALL BEFORE ME!
THE DARK LORD OF MAGIC!
FOR THE LAST FIVE YEARS, IT HAS ALWAYS BEEN ABOUT YOU, CHRISTIAN. I RAISED YOU, WATCHED OVER YOU LIKE YOU WERE MY OWN... ALL IN PREPARATION FOR THIS ONE MOMENT.
I SUMMONED THE SHADOW PEOPLE TO DO MY BIDDING. I USED THE OCULAR ORB TO SEND YOU INTO MY TRAP.
EVEN IN THE CEMETERY THIS VERY EVENING, I WAS WATCHING YOU. WATCHING... AND WAITING.

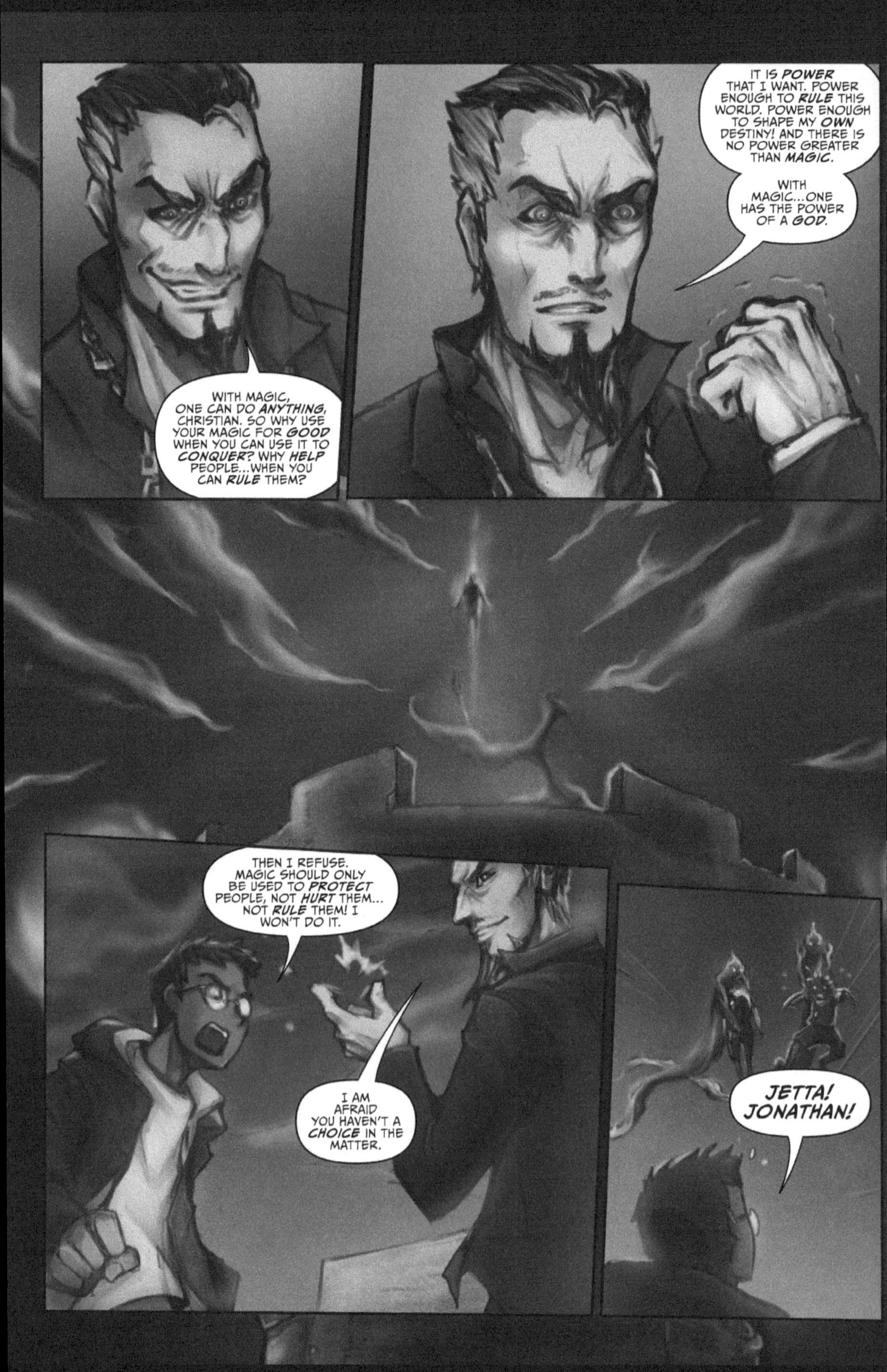
WITH MAGIC, ONE CAN DO ANYTHING, CHRISTIAN. SO WHY USE YOUR MAGIC FOR GOOD WHEN YOU CAN USE IT TO CONQUER? WHY HELP PEOPLE...WHEN YOU CAN RULE THEM?
IT IS POWER THAT I WANT. POWER ENOUGH TO RULE THIS WORLD. POWER ENOUGH TO SHAPE MY OWN DESTINY! AND THERE IS NO POWER GREATER THAN MAGIC.
WITH MAGIC...ONE HAS THE POWER OF A GOD.
THEN I REFUSE. MAGIC SHOULD ONLY BE USED TO PROTECT PEOPLE, NOT HURT THEM... NOT RULE THEM! I WON'T DO IT.
I AM AFRAID YOU HAVEN'T A CHOICE IN THE MATTER.
JETTA! JONATHAN!

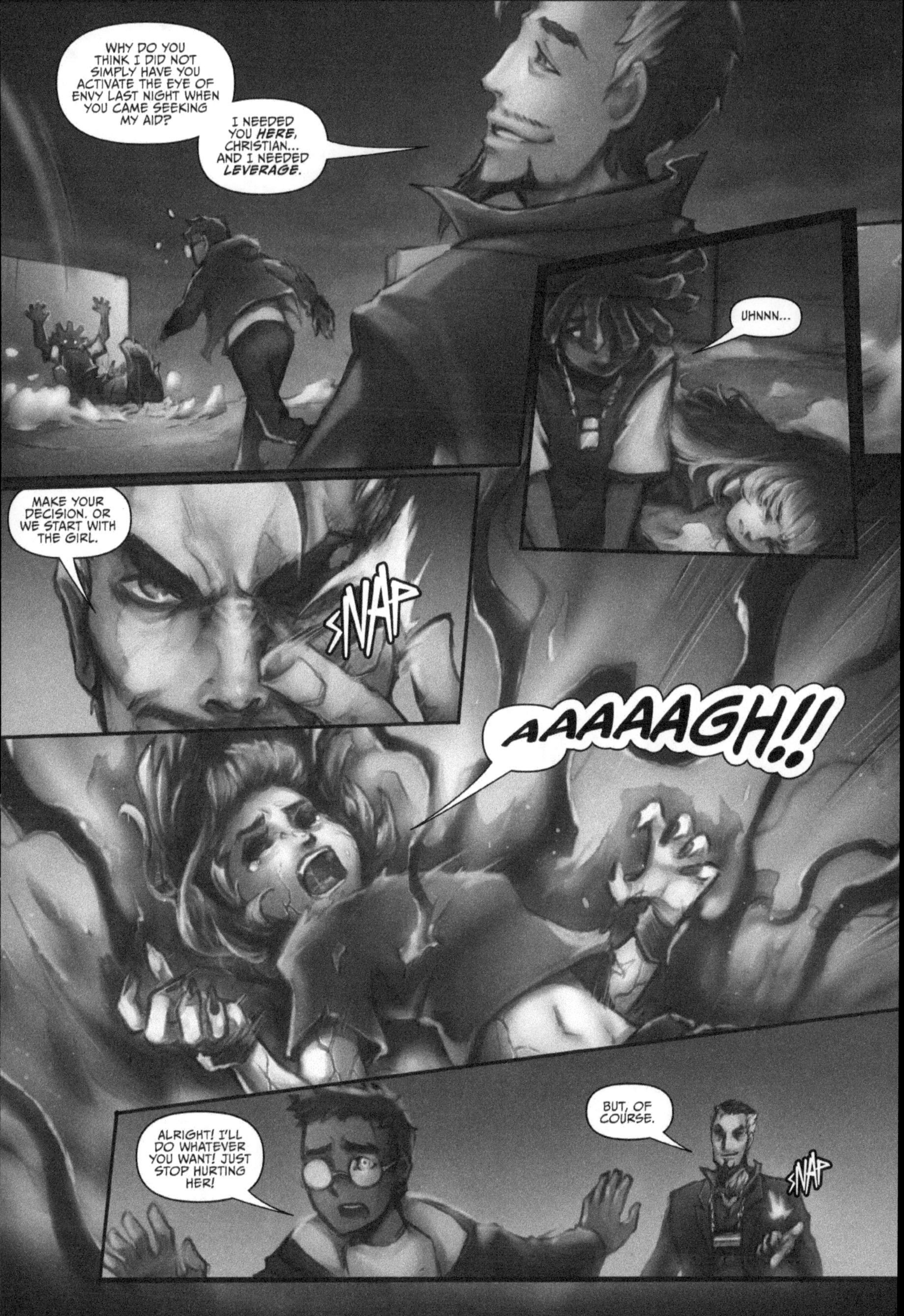

WHY DO YOU THINK I DID NOT SIMPLY HAVE YOU ACTIVATE THE EYE OF ENVY LAST NIGHT WHEN YOU CAME SEEKING MY AID?
I NEEDED YOU *HERE*, CHRISTIAN... AND I NEEDED *LEVERAGE*.
UHNNN...
MAKE YOUR DECISION. OR WE START WITH THE GIRL.
SNAP
AAAAAGH!!
ALRIGHT! I'LL DO WHATEVER YOU WANT! JUST STOP HURTING HER!
BUT, OF COURSE.
SNAP

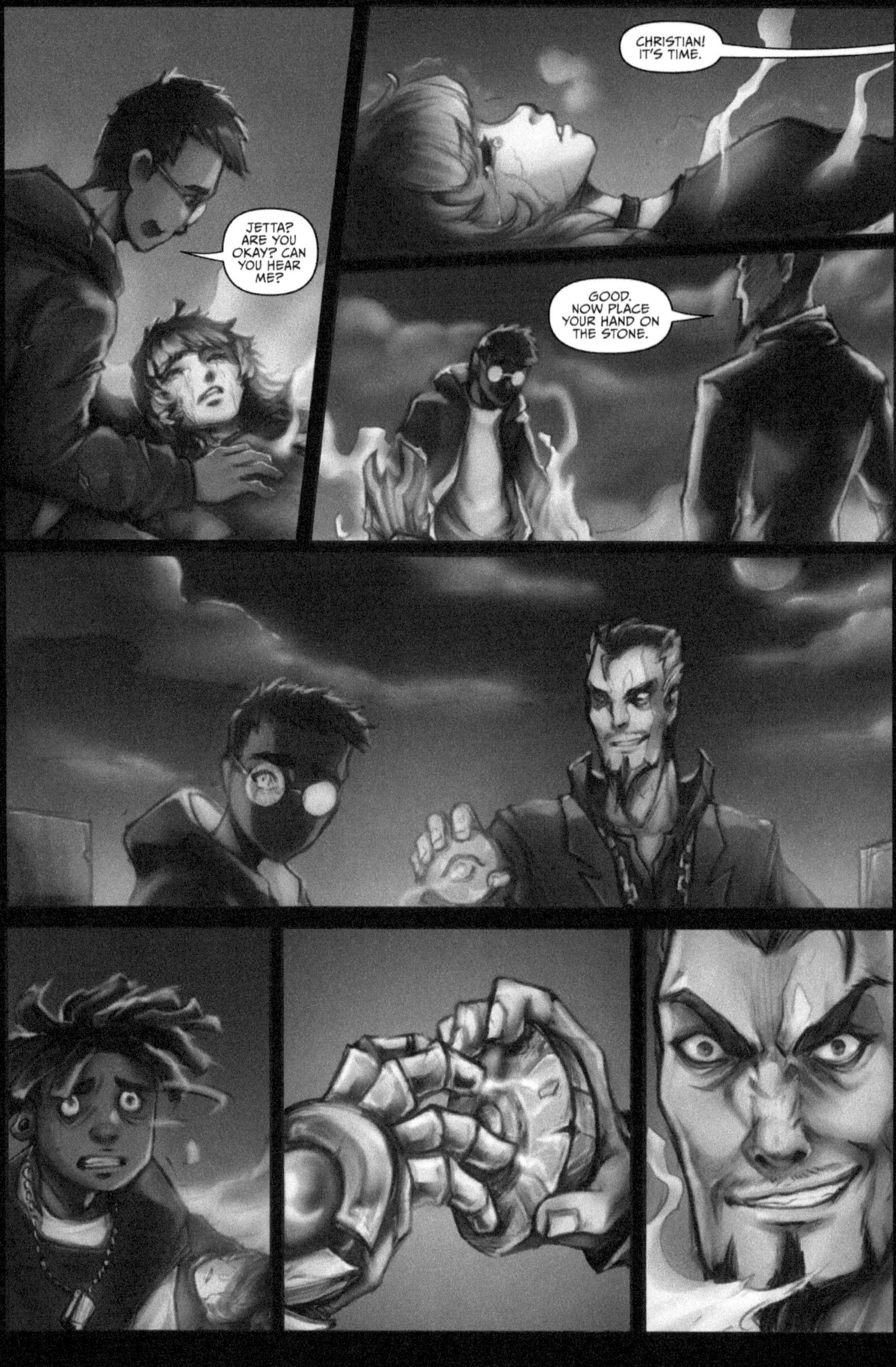
JETTA? ARE YOU OKAY? CAN YOU HEAR ME?
CHRISTIAN! IT'S TIME.
GOOD. NOW PLACE YOUR HAND ON THE STONE.

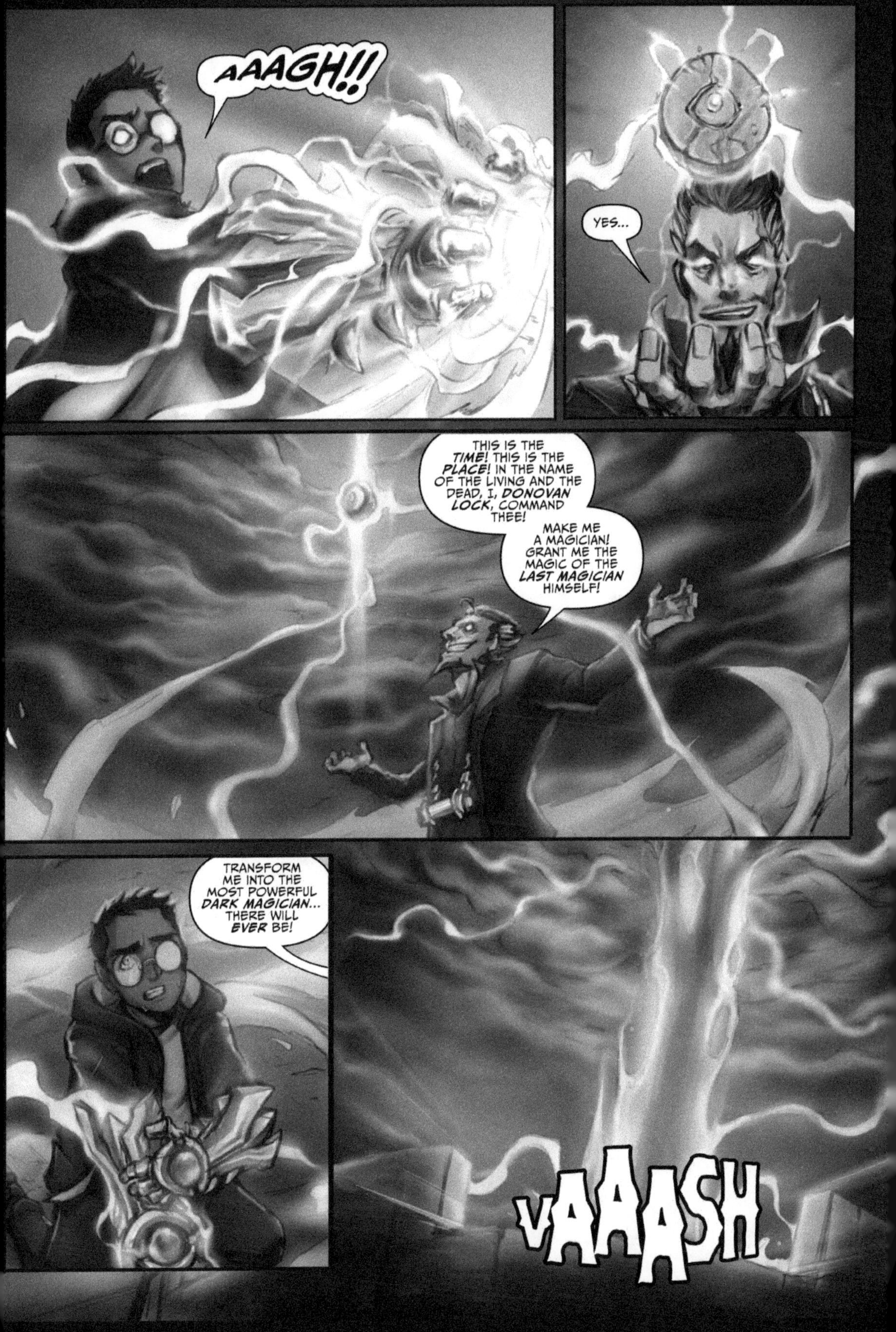
AAAGH!!
YES...
THIS IS THE TIME! THIS IS THE PLACE! IN THE NAME OF THE LIVING AND THE DEAD, I, DONOVAN LOCK, COMMAND THEE!
MAKE ME A MAGICIAN! GRANT ME THE MAGIC OF THE LAST MAGICIAN HIMSELF!
TRANSFORM ME INTO THE MOST POWERFUL DARK MAGICIAN... THERE WILL EVER BE!
vAAASH

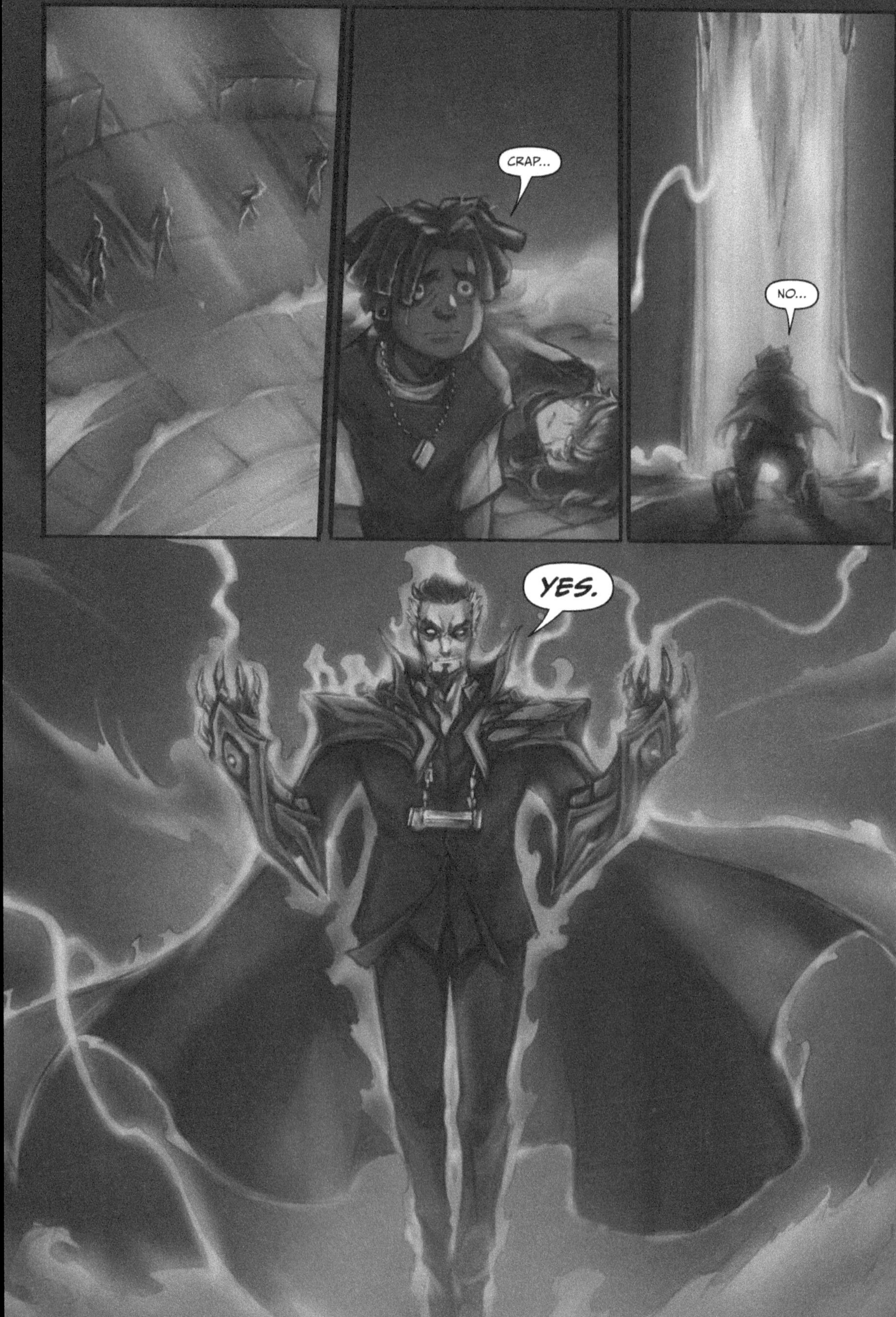
CRAP...
NO...
YES.

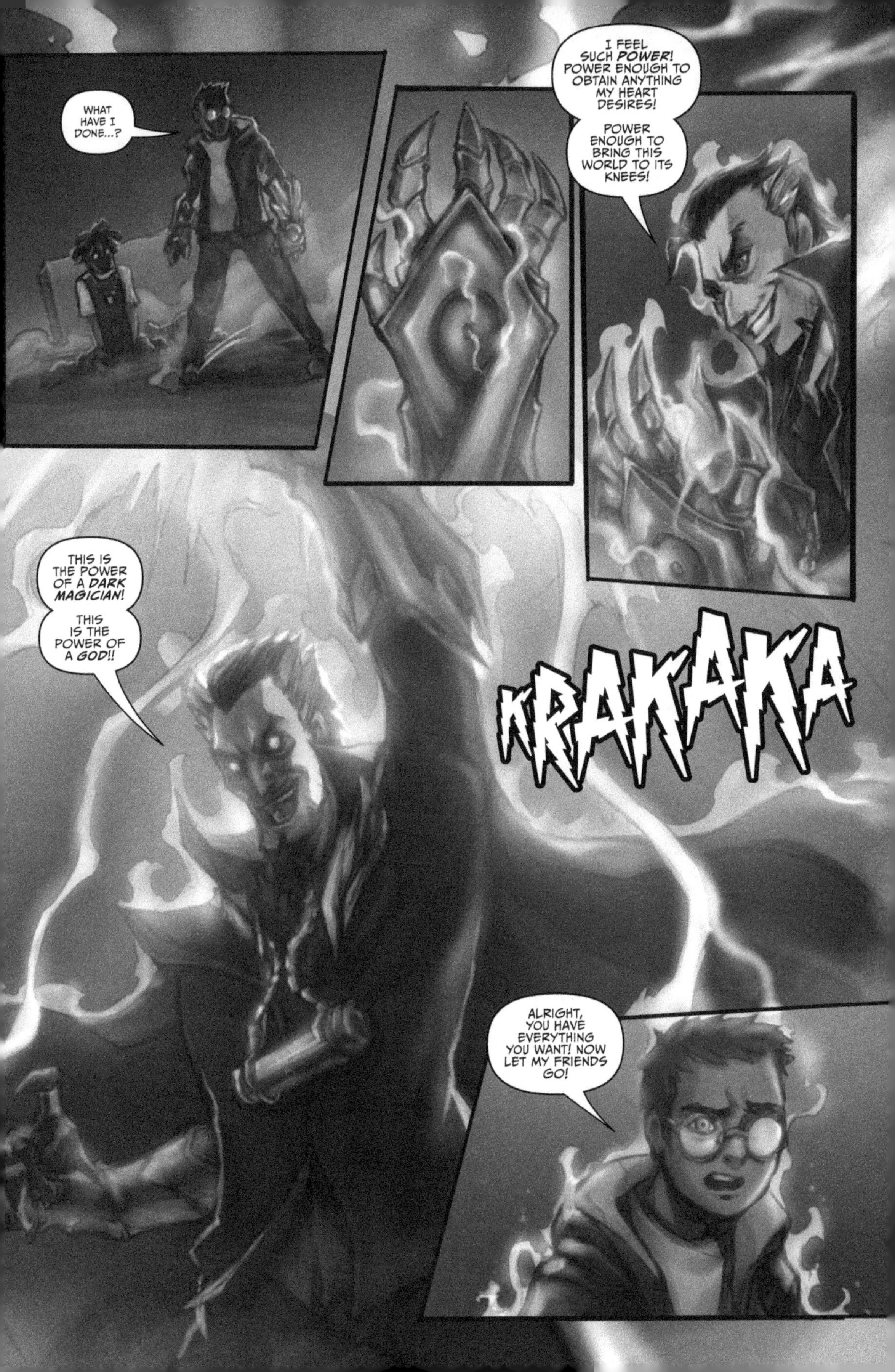

WHAT HAVE I DONE...?
I FEEL SUCH POWER! POWER ENOUGH TO OBTAIN ANYTHING MY HEART DESIRES!
POWER ENOUGH TO BRING THIS WORLD TO ITS KNEES!
THIS IS THE POWER OF A DARK MAGICIAN!
THIS IS THE POWER OF A GOD!!
KRAKAKA
ALRIGHT, YOU HAVE EVERYTHING YOU WANT! NOW LET MY FRIENDS GO!

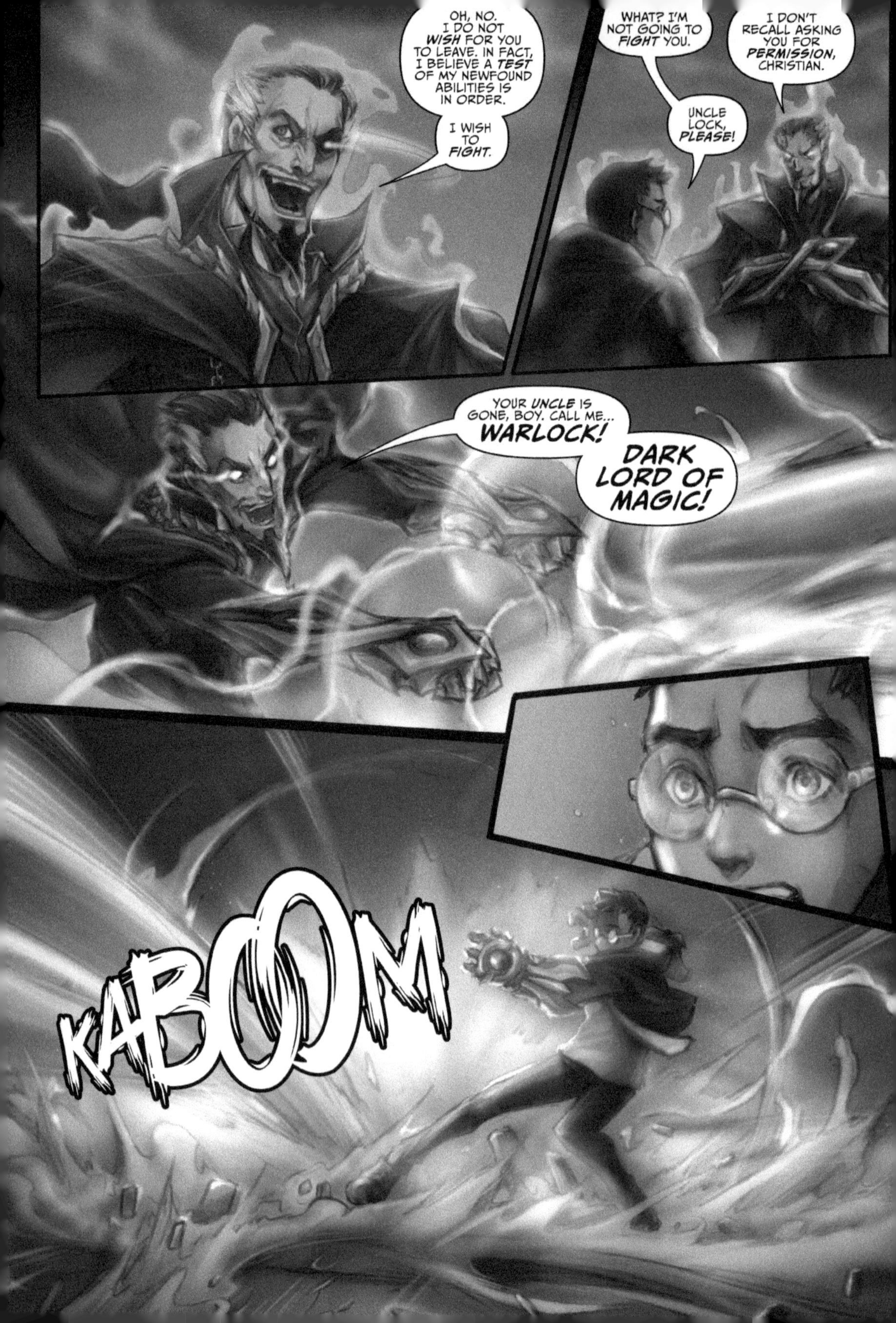
OH, NO. I DO NOT WISH FOR YOU TO LEAVE. IN FACT, I BELIEVE A TEST OF MY NEWFOUND ABILITIES IS IN ORDER.
I WISH TO FIGHT.
WHAT? I'M NOT GOING TO FIGHT YOU.
UNCLE LOCK, PLEASE!
I DON'T RECALL ASKING YOU FOR PERMISSION, CHRISTIAN.
YOUR UNCLE IS GONE, BOY. CALL ME... WARLOCK!
DARK LORD OF MAGIC!
KABOOM

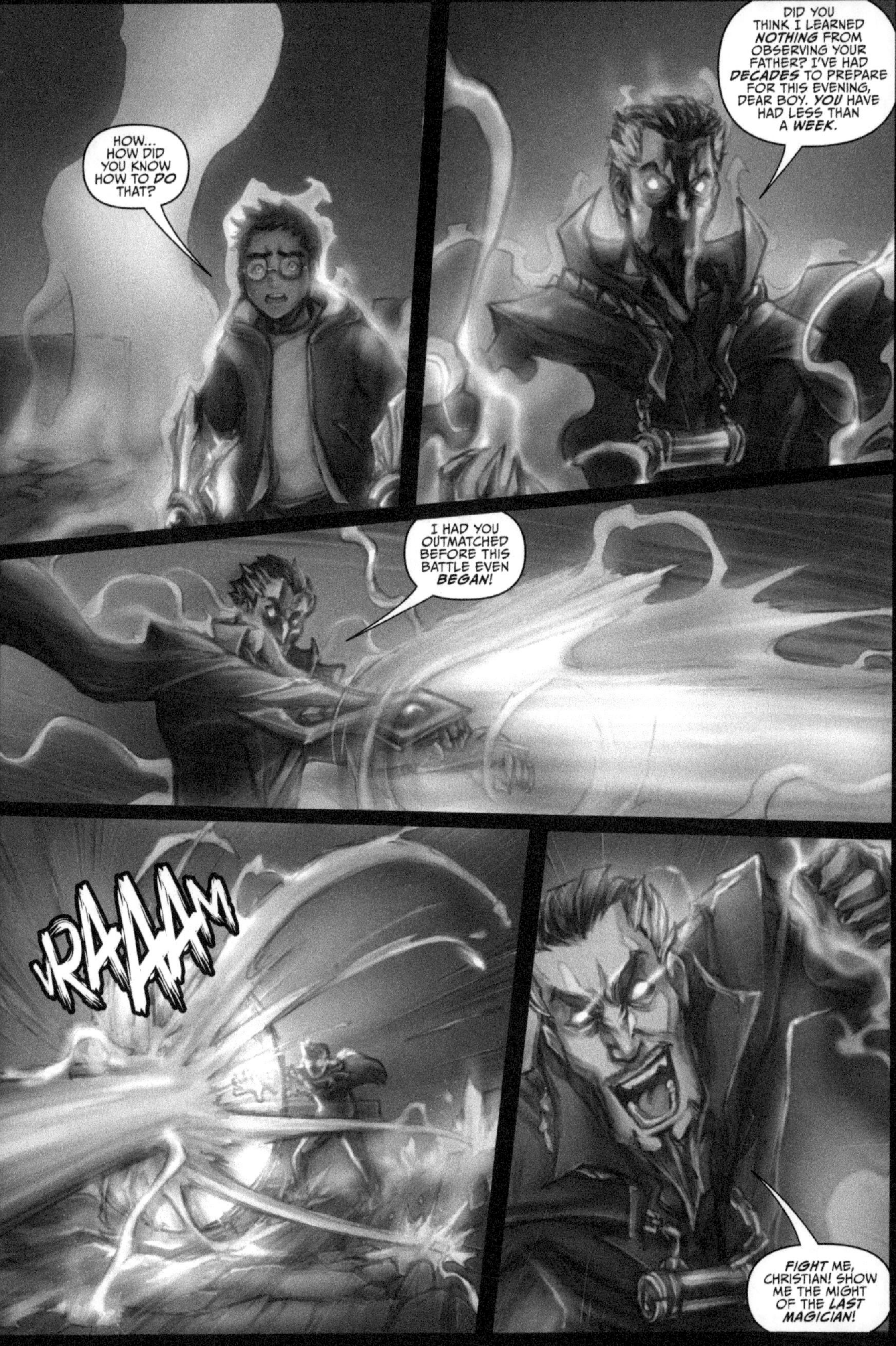
HOW... HOW DID YOU KNOW HOW TO DO THAT?
DID YOU THINK I LEARNED NOTHING FROM OBSERVING YOUR FATHER? I'VE HAD DECADES TO PREPARE FOR THIS EVENING, DEAR BOY. YOU HAVE HAD LESS THAN A WEEK.
I HAD YOU OUTMATCHED BEFORE THIS BATTLE EVEN BEGAN!
VRAAAM
FIGHT ME, CHRISTIAN! SHOW ME THE MIGHT OF THE LAST MAGICIAN!

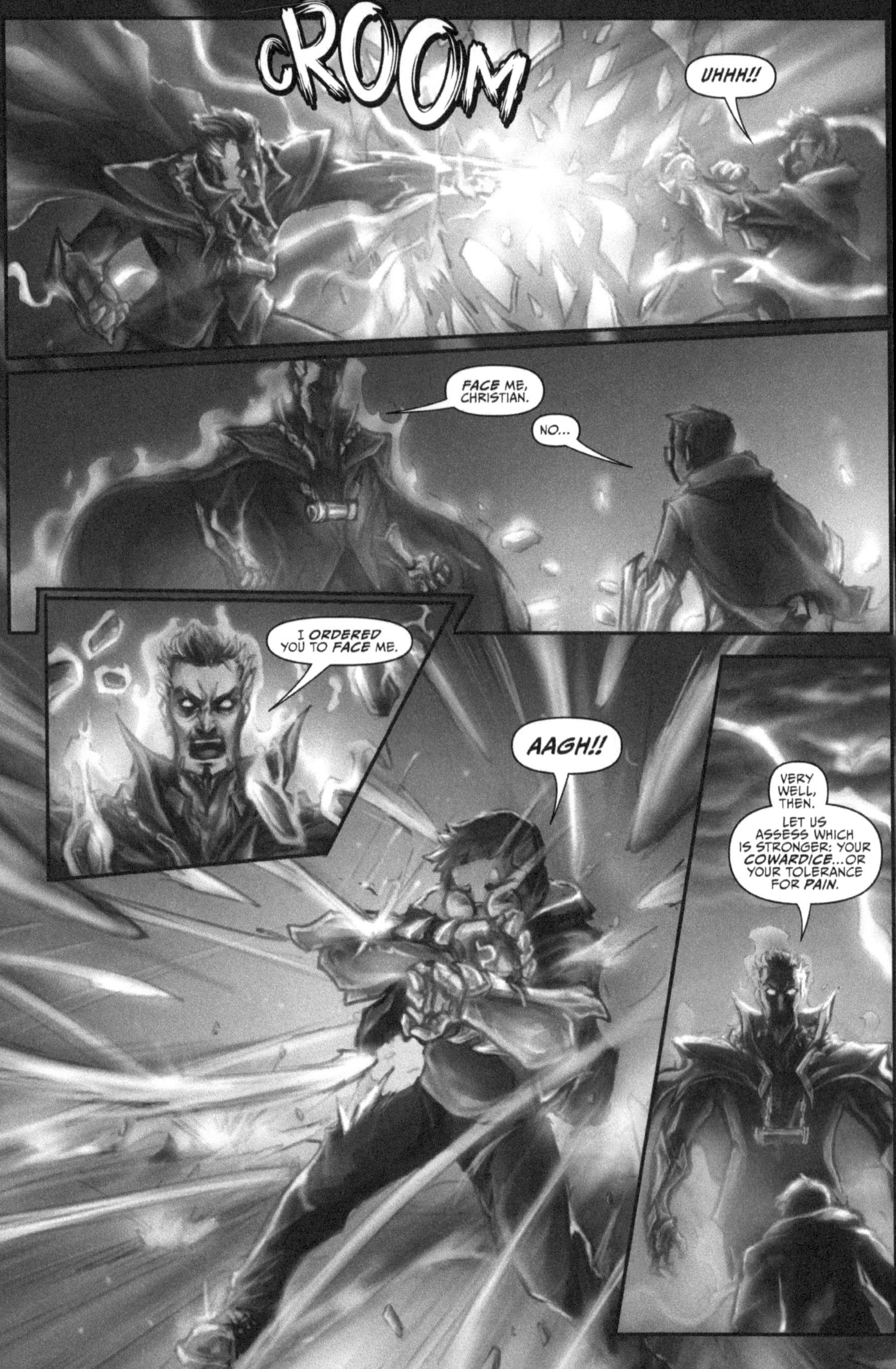
CROOM
UHHH!!
FACE ME, CHRISTIAN.
NO...
I ORDERED YOU TO FACE ME.
AAGH!!
VERY WELL, THEN.
LET US ASSESS WHICH IS STRONGER: YOUR COWARDICE...OR YOUR TOLERANCE FOR PAIN.

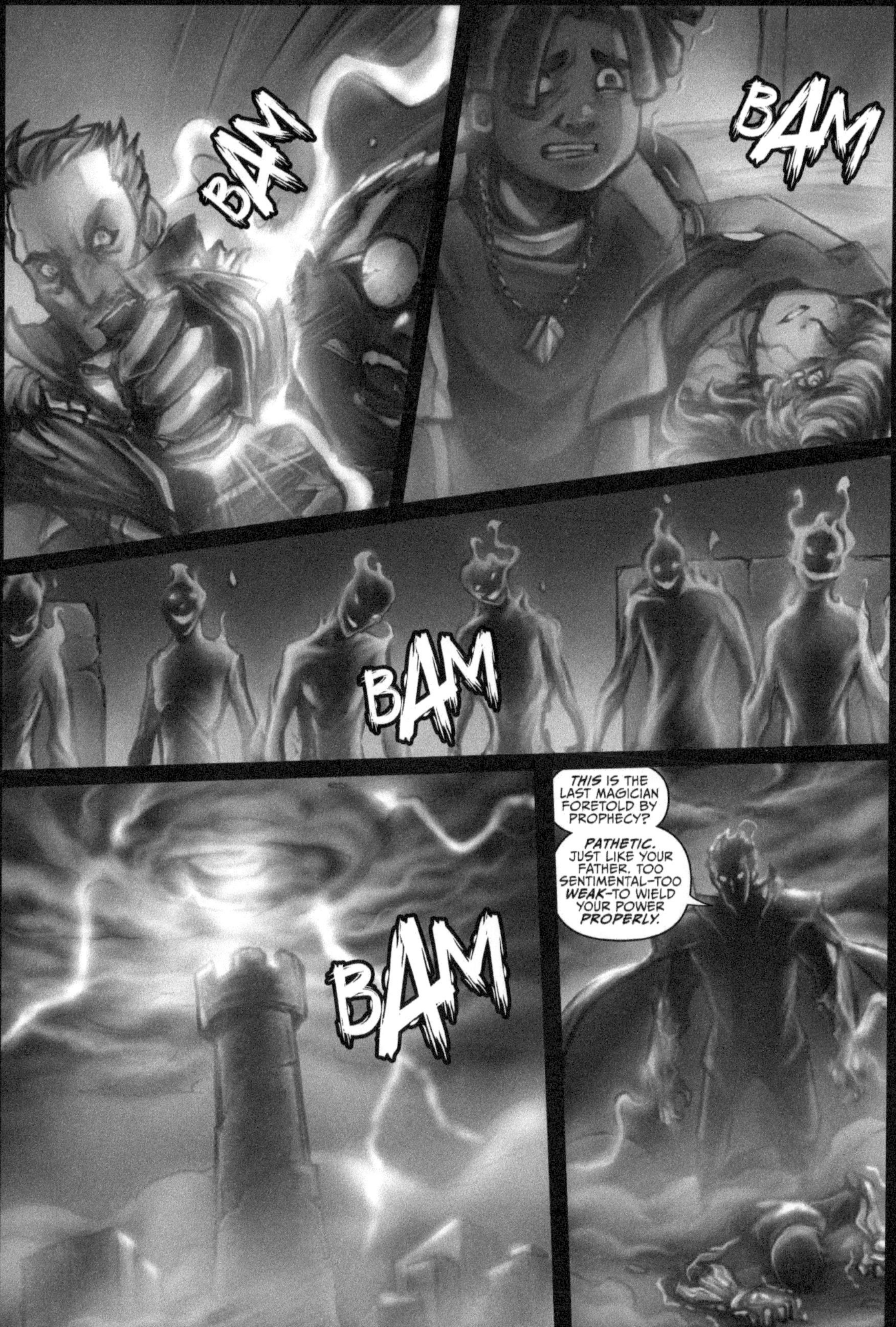
BAM
BAM
BAM
BAM
THIS IS THE LAST MAGICIAN FORETOLD BY PROPHECY?
PATHETIC. JUST LIKE YOUR FATHER. TOO SENTIMENTAL–TOO WEAK–TO WIELD YOUR POWER PROPERLY.

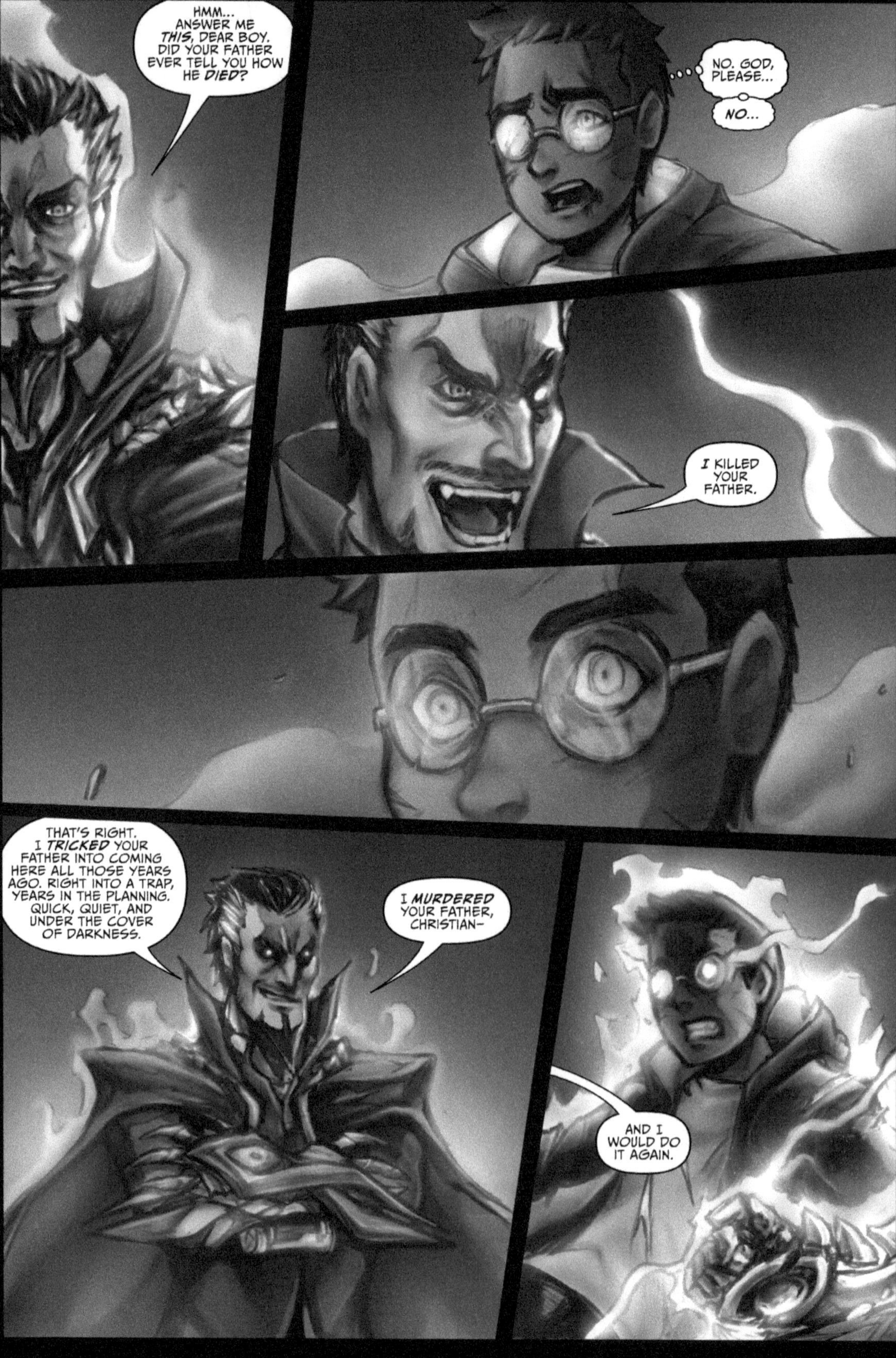
HMM... ANSWER ME THIS, DEAR BOY. DID YOUR FATHER EVER TELL YOU HOW HE DIED?
NO. GOD, PLEASE...
NO...
I KILLED YOUR FATHER.
THAT'S RIGHT. I TRICKED YOUR FATHER INTO COMING HERE ALL THOSE YEARS AGO. RIGHT INTO A TRAP, YEARS IN THE PLANNING. QUICK, QUIET, AND UNDER THE COVER OF DARKNESS.
I MURDERED YOUR FATHER, CHRISTIAN–
AND I WOULD DO IT AGAIN.

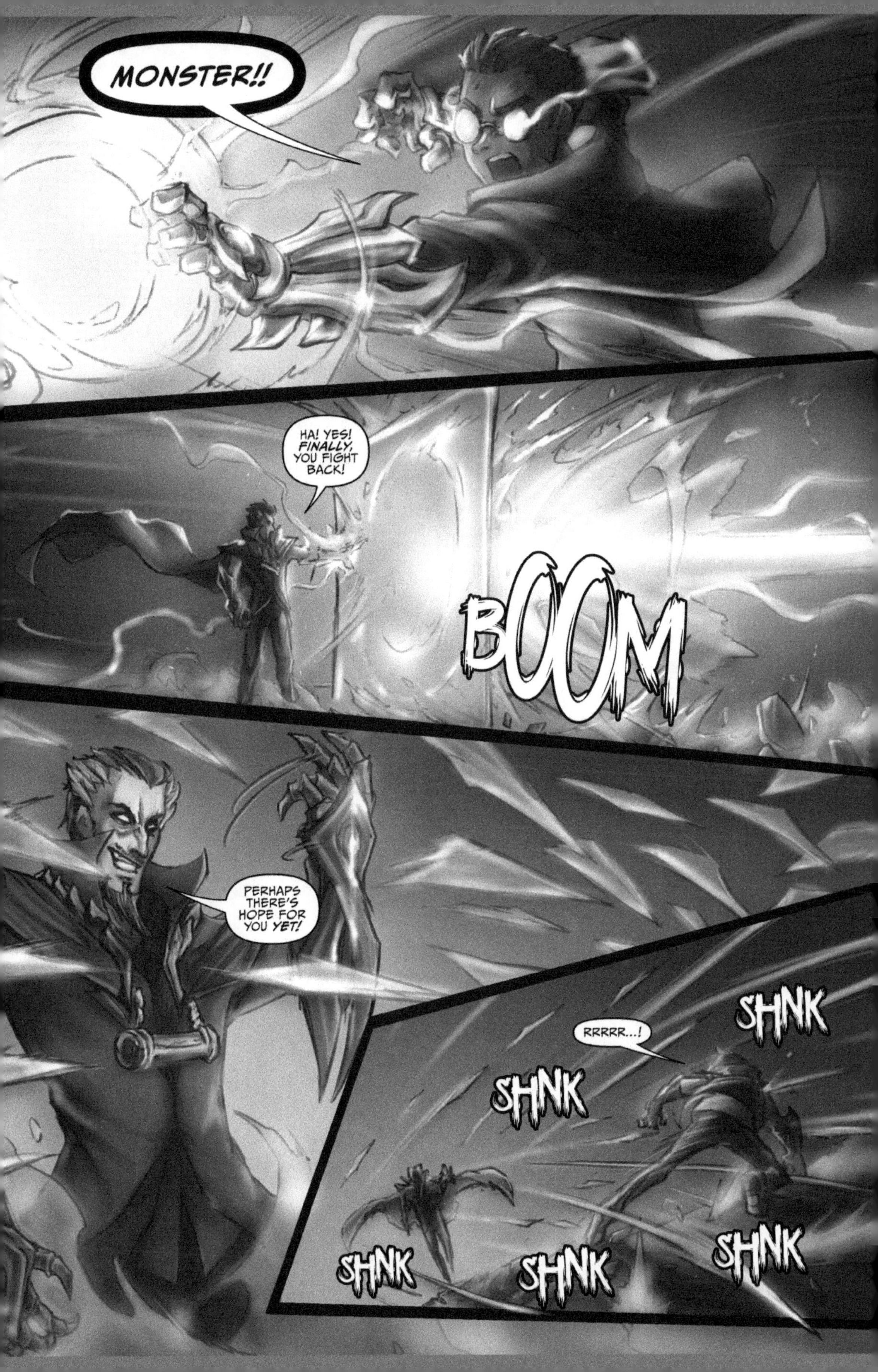
MONSTER!!
HA! YES! FINALLY, YOU FIGHT BACK!
BOOM
PERHAPS THERE'S HOPE FOR YOU YET!
SHNK
RRRRR...!
SHNK
SHNK
SHNK
SHNK

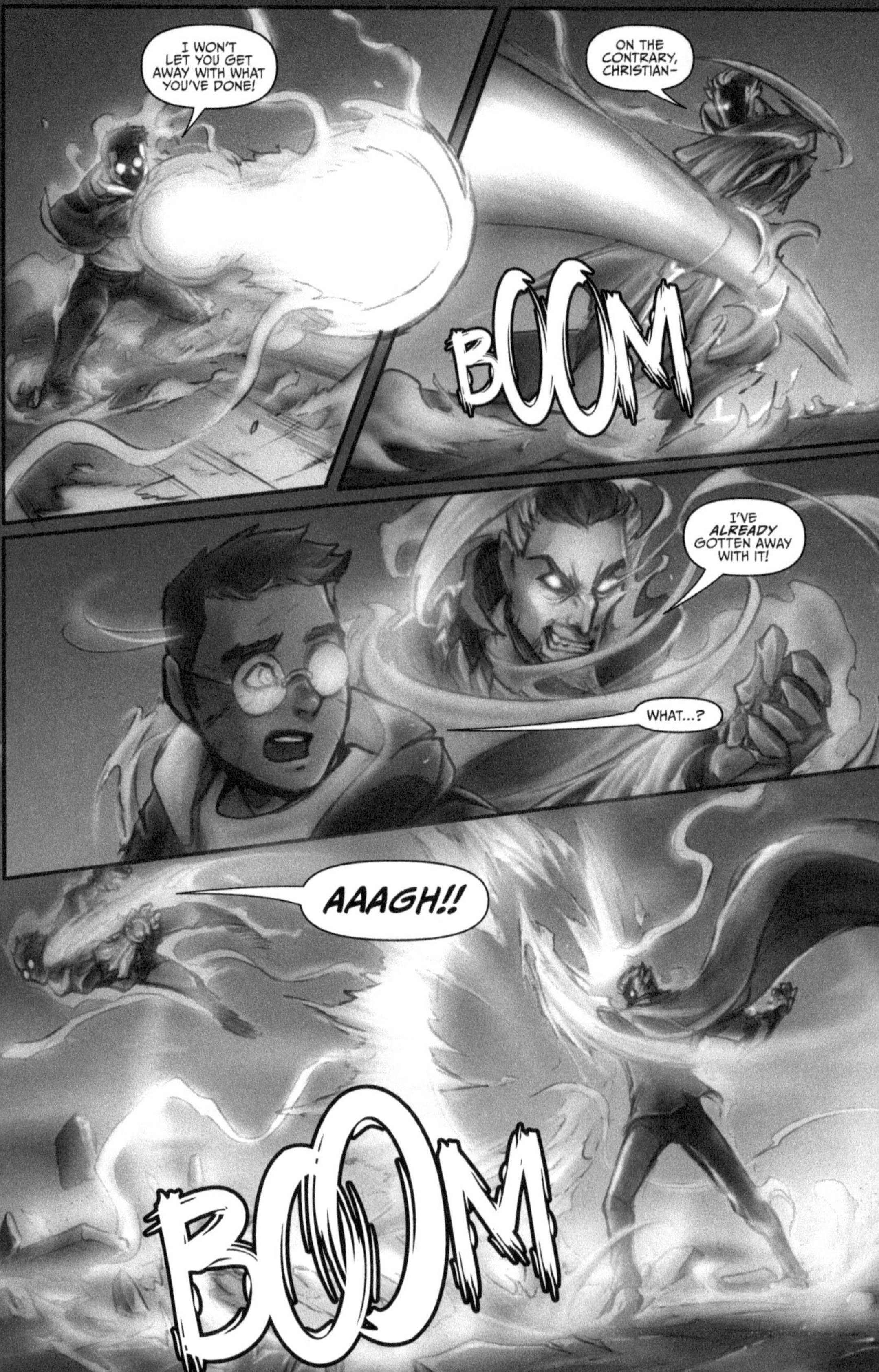
I WON'T LET YOU GET AWAY WITH WHAT YOU'VE DONE!
ON THE CONTRARY, CHRISTIAN-
BOOM
I'VE *ALREADY* GOTTEN AWAY WITH IT!
WHAT...?
*AAAGH!!*
BOOM

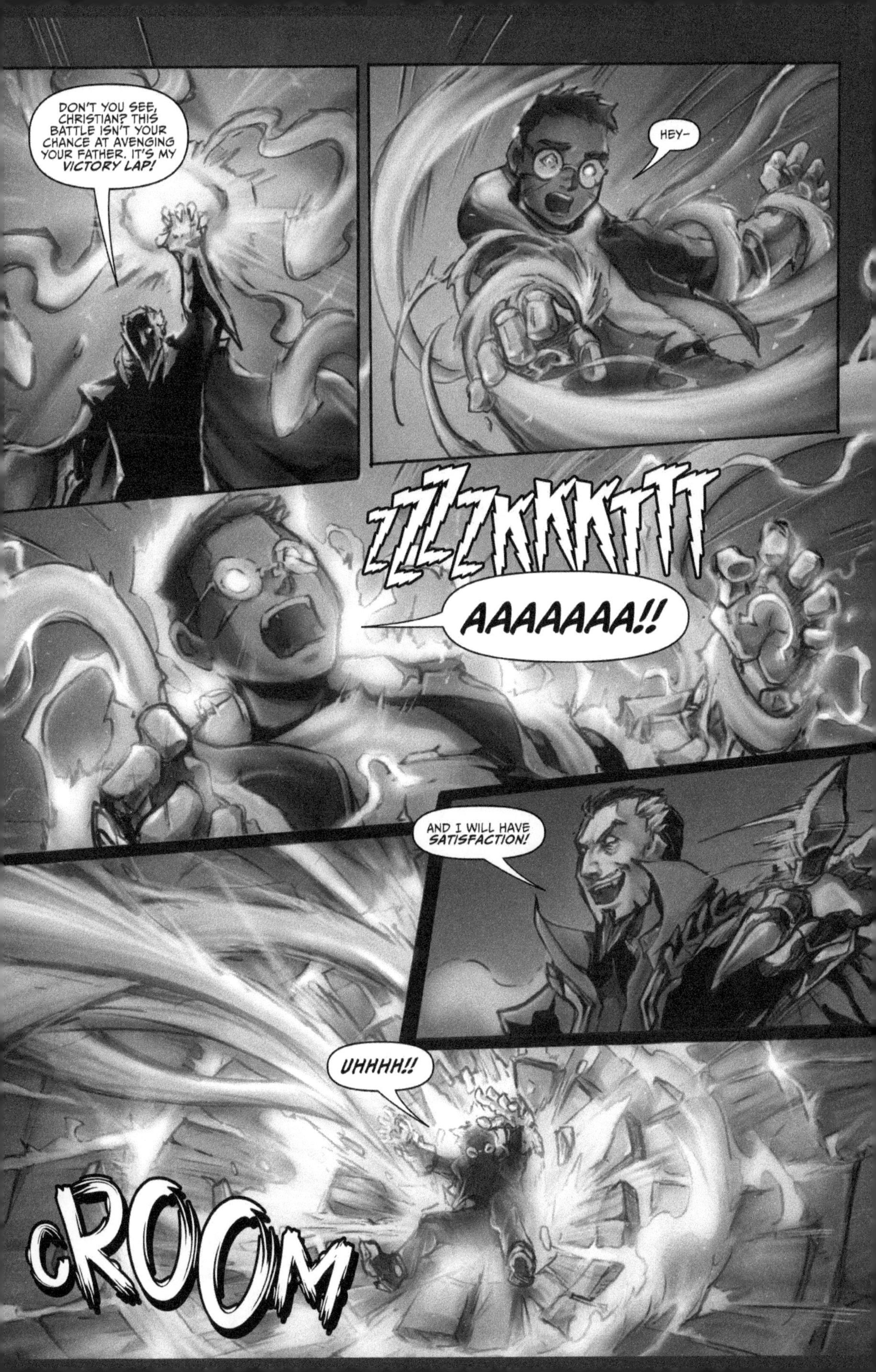
DON'T YOU SEE, CHRISTIAN? THIS BATTLE ISN'T YOUR CHANCE AT AVENGING YOUR FATHER. IT'S MY *VICTORY LAP!*
HEY–
ZZZKKKTTT
AAAAAAA!!
AND I WILL HAVE *SATISFACTION!*
UHHHH!!
CROOM

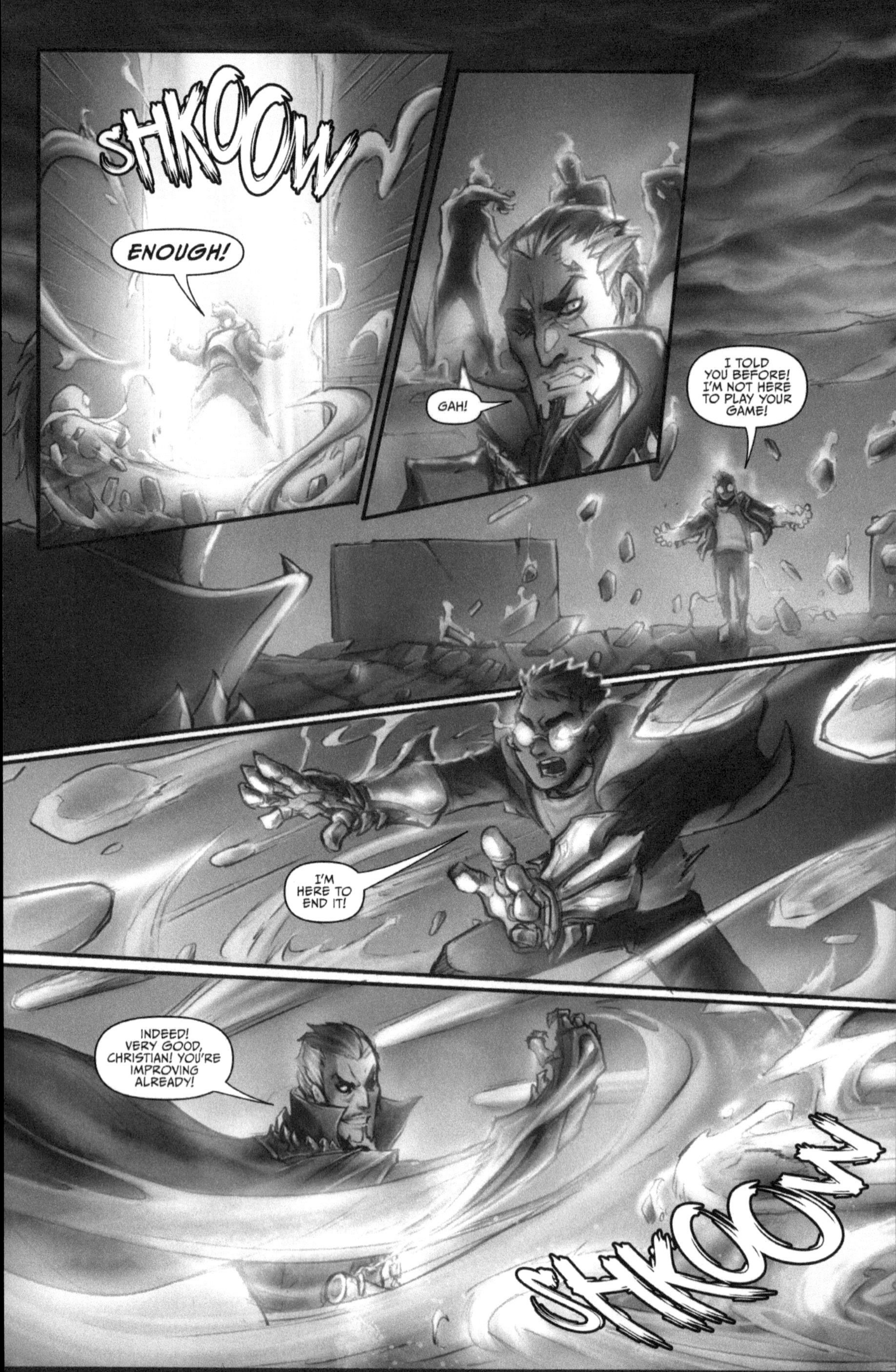
SHKOOOW
ENOUGH!
GAH!
I TOLD YOU BEFORE! I'M NOT HERE TO PLAY YOUR GAME!
I'M HERE TO END IT!
INDEED! VERY GOOD, CHRISTIAN! YOU'RE IMPROVING ALREADY!
SHKOOOW

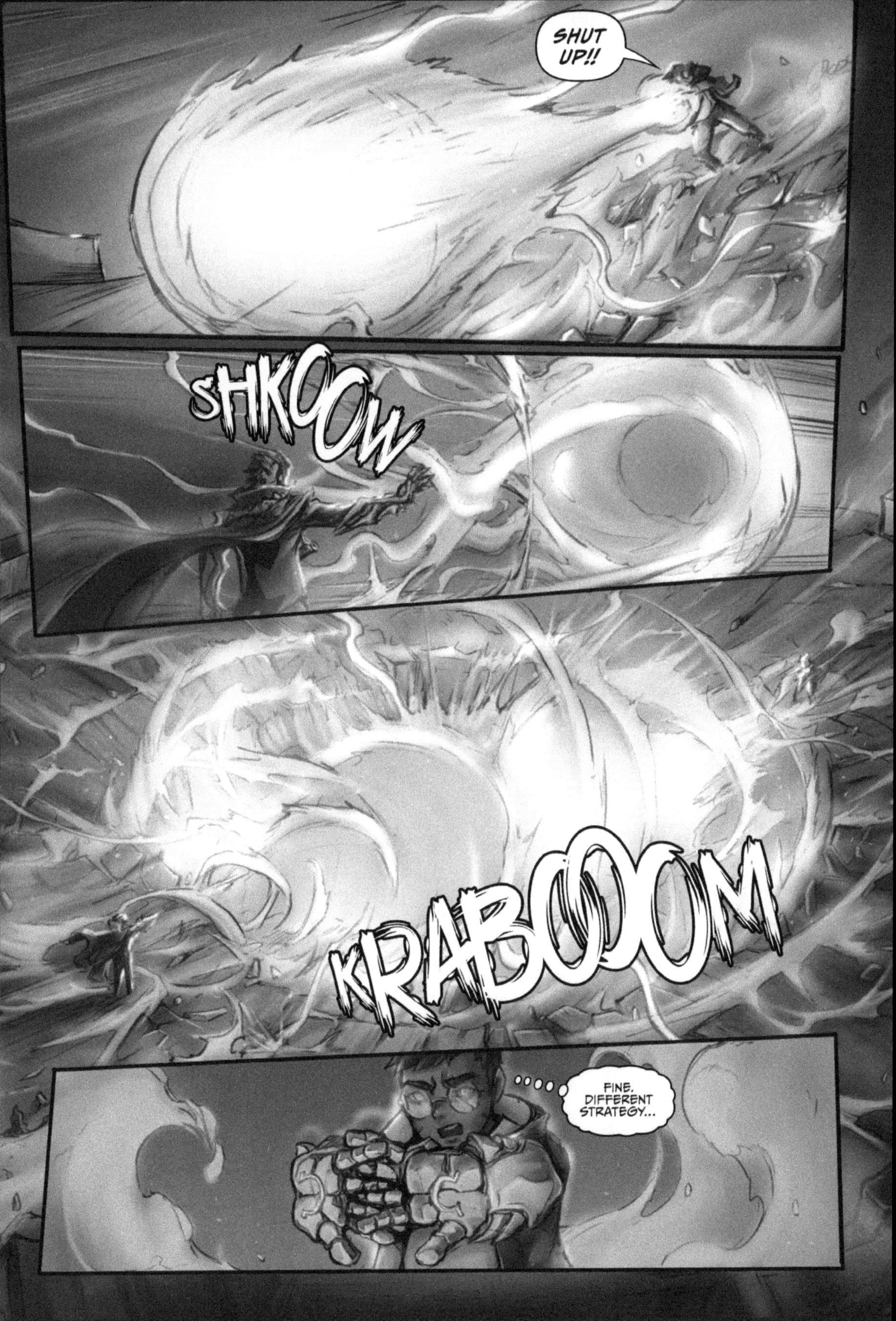
SHUT UP!!
SHKOOOW
KRABOOOM
FINE. DIFFERENT STRATEGY...

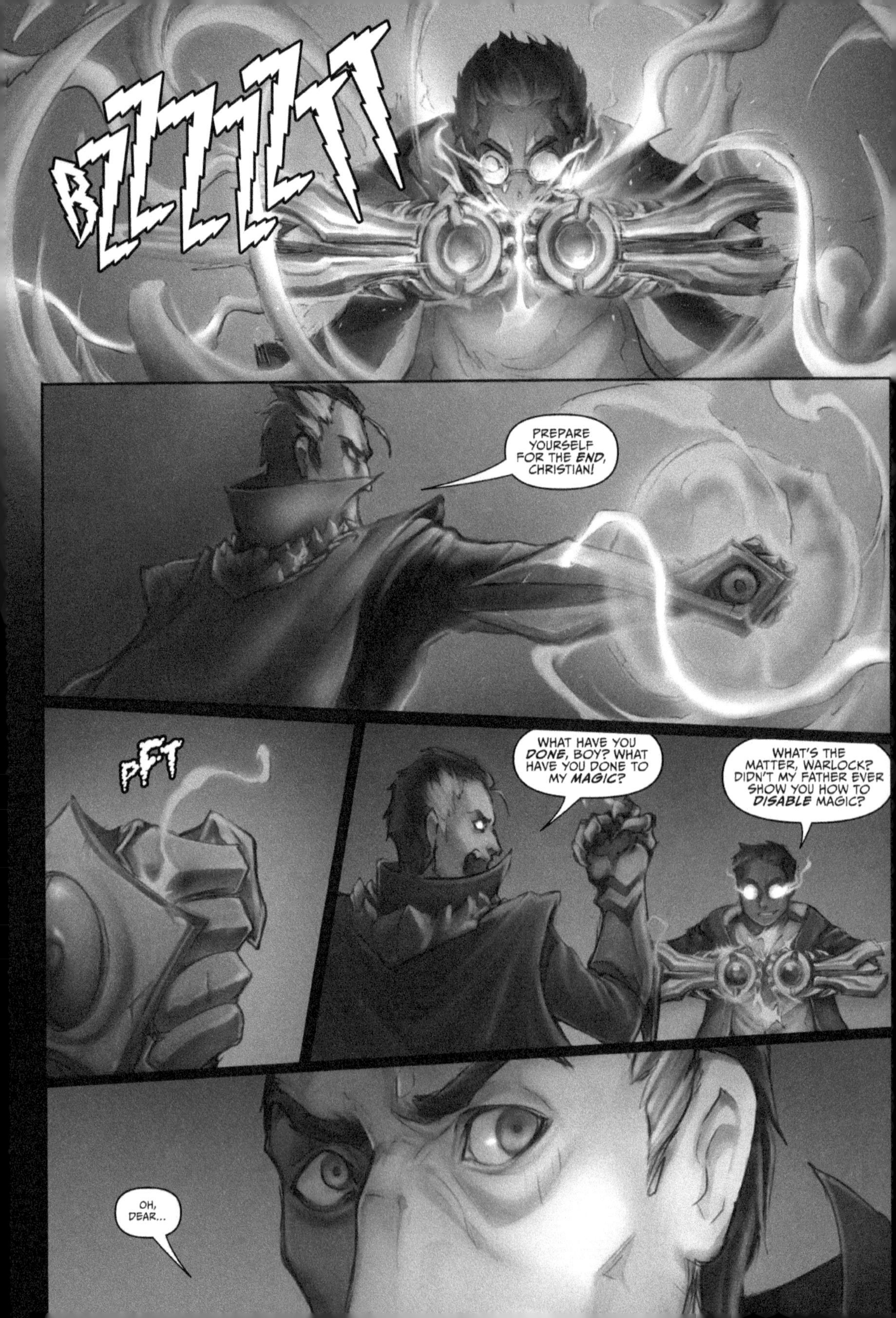
BZZZZZTT
PREPARE YOURSELF FOR THE END, CHRISTIAN!
pFT
WHAT HAVE YOU DONE, BOY? WHAT HAVE YOU DONE TO MY MAGIC?
WHAT'S THE MATTER, WARLOCK? DIDN'T MY FATHER EVER SHOW YOU HOW TO DISABLE MAGIC?
OH, DEAR...

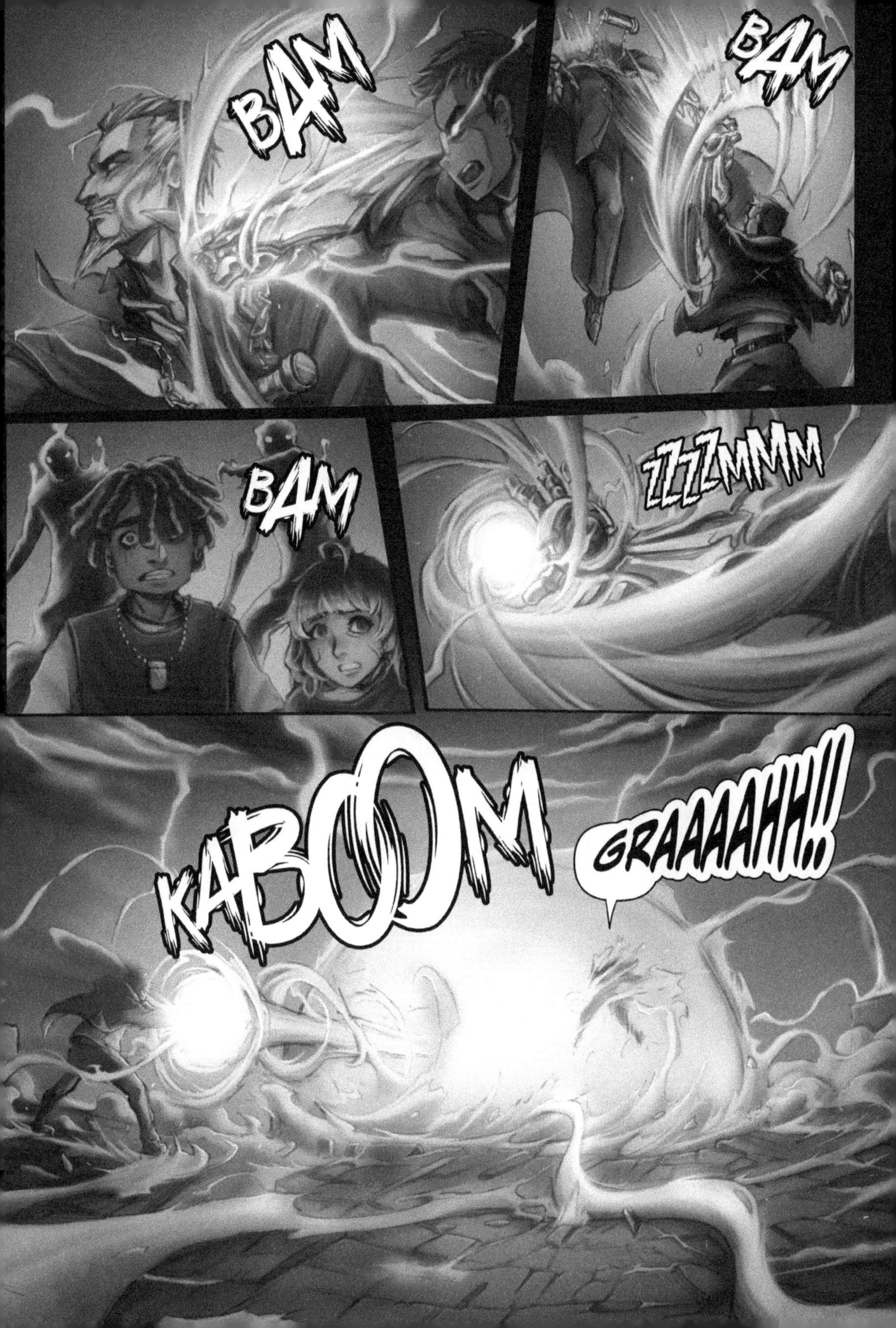
BAM
BAM
BAM
ZZZZMMM
KABOOM
GRAAAAHH!!

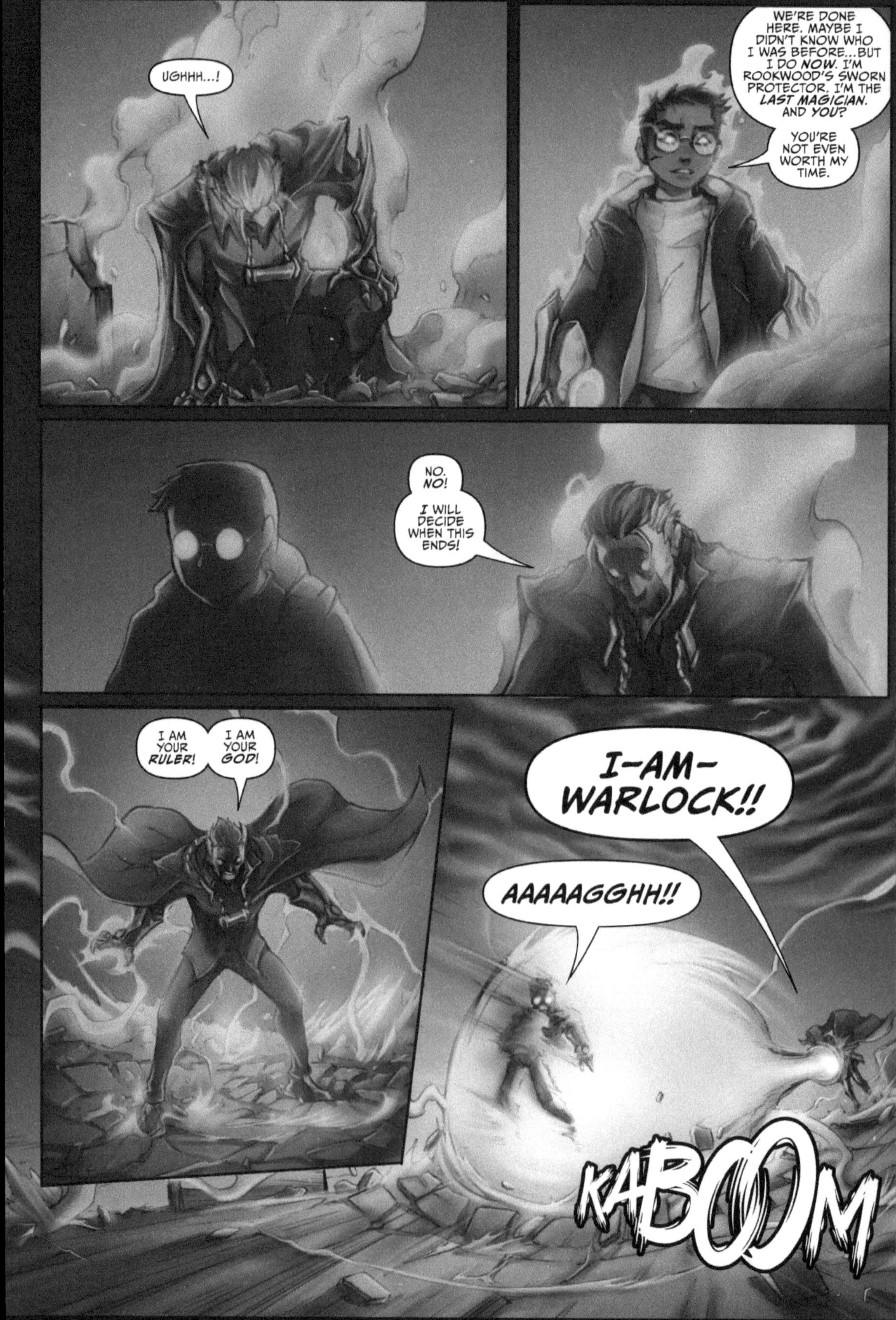
UGHHH...!
WE'RE DONE HERE. MAYBE I DIDN'T KNOW WHO I WAS BEFORE...BUT I DO NOW. I'M ROOKWOOD'S SWORN PROTECTOR. I'M THE LAST MAGICIAN. AND YOU?
YOU'RE NOT EVEN WORTH MY TIME.
NO. NO!
I WILL DECIDE WHEN THIS ENDS!
I AM YOUR RULER!
I AM YOUR GOD!
I-AM-WARLOCK!!
AAAAAGGHH!!
KABOOM

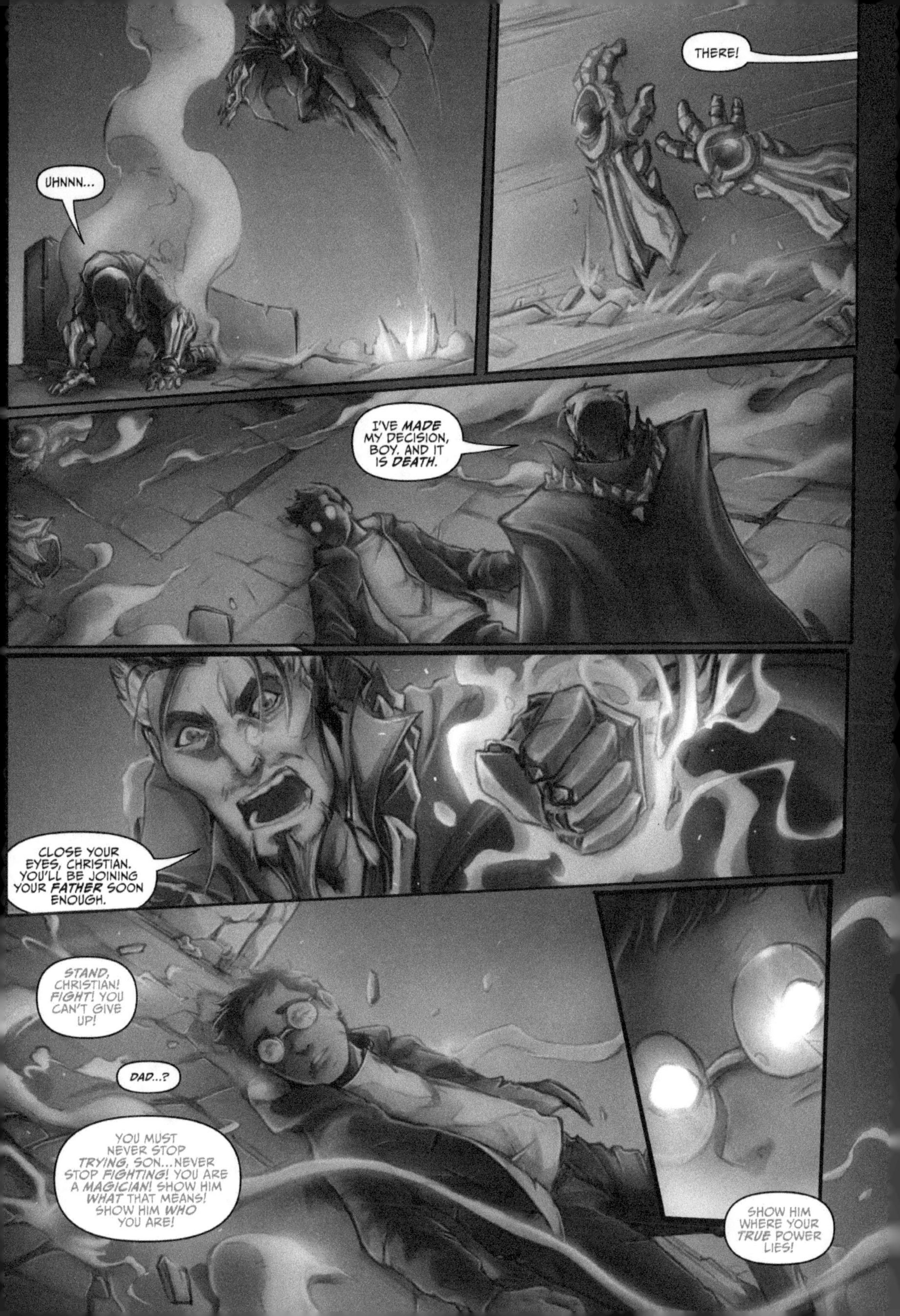
UHNNN...
THERE!
I'VE *MADE* MY DECISION, BOY. AND IT IS *DEATH*.
CLOSE YOUR EYES, CHRISTIAN. YOU'LL BE JOINING YOUR *FATHER* SOON ENOUGH.
*STAND*, CHRISTIAN! *FIGHT*! YOU CAN'T GIVE UP!
*DAD...?*
YOU MUST NEVER STOP *TRYING*, SON...NEVER STOP *FIGHTING*! YOU ARE A *MAGICIAN*! SHOW HIM *WHAT* THAT MEANS! SHOW HIM *WHO* YOU ARE!
SHOW HIM WHERE YOUR *TRUE* POWER LIES!

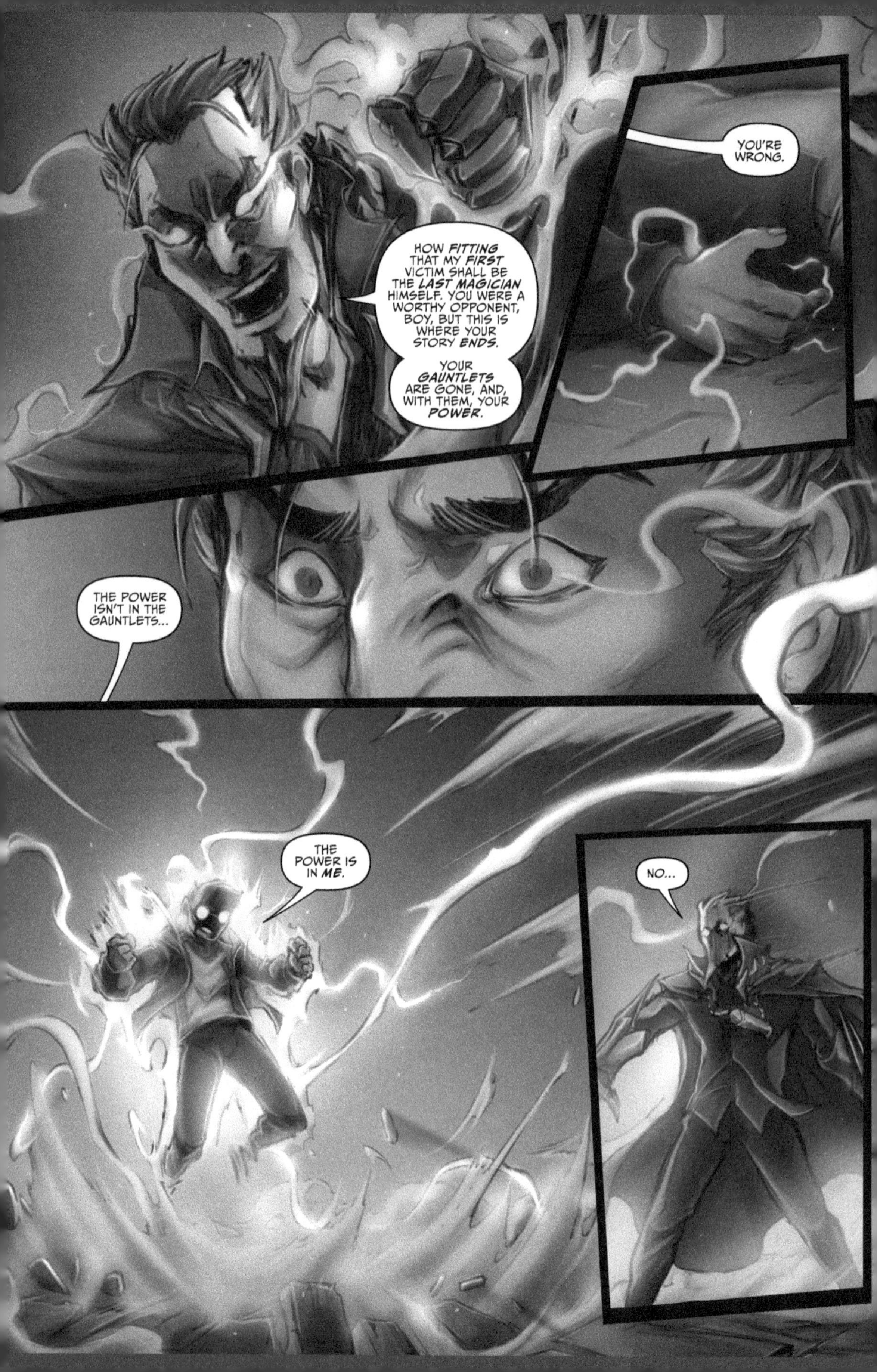
HOW FITTING THAT MY FIRST VICTIM SHALL BE THE LAST MAGICIAN HIMSELF. YOU WERE A WORTHY OPPONENT, BOY, BUT THIS IS WHERE YOUR STORY ENDS.
YOUR GAUNTLETS ARE GONE, AND, WITH THEM, YOUR POWER.
YOU'RE WRONG.
THE POWER ISN'T IN THE GAUNTLETS...
THE POWER IS IN ME.
NO...

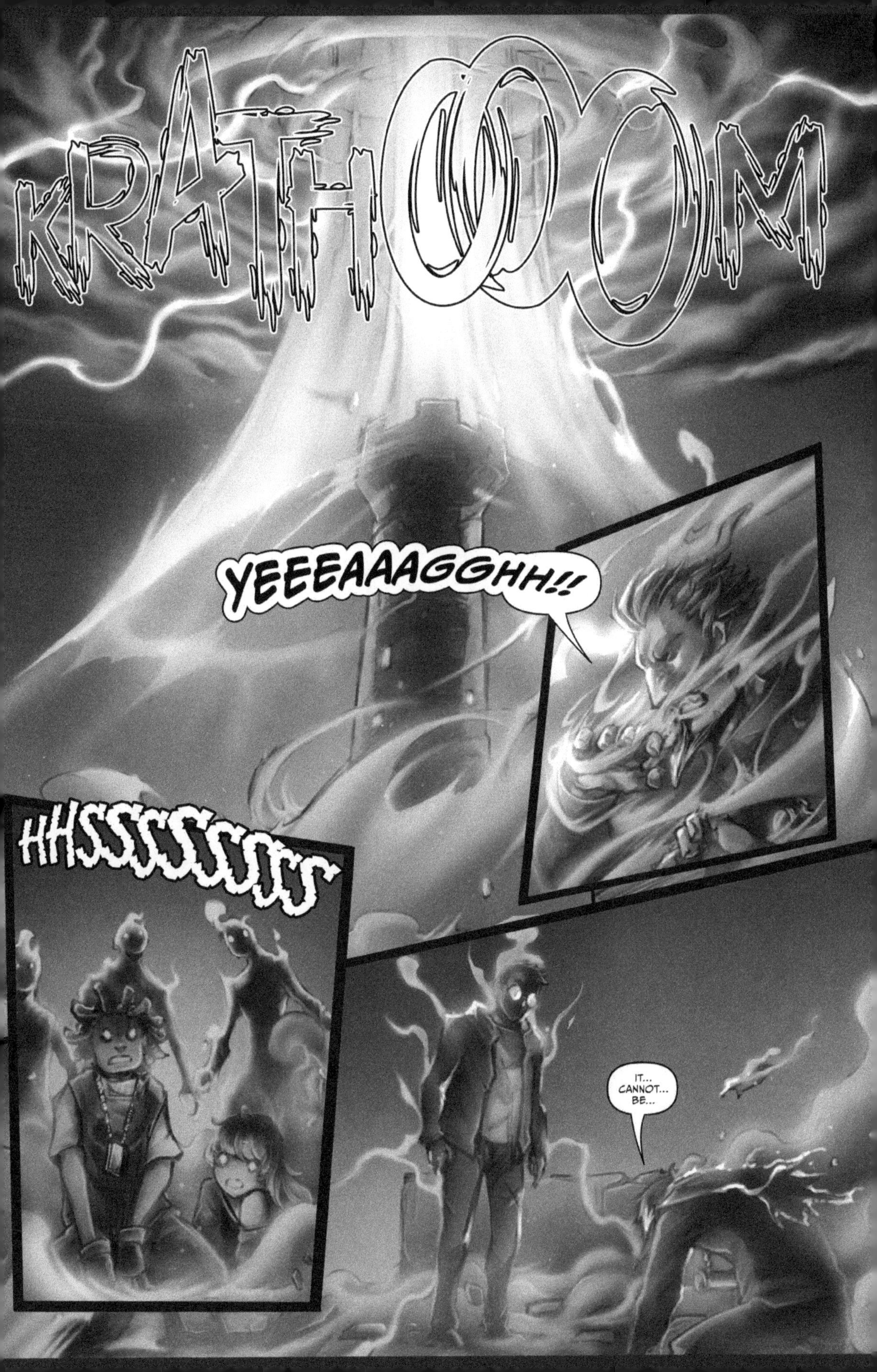
KRATHOOOM
YEEEAAAGGHH!!
HHSSSSSSSSSS
IT... CANNOT... BE...

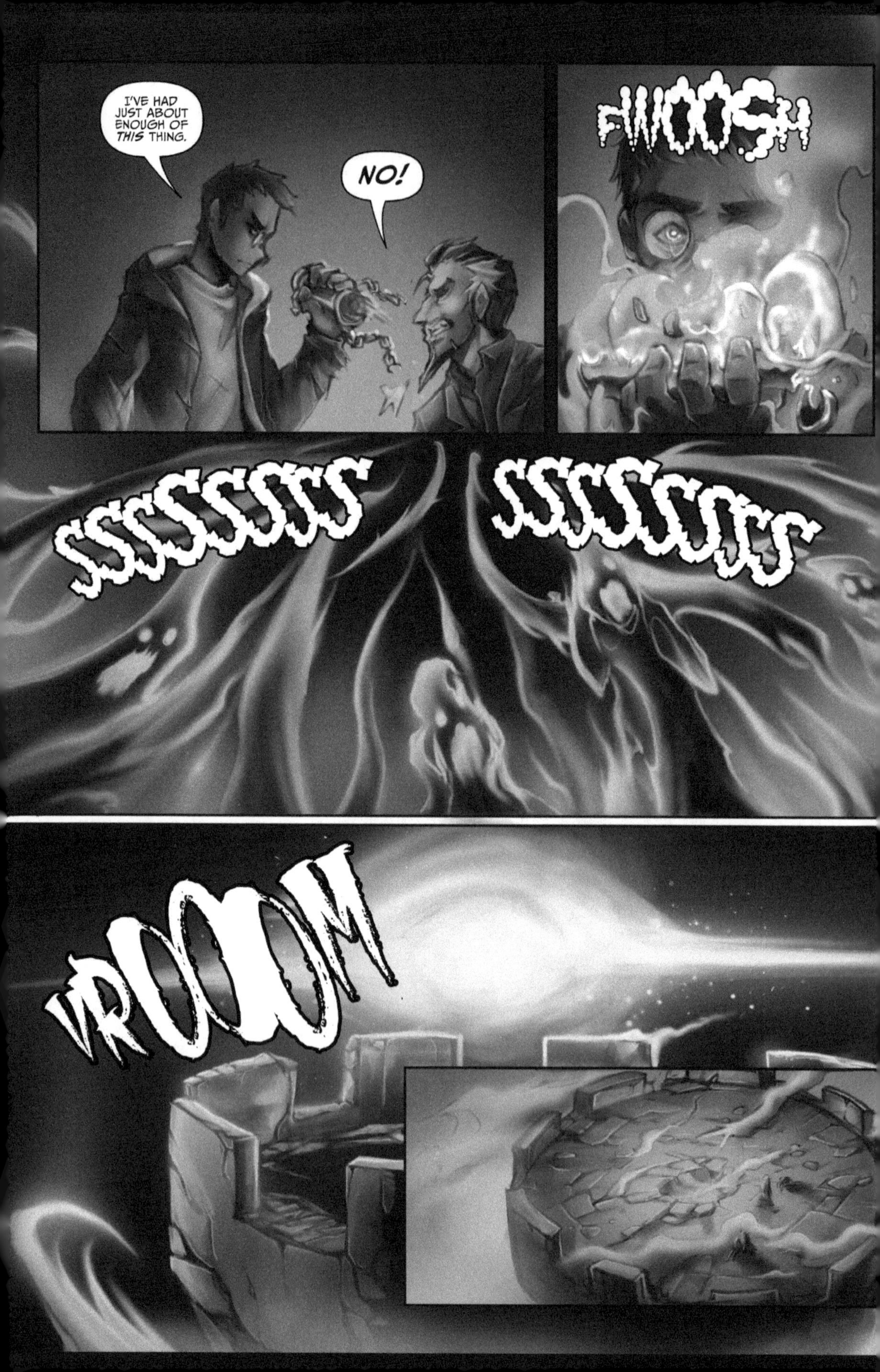
I'VE HAD JUST ABOUT ENOUGH OF *THIS* THING.
NO!
FWOOSH
SSSSSSSSSS
SSSSSSSSSSS
VROOOM

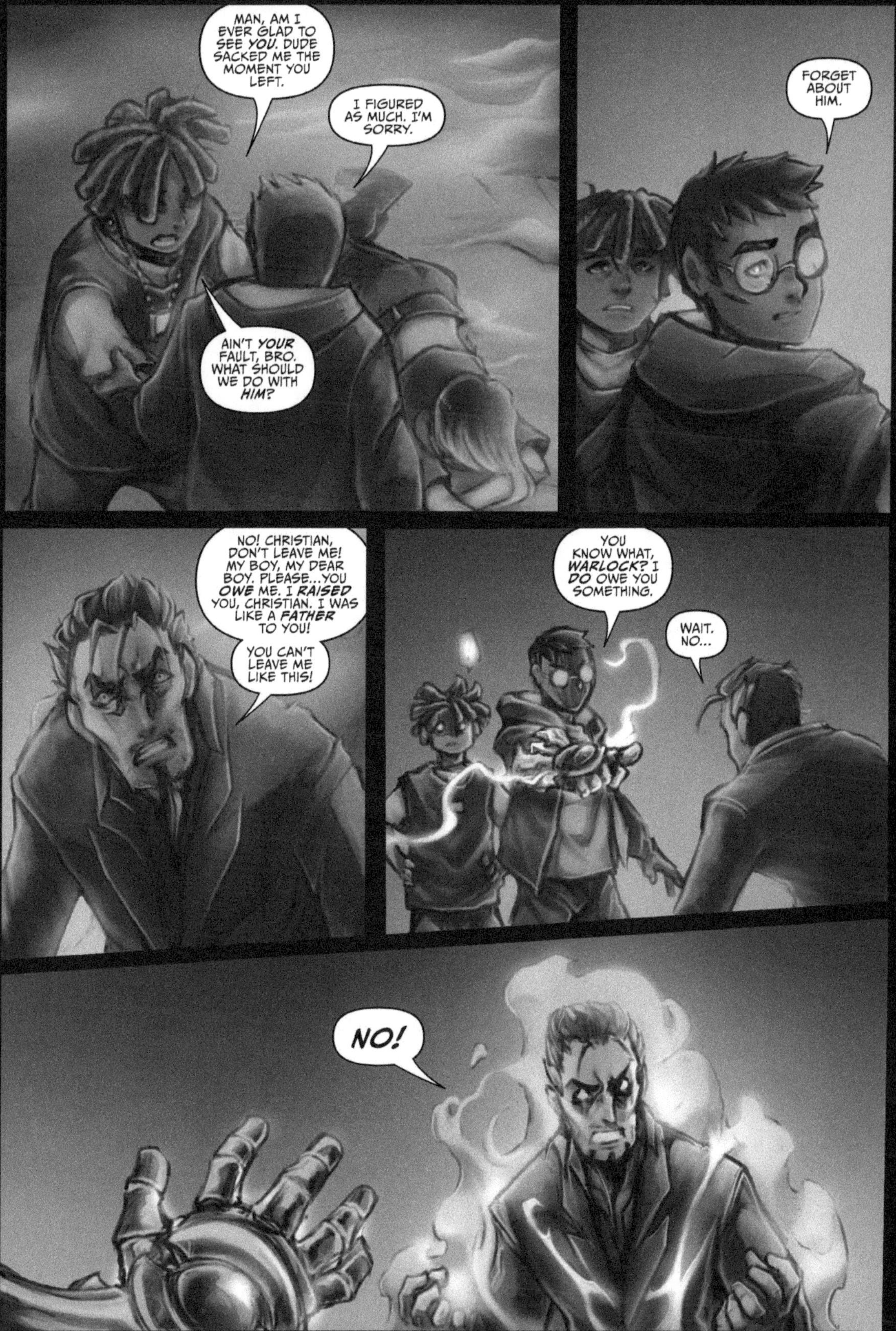
MAN, AM I EVER GLAD TO SEE YOU. DUDE SACKED ME THE MOMENT YOU LEFT.
I FIGURED AS MUCH. I'M SORRY.
AIN'T YOUR FAULT, BRO. WHAT SHOULD WE DO WITH HIM?
FORGET ABOUT HIM.
NO! CHRISTIAN, DON'T LEAVE ME! MY BOY, MY DEAR BOY. PLEASE...YOU OWE ME. I RAISED YOU, CHRISTIAN. I WAS LIKE A FATHER TO YOU!
YOU CAN'T LEAVE ME LIKE THIS!
YOU KNOW WHAT, WARLOCK? I DO OWE YOU SOMETHING.
WAIT. NO...
NO!

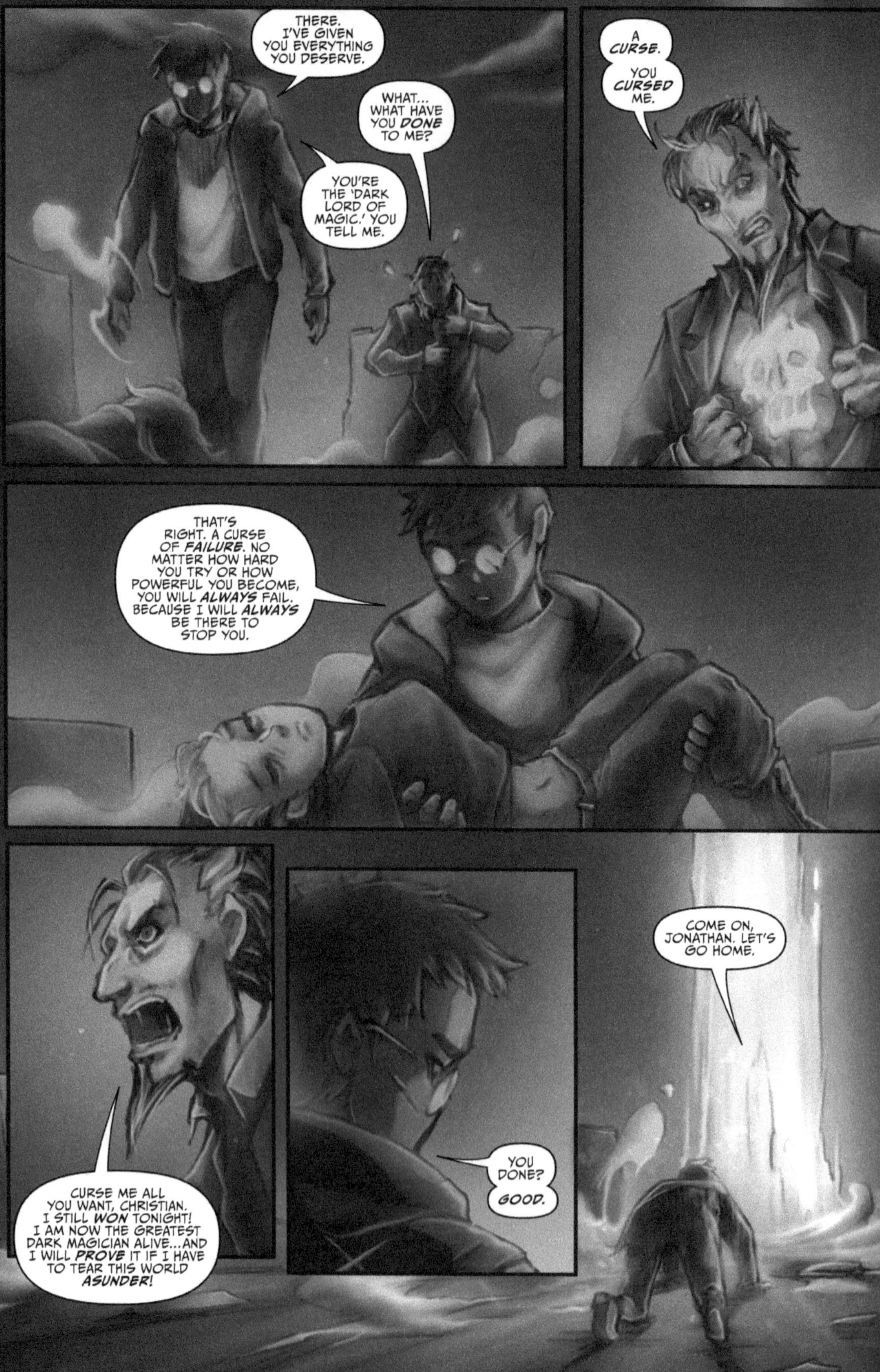
THERE. I'VE GIVEN YOU EVERYTHING YOU DESERVE.
WHAT... WHAT HAVE YOU DONE TO ME?
YOU'RE THE 'DARK LORD OF MAGIC.' YOU TELL ME.
A CURSE. YOU CURSED ME.
THAT'S RIGHT. A CURSE OF FAILURE. NO MATTER HOW HARD YOU TRY OR HOW POWERFUL YOU BECOME, YOU WILL ALWAYS FAIL. BECAUSE I WILL ALWAYS BE THERE TO STOP YOU.
CURSE ME ALL YOU WANT, CHRISTIAN. I STILL WON TONIGHT! I AM NOW THE GREATEST DARK MAGICIAN ALIVE...AND I WILL PROVE IT IF I HAVE TO TEAR THIS WORLD ASUNDER!
YOU DONE? GOOD.
COME ON, JONATHAN. LET'S GO HOME.

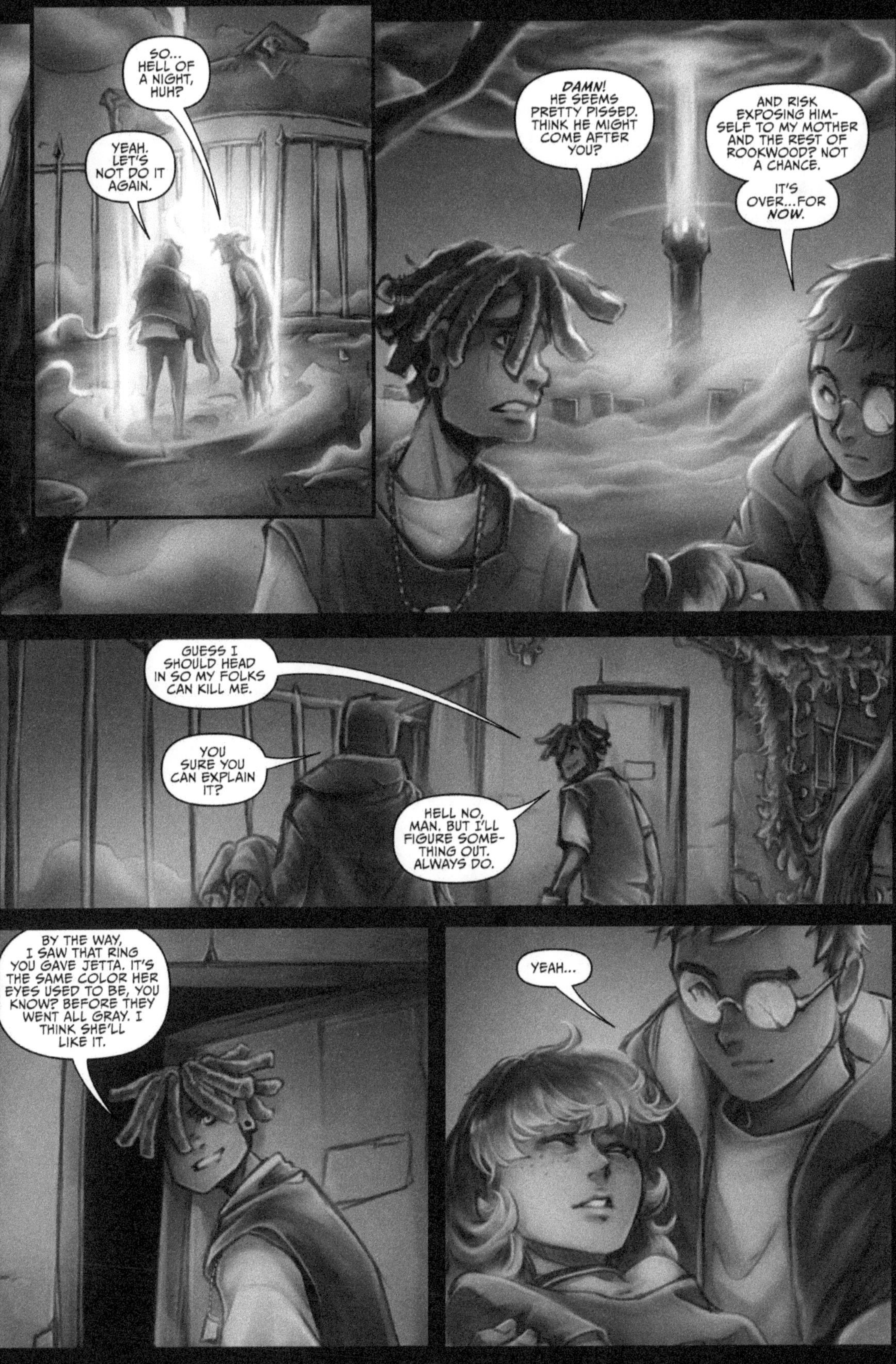
SO... HELL OF A NIGHT, HUH?
YEAH. LET'S NOT DO IT AGAIN.
DAMN! HE SEEMS PRETTY PISSED. THINK HE MIGHT COME AFTER YOU?
AND RISK EXPOSING HIM-SELF TO MY MOTHER AND THE REST OF ROOKWOOD? NOT A CHANCE.
IT'S OVER...FOR NOW.
GUESS I SHOULD HEAD IN SO MY FOLKS CAN KILL ME.
YOU SURE YOU CAN EXPLAIN IT?
HELL NO, MAN. BUT I'LL FIGURE SOME-THING OUT. ALWAYS DO.
BY THE WAY, I SAW THAT RING YOU GAVE JETTA. IT'S THE SAME COLOR HER EYES USED TO BE, YOU KNOW? BEFORE THEY WENT ALL GRAY. I THINK SHE'LL LIKE IT.
YEAH...

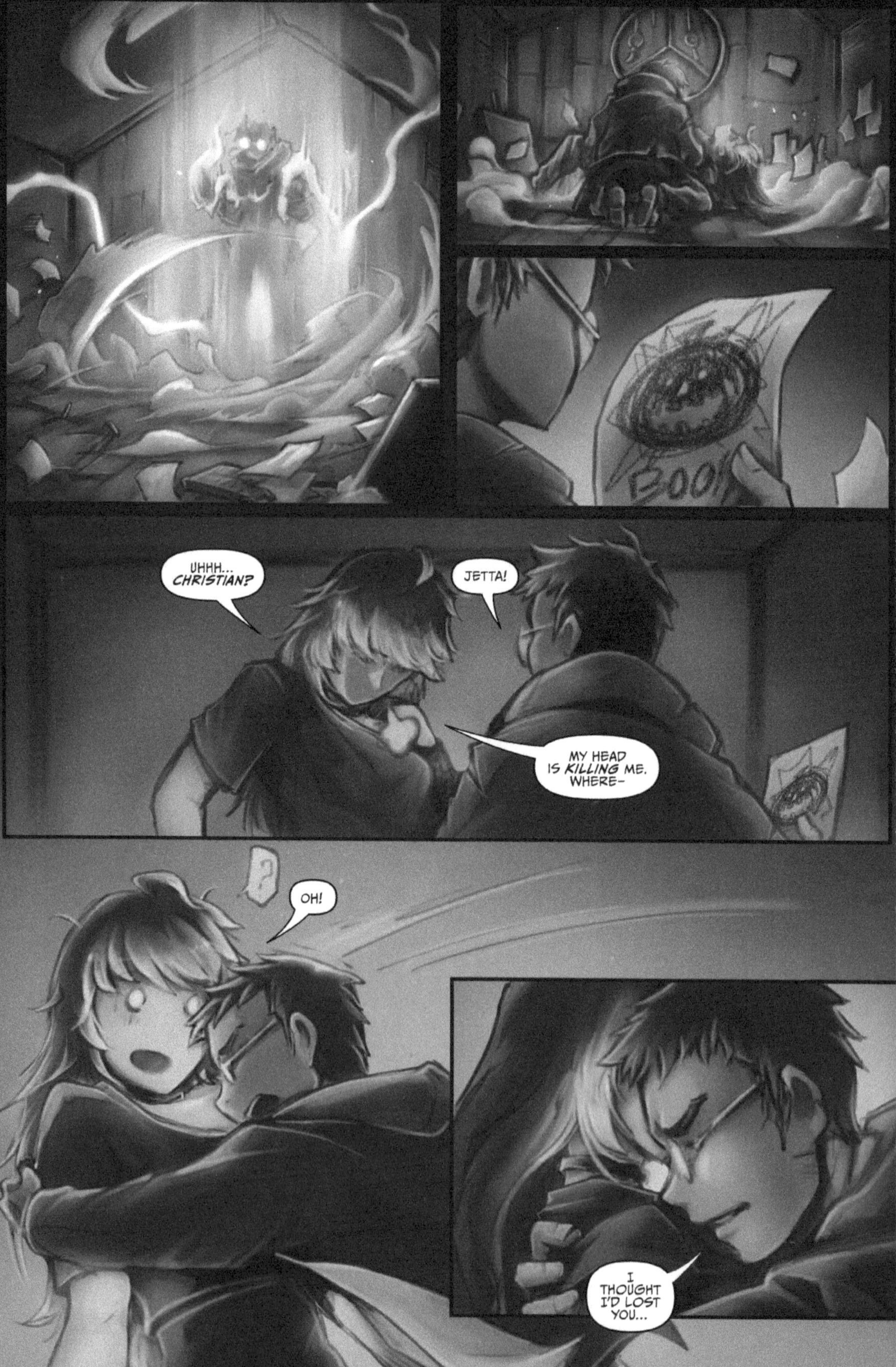
BOO!
UHHH... *CHRISTIAN?*
JETTA!
MY HEAD IS *KILLING* ME. WHERE-
OH!
I THOUGHT I'D LOST YOU...

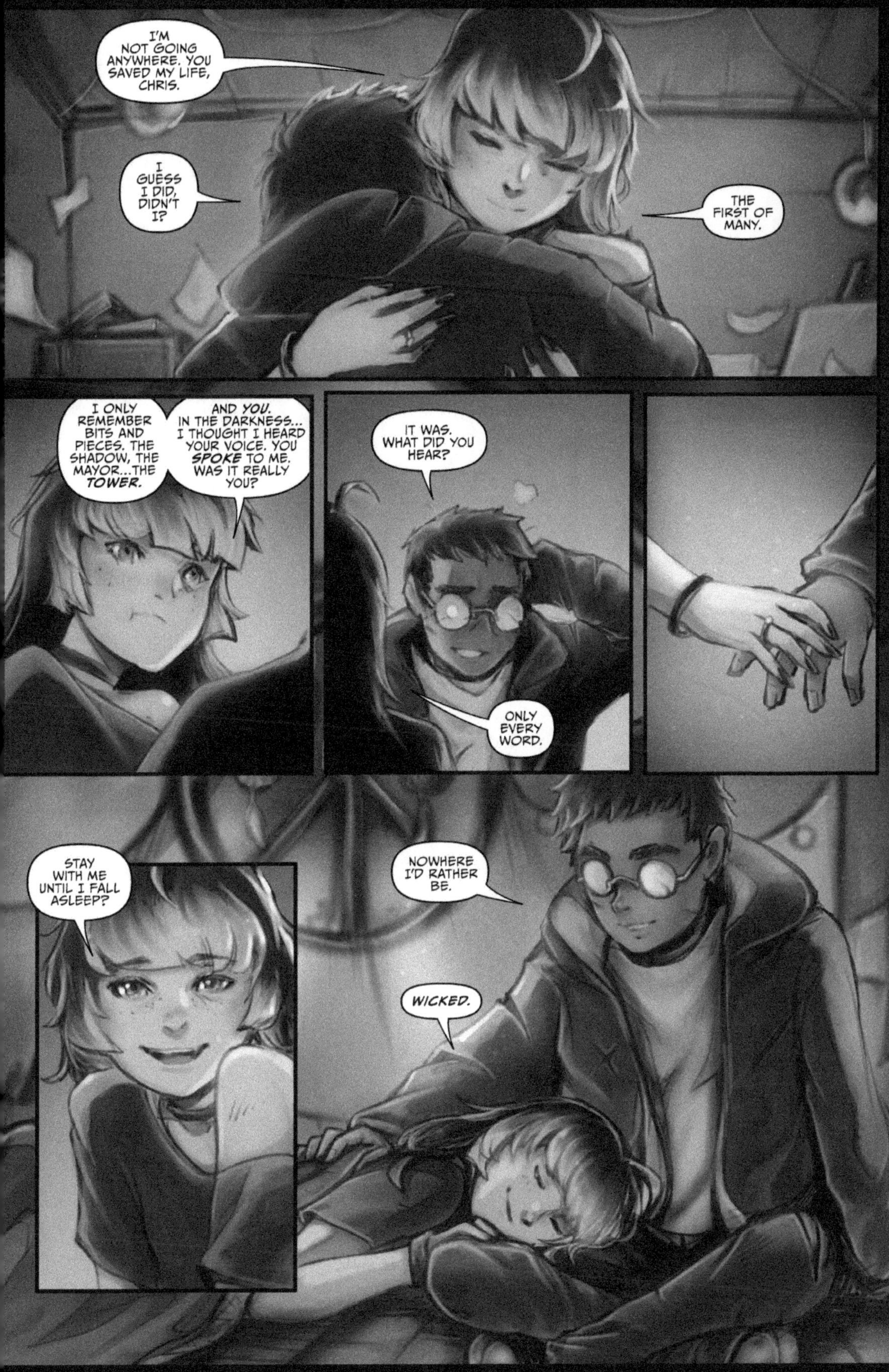
I'M NOT GOING ANYWHERE. YOU SAVED MY LIFE, CHRIS.
I GUESS I DID, DIDN'T I?
THE FIRST OF MANY.
I ONLY REMEMBER BITS AND PIECES. THE SHADOW, THE MAYOR...THE *TOWER.*
AND *YOU.* IN THE DARKNESS... I THOUGHT I HEARD YOUR VOICE. YOU *SPOKE* TO ME. WAS IT REALLY YOU?
IT WAS. WHAT DID YOU HEAR?
ONLY EVERY WORD.
STAY WITH ME UNTIL I FALL ASLEEP?
NOWHERE I'D RATHER BE.
*WICKED.*

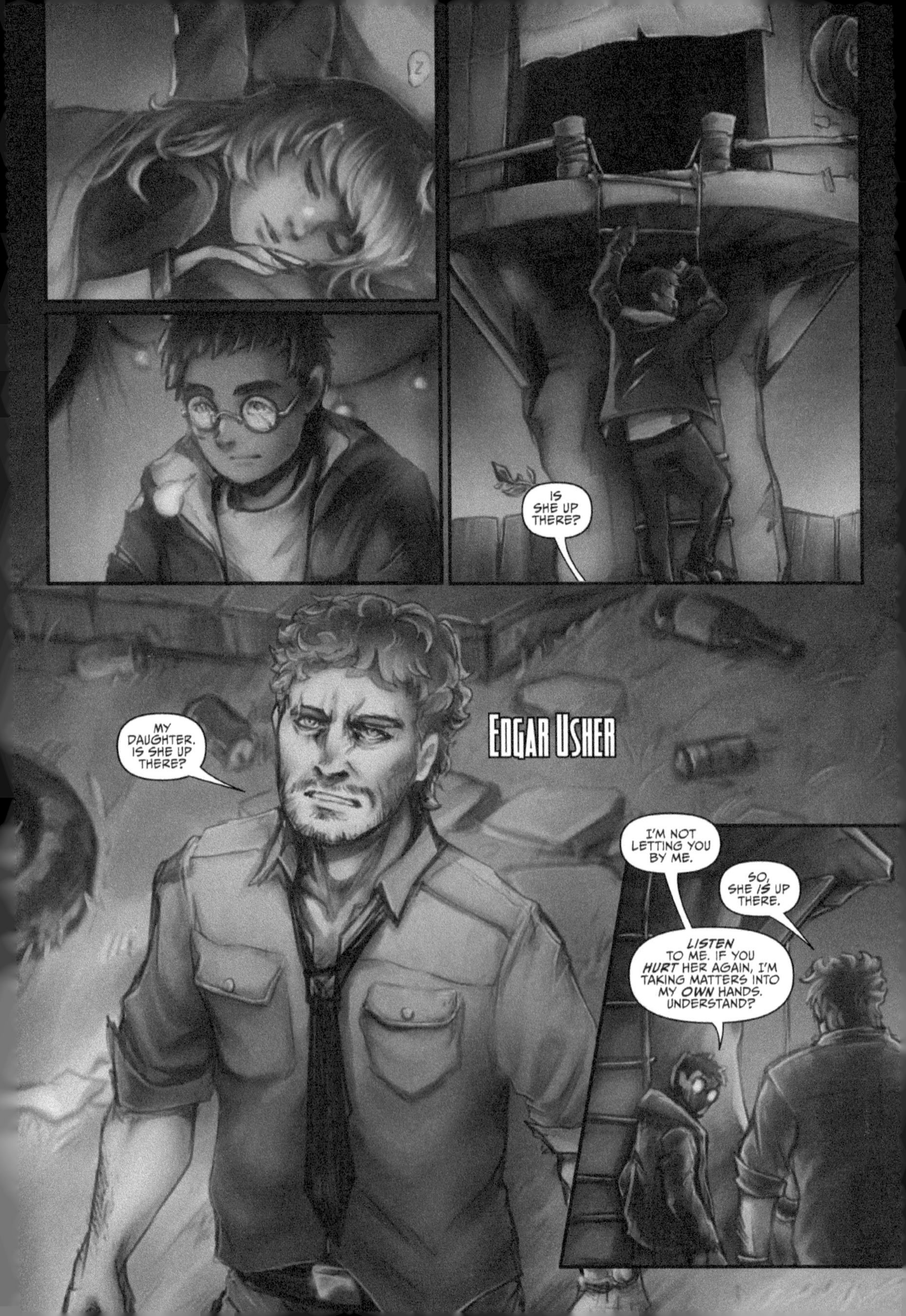
IS SHE UP THERE?
MY DAUGHTER. IS SHE UP THERE?
EDGAR USHER
I'M NOT LETTING YOU BY ME.
SO, SHE *IS* UP THERE.
***LISTEN*** TO ME. IF YOU ***HURT*** HER AGAIN, I'M TAKING MATTERS INTO MY ***OWN*** HANDS. UNDERSTAND?

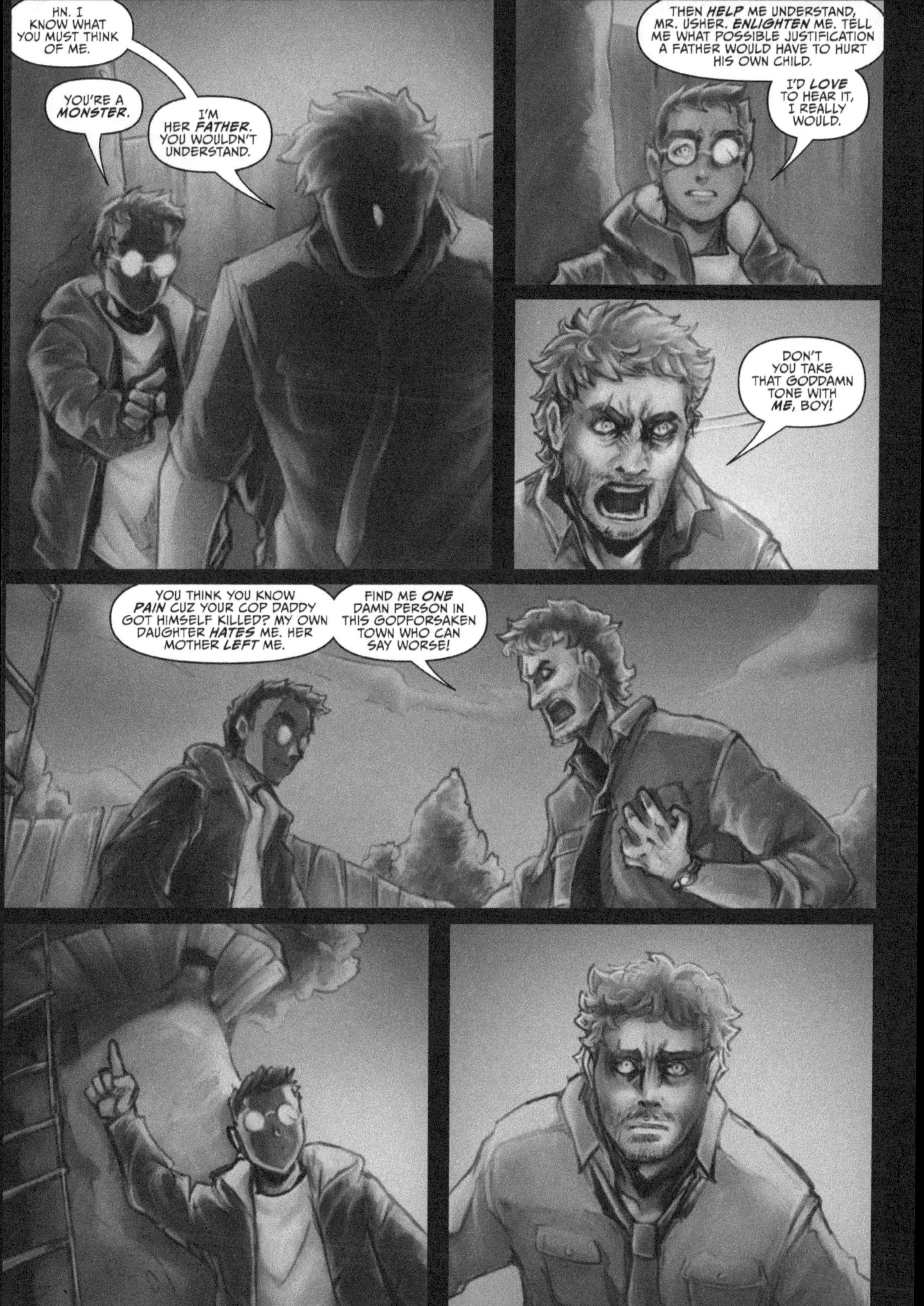
HN. I KNOW WHAT YOU MUST THINK OF ME.
YOU'RE A *MONSTER*.
I'M HER *FATHER*. YOU WOULDN'T UNDERSTAND.
THEN *HELP* ME UNDERSTAND, MR. USHER. *ENLIGHTEN* ME. TELL ME WHAT POSSIBLE JUSTIFICATION A FATHER WOULD HAVE TO HURT HIS OWN CHILD.
I'D *LOVE* TO HEAR IT, I REALLY WOULD.
DON'T YOU TAKE THAT GODDAMN TONE WITH *ME*, BOY!
YOU THINK YOU KNOW *PAIN* CUZ YOUR COP DADDY GOT HIMSELF KILLED? MY OWN DAUGHTER *HATES* ME. HER MOTHER *LEFT* ME.
FIND ME *ONE* DAMN PERSON IN THIS GODFORSAKEN TOWN WHO CAN SAY WORSE!

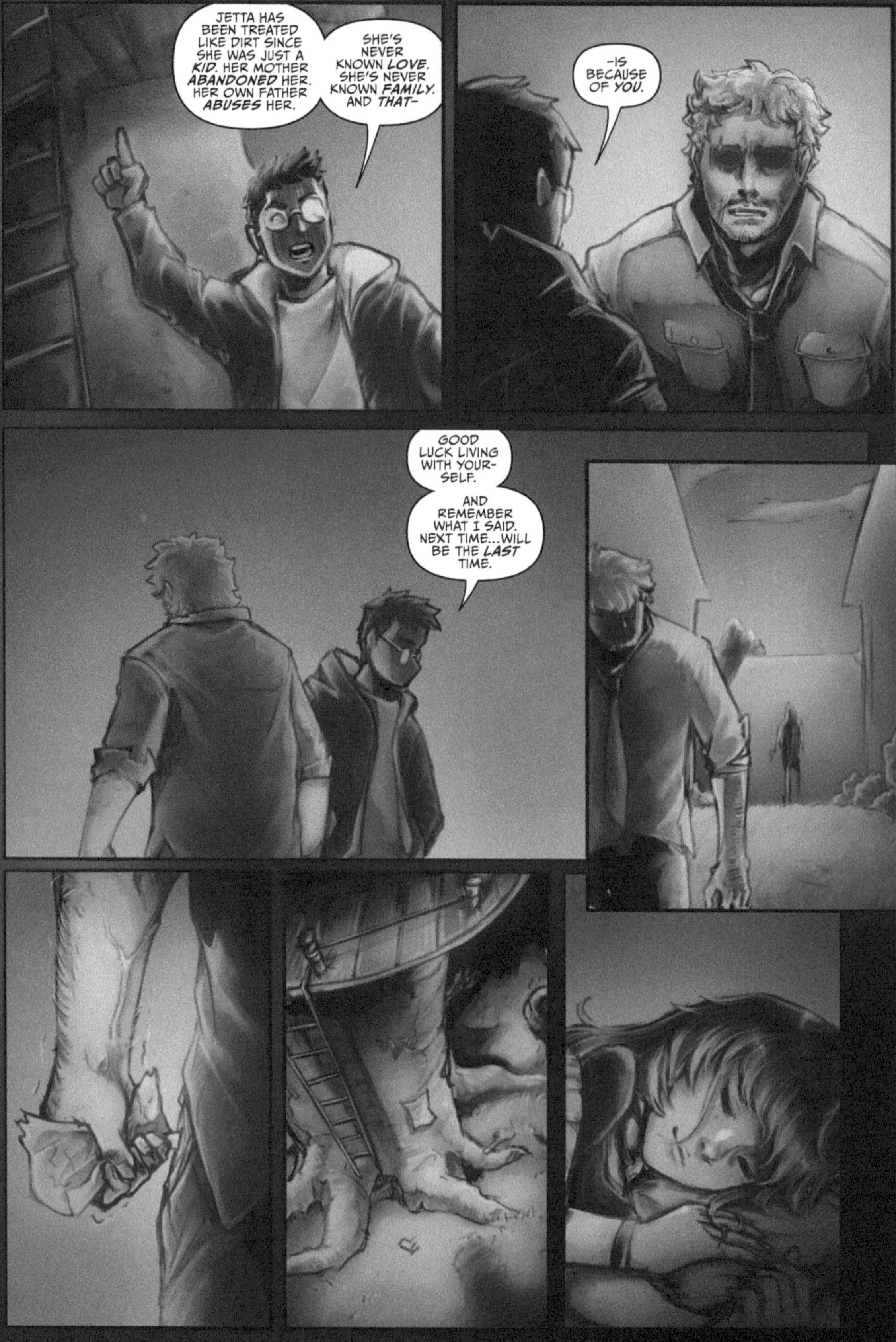
JETTA HAS BEEN TREATED LIKE DIRT SINCE SHE WAS JUST A *KID*. HER MOTHER *ABANDONED* HER. HER OWN FATHER *ABUSES* HER.
SHE'S NEVER KNOWN *LOVE*. SHE'S NEVER KNOWN *FAMILY*. AND *THAT*–
–IS BECAUSE OF *YOU*.
GOOD LUCK LIVING WITH YOUR-SELF.
AND REMEMBER WHAT I SAID. NEXT TIME...WILL BE THE *LAST* TIME.

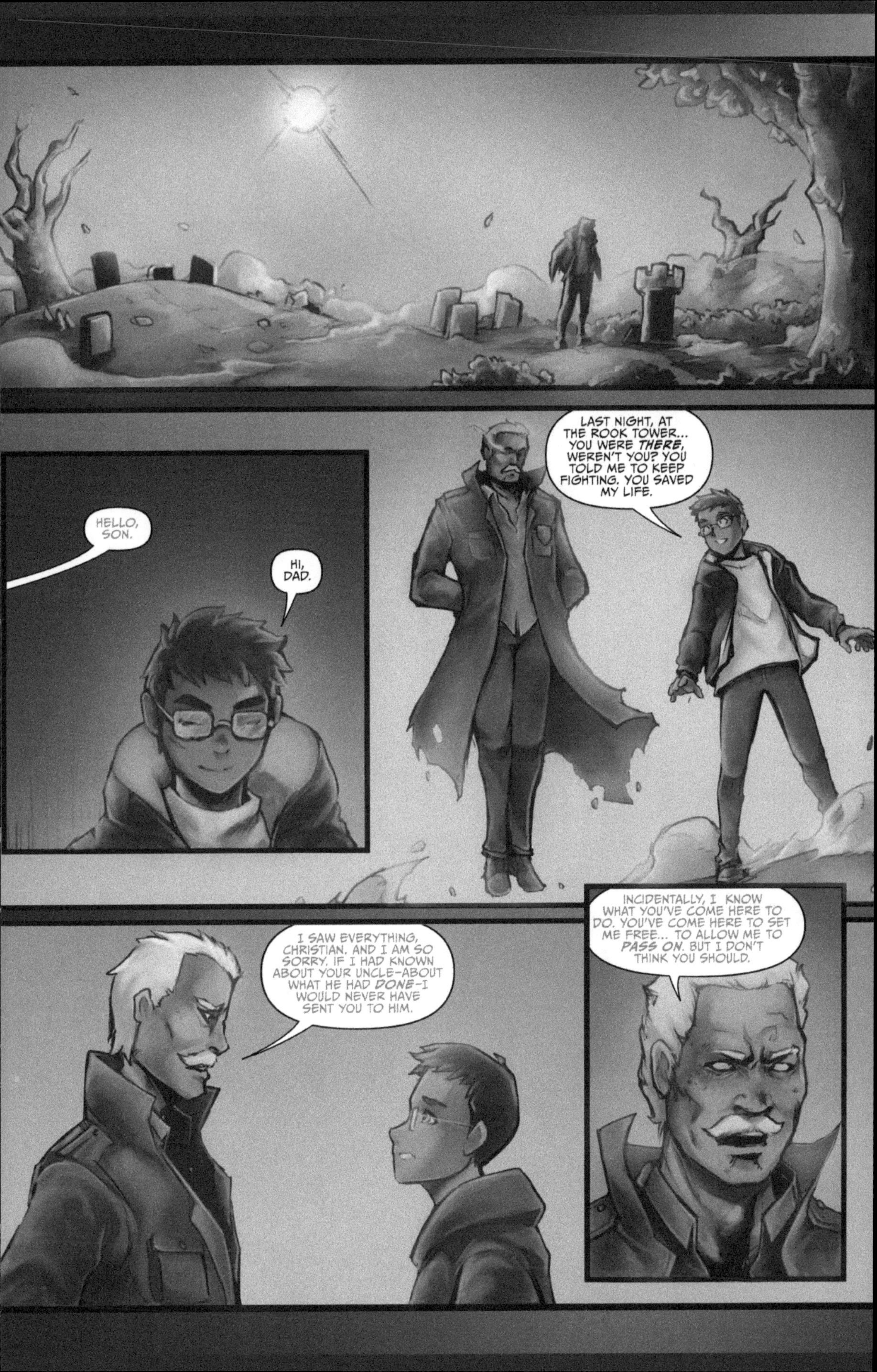
HELLO, SON.
HI, DAD.
LAST NIGHT, AT THE ROOK TOWER... YOU WERE THERE, WEREN'T YOU? YOU TOLD ME TO KEEP FIGHTING. YOU SAVED MY LIFE.
I SAW EVERYTHING, CHRISTIAN. AND I AM SO SORRY. IF I HAD KNOWN ABOUT YOUR UNCLE–ABOUT WHAT HE HAD DONE–I WOULD NEVER HAVE SENT YOU TO HIM.
INCIDENTALLY, I KNOW WHAT YOU'VE COME HERE TO DO. YOU'VE COME HERE TO SET ME FREE... TO ALLOW ME TO PASS ON. BUT I DON'T THINK YOU SHOULD.

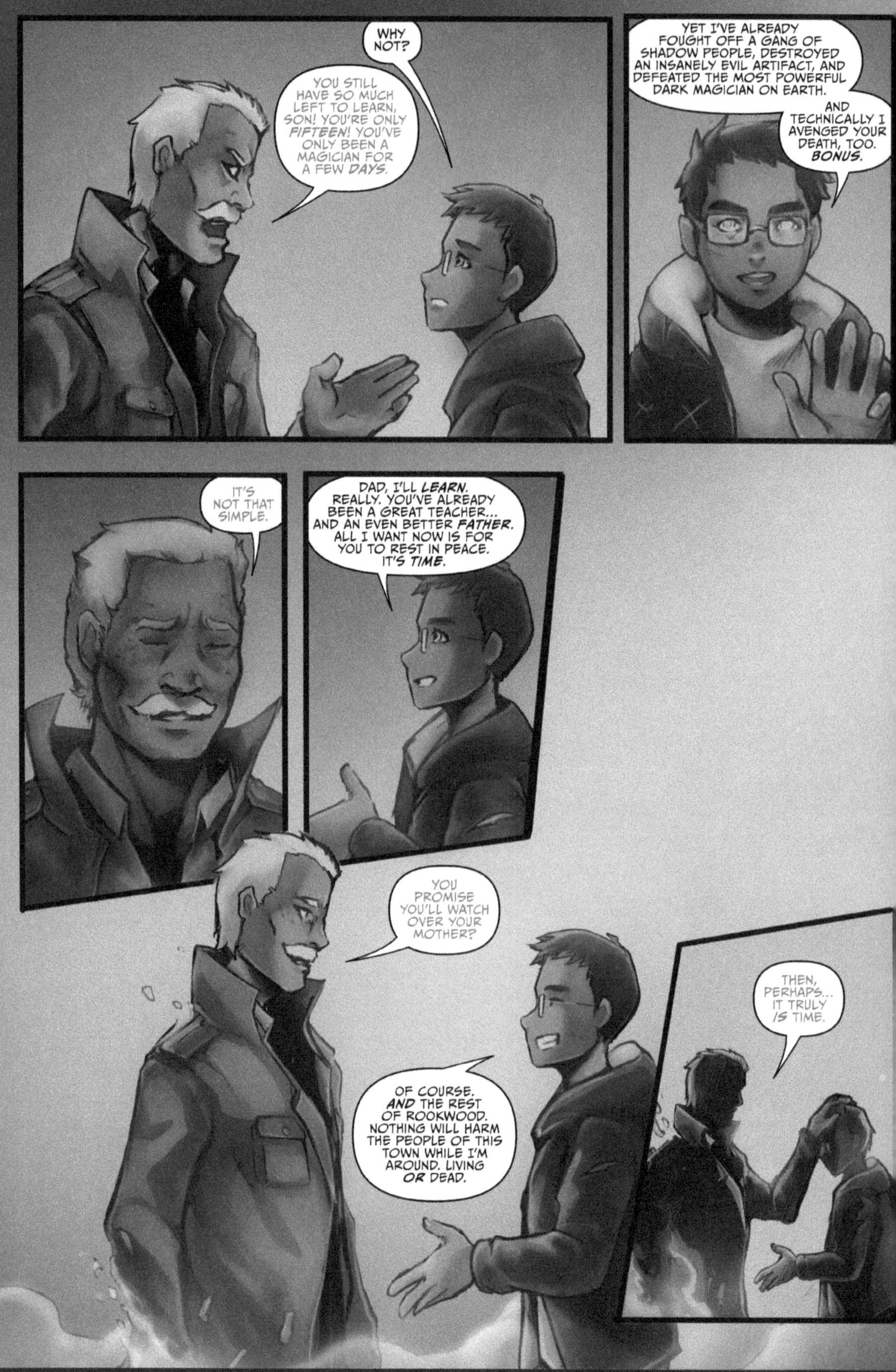
YOU STILL HAVE SO MUCH LEFT TO LEARN, SON! YOU'RE ONLY FIFTEEN! YOU'VE ONLY BEEN A MAGICIAN FOR A FEW DAYS.
WHY NOT?
YET I'VE ALREADY FOUGHT OFF A GANG OF SHADOW PEOPLE, DESTROYED AN INSANELY EVIL ARTIFACT, AND DEFEATED THE MOST POWERFUL DARK MAGICIAN ON EARTH.
AND TECHNICALLY I AVENGED YOUR DEATH, TOO. BONUS.
IT'S NOT THAT SIMPLE.
DAD, I'LL LEARN. REALLY. YOU'VE ALREADY BEEN A GREAT TEACHER... AND AN EVEN BETTER FATHER. ALL I WANT NOW IS FOR YOU TO REST IN PEACE. IT'S TIME.
YOU PROMISE YOU'LL WATCH OVER YOUR MOTHER?
OF COURSE. AND THE REST OF ROOKWOOD. NOTHING WILL HARM THE PEOPLE OF THIS TOWN WHILE I'M AROUND. LIVING OR DEAD.
THEN, PERHAPS... IT TRULY IS TIME.

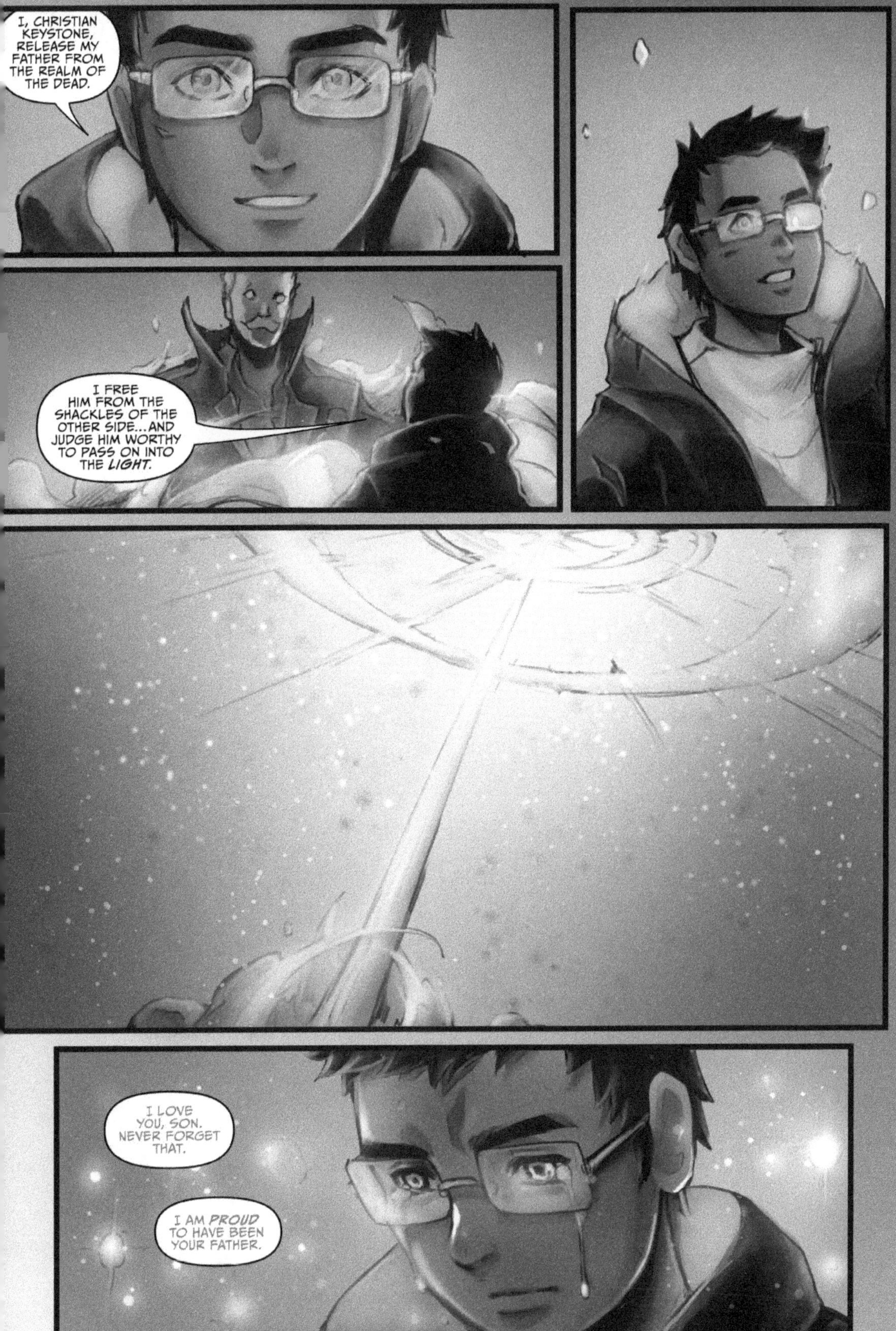
I, CHRISTIAN KEYSTONE, RELEASE MY FATHER FROM THE REALM OF THE DEAD.
I FREE HIM FROM THE SHACKLES OF THE OTHER SIDE...AND JUDGE HIM WORTHY TO PASS ON INTO THE *LIGHT*.
I LOVE YOU, SON. NEVER FORGET THAT.
I AM *PROUD* TO HAVE BEEN YOUR FATHER.

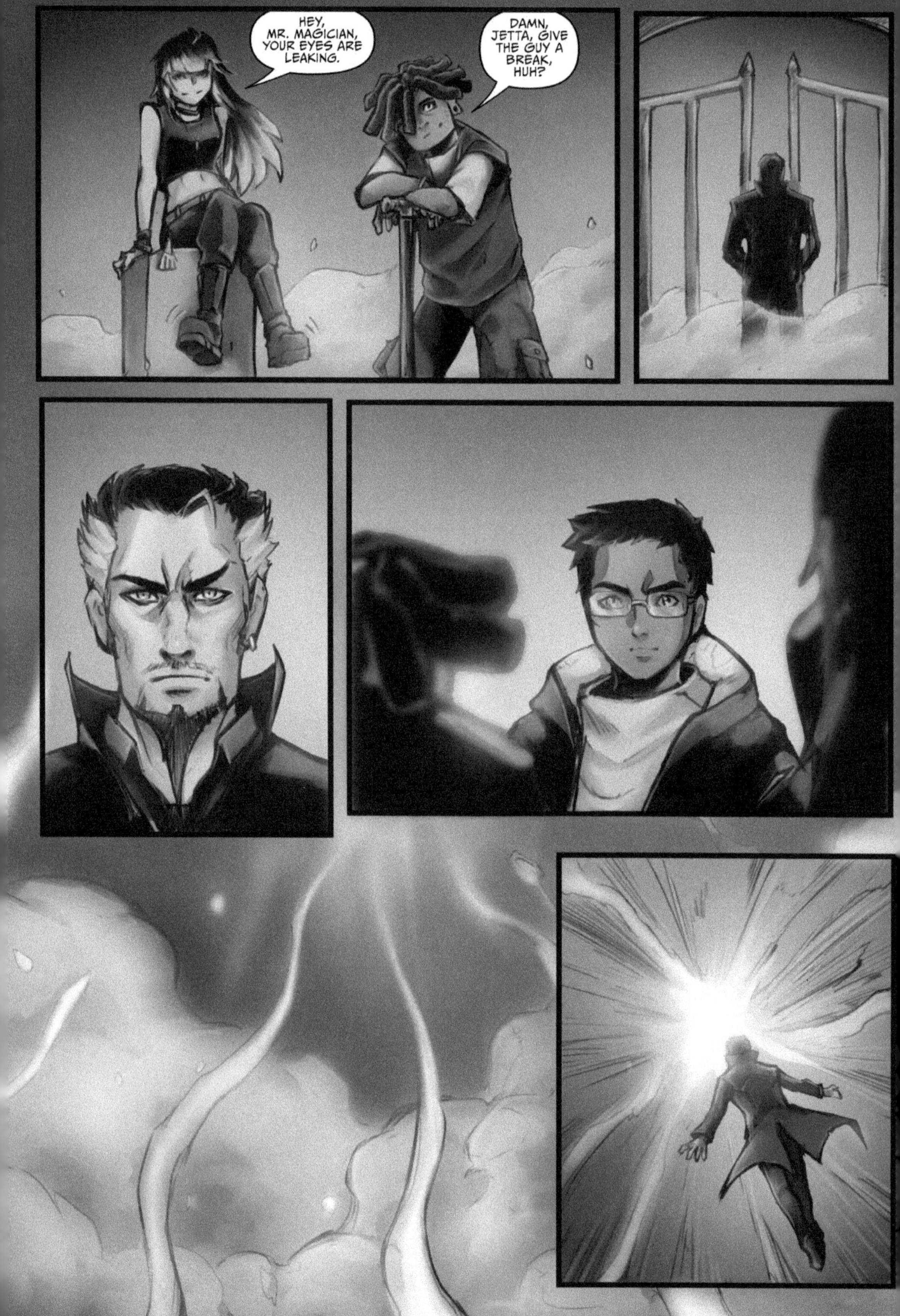
HEY, MR. MAGICIAN, YOUR EYES ARE LEAKING.
DAMN, JETTA, GIVE THE GUY A BREAK, HUH?

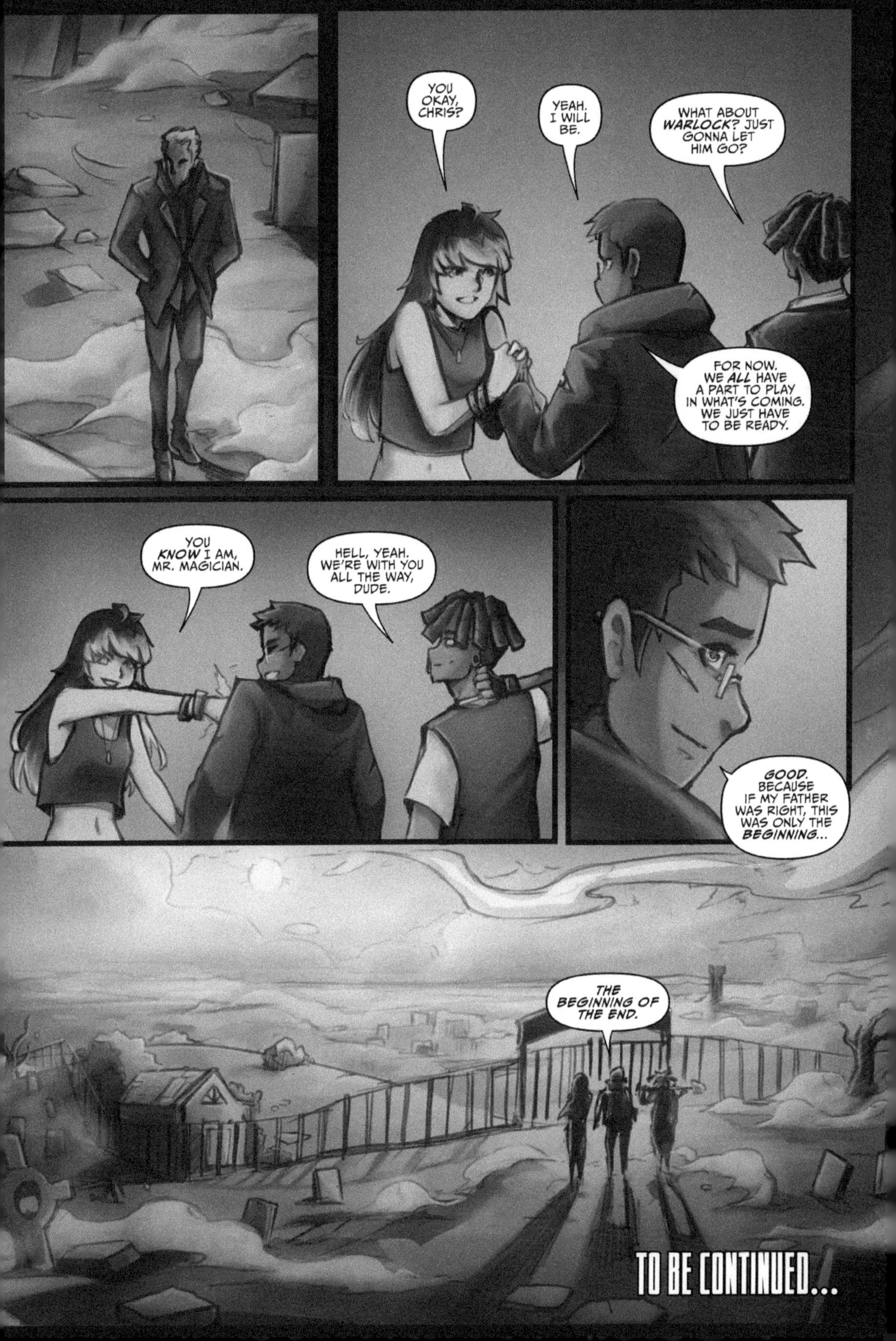
YOU OKAY, CHRIS?
YEAH. I WILL BE.
WHAT ABOUT WARLOCK? JUST GONNA LET HIM GO?
FOR NOW. WE ALL HAVE A PART TO PLAY IN WHAT'S COMING. WE JUST HAVE TO BE READY.
YOU KNOW I AM, MR. MAGICIAN.
HELL, YEAH. WE'RE WITH YOU ALL THE WAY, DUDE.
GOOD. BECAUSE IF MY FATHER WAS RIGHT, THIS WAS ONLY THE BEGINNING...
THE BEGINNING OF THE END.
TO BE CONTINUED...

MARKOSIA

CPSIA information can be obtained
at www.ICGtesting.com
Printed in the USA
BVHW012056130223
658422BV00015B/208